Worship

THE GOLDEN THREAD

Worship
THE GOLDEN THREAD

WEAVING WORSHIP
THROUGH THE
FABRIC OF LIFE

BRUCE W. TRIPLEHORN

BMH
www.bmhbooks.com
Winona Lake, IN 46590

Worship, the Golden Thread

Copyright © 2008 by
Bruce W. Triplehorn

Published by BMH Books
P.O. Box 544, Winona Lake, IN 46590 USA
www.bmhbooks.com

ISBN 978-0-88469-309-3
RELIGION / Christian Life / Spiritual Growth

Scripture references are from the New American Standard Bible,
Copyright © 1960, 1962, 1963, 1968, 1971, 1972, 1973, 1975, 1977, 1995
by The Lockman Foundation. Used by permission. (www.Lockman.org)

Printed in the United States of America

Dedication

To my wife, Lisa, my soul mate,
who has taught me more
about worship through her life
than I have learned
from any book.

Acknowledgments

I am indebted to many who have helped to rescue me from a religious life and to shape me into a worshiper. Bruce Erickson, Dick Sellers, Bob Fetterhoff, Dan Green, George Johnson, Bill Burk, Ron Sauer, Dan Allan, Tom Julien, and Dave Guiles have all had an influence on my life in different ways. I am grateful for Brazilian friends like Ray, Nonato, Eslon, Edson, Luis, Vicente, Manuel, Pedro, Pingo, Luiz, Alberto, and Jeú who have taught me so much as we have been seeking God together.

I would like to thank Tom Julien and Terry White who encouraged me to continue writing. Without their encouragement, I would have given up.

I am grateful to George Johnson, Butch Pursley, Jeff Bogue, Bob Combs, and Neil Cole for their comments on the material included in this book.

I appreciate the patience and the thorough work of Jesse Deloe in editing the manuscript.

I am especially grateful for my wife, who has been such a great example to me as well as an encouragement. Without her help in listening, commenting, and extensive editing, this book would not have become a reality.

Finally, I am grateful to my Lord Jesus Christ, who called me out of the darkness and has so patiently worked with me as I have learned the joy of worshiping Him.

Bruce Triplehorn
Belénado Pará, Brazil
September 2008

Table of Contents

Preface

One of the greatest challenges in studying the Scriptures is to discover what gives each book cohesiveness. Various themes are woven into all 66 books of the Bible. What is it that ties each book together into a whole? Even more important, what is the "golden thread" throughout the entire Bible?

The reason for studying the Word is not just to obtain cognitive knowledge, but to know how to live a life pleasing to God, both individually and collectively as the body of Christ. By discovering foundational issues in the Bible, we can discover what God wants from us and what the Christian life is all about. I don't want just to live "religious moments" periodically, as a mediocre Christian. I want to know what God really wants of me and to live a life radically committed to Jesus.

I believe that *worship is the golden thread that ties the Bible together.* It is overtly emphasized or is the underlying theme from Cain and Abel's worship in Genesis to the worship of the Lamb in Revelation. From the Creation to the New Jerusalem, God is to be exalted and worshiped. Kings of Israel and Judah were evaluated, not on their foreign or domestic policies, but by their worship.

The Scriptures are a history of God's relationship with man through worship. It is the underlying theme of every page and the glue that ties its long history together. It is the key that unlocks the meaning of the Bible and the foundation of God's redemptive plan. It becomes obvious, then, that *worship is the golden thread of the Christian life and is to be woven into the fabric of believers' lives, ministries, and churches.* God wants us to learn to be worshipers!

All the great men of the Bible were called into ministry in the context of worship, which characterized their lives. The great men of church history were worshipers. But, somewhere along the way, the church lost the golden thread and drifted into the religious tendency to divide the Christian life into the sacred and the secular. This religious dichotomy has separated worship from our daily lives.

Worship is the sum total of what we are trying to implement in Brazil. It permeates everything we do from our first contact with someone when we share the gospel until we train and send out leaders. Worship is the foundation of our church structure. It is the goal of our meetings and encounters. Worship is what binds us together. Followers of the Lord Jesus Christ are already worshipers in one sense. John MacArthur says, "All who are saved are true worshipers. There is no possibility of being saved and then *not* worshiping God in spirit and truth. The objective of salvation is to make true worshipers (cf. Phil. 3:3)."[1]

A. W. Tozer writes, "Jesus was born of a virgin, suffered under Pontius Pilate, died on the cross and rose from the grave to make worshipers out of rebels!"[2]

If you have entered into a relationship with Jesus Christ through the new birth, you have before you an open door to a life-attitude of worship. Unfortunately, many of us have allowed the secular/sacred perspective of life to stifle God's supreme purpose for us.

Like me, you may be easily distracted from the practice of God's presence. You may be busy with important activities, but not devoting yourself as much as you should to what is essential. You are a worshiper, but may not be living a life of worship, as you should. The goal of this book is to help you develop as a worshiper, not just on Sunday morning, but throughout your life, allowing worship to overflow into service.

This book is about how to weave the golden thread into the fabric of our lives, our ministries, and the church. Worship is a life-attitude, involving walking by the Spirit. It is cultivated as we live out the reality of the body of Christ. I want to share with you, also, some of my own personal experiences as I have grown in my walk with God.

More than twenty years ago, John MacArthur prefaced his book on worship, saying:

> *My own heart has been relentlessly pursued by the lion of worship as over the years I have traversed the Scripture. My mind*

---

[1] John MacArthur, *The Gospel According to Jesus*, p. 56.
[2] A. W. Tozer, *Whatever Happened to Worship?* p. 11.

has been inescapably stalked by worship's awesome and majestic reality…In my ministry, I have always longed to lead people to a personal encounter with the majesty of our living, holy God, yet for years I fell short of fully understanding what worship was and how it is was to be accomplished. Out of recent personal frustration with my own failures in worship and a deep concern for a contemporary church that seemed to know as little as I about true worship, I sought to better understand the Bible's message that worship is the essential expression of service rendered unto God.[3]

And so, today I am writing with the same heart and pursuit.

Tozer writes, "Is it not a beautiful thing for a businessman to enter his office on Monday morning with an inner call to worship, 'The Lord is in my office—let all the world be silent before Him.' If you cannot worship the Lord in the midst of your responsibilities on Monday, it is not very likely that you were worshiping on Sunday?"[4]

I pray that you would no longer live a divided Christian life, separating the sacred from the secular, the ministry from your daily routine. The Lord's people are called to be full-time priests, full time in the ministry, having been set free from the restraints of religion to worship God in spirit and truth.

As I am writing this book, I am praying for you, the reader, to become the worshiper that God intends you to be.

Bruce W. Triplehorn

---

[3] John MacArthur, *The Ultimate Priority*, p. vii.
[4] Ibid. p. 122.

Introduction

"Our church does the same things your churches do. You just call everything by different names." João[1] said, as we putt-putted through the streets of Uberlândia, Brazil, in his old green Volkswagen. I couldn't believe my ears!

He and I had been good friends for years, having worked and studied the Bible together in the same church at the beginning of my missionary career. Despite our friendship, mutual respect for each another, and our common love for the Lord, it was obvious we had major differences in our views of the Christian life and the church.

I had just finished teaching the book of Ephesians in the Bible Institute at João's church, and he was taking me to catch a bus to return home. Preparing the course and teaching it were rich times of worship for me. I was still in awe of the work of God, His character, and His marvelous bride, the church, as Paul had explained them in that incredible epistle.

God's presence in our classes was obvious to all of us. By the end of the course, the seed truths that were planted had taken root. Strained relationships between pastors and between husbands and wives were resolved. A temporary truce was called in a war of words over different ministry styles. Most importantly, we understood the church as never before.

That is why João's words that afternoon surprised me. He had sat through the course and seemingly understood the concepts along with the rest of us. Our conversation caused me to think deeply about what made our vision of the ministry here in Brazil unique.

---

[1] Not his real name.

About nine years earlier, we had started a movement in Brazil that has resulted in at least six new churches and twenty other groups in various stages of church-development. João had raised questions and even opposed what we were doing. He believed our mobilizing teams of ordinary people from all walks of life for church planting detracted from the high calling of the pastor, which he had even referred to as "priestly." Our training was mentor-based and focused on preparing worshipers to plant churches. It included people who already had jobs to support themselves. Could it be that what we were doing was just a difference in semantics, as João suggested? What was the fundamental difference in the way we viewed the Christian life?

Despite our different views of the church, he tried to find similarity in some of the forms. "You call them 'spiritual families'; we call them 'home worship services.' You call them 'celebrations'; we call them 'worship services.' We even use the evangelism material you developed. You changed the names just to be more modern," João claimed.

He was right in saying that most of the changes people talk about today are simply differences in the way things are done (external forms) rather than substantial paradigm shifts. For example, a couple of the bigger controversies among many North American churches seem to be about music or sermon styles. I agree with João, that much of what is happening is just different ways of doing the same things. Changes are mostly in outward forms and the new names given to them.

As I further reflected on João's statements, I asked myself a number of questions. What true changes were we seeking to implement? What made the church in Acts such a vibrant group? What is really the core value of the church? If we were to strip away the building, the pews, the Sunday School visuals, the instruments, and microphones, what would be left? What is the church in its essence? If we are to plant a church in a new culture, what is the seed we will plant so that we do not merely transplant our culture's way of doing things? These are key questions all believers should be asking. We need to go back to the Bible to see what it teaches about what it is to be a Christian and how Christians are to relate to one another within the church.

Did you ever notice that you often think of a great answer to a question a few hours after the conversation has ended? I didn't express this to my friend, but it later dawned on me that our goal is not just a semantic change, but a renewal of our understanding of the essence of worship as it relates to the Christian life and the church. João, as many Christians, had a religious view of the Christian life, separating the organization of the church from its spiritual considerations.

Our differences all stemmed from a different view of worship. That influences how we view evangelism, discipleship, church government, the Christian life—everything! When worship is seen as a separate activity, then our Christian life is reduced to a mere allegiance to a religious system.

João is definitely not a hypocrite, nor is he uninvolved. He is very sincere and hard working. He really wants to please God. However, his view of worship has hurt his growth and effectiveness.

As the two of us pulled up to the house where I was to catch the bus, we sat in his VW Beetle and talked of other matters related to business and strategy. Based on the comments he had made earlier, however, it seemed as if we were speaking different languages. Nevertheless, the conversation I had with João challenged me to examine my life and ministry and ultimately led to the writing of this book.

Part 1 searches scriptural teaching about worship, examining the cause, the heart, the power, and the results of worship. Part 2 answers very practical questions. How does worship affect evangelism? What do walking by the Spirit and discipleship mean? What should small groups look like? How do we train leaders? How does worship as a life-attitude work in the church?

At the end of each chapter, you will find practical exercises to help build the chapter's concepts into your life. They are important in developing a worshipful life-attitude.

May God bless you richly as you explore with me the depths of God's purpose for your life.

Part One

WORSHIP
AS A
LIFE-ATTITUDE

Part One Introduction

WORSHIP
AS A
LIFE-ATTITUDE

The more I investigate and write about worship, the more I feel like a beginner, still on a steep learning curve. I had intended to write a one-chapter definition of worship, but a 20-year spiritual journey could not be confined to a few pages.

I have moved in a variety of circles, from the secular academic world to seminary, from the Northern Hemisphere to the Southern, and from Ozzy Osbourne to Keith Green. These changes stripped away much of my cultural narrowness and freed me from a lot of the religious habits and concepts acquired over the years. They enabled me to see the essence of Christianity, which deepened my intimacy with God. This growth in worship has been the single most transforming influence in my life. It is what changed me from a sinner to a saint, from a university professor to a missionary, from having a mediocre marriage to having a great relationship with my wife, and from being a frustrated Christian to a fruitful servant of the Lord.

A friend once said that if you cannot express your sermon in one sentence, you shouldn't preach it. I suppose the same is true for a book. The following definition and summary statements give an overview of what we will be developing throughout the first section of this book:

Worship is experiencing intimacy with God, seeking and enjoying constant spiritual fellowship with Him.

Worship results from *a believer's* choosing *to seek* such intimacy *by learning to see* God *through His Word and growing in* the *fear, honor, and love* of *God.* It involves the believer's constant offering of himself to God's *guiding presence, resulting in his being transformed into Christ's image and* continually involved in loving *service.*

The definition is fairly simple, and although the summary statements may seem a little cumbersome at first, they sum up well the biblical teaching on worship as found in John 4:23 and Romans 12:1-3.

Jesus used metaphors to simplify deeper spiritual principles. Taken from everyday life, these illustrations help simplify abstract biblical truths so that they can be applied to daily living more easily. In the pages that follow, we will use a marriage metaphor to illustrate the unity we can experience in our relationship with God.

I refer to worship as a life-attitude. This attitude goes much deeper than the "I never miss church on Sunday!" type of commitment. Rather, it is the heart of a true worshiper. Biblically, our hearts are more than just our emotions, but also include the "center and source of the whole inner life, with its thinking, feeling, and volition."[1] This includes our attitudes, values, thoughts, beliefs, emotions, desires, and worldview. Worship begins deep within us. It is a mind-set, a conscious choice shaped by the Bible. Keep this diagram in mind as you read.

LIFE-ATTITUDE ➡ LIFESTYLE
(Attitudes)   *(Actions)*

The lifestyle we are describing engenders actions that flow from a life-attitude of genuine worship as opposed to the "religious moments" practiced by many people.

Jonathan Edwards, a key figure in America's Great Awakening, was a dedicated, religious person. He talked a lot about God and prayed five times a day. He even mobilized his friends to build a prayer booth in the woods so he could pray in secret. However, he commented:

---

[1] Walter F. Bauer, F. Wilbur Gingrich, and Frederich W. Danker, *A Greek-English Lexicon.*

But in the process of time, my convictions and affections wore off; and I entirely lost all those affections and delights and left off secret prayer, at least as to any constant performance of it; and returned like a dog to his vomit, and went on in the ways of sin.

The first instance that I remember of that sort of inward sweet delight in God and divine things that I have lived much in since, was on reading those words, 1 Tim. 1:17, *Now unto the King eternal, immortal, invisible, the only wise God, be honor and glory forever and ever, Amen.* As I read the words, there came into my soul, and was as it were diffused through it, a sense of the glory of the Divine Being.[2]

Jonathan Edwards was sincere, fervent, and disciplined in his religious practices, but he was, nevertheless, still just a religious sinner. The experience he describes was the first time he tasted real worship and intimacy with God.

The principles we shall develop further in this book should guide you to comprehend and practice worship as a life-attitude. Begin reading in an attitude of prayer. Ask God to use these seed truths to build worship into the center of your life as you walk with Him.

May the golden thread of worship be woven deeply into your life.

For the crooked man is an abomination to the Lord; But He is intimate with the upright (Prov. 3:32).

Chapter 1

Misconceptions about Worship

Leaving Behind the Religious Life to Live Worship

"But an hour is coming, and now is, when THE TRUE WORSHIPERS *shall* WORSHIP THE FATHER *in spirit and truth; for such people* THE FATHER SEEKS TO BE HIS WORSHIPERS" (John 4:23).

SEED TRUTH: TO DEVELOP AS WORSHIPERS, WE CANNOT DIVIDE OUR LIVES INTO THE SACRED AND SECULAR, BUT WE MUST LEARN TO ALLOW EVERYTHING WE DO TO FLOW FROM WORSHIP. *Worship is not singing, nor is it a religious event, nor is it something isolated from our daily lives. Religious people tend to equate worship with music. They divide their existence into religious and secular activities and don't see the relationship between worship and their daily lives. Genuine worship is not a religious activity nor is it limited to music. It is life itself. It is the golden thread that ties everything in life together and gives it meaning.*

Worship has been my passion for more than twenty years. I awoke out of spiritual slumber four years after coming to Christ, when I discovered that worship was more than singing songs. The first message I ever preached was on worship. When we were raising our missionary support, the messages I preached were on worship. It is central in our discipleship and leadership training here in Brazil. One of my students recently commented that one of every four words I spoke in class was "worship."

WORSHIP IS LIFE ITSELF.
IT IS THE GOLDEN THREAD THAT TIES EVERYTHING IN LIFE
TOGETHER AND GIVES IT MEANING.

I was invited to speak at our youth camp in Brazil. I had been too busy to go in previous years. However, when I heard that worship was the theme, I eagerly accepted.

I gave it my all at this camp, trying to plant seeds that would sprout in these young lives, raising up true worshipers. I wanted them to experience united lives, joined to God with a single passion. I shared my favorite passages and my life, explaining how worship had changed me.

Toward the end of the camp, we had a panel discussion with others who had also taught on the subject during the retreat. A question about dancing was raised, because customarily at retreats the kids have a "social" time that is a folk dance, a cross between square and line dancing.

When one of the leaders condemned dancing as an expression of worship, someone pointed out sarcastically that maybe we should all ask God's forgiveness for the "social." One of the leaders called out, "Wait a minute. The social is one thing and worship is quite another. Don't mix the two."

Don't mix the two? Well then, don't do the social! If something can't be done with an attitude of worship and a consciousness of God's presence, maybe we shouldn't be doing it. Sure, there is a difference between corporate worship, where there should be a more serious atmosphere, and a time for youth just to play around. But this leader talked as if God were not present during fun activities.

His response made me wonder what he understood about worship. Had he listened to the teaching? Had he reflected on the theme of the retreat?

When we got out on the soccer field that afternoon, however, it was clear that the game did not fall into his worship category. At first, I thought he was kidding, the way he yelled at his teammates. It was just a pick-up game, but he was arguing with the ref and shouting criticisms at the other players. Since he is a good singer and often is invited to lead "worship," he considers it to be only music. By his play on the soccer field, he obviously divides his life into the sacred and secular. Worship to him is a religious event.

Before we can more fully develop our definition of worship, we must clear up some common misconceptions. Worship goes beyond any religious practice including singing and music, no matter what style we prefer. Worship is not something isolated from our daily lives that we tack on to our already busy schedules. Worship is our life.

THE MARRIAGE METAPHOR

Marriage is used extensively in the Scriptures to illustrate our relationship with God (Isa. 62:5; Jer. 31:32; Ezek. 16:32; Eph. 5:31-32; Rev. 19:7; 21:2). Even the adultery of Gomer, Hosea's wife, is used as a vivid illustration of the deep hurt God felt over Israel's unfaithfulness (Hos. 2:2). Thus, marriage can help us understand worship better.

Marriage is the joining of two lives into one. Although some may view marriage as adding a spouse to their list of other activities or responsibilities, it is really a new way of life and a new life-attitude. Many think they have their careers, their friends, their weekend sports, their relatives, etc., and now, when they marry, they simply add one more *thing* to their lives. The conflicts begin when the spouse starts interfering with the already established areas.

In the last few years I have begun to learn what it means to be one with my wife. My relationship with her affects everything, influencing my attitudes and actions. Outwardly, my marriage may not look much different than it was a few years back when I neglected her. I am still involved in many of the same activities, and I travel quite a bit. However, there are some attitude changes that have influenced the whole dynamic of our relationship.

Now she is my best friend, and, therefore, she is in the back of my mind all the time. When I hear something new, I think, "Oh, Lisa will be interested in that." When I go someplace new, I think, "Wow, Lisa would really enjoy this. I wish she were here."

Some couples take separate vacations because they "need their space." It's a "his and hers" mentality characteristic of many relationships. However, marriage is full time and not just an important *part* of one's life.

We cannot be part-time worshipers any more than we can be part-time husbands or wives. Worship and our relationship with God are not additions to our lives, but the very center of our being. It is unthinkable that we would take a break from our relationship with God or tell Him we "need our space," although we may often act that way. We are one spirit with God (1 Cor. 6:17).

> WE CANNOT BE PART-TIME WORSHIPERS ANY MORE THAN WE CAN BE PART-TIME HUSBANDS OR WIVES.

God does not want first place in our lives; He wants the only place. Our relationship with Him governs everything we do. Instead of having God first, family second, job third, etc., we should involve Him intimately in all of them. He is the Master over all. Only in this way can we live consistently with what it truly means to be a Christian. Referring to money, Jesus said we cannot serve two masters (Matt. 6:24). James called people who are friends with the world "adulterers" and "enemies of God" (James 4:4).

Our goal is a unified life that results from the continual process of submitting all things to God. *Worship unites every aspect of our lives with the Lord.* Those things that used to seem so important or attractive diminish as we become increasingly aware of His presence and less distracted by the things of this world.

MISCONCEPTIONS ABOUT WORSHIP

WORSHIP IS NOT JUST MUSIC.

Most Christians seem to believe that the Sunday morning service is the time when we are supposed to worship. Many think worship is expressed primarily by praise and that praise most commonly involves music. Hence, musicians usually lead worship services. But leading a group in worship effectively does not require musicians. Anyone who can bring hearts together in God's presence can lead worship.

Worship is often looked upon as a feeling of God's presence created by the circumstances. That is why music is often confused with worship. Our tastes in music may affect our ability to *feel* God's presence, because music can produce a sense of the sacred.

I did not relate well to the church in which I was raised. The preacher was a very sincere man who gave interesting messages, but there was little biblical content. When the organ hit certain chords, it was a cue to sit up, stand up, read a responsive reading, or start talking and go home. The organ led the service.

Even though the music and rituals were not my style, I felt good about going to church. Perhaps I felt I had witnessed something sacred and had fulfilled my religious duty. I had no idea, however, what it meant to have a relationship with the Lord, let alone what worship was all about.

When I became a believer, I attended a more progressive church where we sang "Scripture songs" accompanied by guitars. I could really relate to the music and the practical study of the Bible. When we moved into a new building, however, an organ was used, and we started singing hymns. I just couldn't "worship" because the music got in the way of my "feelings of worship." In our former location I suspect the guitar music would have gotten in the way of the older people's "feelings of worship."

Since that time, however, I have grown, and the style of music does not interfere with my fellowship with God. My worship is no longer confined to music.

As Herbert Bateman says, "The overemphasis on music in worship … has led some worship leaders to erroneously place it at the center. Sometimes music is equated with authentic worship."[1]

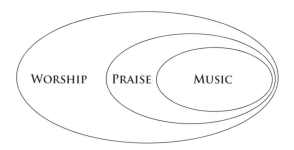

---

[1] Herbert W. Bateman IV, "A Call for Authentic Worship" in Bateman, *Authentic Worship*, p. 50.

By making worship music and praise the same, it becomes easier unconsciously to divide our lives into the sacred and secular. When I am praising, I am worshiping. When I am not praising, I am not worshiping and I carry on my life as usual without thinking about God. Our goal is to worship God 24-7. We frequently express our worship in praise and sometimes by praising in song as in the figure above.

Is there anything wrong with praise or is it somehow inferior to worship? Not at all. Praise is an important expression of a worship lifestyle.

Keep in mind that praise can be expressed not only in song, but also with words, gestures, and even dance. Psalm 87:7 talks about speaking, singing, and dancing as expressions of praise.

Someone asked me what kind of God takes delight in the singing of hymns to Him. From a human perspective a desire to be praised seems rather egotistical. God's delight in our expressions of praise, however, is not because He has a need to hear encouraging words about Himself, but such singing expresses and reinforces the truth about Him. He finds joy when praise is a spontaneous outpouring of our love and respect for Him.

A friend of mine, attending a worship seminar, listened in amazement as all the presentations told of the techniques of music, lighting, and sound. Someone commented that if you had a twenty thousand dollar sound system, you could really do things up right. My friend pointed out that they had forgotten the most important element: God Himself.

WORSHIP IS NOT RELIGION.

I once visited an older gentleman in a hospital in Belém, where we live. Since he did not know the Lord, his daughter was eager for me to share Scripture with him. When I opened my Bible, the nurse came in with his dinner and he became distracted. His wife admonished him, "Not now, dear. We are having a religious moment. It is important for us to have these religious moments. Your dinner can wait."

"Religious moment! Ha!" I smiled to myself. That is typical thinking for many Brazilians who do not have a relationship with Christ, but I had never actually heard anyone say it out loud. The more I thought about it, however, the more I realized that many people view the Christian life that way.

I have an aunt who thinks it's wonderful that I am "religious." Although I realize she means it as a compliment in seeing me as someone committed to God, I really don't like being called religious. I consider religion to be the opposite of genuine Christianity and in stark contrast to genuine worship.

However, the Bible *does* use the word "religion." Festus lumped Paul's faith in Jesus into the broad category of religion along with Judaism (Acts 25:19). Paul himself described his life as a Pharisee as belonging to a strict "sect of our religion" (Acts 26:5; Gal 1:13). He also described the Athenians as "religious"[2] (Acts18:22) as a bridge to expose them to the true God.

The word translated as "religion" in these passages emphasizes not the life-attitudes, but rather the outward expressions of worship.[3] It usually has a negative connotation, because it emphasizes only the external manifestations of a supposed relationship with God independent of any inner reality. Thus, the empty sacrifices and rituals were condemned by God in Isaiah 1:10-20. Jesus echoed these words, saying, "This people honors Me with their lips, But their heart is far away from Me. But in vain do they worship Me…" (Mark 7:6-7). Vain worship is the right actions without the inward relationship with God.

There is a notable exception to the generally negative use of this word. James 1:26-27 says, "If anyone thinks himself to be religious, and yet does not bridle his tongue but deceives his own heart, this man's religion is worthless. Pure and undefiled religion in the sight of our God and Father is this: to visit the orphans and widows in their distress, and to keep oneself unstained by the world."

---

[2] Paul uses the word deisidaímōn, which generally means to be superstitious, but in this context it is positive. It basically means to reverence or fear deity.

[3] Kittel and Fredrich say, "It has to do mostly with the externals of worship, and makes them a matter of taste or choice. Synonyms…are similarly rare in the NT. This indicates that expressions denoting a religious attitude to God find little place in NT Christianity, for here one's attitude to God is the response to God's claim, and in distinction from cultus, the Bible speaks of faith as the obedience of the whole person to God." Gerhard Kittel and Gerhard Friedrich, *Theological Dictionary of the New Testament*.

What James is saying is that the real external manifestation of worship is not expressed in mere religious moments when we sing praises. It is not a ritual or a system of rules. Real "religion," or the real outward expression of worship, is seen in the way we treat the most needy people around us.

"Religion," for the remainder of this book, will be used to describe the empty, outward expression of a supposed relationship with God by those who live a divided life. Since religion emphasizes external appearances, there will be a tendency for ritualism, legalism, individualism, and hypocrisy.

I have been fighting to free myself from the vestiges of religion that I still carry because it interferes with my own worship. We have found that the greatest barrier to people coming to Jesus in Brazil is the culture's religious mind-set. People are drawn to religion and want to add Jesus to their other good luck charms in order to be blessed rather than submit to Him. Even those who know Him can easily slide into a benefit-seeking religious mentality.

On the other hand, real worship expresses itself outwardly, but not just during specific religious moments. Real worship will always be practiced as a lifestyle. Religion is characterized by a divided life, separating worship of God from beliefs, attitudes, actions, and ministry.

AN EXAMPLE

Although this is a fictitious story, it could very well have been my life. It could be your life. Try to put yourself in the shoes of Jim.

Even though Jim was raised going to church, it was only when he went away to Winchester State University that he heard the plan of salvation. A couple of guys on his dorm floor who were involved in a campus ministry explained a tract that showed him how he could have a fulfilling life through Jesus Christ. Things made sense and he asked Jesus to come into his heart.[4] He soon started attending

---

[4] This terminology, considered central to the modern gospel, is based on an erroneous interpretation of Rev. 3:20. The New Testament calls us to respond to the Gospel by repenting and believing. Although many, including myself, make decisions as Jim did, this initial step often leads the person to read the Scriptures and come to true salvation.

campus Bible studies and couldn't seem to get enough. He also talked with others about getting saved and even led some Bible studies. He loved the group times. They were dynamic and the praise music really moved him.

Jim learned how to live by Christian standards. Although drinking, drugs, and illicit sex were the norm in his dorm, he learned how to control his desires and avoid those pitfalls. Jim found that memorizing Scripture and his quiet time were very important in resisting temptation. He also had a prayer partner who held him accountable and helped him overcome some of his bad habits and to resist temptation.

During summer break, Jim felt strange going back to his home church. It seemed so cold and the old hymns seemed so dry. It wasn't at all like the spontaneous, fun, and meaningful times he had in the campus group.

The summer before his senior year, Jim went on a ministry trip. He was amazed at how open the people were in the Latin American country. Many people made decisions. He was especially moved by the way the people in the small church sang. Although they were sometimes off-key, the songs they sang were not at all like those in his home church. What made them different?

When he returned for his senior year, Jim prayed about going into ministry full time. He met Sarah, a girl who was also involved in the group. After praying about it, they decided that God was leading them to marry.

As soon as they graduated, Jim and Sarah were married. Although they wanted to serve God and maybe even become missionaries, they still had debts from college. They both got jobs and started working. They found a local church that was somewhat like their campus group. The music was upbeat and meaningful. The messages were interesting and always touched on practical areas of their lives.

After their kids came along, the idea of full-time ministry gradually faded. However, they were faithful in their church attendance and their giving, and they were known as hard-working, honest employees. When they had a chance, they invited people to church or talked about how meaningful it was to know Jesus. They went on several short-term missions trips. Jim even became the teacher of his adult Sunday School group and joined the elder board. People who knew them said what a great Christian couple they were.

Some problems hovered underneath the surface, however, and Jim knew it. Although there were no arguments, the passion had gone out of their marriage and everything had become routine. Although they had prayed together when they were dating, they rarely talked about Jesus with each other now. They just dutifully bowed their heads for prayer every meal, wanting to set that example for the kids.

Jim was constantly stressed with the pressures of his job. Sarah was caught up in being a mother, shuttling her kids from one activity to another. Neither had much time to read the Bible any more, although they rarely missed a church service. When they were in college, they had already memorized all the key passages. They knew well most of the stories in the Bible, especially the stories about Jesus. Most of the time, they pretty much knew what the pastor was going to say.

But Jim knew something was missing. Although he never did anything illicit or immoral, he struggled like everyone else with certain sins that just wouldn't go away. Whenever he talked with real worshipers, he listened quietly, wishing he were the same and vowing that he would start reading the Bible more. He knew something was missing but was at a loss to know what to do. Why did they seem so much more committed than he? After all, he thought he was doing the right things and did his best to maintain a "good testimony" before everyone.

Is it possible that Jim would come to the end of his life, stand before the Lord and say, "But Lord, did I not teach Sunday School in your name, serve on the church board in your name, go on missions trips in your name?" and God would answer, "Depart from Me, you never worshiped Me"? (cf. Matt. 7:22-23).

Is it possible that Jim merely embraced a religion rather than Christ and was never really saved? Could it be that his worship was only an emotional response to music? Might it be that his behavior was only an application of the Christian ethic and his church attendance was merely a religious duty?

Of course, it is also possible that Jim, somewhere along the line in his study of the Scriptures, truly became a new creature in Christ

(2 Cor. 5:17), but in his discipleship, he never learned the centrality of true worship, intimacy with God, or what it means to walk by the Spirit. He thought as long as he didn't violate the Christian moral ethic and did fulfill his responsibilities, he was being a good Christian.

Perhaps he read his Bible to learn more about God instead of to know Him more intimately.

It is possible that he sought to do the right thing as a good testimony instead of seeking to be right in His relationship with God.

Maybe he prayed to tell God what he wanted instead of to know God's heart and pray according to God's will.

Maybe he went to church only to be fed and to sing rather than to join his heart with other worshipers in God's presence in mutual edification.

Perhaps he merely contributed money to missions instead of experiencing the Great Commission (Matt. 28:19-20) as a result of His intimacy with God.

Most of all, it is almost certain that, although he had been moved emotionally, he never learned the joy of walking daily in God's presence. Jim had learned to remember God only at certain times. Worship was merely an activity tacked on to his life rather than the golden thread that tied his life together. He had never learned the art of worshiping and thus his life produced only wood, hay and stubble (1 Cor. 3:12-15).

WORSHIP IS NOT A LIFE DIVIDED INTO SECULAR AND SACRED.

A Brazilian pastor spoke at one of our national conventions in northern Brazil and was used by God to open people's eyes to their spiritual state. A friend later told me you could hear a pin drop as everyone sat in awe of God after the message.

I asked how the main business session went that afternoon in light of God's presence in the morning worship time. He grinned, shaking his head, "It was the same old thing." Apparently, petty fights and outbursts of anger were evident. In the minds of the attendees, business was one thing and worship another.

A couple years later, at another conference, I spoke on walking with God as it relates to worship. After the third message, I asked my friend João whom I mentioned in the introduction what he thought of the material I had presented. Once again, I couldn't believe my ears at his response.

"I really liked what you had to say," João replied. "I enjoy hearing you speak about worship and walking with God. It is obvious that there has been a more spiritual emphasis in the churches of Belém since you arrived. But your problem, Bruce, is all you think about is the spiritual. You don't think about the political aspects of the church." My friend still had a dichotomous view of the Christian life and the church. In his mind, the spiritual and the political are separate.

Many people have a divided view of life, splitting their lives between the sacred and the secular.

Of course, we need to set aside moments for personal and corporate praise when we train our minds to focus on God. But worship is not to be an isolated, weekly activity when we recall God's presence then resume our "normal lives" with our batteries recharged. As Joseph Carroll comments, "To worship Him in our quiet time is not the end. It is only the beginning. You are merely tuning your instrument to face the day."[5]

> MANY PEOPLE HAVE A DIVIDED VIEW OF LIFE, SPLITTING
> THEIR LIVES BETWEEN THE SACRED AND THE SECULAR.

I could cite many examples of people living an almost "Jekyll and Hyde" life, acting one way during *spiritual* times, only to turn around to treat business matters as if God were not present. With such people, there is no singleness of purpose under the one Master.

The Divided Life and Attitudes

"This people honors Me with their lips, But their heart is far away from Me. But in vain do they worship Me, teaching as doctrines the precepts of men" (Mark 7:6-7, quoting Isaiah 29:13).

Nothing is worse than doing right things for wrong reasons. Expressions of reverence, praise, obedience, or even good works that

---

[5] Joseph Carroll, *How to Worship Jesus Christ,* p. 23.

do not flow from worship are hypocritical and "in vain," or empty. Sin is not only doing wrong, but also doing what is right, even what God has commanded, with a wrong attitude or motivation.

In the context of Mark 7, it may seem to us that the disciples lacked personal hygiene, because they did not wash their hands. Certainly, nothing is wrong with washing one's hands after coming from the market; in fact, it is a pretty good idea. The Pharisees' motivation, however, was to purify themselves ritually and externally, but they had no concern about their internal purity.

The word "honor" as Jesus used it in this passage referred to the Jews' religious moments rather than a life-attitude of worship. To honor God truly means to value Him as one's treasure. Their forms of worship were empty because they were devoid of valuing, treasuring, esteeming, and honoring God in their heart or innermost being. Their worship was mere lip service.

Our lives are divided because we do not have just one treasure, Jesus Christ. We often find our meaning and value in the same things the world does.

The Divided Life and Beliefs

When asked why she converted to Catholicism, a colleague of my father replied that she wanted a religion that told her exactly what to believe and what to do. As long as she went to Mass and did what she was told, she would fulfill her religious obligation and would not have to think about it the rest of the week. She said she wanted to fulfill her religious duty and not be bothered anymore. She was not drawn to authentic worship as a life-attitude, but was attracted to religion that she could easily lay aside while continuing her scientific activities.

My father asked another scientific colleague, a priest, how he could reconcile the theory of evolution and the priesthood. The priest replied that he wore two hats, a scientific hat and a priestly hat. He did not mix the two. His religion was distinctly separate from his life as a scientist.

It is not only Catholics who think that way. This dichotomy exists in every religion, including some evangelical, conservative born-again Christians.

We have often heard politicians who try to appease both sides of the abortion debate say, "I am personally opposed, but I support the right of . . .."

If someone's "beliefs" are contradicted by his attitudes or actions, those beliefs are not truly beliefs at all, but merely religious dogma. The divided life leads to a contradictory and inconsistent belief system.

That is why Jesus said, "Rightly did Isaiah prophesy of you hypocrites, as it is written, 'This people honors Me with their lips, But their heart is far away from Me. But in vain do they worship Me, teaching as doctrines the precepts of men.' Neglecting the commandment of God, you hold to the tradition of men" (Mark 7:6-8).

The Divided Life and Ministry

Because they see worship as something tacked on to the Christian life, many church members make the distinction between those "in the ministry full time" and "laymen." Even the lives of those who are "in the ministry," are often divided into ministry and personal activities.

Jesus didn't divide His life into such compartments. On one occasion He was ready to go on a retreat with His disciples when they returned from a ministry trip (Mark 6:30-32), and a multitude came after Him. Jesus felt compassion for them and ministered to them (Mark 6:34), feeding five thousand men plus women and children, involving His disciples in the ministry.

Often, at just those moments when I think of taking a break, God presents an opportunity to share my faith with someone. Consequently, nothing I do is not somehow related to ministry. It is being on call 24-7. There is no retiring to the beach or sitting on the porch in a rocking chair. Retirement starts when my body is either very weak[6] or six feet under and I am finally fulfilled in my worship in His presence.

---

[6] Since worship is the heart of ministry, it still continues when we are weak or disabled. We may not be able to walk around, but we are still ministering and our lives are having an impact we may never recognize.

The Divided Life Condemned

The "Sermon on the Mount" (Matt. 5-7) is a masterful exposition, condemning the divided religious life. Jesus knew that many of the Jews of His day were comfortable and self-confident in their outward obedience of the Ten Commandments and their mechanical temple rituals. They thought as long as they fulfilled their religious obligations and didn't overtly violate God's righteous standard, they were pleasing Him.

In his classic book, *How to be a Christian without being Religious*, Fritz Ridenour writes that religious people "prefer religious effort—dealing with God on their own terms. This puts them in control. They feel good about 'being religious'… Instead of responding to God's love, we reach out for it—and neatly keep God at arm's length while we do so."[7]

Jesus condemned a religious mind-set with its emphasis on outward forms, and He constantly taught that our actions should flow from a worshipful relationship with God.

Jesus started His message in Matthew 5:1-12 by describing the inward attitudes (vv. 3-6) and the fruit of those who are true worshipers (vv. 7-12).

He demonstrated the futility of outward actions that do not correlate with inward attitudes (murder, adultery, divorce, oaths). Worship not only changes our actions, but also transforms our attitudes (Matt 5:13-48).

Jesus recognized that spiritual disciplines (prayer and fasting) could become mere religious activities if not motivated by a love for God. The disciplines are to help weave the golden thread of worship into our lives, not to show us to be religious (Matt. 6:1-18).

> WORSHIP NOT ONLY CHANGES OUR ACTIONS,
> BUT ALSO TRANSFORMS OUR ATTITUDES.

Genuine worship, as Jesus taught, influences our values. Our treasure is no longer to be in the goods we acquire or in our fame. We are to desire and seek intimacy with Him (Matt. 6:19-7:12).

---

[7] Fritz Ridenour, *How to Be a Christian*, p. ii.

Jesus warned about false teachers who would point people to the broad gate of religion rather than the narrow gate of walking with Him (Matt 7:13-14). The lives of these false, religious teachers contradict their teaching (Matt. 7:15-20). Those who follow false teachers will find out one day that their religion did not save them. At the judgment, they will discover their religious activities were no substitute for knowing God (Matt. 7:21-23). At the end of His message, Jesus compares people who follow a life that is merely religious to those whose house is built on sand. But He compares believers who worship God with an undivided heart to those who build their house upon rock (Matt. 7:24-27).

Jesus' most stinging rebuke of religion is in Matthew 23:3 where He condemns those who live divided lives. With a cutting accusation, He says, "They say things, and do not do them."

Many people proudly claim to be religious, and that is all they are. Jesus calls them hypocrites. Unfortunately, many of us who know the Lord are also living in such a way that our actions are not always consistent with our beliefs and attitudes.

Why the Divided Life?

Why do people try to find meaning in anything other than their relationship with Christ? Why do we divide our interests? Why are we so easily distracted from His presence?

People live divided lives because they are more comfortable doing *than* being. "John's disciples and the Pharisees were fasting; and they came and said to Him, 'Why do John's disciples and the disciples of the Pharisees fast, but Your disciples do not fast?'" (Mark 2:18).

We like to be able to measure our growth and success, but worship and fellowship with God are so intangible we cannot put them in a report. How can you measure love? It can't be quantified or broken down into minutes or hours.

Some of John's disciples who were still bound by religion and hadn't figured things out yet, along with some Pharisees, questioned Jesus. They asked why He and His disciples were not following the traditional forms of fasting. They did not understand that fasting was not to be done as a merely religious ritual.

John MacArthur observes, "Along with alms giving and certain prescribed prayers, twice-weekly fasting was one of the three major expressions of Orthodox Judaism during Jesus' day."[8] Although fasting may have started with good intentions, it had become an empty custom.

Nothing is wrong with fasting in itself. It is one of several spiritual disciplines of the Christian life. As MacArthur states, however, "Religious ritual and routine have always been dangerous to true godliness… But even when it is not wrong in itself, when a *form* of praying, worshiping or serving becomes the focus of attention, it actually becomes a barrier to true righteousness."[9]

In the Old Testament, fasts were proclaimed at certain critical moments (2 Chron. 20:3; Ezra 8:21; Esther 4:15-16). Some moments were for humility and brokenness before the Lord, and at those times, fasting was appropriate. Other moments were for rejoicing and were accompanied by feasting. Those times can't be programmed, but they should be appropriate to the occasion.

People live divided lives because they prefer to practice forms rather than respond to God. "And Jesus said to them, 'While the bridegroom is with them, the attendants of the bridegroom cannot fast, can they? So long as they have the bridegroom with them, they cannot fast. But the days will come when the bridegroom is taken away from them, and then they will fast in that day'" (Mark 2:19-20).

Jesus' rhetorical question shows the absurdity of an outward expression of sorrow and repentance during a time of joy. The bridegroom's presence is marked by celebration, not mourning. Jesus noted that when He was no longer present, "They will fast in that day," which would be an appropriate reflection of one's dependence on Him.

"No one sews a patch of unshrunk cloth on an old garment; otherwise the patch pulls away from it, the new from the old, and a worse tear results. No one puts new wine into old wineskins; otherwise the wine will burst the skins, and the wine is lost and the skins as well; but one puts new wine into fresh wineskins" (Mark 2:21-22).

Jesus used these two additional analogies to emphasize that the living relationship between God and man could not be mixed with the ritualism that characterized the religion of His day.

---

[8] MacArthur, *The MacArthur New Testament Commentary*, Matthew 8-15, p. 68.
[9] Ibid.

The first analogy was about sewing together two types of cloth—new and old—in making a patch. If the two are incompatible, damage will result at the first washing, as the new cloth shrinks and tears away from the old cloth. Everyone who heard Jesus knew the two types of cloth were incompatible.

The second analogy involved putting new wine in old wineskins, something people of that day knew was unwise. The leather wineskins would stretch and lose their elasticity after wine had fermented in them. When the new wine started fermenting, the wineskins could not stretch any further and would rupture.

The new wine Jesus was describing is more than just the New Covenant. It is a living relationship with God, something new and recent[10] as a result of Christ's sacrifice. The old forms (wineskins) cannot contain a living, dynamic, undivided relationship with God.

The old wineskins are worn out and antiquated religious rituals.[11] They are no longer useful because they have served their purpose. They are not necessarily old in terms of time but in their usefulness. The new wineskins are of a completely different character from the old.[12]

The new wine of our intimacy with God will lead us to seek new wineskins to cultivate our worship. Once we have drunk deeply of the new wine, we long for the freedom to live in God's presence, leading us to new outward expressions. The antiquated religious rituals are no longer appropriate.

Jesus is not talking about replacing the wineskins, but rather partaking of the new wine. Jesus' death and resurrection brought about a change, not only in the form of worship, but also in the essence of worship. Paradigm shifts in worship today are often more about the wineskins than the new wine. There is a tendency to focus on changes in forms of worship rather than on its essence.

Many Old Testament saints walked with God and lived their lives before Him. They were commanded to love God with their whole beings and remember His presence in their daily activities (Deut. 6:4-9). Worship was never meant to be limited to the temple.

---

[10] Greek: *néos* - Something that is new in time, young.
[11] Greek: *palaiós* – Something outdated in terms of years; it belongs to the past.
[12] Greek: *kainós* – Something of a different quality from the old; unused.

God instituted festivals, Sabbaths, and sacrifices. These activities were meant to separate the sacred from the common, but were never intended to bring about the dichotomy that came into existence and led to empty ritualism.

Is it possible that true believers may be prisoners of the old wineskins of religion? Absolutely! Some of John's disciples had not broken free. The book of Acts is the story of the disciples being set free. Every time they discovered their freedom in Christ, the church grew.

When new people were released to do ministry, the church grew (Acts 6:7). When they were forced to leave the proximity of the temple, the church grew (Acts 8). When the church finally realized and declared its freedom from the law, the church grew (Acts 16:4-5). The freedom they discovered was not a fleshly freedom so that they could do as they pleased, but the freedom to live in God's presence at all times. As a result, the church grew and spread.

People live divided lives because they don't like change. They are more comfortable with familiar rituals and no longer seek to grow. "And no one, after drinking old wine wishes for new; for he says, 'The old is good enough'" (Luke 5:39).

People generally don't like change. Familiarity is comfortable. In the beginning of their Christian lives, everything is new and they are always seeking to deepen their worship. But they soon become content, and their passion loses momentum. Change in rituals becomes threatening even though they have lost sight of why the practice was instituted in the first place.

What is needed is not a change in forms but a return to the essence of worship. Simply changing from hymns to contemporary praise songs, for example, is not a real paradigm shift. New architecture or different homiletic styles are all just changes in the wineskins that can occur without really drinking the new wine.

JESUS CORRECTS A RELIGIOUS SINNER

Jesus' conversation with the Samaritan woman is probably the most extensive expression of God's mind about worship. The woman saw worship as a *religious moment* to be observed at a sacred place. She did not see worship as uniting herself to God in such a way that it influenced her daily life.

After breaking down all kinds of cultural, social, and racial barriers, Jesus offered her "living water," which refers to spiritual life that flows from the indwelling presence of the Holy Spirit (John 4:10).

Like us, the Samaritan woman was focused on the physical world. She was unable to comprehend a relationship with God. Her religion was restricted to certain holy moments experienced at holy places, and it certainly didn't affect her lifestyle. But Jesus promised her a truly satisfying relationship (John 4:13-14). He offered her something new, but she continued to ask about the right way to do things.

WORSHIP IS NOT RESTRICTED TO TIME OR PLACE.

When Jesus exposed the woman's lifestyle, she quickly changed the subject to religion. She asked about the correct place to practice religious moments. "'Our fathers worshiped in this mountain; and you people say that in Jerusalem is the place where men ought to worship.' Jesus declares that worship is no longer restricted to holy times and holy places. He said to her, 'Woman, believe Me, an hour is coming when neither in this mountain, nor in Jerusalem, will you worship the Father'" (John 4:20-21).

Virtually every religion has some sort of holy man or woman who performs some kind of sacred ceremony in a sacred location. That was also true of the Jews. The Jewish priests (the holy men) performed their sacrifices (their holy ceremonies) in the temple in Jerusalem (the holy place).

The Samaritans had their own parallel religion with priests and sacrifices on Mount Gerazim. The focus of the Samaritan woman's question was on the proper holy place for worship to take place. She, like most people, saw things this way:

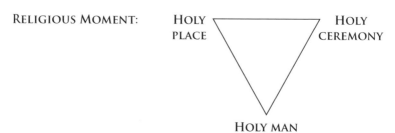

RELIGIOUS MOMENT: HOLY PLACE   HOLY CEREMONY   HOLY MAN

For her, this sacred triangle of religion was necessary to have an appropriate religious moment.

People associate worship with a specific location because it makes life simpler. As Skip Ryan observed, "If we can deal with God in a certain place and at a certain time, the implication is that we are free to live the rest of our lives the way we want to."[13]

Before Christ's death and resurrection, God Himself restricted worship to the sacred triangle (Jerusalem, the priests, the sacrifices). That is why David longed to dwell in the house of the Lord; it was the place where he could worship and commune with God. David sought to unite himself with God in worship but had to go to the temple to do it.

Then Jesus made a monumental statement to the Samaritan woman! Worship would no longer be restricted to either of the places she had mentioned. With Christ's perfect sacrifice, everything changed! His followers would never again be limited in their opportunity to commune with Him.

MacArthur comments, "Our Lord had come into the world to seek and to save the lost. He revealed to a Samaritan woman that His objective in seeking and redeeming sinners is to fulfill God's will in making them true worshipers."[14]

That is why Peter wrote in 1 Peter 2:5, "You also, as living stones, are being built up as a spiritual house [we are the holy place] for a holy priesthood [we are the holy men], to offer up spiritual sacrifices acceptable to God through Jesus Christ [we perform the holy ceremony]."

Look at the change that happened through Jesus' sacrifice:

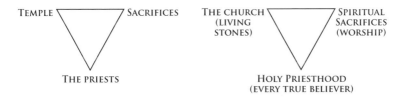

TEMPLE — SACRIFICES

THE PRIESTS

THE CHURCH (LIVING STONES) — SPIRITUAL SACRIFICES (WORSHIP)

HOLY PRIESTHOOD (EVERY TRUE BELIEVER)

---

[13] Joseph Ryan, *Worship: Beholding the Beauty of the Lord*, p. 74.
[14] MacArthur, *The Gospel According to Jesus*, p. 56.

Although there are times to separate ourselves for private and corporate worship, worship should be our constant mind-set. As Madame Guyon says, "It is not enough to be turned inwardly to your Lord an hour or two each day. There is little value in being turned within to the Lord unless the end result is an anointing and a spirit of prayer which continues with you during the whole day."[15]

Rick Warren writes, "You will never grow a close relationship with God by just attending church once a week or even having a daily quiet time. Friendship with God is built by sharing all your life experiences with him."[16]

Worship Is a Constant Life-Attitude.

"But an hour is coming, and now is, when the true worshipers shall worship the Father in spirit and truth; for such people the Father seeks to be His worshipers" (John 4:23).

JESUS TEACHES THAT WORSHIP IS
A CONSTANT LIFE-ATTITUDE.

Later, we will explore in depth the truths Jesus declared in this verse. Suffice it to say now that worship is a subjective, spiritual attitude (in spirit) as well as an objective, conscious, cognitive experience (in truth) that flows from what we know about God, largely from His Word. It is not an either-or activity, but a both-and attitude.

To worship God in *spirit* is the inward communion we have with Him in our spirits. We can think of this as "the pure, inner worship of God, that has nothing to do with holy times, places, appurtenances, or ceremonies."[17] Worship is spiritual in its essence, since God is spirit in His essence.

Worshiping God in spirit also means it is not just an occasional activity, but an inner attitude that follows a person throughout his day. A worshiper's goal is to live constantly in an attitude of reverence,

---

[15] Madame Guyon, *Experiencing Jesus Christ*, p. 71.
[16] Rick Warren, *The Purpose Driven Life*, p. 87.
[17] Bauer et al.

in awe of God's continual presence, because he consciously chooses to join his life to God in worship and fix his mind on things above. There is also the objective aspect of worship *in truth*. Our worship needs to be based on a right concept of God as He has revealed Himself. We need to use all our resources to comprehend what God has said in His Word to provide the basis of our worship. There is no shortcut to spirituality that bypasses the study of the Word.

MacArthur described the Samaritans' worship as animated or enthusiastic heresy while the Jews were guilty of dead orthodoxy."[18] Many churches today could easily fall into either category, failing to worship God in spirit and truth. Many of those committed to the truth are mechanical in their expression of worship while those who show more enthusiasm may have little regard for what the Scriptures say, relying on feelings instead.

Neither the Samaritans nor most of the Jews were truly worshiping God. They were merely being religious.

GOD SEEKS WORSHIPERS.

Jesus declares that God is seeking worshipers: "…for such people the Father seeks to be His worshipers" (John 4:23).

In Brazil, it is easy to find people who want to be religious. It is considered good luck for a person to study the Bible with you. It is not difficult to strike up a casual conversation about spiritual things. To find those interested in becoming worshipers, however, is a different story that we will address in part 2.

The world is full of religious people. But God is looking for people who long to have their lives connected to Him so His presence influences everything they do. He is seeking worshipers.[19]

A UNITED WORSHIPING LIFE (HEART)

"Teach me Your way, O LORD; / I will walk in Your truth; / Unite my heart to fear Your name. / I will give thanks to You, O Lord my God, with all my heart, / And will glorify Your name forever" (Ps. 86:11-12).

---

[18] MacArthur, a "Superconference" message at Liberty University in the early 80s.
[19] The Greek word zētéō carries the idea of zealously seeking out or striving to find.

All of us have divided hearts to some extent. David asked God to "Unite my heart to fear Thy name," or as the NIV translates it, "Give me an undivided heart."

Commenting on Psalm 86, Spurgeon says, "Our minds are apt to be divided [among] a variety of objects, like trickling streamlets which waste their force in a hundred runnels; our great desire should be to have all our life-floods poured into one channel and to have that channel directed towards the Lord alone."[20]

The heart, biblically, is the composite of desires, emotions, thoughts, and the will. When the psalmist asked for a united heart, his plea was for God to create within him a single desire, focus, attitude, and passion.

As we said earlier, "fear" is a worship term. It is not a cowering or recoiling before God or the dread of punishment. It is being in awe of God, having a holy reverence for Him. We become fascinated with God with the result that all our interest is focused on Him.

His *name* is the sum total of His character or, as Paul commonly speaks of it in Ephesians and Colossians, His "fullness." It is so easy to divide God into a list of attributes and lose sight of the entirety of His essence.

The word "awesome" is overused today, but I like to reserve it to describe God. There should be nothing that arrests our attention and is more fascinating than God.

When I first came to Belém, I tried to disciple a few sharp young men. During our study times, we talked about spiritual matters and studied the Bible. Outside of our designated study times, however, we rarely talked about God, but we often talked about church strategy. I noticed when we talked about the Bible, the students gave rote responses and rarely showed a sense of awe. Other subjects, however, would cause their eyes to light up.

That is when I began to be more selective in choosing those in whom I wanted to invest my life. I found that some people genuinely know the Lord but are wasting their lives by placing their affections on things that can never satisfy. They have never tasted true joy and freedom. I now invest in those who are hungry for more intimacy with God.

---

[20] C. H. Spurgeon, *The Treasury of David*, p. 467.

David asked God to unite his heart, giving him a single passion. He did not want to live a merely religious life, fulfilling his duty but having a thousand other interests. If that is your desire, too, ask God for a united heart.

Piper raises hypothetical questions about having a single purpose. He asks, "Can life really have that much 'singleness' of purpose? Can work and leisure and relationships and eating and lovemaking and ministry all really flow from a single passion? Is there something deep enough and big enough and strong enough to hold all that together? Can sex and cars and work and war and changing diapers and doing taxes really have a God-exalting, soul-satisfying unity?"[21]

The answer is a resounding, *YES!* The golden thread of worship is the single purpose in life that ties everything together.

Have you ever heard someone say, "Jesus wants to be a part of your life"? But Jesus doesn't want to be just a part of your life. He wants to *be* your life. Jesus is life. Worship is not tacked on, no matter how high it is on the list.

God has transformed much of my own life by giving me a united heart. After "making a decision" for Christ, I saw no contradiction in partying on Saturday night and being in church on Sunday morning. I sought to follow God from a position of comfort, not allowing my relationship with God to interfere with my personal satisfaction. Even after supposedly sacrificing everything to become a missionary, my ministry was my fulfillment, not my worship relationship with God. Although I am still in the process of discovering what it means to have a united heart, I have learned that He and He alone is my treasure, my identity, my fulfillment, my refuge, my joy, and my life.

TRIVIALIZING WORSHIP

It is possible that by saying everything is worship we risk trivializing it. Someone recently told my wife that she liked Oregon because people don't go to church to worship God; they go out into the woods. To them, any fulfilling experience can be described as worship although it may be devoid of any relationship with God.

---

[21] John Piper, *Don't Waste Your Life*, pp. 43-44.

I have also heard some workaholic evangelists say, "Evangelism is the way I worship God." That statement can be true, as we shall see in chapter 11. For some, however, it is an excuse for their lack of practicing individual and corporate worship. Both are foundational to a worshipful life-attitude.

When we talk about integrating worship into every area of our lives, we are not trivializing worship nor are we saying there is no need for times set aside to focus on God's presence. As Ron Manahan comments in reference to Psalm 15, "… conduct and temple are tied together. *Worship and life are intertwined*" [22] (italics original).

That can happen, however, only when we train our minds to focus on worship. We desperately need focused times of worship.

Anthony B. Robinson says, "In worship we practice the basic skills of our faith. We practice them over and over again so that they become second nature to us, and in becoming second nature, they become the way we see the world and live in it." [23]

In other words, the times that we separate to focus on God individually and with other believers are not merely religious moments separated from daily life. These times serve as springboards to launch into a worshipful life attitude, bringing the presence of God into everything we do.

CONCLUSION

Are you religious or are you a worshiper? Your answer depends on how you view worship. Is your energy divided into many small streams when only one thing is truly important? Are you experiencing the new wine?

If we see worship as an event rather than the golden thread to be woven into every area of our lives, we are merely living from one religious moment to the next. If we focus only on praise or music, we are missing the essence of worship, having focused on the wineskins rather than the new wine. Our worship relationship with God should govern all of our thoughts and activities.

Jesus came to turn sinners into worshipers. He is seeking worshipers who will worship Him in spirit and truth. Because of His

[22] Ronald Manahan, "The Worshiper's Approach to God" in Bateman, p. 71.
[23] Anthony B. Robinson, in Leanne Van Dyk, *A More Profound Alleluia*, p. 137.

sacrifice on the cross, we are no longer restricted to holy times and holy places with the need for holy men. We have been set free from religious restraints to worship God as a life attitude, to live a life radically committed to Jesus Christ. There is no longer a dichotomy between the secular and the sacred because God's presence in our lives makes everything sacred.

Our goal should be to drink deeply of the new wine and to weave the golden thread of worship into everything we do, forsaking a divided life-attitude.

GOD'S PRESENCE IN OUR LIVES
MAKES EVERYTHING SACRED.

THE PARADIGM SHIFT

It is often useful to think in terms of contrasts, putting two contrasting concepts side by side to examine our thinking. Using the following table, examine your own life in light of what you have just read. Are you living a religious lifestyle or a worshipful life attitude?

RELIGIOUS MOMENTS	WORSHIP AS A LIFE ATTITUDE
1. OBJECTIVES: • To feel inspired and fulfilled • To fulfill a religious duty • To experience His presence	1. OBJECTIVES: • To please and enjoy God • To offer our lives to Him constantly as an outflow of worship • To live in His presence
2. MEANS: *Worship at certain designated times through a specific stimulus* • In corporate settings: Praise and music • Individually: Quiet times and prayer at meals	2. MEANS: *A mind trained to contemplate God at all times in:* • The Word • Nature • In the Body of Christ • Other people • The circumstances of life
3. CHARACTERISTICS: • Limited to holy places and holy events • Dependent on the musicians, the style of music, and the atmosphere • A divided heart	3. CHARACTERISTICS: • Unlimited: A life attitude • Independent of the surroundings • A united heart
4. RESULT: • A temporary change • Pleases the congregation • A divided lifestyle	4. RESULT: • A permanent transformation • Pleases God • A united worship life attitude with His presence integrated into everything

WHERE TO START?

1. **EXAMINE YOUR RELATIONSHIP WITH THE LORD.** Many people have "made decisions" for Christ, but they have merely embraced the Christian religion without ever becoming worshipers. Maybe you have been baptized and a part of your church for years but have not come into intimacy with God. Perhaps now is the time for you to "fall on [your] face and worship God" (1 Cor. 14:25) and unite your life to Him.

2. **ASK GOD TO EXAMINE YOUR WORSHIP.** It is nearly impossible for us to perceive religious attitudes in our lives unless God alerts us. Ask Him to examine your worship to show you where you are just going through the motions and the areas of your life that have not been integrated into your worship. How divided is your thinking? How much of your thought life is independent of God? Do you read the Scriptures, pray, and go to church as religious moments? Are you doing these things out of your love for God, or do you think God will love you more if you do them?

3. **ASK GOD TO GIVE YOU A UNITED HEART.** This is the process of offering your interests to Him and inviting His presence into everything you do.

4. **LEARN TO CONTEMPLATE GOD IN THE SCRIPTURES.** Every day this week, read one chapter of Isaiah 40-46. Every time you come across a quality of God, write it in a notebook and immediately take time to praise God for that aspect of His character. After you have finished praising Him, continue reading, repeating the same process when you find another quality of God. This is part of training your mind to stay fixed on His presence.

5. **LEARN TO FOCUS YOUR MIND ON GOD.** Sometime this week, while you are waiting in line or in traffic, look around at everything through God's eyes, thanking and praising Him for what you see. See if you can focus on Him for 15 minutes, without allowing your mind to wander.

DISCUSSION QUESTIONS

1. Why do most people view their Christianity in terms of "religious moments"?

2. How does the marriage metaphor relate to worship? How is marriage like worship?

3. Explain the parable of the new wine in old wineskins as it relates to worship.

4. What did the Samaritan woman understand about worship?

5. How did Jesus correct her view of worship?

6. What are some of the things that inhibit you from living a life of worship?

7. Why is worship central in our walk with God?

8. How does the "holy triangle" (holy man-holy place-holy ceremonies) influence people's views of worship?

9. How does worship influence your life?

10. What is a united life as opposed to a divided life?

11. What did you learn from using the Scriptures as the basis for your worship?

12. Examine the "paradigm shift" table. In what areas are you still living "religious moments" in your outlook?

13. What is the most important truth you learned from this chapter?

14. How has this chapter helped you be a better worshiper?

Chapter 2

WORSHIP IS IN SPIRIT

GOING BEYOND THE INTELLECTUAL OR EMOTIONAL INTO SPIRITUAL INTIMACY

But an hour is coming, and now is, when the true worshipers shall WORSHIP THE FATHER IN SPIRIT *and truth; for such people the Father seeks to be His worshipers* (John 4:23).

SEED TRUTH: WORSHIP IS SPIRITUAL, GOING BEYOND THE INTELLECTUAL AND EMOTIONAL. *Worship is spiritual intimacy with God. People who are merely religious respond intellectually or emotionally to corporate praise, but they are not affected spiritually. Spiritual worship is independent of circumstances, but it is dependent on seeking communion with God. To become worshipers, we must go beyond mere knowledge and emotionalism and seek to relate to God on a spiritual level. The golden thread of worship needs to be woven deeply within our spirits and not be merely an external practice.*

During a visit to the U.S., I told a veteran missionary friend that I had dropped from my vocabulary the word, *crente,* the popular Portuguese word for a believer. I explained it was because the word had become meaningless in Brazil. It was used to refer to anyone who was religious but wasn't Catholic. That included Jehovah's Witnesses, Mormons, and other groups. Furthermore, it had become a negative term to many because it is associated with the corruption in the so-called evangelical church.

Instead of *crente* (believer), we have come to use the somewhat cumbersome phrase, "those who have entered into an intimate relationship with God." That phrase communicates not only what a true Christian is, but also what his or her goal is. Many people believe that Jesus died for us just so that we could be saved and go to heaven. Therefore, they act as if they have reached their goal at the moment of conversion. We all rejoice when a person makes "a decision" but we too often stop investing in the person's life, and as a result they fail to grow in their walk with Him. These new "crentes" (believers) may sit in the pew satisfied that they are going to heaven and live from one *religious moment* to the next. Many of those who have "made a decision" do not even know the Lord and those who are truly converted aren't always seeking to deepen their intimacy with God. That is why I no longer use the word *crente*.

The morning after our discussion, my missionary friend, still in his bathrobe, came into the room where I had been sleeping. It was obvious something was on his mind. He asked, "Where do you find a reference in the Bible to an intimate relationship with God?"

I had never been asked that before, but I suggested a number of key passages, emphasizing John 17:3, where "knowing" describes intimacy as the essence of eternal life. John could have chosen a number of different words to communicate cognitive knowledge about God, but he chose one that emphasizes relationship.

"I like your answer," he responded. "But to be honest, I had not heard much about an intimate relationship with God until recently. Even in seminary, it was not emphasized. Did we somehow miss something?"

I have great respect for my friend. He had a big influence on our becoming missionaries and his life has always been an example to me. I consider him to be a spiritual man. Maybe Christians of his generation focused on obedience, doctrine, evangelism, and missions. Perhaps they took intimate fellowship with God for granted and so they didn't talk much about it. It is possible that many shied away from the spiritual dimension of a relationship with God as a reaction against the excesses of some groups. Instead, some equated biblical knowledge and outward obedience with spirituality.

On the other hand, maybe my generation, the "love generation," talked about a relationship with God so much that the concept has lost its meaning. Many, in their search for intimacy, have shunned objective study of the Scriptures, preferring to experience God. The results have also led many to be superficial in their relationship with God.

Just reading and studying the Bible are not enough. If intimacy with God is not the aim, Bible reading may be interesting, but it lacks life and the power to transform lives.

Worship is about a spiritual relationship with God. We were made in His image so that this would be possible. Although it is intimate and real, it is essentially spiritual. Through the indwelling presence of God's Spirit, we are able to have spiritual communion with Him at any time and any place.

In this chapter we will explore the spiritual nature of our being as the basis for union with Christ.

THE MARRIAGE METAPHOR

Today, the sexual relationship between two people has been brought down to an animal level. Through scientific studies, we now know the physiological basis of the sex drive, and it can even be influenced medically. Because humans are considered just another animal species, the biological reproductive instincts in the living world have become the basis for human sexual behavior.

Crosby, Stills, Nash, and Young, the famous folk rock group from the Woodstock era, sang, "If you can't be with the one you love, love the one you're with." This philosophy represents an individualist view of relationships. In other words, "If my wife isn't around to meet *my* needs, then I will find someone who will. After all, we all have our physiological needs, don't we?" That idea isn't really new; it was floating around Corinth in Paul's day. The popular statement, "Food is for the stomach, and the stomach is for food" (1 Cor. 6:13) had reduced sexual intimacy to a physiological drive on the same level as hunger, thirst, and self-preservation.

Citing Genesis 2:24, Paul says, "the one who joins himself to a prostitute is one body with her" (1 Cor. 6:16). He asserts that our physical bodies are temples of the Holy Spirit (1 Cor. 6:19) to show how absurd it is to join one's body to a prostitute.

Paul condemned sexual immorality principally because of the spiritual implications of the union. He writes, "Every other sin that a man commits is outside the body, but the immoral man sins against his own body" (1 Cor. 6:18). Apparently, gluttony and drunkenness do not affect the core of our being like sexual immorality does. They are considered to be outside the body, not influencing our whole being as does the sexual relationship. It involves joining the essence of who we are with our spouses to whom we have made an exclusive commitment. *The heart of real sexual union is spiritual intimacy.*

Then Paul makes the most intriguing statement in the whole passage in verse 17, "But the one who joins himself to the Lord is one spirit with Him." He makes it clear that our relationship with the Lord is a spiritual union. At the same time, Paul shows the contradiction between the physical union with a prostitute and a spiritual union with God through worship. It is unthinkable that these two diametrically opposed relationships could exist in the same being.

However, when there is physical union between two married people who have joined themselves to the Lord, there is an incredible spiritual union that defies explanation. That is why Paul said, "Great is this mystery." But he shows that the spiritual union to which he is referring is beyond marriage when he says, "But I am referring to Christ and the church" (Eph 5:32).

This biblical metaphor takes worship far beyond a mere cognitive knowledge of God or an emotional rush. *Worship is lovingly joining ourselves spiritually to the Lord.* In the Scriptures, the term "to join"[1] means "to cling, to bind, or enter into close contact with." Such spiritual oneness defies explanation. Unless someone has had his spirit touched through communion with God, he can never fully understand the joy and pleasure of worship.

LIFE IS INTIMACY WITH GOD

There are so many interesting pursuits in this life that we need a couple of lifetimes to do everything we would like. I like camping, backpacking, running, playing volleyball, reading, writing, watching movies, playing games, eating—I could go on and on. Each of us

---

[1] *Kalláō* in the Greek.

could fill a couple of pages, listing things we like to do. But what really defines us and gives us meaning?

When I taught at Liberty University, our goal was to train young Christians to take the gospel light into virtually every area of life, whether as teachers, lawyers, nurses, musicians, scientists, etc. However, those careers were never to be the main purpose or to provide the identity of those persons. Rather, their work was to be a reflection of their intimacy with God.

I noticed that some of the freshmen entering our pre-med program wanted the prestige of being a physician under the guise of serving the Lord. They were hedging their bets, trying to find identity in both their careers and their service to God. Most of them with that attitude did not last long and soon dropped out of the program.

On the other hand, we saw several become brilliant scientists and skilled physicians. Their identities were not in their careers, but in their relationship with God.

Every person attempts to find meaning in something. After we have satisfied our basic physical needs, the question that most haunts us is the purpose of life. We have a deep longing to know who we are, from where we came, and where we are going. To seek the answers is a "burdensome task" (Eccl. 1:13, NKJV).

From the experience of Adam and Eve, we can discover the origin of this longing for meaning. God had created a perfect world for them. He met all their needs and they were satisfied in Him. God did not ask Adam what he wanted or force him to make any choices except for one—to obey or disobey. Adam always trusted God to give him what was best, which was God Himself. Adam and Eve had perfect communion with God and their lives were joined to His.

Then sin entered the world. Adam and Eve yielded to the temptation to eat from the tree of knowledge of good and evil out of a desire (as Satan put it) to be "like God, knowing good and evil," enabling them to make decisions independently of God (Gen. 3:5).

They not only disobeyed a direct order from God, but they chose a path of independence from God. They wanted to be like Him, to be "the master of [their] fate and the captain of [their] soul." *Sin is any action or attitude that is independent from God.*

In his book on the identity of the Christian, David Needham comments, "Somehow, under the tree of the knowledge of good and evil, our first parents acquired this deathly nature. To be more accurate, the Bible focuses on what they *lost* rather than on what they acquired."[2] He continues, "What then really happened to those two tragic people? Though still 'living' they had lost *life*. Eventually, they would lose physical life. But right at that moment of disobedience they lost true life"[3] (italics original).

The fall led to a break in the worship relationship. No longer were their lives joined to God, and since that time, sinful man, in his groping for life,[4] has tried to find life in any source but God.

HUMAN BEINGS ARE DESPERATE
TO FIND LIFE AND MEANING.

Ecclesiastes says that God has "set eternity in their heart, yet so that man will not find out the work which God has done from the beginning even to the end" (Eccl. 3:11). Referring to this verse, MacArthur comments, "God made men for His eternal purpose, and nothing in post-Fall time can bring them complete satisfaction."[5] In other words, human beings are desperate to find life and meaning.

Augustine said, "My sin was this, that I looked for pleasure, beauty, and truth, not in Him, but in myself and in other creatures. And that search led me instead to pain, confusion, and error."[6]

In desperation to recover the life they have lost, some seek to find life in what is generally recognized as sinful behavior, such as drunkenness, drugs, illicit sex, violence, etc. These are generally not socially acceptable behaviors, so often they are pursued secretly. Some try to find fulfillment indirectly through pornography, violent films, and fantasies. None of these finds approval in the Christian world.

---

[2] David Needham, *Birthright, Christian, Do You Know Who You Are?* pp. 20-21.
[3] Ibid. p. 21.
[4] The Greek word *Zōé* means more than mere existence, indicating a quality of life.
[5] MacArthur, *The MacArthur Study Bible*, p. 930.
[6] Augustine, quoted by Ryan, *Worship*, p. 18.

Other "life-seeking" activities are not viewed as overtly sinful so long as one doesn't go to excess. The pursuit of money is fine, if it isn't motivated by greed and doesn't involve dishonesty. Being a sports fanatic is great so long as I don't miss church too much and don't use nasty language to describe the referee. Food is fantastic if I don't overindulge. My life can be my career so long as I don't completely neglect my family and I am in church on Sunday.

And, of course, no one will criticize a person who finds his life in the ministry where it is honorable to put in seventy-hour weeks for the Lord. We missionaries love to fill our prayer letters with all our activities. Nor will anyone criticize someone who finds identity in his or her family.

When we get right down to it, however, none of these truly satisfies. Maybe our activities temporarily distract us from our emptiness. Some of these activities might be fun and many are noble, but they are not the purpose for our lives.

LIFE IS FOUND IN WORSHIP AND OBEDIENCE,
IN THAT ORDER.

Solomon set out to find meaning. He had the honesty and wisdom to conclude, "all was vanity and striving after wind and there was no profit under the sun" (Eccl. 2:11). What was the conclusion of his search for life? "Fear God and keep His commandments" (Eccl. 12:13). "Fear" is a worship term. Solomon's conclusion: *Life is found in worship and obedience, in that order.*

Jesus came that we might have life, but that does not just mean eternal existence.[7] Here is a small sampling of references describing Jesus (emphasis mine).

"In Him was *life,* and the life was the Light of men"
(John 1:4).

---

[7] If the Bible meant that man would simply exist eternally, the Greek word would have been *bíos* from which we get the word "biology." However, the Bible uses the word *zōé* to speak of the quality of life Jesus offers for all eternity.

"For just as the Father raises the dead and gives them *life*, even so the Son also gives *life* to whom He wishes"
(John 5:21).[8]

"I am the bread of *life*; he who comes to Me shall not hunger..."
(John 6:35).

"'The words that I have spoken to you are spirit and are *life*'"
(John 6:3).

"'I am the light of the world; he who follows Me shall not walk in the darkness, but will have the Light of *life*'"
(John 8:12).

"'I came that they might have *life*, and might have it abundantly'"
(John 10:10).

"'I am the resurrection and the *life*; he who believes in Me shall live even if he dies'"
(John 11:25).

"'I am the way, and the truth, and the *life*'"
(John 14:6).

"'And this is eternal *life*, that they may know Thee, the only true God, and Jesus Christ whom Thou hast sent'"
(John 17:3).

Furthermore, Jesus is called "The Prince of *life*" (Acts 3:15). The disciples were commanded to preach "the whole message of this *Life*" (Acts 5:20). The disciples were amazed that the gentiles were granted "repentance that leads to *life*" (Acts 11:18).

Of all the references to life in the Epistles, I want to highlight just one important passage, 2 Peter 1:3. Peter writes that we have been given "everything pertaining to *life* and godliness, through the true knowledge of Him who called us by His own glory and excellence" (emphasis added).

---

[8] This passage speaks of giving life to the spiritually dead, not the resurrection from the dead as in John 5:28-29.

This means that the fullness of life has already been granted to believers.[9] It also says that we have been granted the resources for godliness. By definition, it is a worship term as well. It is similar to "fear" in that worship carries over into every area of one's life.[10]

Everything we need for life has been granted through intimacy with God. It was His grace and the glory and excellence of His character that drew us to Him. Only those who are interested in becoming worshipers will be drawn by who He is.

Jesus is our life. Although true worshipers are certainly involved in many activities and pursue many interests, their identity, treasure, meaning, comfort, and refuge are found in their intimacy with Him.

WORSHIP AND SPIRITUAL INTIMACY

Worship and intimacy with God are not the same thing, but they are inseparable. It is impossible to have one without the other. They are two golden threads woven together into one strand. They are the pure new wine that would be diluted if one were missing.

DEFINING INTIMACY WITH GOD

John 17:3 was the first passage that came to mind when my friend asked about intimacy with God. Jesus defines the essence and purpose of eternal life: knowing God. The key word is "*know.*"[11] The word "conveys the thought of connection or union, as between man and woman" (Matt.1:25 and Luke 1:34, both KJV).[12] It is a relational and experiential term. It means to come to realize something through personal experience.

Many times, Brazilians convey this idea when they are learning English. They may ask, "Do you know Brazil?" They are not asking if you have heard of Brazil, but if you have ever personally been there and experienced their country. Although *ginōskō (to know)* is not always used in terms of a relationship with God, it certainly does imply more than just an intellectual understanding of Him.

---

[9] To underscore the permanence of what has been granted to us, Peter uses a perfect tense verb in the Greek.

[10] *Eusébeia* in the Greek. *Eu* means "well." *Sebeia* means "to be in awe." A godly person is one who lives in awe of God.

[11] *Ginōskō* in the Greek.

[12] W. E. Vine, *An Expository Dictionary of New Testament Words.*

Jesus told Thomas, "If you had *known* Me, you would have *known* My Father also; from now on you *know* Him and have seen Him" (John 14:7). Jesus is not talking about cognitive knowledge, but a real friendship with the Father, which is possible only through intimacy with the Son.

Paul described the nature of our fellowship with God, saying, "But now that you have come to *know* God, or rather to be *known* by God, how is it that you turn back again to the weak and worthless elemental things" (Gal. 4:9). Obviously, God knows everyone, but He does not have an intimate relationship with everyone. The question here is "How could you be so close to God and then go back into legalistic, ritualistic religion?"

Paul often used a stronger word for knowing[13] when he said that the goal of our sanctification is a closer walk with Him. He referred to "...the new self who is being renewed to a true *knowledge* according to the image of the One who created him" (Col. 3:10).

Intimacy Is Enjoying God's Presence

John says, "Our fellowship is with the Father, and with His Son Jesus Christ" (1 John 1:3). Communion[14] with God. What an incredible idea!

That is why David marveled, "What is man that You take thought of him, And the son of man that You care for him?" (Ps. 8:4). "Caring" for us carries the idea that God would actually bend over and come down to our level and consider us. Who are we to think that God would even care about us?

He is a holy God, the Creator of the Universe. We are but dust. One has to be in awe that this great and mighty God has chosen to have fellowship with us.

To many religions such as Islam, the idea of intimacy with God is absurd. God is seen as so transcendent that the idea of a relationship between man and God is unthinkable. Thus, the prayers of Muslims are not personal, but ritualistic. High religions with rituals reinforce the idea that God is distant and unapproachable.

---

[13] *Epígnōsis* in the Greek.
[14] *Koinōnía* in the Greek, meaning, "to share in common."

How does spiritual intimacy happen? We have ready access to God at all times because His Holy Spirit indwells our spirits. Thus, we are capable of living above the earthly, physical world and in the spiritual realm. That is why Paul exhorted the Colossians to fix their minds on things that are above and not on the things of this earth (Col. 3:2). That is possible only because of the presence of His Spirit within us.

Joseph Carroll tells the story of a fellow soldier who learned how to live in the realm of worship, fixing his mind on God's presence. After missing roll call several times, Tom Watson was called before the Colonel for discipline. His explanation was, "Well, Colonel, I begin to worship my Lord Jesus [he used to call Him his beautiful Lord Jesus]; and I cannot hear anything. I do not hear the bugle. I do not hear the men. I do not hear anything. I'm sorry."[15]

Intimacy Is Being God's Friend

Deep fellowship with God happens only when we move from the formalities to a genuine friendship. Friends enjoy being together. They know about each other's lives and still want to know more. They never run out of things to talk about. At times, they don't need to say anything, but just enjoy each other's company. Many of their likes and dislikes are similar or at least they learn to appreciate each other's interests. They let each other enter into every area of their lives.

Our friendship with God should be much the same way. Although we never lose the awesome sense of His presence, we enjoy Him as a friend. As Rick Warren says, "Your relationship to God has many different aspects: God is your Creator and Maker, Lord and Master, Judge, Redeemer, Father, Savior, and much more. But the most shocking truth is this: Almighty God yearns to be your Friend!"[16]

Friendship is based on honesty. Warren states, "God doesn't expect you to be perfect, but he does insist on complete honesty."[17] The Psalms are full of such honest feelings and confessions to God.

---

[15] Carroll, p. 90.
[16] Warren, *Purpose Driven Life*, p. 85.
[17] Ibid. p. 92.

Friends often come to share the same values. We need to learn to love the things God loves and hate the things He hates. As we worship and relate to God, His values are instilled in us. In a human friendship, it is a two-way street, but with God, we are the ones who are changed.

Friends enjoy being together. We come to God because we enjoy His presence. As Piper says, "When worship is reduced to disinterested duty, it ceases to be worship."[18] It is not a relationship, but a task.

John records an amazing statement by Jesus. "No longer do I call you slaves, for the slave does not know what his master is doing; but I have called you friends, for all things that I have heard from My Father I have made known to you" (John 15:15). This gives us a clear indication that God doesn't want just the mechanical obedience of a slave,[19] but the trusting obedience of a friend.[20]

A few years ago, I dedicated myself to walking in fellowship with God. I was seeing everything through His eyes and overflowing with joy in His presence. One day, Lisa and I went out to Marituba, a nearby town. She met with the pastor's wife at their home while I met with the pastor in his office. She dropped me off and was supposed to pick me up at 11:30 to give us plenty of time to get home for lunch with the kids.

She was late and so we missed each other. Normally, I would have been very upset, but since I was walking in fellowship with God, I saw His hand in it. For the next few hours, God and I walked around Marituba, meeting with people as He guided my steps. Even on the way home, God's hand was evident.

When I walked in the door, Lisa said, "Wow, five o'clock and you're just getting home?"

Immediately, I sensed myself saying to God, "I'll take it from here."

"Well, you're the one who left me in Marituba." I replied with a tone of slight irritation.

---

[18] John Piper, *Dangerous Duty*, p. 54.
[19] *Dŏulŏs* in the Greek.
[20] *Philŏs* in the Greek.

The problems and difficulties never bothered me when, through my intimacy with God, I was seeing His hand in everything. The minute I allowed myself to be distracted from His presence, I became selfish and irritable.

All of this happened when I began to understand the spiritual nature of our intimacy with God that I will describe below. It is something I am still learning to put into practice as I come to a greater understanding of His Word.

Our Access to Intimacy with God

Paul says that through Christ, "we have obtained our introduction by faith into this grace" (Rom. 5:2). The word that translates "introduction"[21] carries the idea of someone taking us into the throne room and personally presenting us to the King. Paul uses this same word in Ephesians 2:18 and 3:12. Jesus Christ has personally taken us into the Father's presence.

My great-uncle, Howard Triplehorn, played football for the University of Michigan with the late Gerald Ford. After Ford became vice president of the United States, I found an old program from a football game in 1934 with a picture of the two of them.

I sent a letter, asking if Mr. Ford would autograph the picture. To my surprise, we were given an appointment with him. To enter his office involved a great deal of formal procedure and security.

I was overwhelmed with the sense of not deserving to be in that office. Diplomats and political leaders were waiting to see him. If it were not for the name of my great-uncle, we would never have passed all the security checkpoints.

A receptionist personally presented us to the vice president. I was utterly in awe and at a loss for words at being introduced to the second most powerful man in our country, right there in his own office.

That is the kind of introduction we have with our Heavenly Father. We can come boldly into His presence, but at the same time, we are awestruck, aware that we are undeserving and that we would be utterly destroyed if not for the righteousness of Jesus Christ.

---

[21] *Prŏsagōgē* in the Greek, meaning, "to lead forward, access."

WORSHIPING GOD IN SPIRIT

JESUS' DESCRIPTION OF WORSHIP

But an hour is coming, and now is, when the true worshipers shall worship the Father in spirit and truth; for such people the Father seeks to be His worshipers (John 4:23).

In the context of this passage, the Samaritan woman had asked which was the correct location to worship God. The Jews had been divided into two kingdoms after the reign of king Solomon. The southern kingdom, Judah, retained Jerusalem as its capital where the temple had been built. The northern kingdom set up a separate capital in Samaria and parallel worship systems in Bethel, Dan, and later on Mount Gerizim, to which the woman referred.

The northern kingdom had fallen to the Assyrians and was later resettled with both Jews and Gentiles. The result was a hybrid race and religion. Although they were known for their spirited festivals, they had a distorted understanding of God.

The Jews were not much better than the Samaritans. They "worshiped," using the forms that they had been taught, but they were guilty of dead orthodoxy. They had the truth but there was no seeking of intimacy with God.

The Samaritan external form of worship was emotional and devoid of truth. The Jewish worship was a cold religious duty, performed without any feeling. Neither was true worship because both lacked the essential spiritual element in their relationship with God.

That is why Jesus said true worshipers worship "in spirit and truth." Worship is in spirit, that is, independent of holy times or holy places, but flowing out of inward communion with God.[22] Although it always involves our minds and understanding (1 Cor. 14:15-16), it goes beyond the intellectual to the spiritual. Emotions will often accompany true worship, but they are not its essence.

The Samaritan woman had a religious mind-set and she thought of worship as restricted to certain locations. For her, worship was an occasional activity and not a life-attitude.

---

[22] See Bauer et al. for a definition of worshiping God in spirit.

God is spirit in His essence and can be worshiped only in spirit, independent of outward circumstances.[23] Brother Lawrence knew the spiritual nature of worship as he practiced the presence of God among the steamy pots and pans in the monastery kitchen. He learned the essence of worship because he lived worship. The essence of worshiping God in spirit is that it is constant, uninterrupted communion with Him.

HOLY GROUND IS WHEREVER GOD AND MAN MEET
FOR INTIMATE, SPIRITUAL FELLOWSHIP.

Although God had designated Jerusalem and the temple as His dwelling place and for offering sacrifices, worship in the Old Testament was not restricted to a particular place. In fact, one of Stephen's arguments in Acts 7 is that throughout Israel's history, people had communion with God outside of the Promised Land. They were not restricted to the land or the temple. Holy ground is wherever God and man meet for intimate, spiritual fellowship.

Averbeck writes, "Part of the point is that, since he is 'spirit,' the physical place of worship is not the real issue and it never was, even though the Jerusalem temple was the assigned place in Jesus' day, not Mount Gerizim."[24]

Jesus said to the Samaritan woman, "An hour is coming and now is," indicating that a change was about to take place. Since Jesus' sacrifice was perfect, there was no longer a need for a specific place to sacrifice. Jesus fulfilled the imagery of the Old Testament festivals and rituals, so pilgrimages to Jerusalem were no longer necessary. Jesus revealed the truth about God, correcting misunderstandings

---

[23] This is one of four essence statements about God that use a noun as a metaphor to describe Him. The others are "God is love" (1 John 4:8), "God is light" (1 John 1:5), and "God is a consuming fire" (Heb. 12:29). It is also interesting to look at the statements that use an attributive genitive to describe God. He is the "God of love and peace" (2 Cor 13:11, Phil. 4:9), the "God of patience" (Rom 15:5, NKJV), "The God of hope" (Rom 15:13), "The God of grace" (1 Pet. 5:10), and the "God of comfort" (2 Cor 1:3). He is also the "Father of spirits" (Heb. 12:9), "Father of lights" (James 1:17), and "Father of mercies" (2 Cor 1:3).
[24] Richard Averbeck, "Worshiping God in Spirit" in Bateman, p. 83.

and advancing the Old Testament revelation of God. Because of what Jesus did on the cross, New Testament believers are truly able to worship God in spirit and truth any place and at any time. My body is now a temple of the Holy Spirit (1 Cor. 6:19), so I have the "holy place" with me at all times.

Some interpret worshiping "in spirit" (John 4:23) to mean that worship is directed by the Holy Spirit. While it is certainly true that the Holy Spirit glorifies Jesus (John 16:14), leading us to worship Him, this passage describes the believer's regenerated spirit that has been joined to the Holy Spirit.[25]

Morgenthaler writes,

> Spirit and truth must be the fundamental building blocks of any valid worship experience. It is significant, however, that these elements are always found in the context of a relationship with God. Without the give and take of relationship, without interaction between God and God's people, spirit and truth cannot be expressed. And if spirit and truth are not expressed, no worship takes place.[26]

WORSHIPING IN SPIRIT IS MORE THAN EMOTIONS.

"When do you best worship God?" is a good analytical question to help discover where people are in relation to worship. A friend of mine asked that question during a retreat in France. The answers were varied: "During a walk in the woods." "Listening to Bach on the organ." "When I am in church," and so forth.

In all cases, worship was reduced to what they described as "*sens du sacré*," "a sense of the sacred," or a feeling associated with their outer circumstances. These moments can be fairly easily orchestrated. Music, for example, can stir our emotions and make us feel good and lead us to believe we have had some sort of religious experience.

---

[25] In both of these cases, there is no article before the word "spirit." Although this is not an absolute rule, there is generally an article of specific designation before the noun when referring to the Holy Spirit. Furthermore, the context of both of these passages contrasts the empty external forms of worship with true inner worship.
[26] Sally Morgenthaler, *Worship Evangelism: Inviting Unbelievers into the Presence of God*, p.47.

Elmer Towns says, "America's Protestants choose churches on the basis of what affirms us, entertains us, satisfies us or makes us feel good about God and ourselves."[27] In other words, people choose their churches by their outward forms, caring more about personal experience than substance. They choose what will give them the greatest sense of the sacred.

Real worship goes beyond our emotions, to a spiritual joy deep in our spirits.

WORSHIPING IN SPIRIT IS MORE THAN A MENTAL EXERCISE.

Although knowing the truth is foundational to intimacy with God, worship cannot be thought of as merely an intellectual activity. How could a finite mind even begin to grasp the greatness of God so as to worship Him?

Warren Wiersbe says, "I'm no longer analyzing texts in order to organize sermons; I am meeting God in His Word and discovering the reality of a song I have sung but little understood, 'Beyond the sacred page, I seek Thee, Lord; My spirit pants for Thee, O living Word!'"[28]

Real worship goes beyond our thoughts to a knowledge of Him in our spirits.

OUR SPIRITUAL NATURE

What is our "spirit" through which we have fellowship with the Living God?

It is difficult to make clear distinctions between the various aspects of our being. When considering the inner man, nothing is cut-and-dried. Each human should be viewed as complete, rather than a composite of his parts. Human beings are complex. It is important, however, to understand who we are so we can appreciate what worship is and how it affects us. This understanding will impact our view of sanctification and our growth as Christians.

There are two major viewpoints of the internal makeup of humans, differing in their ideas on the soul and spirit. The "trichotomist view" argues that man is made up of a body, a soul, and a spirit. The

---

[27] Elmer Towns, in Morgenthaler, p.19.
[28] Warren Wiersbe, *Real Worship: Playground, Battleground, or Holy Ground?* pp. 17-18.

"dichotomist view" holds that there is a material and an immaterial part in humans, treating the soul and the spirit as synonymous.

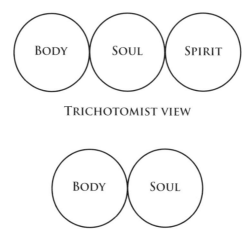

Trichotomist view

Dichotomist view

Although there are differences, they are not as clear-cut as either diagram illustrates. For example, there is a physiological basis for much of our behavior. Our memory can be lost through an accident or brain damage. Also, hormones can affect our emotions, as in post-partum depression. On the other hand, in Luke 16, Jesus describes the thoughts of a person who had died.[29] The rich man remembered (v. 28), had feelings (vv. 24-25), had a will (v. 27), and even reasoned (v. 30). The essence of who the rich man was did not seem to be limited to his physical existence, but continued after death.

Although we cannot draw rigid lines between the various aspects of our beings, that should not keep us from trying to understand them. I believe "soul" and "spirit" should not be treated as one. To do so seriously handicaps our understanding of regeneration, sanctification, and especially worship.

---

[29] There are some groups, most notably the Adventists and Jehovah's Witnesses, who advocate "soul sleep" because they claim that the immaterial part of a person cannot exist apart from the body. They cite the term "sleep" or "asleep" as proof (1 Cor. 15:6; 1 Thess 4:13-15; 2 Pet. 3:4). However, Paul clearly taught that he longed to be absent from the body and present with the Lord 2 Cor 5:6-8. The term "asleep" is merely a euphemism for death.

Paul said the natural or "soulish"[30] man is incapable of understanding the things of the Spirit of God (1 Cor. 2:14). For our purposes here, I will treat the soul[31] as more or less synonymous with the mind.[32] Our will, emotions, and how we see and interpret life are processed through our mind.

On the other hand, our spirits[33] were made to have communion with God. We worship in spirit. It is our spirits that are regenerated and indwelt by His Holy Spirit. That is what makes us new creatures in Christ (2 Cor. 5:17), having been given a new spirit (Ezek. 36:26-27). And our spirits bear witness that we are His children (Rom. 8:16).

Because we have a new spirit, we comprehend spiritual truth (1 Cor. 2:15). The person who has not been regenerated cannot comprehend unless God opens his spiritual perception. Our spirits make us God-conscious and we are able to have communion with Him that goes beyond the limitations of our minds while, at the same time, enlightening our understanding.

Carroll put it this way, "We know that the body has senses; but the spirit also has senses, and it is by the senses of our spirit that we are made conscious of the presence of Christ. 'God is Spirit' who can only be worshiped by that which is spiritual in us, by our spirits."[34]

Although soul and spirit are used interchangeably in some places, several passages indicate a difference (1 Thess. 5:23; Heb. 4:12; 1 Cor. 2:14-15). Many theologians are hesitant to make any distinction between the soul and spirit because of the tendency to consider the spirit as superior to the soul. Those who make a distinction often think that being in the realm of our spirits is irrational, putting our minds in neutral. The Bible is clear, however, showing that the mind and the spirit do not act independently, but in conjunction. Paul said, "I will pray with my spirit, but I will also pray with my mind" (1 Cor. 14:15). He is not describing two independent activities, but

---

[30] Psuchekos in the Greek means "that which pertains to the soul or the natural existence" in this world in contrast to the supernatural world (Bauer et al.).

[31] Psuchē in the Greek. We get our word "psychology" from this word.

[32] Two Greek words are translated as "mind": noûs has to do with the filters by which we process and interpret what happens around us whereas phrŏnēma has to do with the thought process or mind-set.

[33] Pnĕuma in the Greek.

[34] Carroll, p. 38.

one that involves both spiritual and cognitive understanding and communion with God.

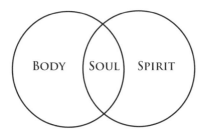

This drawing reflects the overlap that exists. One of the weaknesses of this model is that it reduces the soul to being a subset of the spirit. It does, however, show the overlap and illustrates that the mind or soul is neither purely physical nor spiritual.

When God created Adam, we are told that He "formed man of dust from the ground, and breathed into his nostrils the 'breath of life';[35] and man became a living being" (Gen. 2:7). God made Adam's physical body from dust. The joining of the body and the breath is what made Adam a living "soul."[36]

The mind or the soul is both spiritual and material in its nature. If the spirit is not regenerated, the mind will not be able to perceive the things of God. With the new spirit, however, the mind is progressively becoming more attuned to God through being renewed (Eph. 4:23).[37]

Why is this important to our understanding of worship?

First, we must understand that our fellowship with God and our worship are not merely mental or emotional exercises of our brain. It is not possible to worship an infinite God with our limited fallen minds and emotions without the illumination of our minds through our spirits' being joined to God's.

[35] The Hebrew *neshamah* can mean breath, life, or spirit. The Septuagint uses the Greek word *pnoé* to translate breath. It is related to pneuma or spirit. This word can refer to either God's spirit or man's.

[36] *Psuchē* in the Greek. It can have the sense of the inner person or soul, or it could be translated as Adam's simply becoming a living being.

[37] Paul uses a present passive infinitive to describe the progressive renewing of the spiritual state of a believer's mind while using two aorist infinitives to indicate that the "old self" has been completely laid aside and the "new self" has been "created" in us at the moment of salvation (Eph 4:22-24).

Worship is spiritual communion with God
in which our minds are actively involved.

Second, although worship is spiritual, it is not irrational. Our minds and our comprehension are enlightened through worship. As He gives us spiritual understanding of His character, we respond in worship. Worship is spiritual communion with God in which our minds are actively involved.

Third, emotionalism is not worship, but worship will involve our emotions. John Piper, in several books, demonstrates that our relationship with God is not a cold duty, but involves spiritual joy in God's presence.

Finally, worship and intimacy with God are what drive this growth (Rom. 12:1-2). Thus, we are said to have the "mind of Christ" (1 Cor. 2:16).

By recognizing the spiritual dimension of our beings, we can ask God to strengthen us spiritually. That's how Paul prayed for the Ephesians, asking that they might be spiritually able to understand wisdom and the revelation that God had given them through His Word (Eph. 1:17). He asked that the eyes of their hearts would be enlightened to comprehend spiritual truth (Eph.1:18). And he prayed that they would have their inner man strengthened to understand the church and God's love (Eph. 3:16-19).

Understanding this is not just an interesting topic. It has tremendous bearing on how we see ourselves. My comprehension of these principles has enabled me to understand the nature of my relationship with Him so that I can seek Him spiritually. It has enabled me to approach God's Word as a means of growing closer to Him.

Worshiping with Our Whole Being

Real worship begins with our spirits, but let's look at how Paul inseparably links our minds and spirits in 1 Corinthians 14:15.

I believe the subject of 1 Corinthians 12 to 14 is *not* spiritual gifts, but the working of the Holy Spirit in our lives. Paul introduces the topic, speaking not about spiritual gifts,[38] but spiritual things.[39] He uses the same word here that he uses to describe the "spiritual man" in 1 Corinthians 2:15.

When the Corinthians followed demonic idols, they were passively led astray (1 Cor. 12:2).[40] Their minds were not involved when they became possessed and did irrational things. They passively submitted to the spirit world.

As in Corinth, many Brazilians who have practiced their dark arts have come into the church, read about the Holy Spirit in the Bible, and assumed that His actions were much like the spirits in their Macumba ceremonies. In Brazilian spiritist sessions (Macumba, Candomblé, Umbanda, Kardekism, etc.), the spirits come down upon those who are open, leading them to do supernatural and often irrational things. Some amazing things really happen through demonic powers at those meetings.

American charismatics would raise their eyebrows if they knew what really goes on in some of even the more conservative charismatic groups in Brazil. They would be more reluctant to affirm that Brazil is evangelized and experiencing a revival, as some claim.

In 1 Corinthians 12, Paul demonstrates that the kind of spiritual gift one has been given is not an indication of his level of spirituality. The real indication of someone's spirituality is love, according to chapter 13. Love is the motive for using our spiritual gifts, because love will lead us to fulfill the purpose of the gifts: the edification of the church, not personal benefit. Paul doesn't mention the object of the love. In this case, especially considering the "Great Commandment" (Matt 22:34-40), he is no doubt referring to our love for God (wor-

---

[38] When speaking of spiritual gifts, Paul uses the term *charisma* or the plural *charismata*. Although he addresses this subject in 1 Cor. 12-14 as part of his broad discussion of spirituality, it is not the main point. It is interesting to note that the term is based on the word *charis*, which means grace. These gifts are not measures of spiritual maturity, but a result of God's grace.

[39] Paul uses the term *pněumatikōes* to introduce the subject, not charismata. This is the same term he uses in 1 Corinthians 2 to describe the "spiritual man" (1 Cor. 2:15) and the "spiritual thoughts" as well as "spiritual words" (1 Cor. 2:13).

[40] Paul uses an imperfect passive form of *agō* to show the continuous nature of being led astray and then combines it with a present passive participle of apagō to drive home this point.

ship) and its overflow into our love for others. That love is expressed in action, because worship will always influence what we do.[41]

Paul concludes in 1 Corinthians 14:15: "I will pray with the spirit and I will pray with the mind also; I will sing with the spirit and I will sing with the mind also." He is not describing two separate types of prayer, but one. Spiritual prayer and praise will involve both the mind and the spirit.[42] The Holy Spirit does not act outside of our consciousness when He leads us in prayer and worship. The Spirit works with our spirits, involving our minds.

MacArthur says, "Spirituality involves more than the mind, but it never excludes the mind (cf. Rom. 12:1-2; Eph. 4:12; Col. 3:10). In Scripture, and certainly in the writings of Paul, no premium is placed on ignorance."[43]

WORSHIP INVOLVES OUR EMOTIONS.

Worship that is emotionless is a mere duty. Real worship deeply influences our emotions.

John Piper has promoted the concept of "Christian hedonism" which encourages us to seek joy and satisfaction in our relationship with God. For too long, Bible-believing Christians have been afraid of feelings, because they didn't want to fall into the excesses of Pentecostalism. This fear has probably done more to hinder real worship than anything else.

Piper emphasizes that:

> Pursuing joy in God and praising God are not separate acts. Praise not merely expresses but completes the enjoyment. Worship is not added to joy, and joy is not the by-product of worship. Worship is valuing of God. And when this valuing is intense, it is joy in God. Therefore the essence of worship is delight in God, which displays His all-satisfying value.[44]

---

[41] All of the words translated as adjectives (patient, kind, not jealous, etc.) are actually present tense verbs in the Greek, implying a continuous action on the part of the worshiper.

[42] Although the Greek includes a definite article before the word for "spirit" in this verse, it should be taken as a possessive pronoun and translated as "my spirit."

[43] MacArthur, *1 Corinthians*, p. 377.

[44] Piper, *Dangerous Duty*, p. 24.

Worship will come from and stir up a feeling of awe and wonder. A. W. Tozer repeatedly emphasizes being in awe of God. He writes, "When we come into this sweet relationship, we are beginning to learn astonished reverence, breathless adoration, awesome fascination, lofty admiration of the attributes of God and something of the breathless silence that we know when God is near."[45]

A correct understanding of God leads us to deep feelings, especially a sense of awe of Him

WORSHIP INVOLVES OUR WILLS.

Worship is not passive, but it involves a surrender of our wills. We make conscious choices to respond to God.

Rick Warren says, "True worship—bringing God pleasure—happens when you give yourself completely to God…offering yourself to God is what worship is all about."[46]

Referring to the worship of Revelation 4:11, Joseph Carroll describes it:

What have they [the 24 elders] done? They have abdicated and cast their crowns before the throne, divesting themselves of their glory and saying, "Thou art worthy to receive glory, and Thou alone." Honor and power follow. These three things are what men seek: to be glorified, to be exalted, and to be honored. Therefore, to worship Jesus Christ we must divest ourselves of all desire for glory and honor and power; for He and He alone is worthy of such.[47]

This implies an emptying of any selfish personal desires so that Jesus becomes the most important.

WORSHIP WILL AFFECT OUR BODIES (ACTIONS).

Paul urged us to "present our bodies as living sacrifices" (Rom. 12:2) and to offer the members of our bodies as "instruments of righteousness" (Rom 6:13).

[45] Tozer, *Worship*, p. 30.
[46] Warren, *Purpose Driven Life*, p.78.
[47] Carroll, p. 37.

MacArthur emphasizes this idea when he says,

> True worship includes many things besides the obvious ones
> of prayer, praise, and thanksgiving. It includes serving God
> by serving others in His name, especially fellow believers.
> Sacrificial worship includes "doing good and sharing; for with
> such sacrifices God is pleased" (Heb. 13:15-16; cf. Phil. 4:14).
> But above all else, our supreme act of worship is to offer our-
> selves wholly and continually to the Lord as living sacrifices.[48]

WORSHIP INVOLVES ALL WE ARE.

Warren Wiersbe describes the totality of worship in this way:

> When we consider all the words used for worship in both the
> Old and New Testaments, and when we put their meanings
> together, we find that worship involves both attitudes (awe,
> reverence, respect) and actions (bowing, praising, serving).
> It is both a subjective experience and an objective activity.
> Worship is not an unexpressed feeling, nor is it an empty
> formality. True worship is balanced and involves the mind,
> the emotions, and the will. It must be intelligent; it must
> reach deep within and be motivated by love; and it must
> lead to obedient actions that glorify God. [49]

Packer adds,

> The emotional side of knowing God is often played down
> these days, for fear of encouraging a maudlin self-absorp-
> tion. It is true that there is nothing more irreligious than
> self-absorbed religion, and that it is constantly needful to
> stress that God does not exist for our "comfort," or "hap-
> piness," or "satisfaction," or to provide us with "religious
> experiences"…But for all this, we must not lose sight of the
> fact that knowing God is an emotional relationship, as well
> as an intellectual and volitional one, and could not indeed
> be a deep relationship between persons were it not so.[50]

---

[48] MacArthur, *Romans 9-16*, p. 138.
[49] Wiersbe, pp. 20-21.
[50] J. I. Packer, *Knowing God*, p.35.

Jesus said it best when He identified the highest calling and most important commandment. "You shall love the Lord your God with all your heart, and with all your soul, and with all your mind" (Matt. 22:37; cf. Deut. 6:5). All these terms are internal, reflecting a deep passion from the very center of one's being. The internal life-attitude of worship described here stands in stark contrast to the empty outward ritual of the Pharisees that so deeply offended Jesus.

EXAMPLES OF INTIMACY WITH GOD

One of the reasons the Bible was written was to describe how God developed a deep relationship with men and women throughout history. By studying the lives of these ordinary people just like you and me, and by seeing how they were transformed through their growing relationship with God, we, too, can learn and grow in the depth of our walk with Him. The lives of the men and women listed below have had a tremendous impact on my own life.

MARY, THE MOTHER OF JESUS

My soul exalts the Lord, and my spirit has rejoiced in God my Savior (Luke 1:46-47).

Mary's Magnificat is a spontaneous, poetic expression of praise that reveals deep insight into the spiritual nature of worship. Her words are full of Old Testament references, showing that Mary meditated on the Word, and her worship flowed from her knowledge of the Scriptures.

The passage is a Hebrew parallelism, repeating the same activity in different words. Some think it is used to show that the spirit and soul are synonymous. However, there are three distinctions between the parallel phrases.

First, there is a difference in the timing of the two verbs. The magnifying of the Lord is in the present tense, indicating that as she was talking, her soul was magnifying Him. Mary first rejoiced in God in her spirit and then, as she spoke, was exalting the Lord with her soul.

The second difference is in the meaning of the verbs themselves. The word translated "exalts" or "magnify"[51] means "to extol, glorify or praise." It is an outward expression describing what Mary was

---

[51] *Mĕgalunō* in the Greek.

doing at that very moment with her soul. She was praising God. On the other hand, the word translated "to rejoice"[52] conveys the idea of joy as an inward state of her spirit.

The third obvious difference between the two phrases is in the soul and spirit. These two represent two different realms that are inseparably linked.

What Mary experienced was a deep joy in her spirit through her communion with God because He was her Savior. She understood in her soul what the Lord had done and expressed that praise by extolling Him, using passages of Scripture from the Old Testament that the Spirit brought to her memory. Mary's worship was complete, involving her whole being. Her understanding was enlightened as it bubbled over into magnificent praise.

ENOCH

There is a lot of extra-biblical speculation about Enoch's life, but there is one astounding fact about this man: He "walked with God" (Gen. 5:22). There may be a connection between his walk and his becoming a father, since the two apparently coincided. Is it possible that the responsibility of fatherhood led Enoch to begin to walk with God? That may be an interesting comment on parenting.

Walking, of course, denotes a continuous activity, a daily lifestyle and a life-attitude. That is why there are admonitions to "walk in a manner worthy of the calling" (Eph.4:1), to "walk no longer just as the Gentiles also walk" (Eph. 4:17), to "walk in love" (Eph. 5:2), to "walk as children of light" (Eph. 5:8), and to "be careful how you walk" (Eph. 5:15).

The only other person that is said to have walked with God is Noah (Gen. 6:9). Keil and Delitzsch say that the phrase "denotes the most confidential intercourse, the closest communion with the personal God, a walking as it were by the side of God."[53]

MOSES

The mention of Moses often brings to mind Charlton Heston's authoritative and self-confident portrayal of Moses in the *The Ten*

---

[52] *Agalliaō* in the Greek.
[53] C. F. Keil and F. Delitzsch, *Commentary on the Old Testament. The Pentateuch*, p. 125.

Commandments. A closer look at Scripture, however, shows a Moses that had some of the same struggles we all have. The Bible tells us he was very humble or meek (Num. 12:3).

Acts 7 informs us that Moses knew he had been called by God to deliver Israel. Because he attempted to do this in his own strength, he fled at the first opposition (Acts 7:22-39). How God initially called him and how much Moses knew about God's plan at that time when he was forty years old, we cannot be sure. The Scriptures are silent.

Moses spent the next forty years wandering, and probably being humbled, before he had an encounter with the living God. Then, when God appeared to him, Moses had a number of questions.

First, he asks, "Who are you?" He says, "Behold, I am going to the sons of Israel, and I shall say to them, 'The God (*Elohim*) of your fathers has sent me to you.' Now they may say to me, 'What is His name?' What shall I say to them?" (Ex. 3:13).

To know the name of this God (*Elohim*) implies a closeness to Him. It is not just an epithet by which to address Him. To know His name is to know Him.

God's answer is "I AM WHO I AM" (Ex. 3:14). It is from this Hebrew expression that the name *YHWH* or *Yahweh* is derived. God reveals it as His covenant name to be used by His people. It is not that the name itself has some sort of special power, but it is the intimate name to be used by those who worship Him.

Despite God's promises that they would pay heed to him (Ex. 3:18), Moses asks, "What if they will not believe me?" (Ex. 4:1). God gives Moses the power to perform signs as proof that he was sent by God.

Third, he asks, "Who am I?" (paraphrase of Ex. 4:10). Perhaps he is remembering how he had been rejected and had fled forty years earlier. But God promises to empower Moses for the task.

Finally, Moses gives his "Here am I, Lord. Send Aaron" speech.

Moses did as the Lord told him, probably not with a lot of faith that it would work. Afterward, he says to God, "See, God! I knew this was going to happen. That is why I didn't want You to send me. Pharaoh is mad at me. The Jews are mad at me. And You haven't done anything to free Your people" (Ex. 5:22-23, author's paraphrase).

God explains to him that everything was going according to plan. Then He says, "I am the LORD (*Yahweh*) and I appeared to

Abraham, Isaac, and Jacob, as God Almighty (*El Shaddai*), but by My name, LORD (*Yahweh*), I did not make Myself known to them" (Ex. 6:2-3).

I once talked to a rabbi about this passage. He explained that this was God's way of saying He was going to have much more intimacy with Moses than he ever did with Abraham, Isaac, and Jacob. God entered into a deeper relationship with Moses through revealing more of His character to him.

Moses never really questioned God after that. In fact, in Exodus 33:11 we read, "The LORD used to speak to Moses face to face, just as a man speaks to his friend." That is not literal as the following passage shows. Moses never actually saw the face of God, but it does reveal the degree of communion he enjoyed with the Lord.

Once Moses had a taste of intimacy with God, he wanted more. He says, "Now therefore, I pray You, if I have found favor in Your sight, let me know Your ways, that I may know You, so that I may find favor in Your sight" (Ex. 33:13).

Moses reminds God that he was the object of His grace. Because that was true, he wanted to know God's ways. His ways are more than just His actions. It means that Moses wanted to know God's plans and have a vision for what He was doing. If he learned of God's ways, he would certainly know God more intimately. If he knew God more intimately, he would, in turn, find even more favor with God.

Moses then cried out, "I pray You, show me Your glory!" (Ex. 33:18). Wow! What a request! Moses wasn't satisfied with talking with God face-to-face like someone talks to a friend. He wanted more, much more. And God showed him as much as he could handle.

PAUL

Saul may have already known the answer when he asked the most important question of his life on the road to Damascus, "Who are You, Lord?" (Acts 9:5, NIV). Then came the crushing answer, "I am Jesus whom you are persecuting."

For the first time, Saul felt the weight of the law on him. Although he was zealously religious, he realized he did not know the Author of the law. I believe that is what he was referring to when he later writes, "When the commandment came, sin became alive, and I died" (Rom. 7:9). God left him broken for three days. He was so crushed he didn't eat or drink during that time. Then God sent Ananias to offer the perfect solution: intimacy with Jesus Christ (Acts 9:10-18).

Philippians 3 most clearly expresses Paul's zeal for intimacy with God after he was saved. After condemning the legalistic Judaizers, Paul cites his fleshly, religious credentials in which he had trusted up until his Damascus road experience.

He says, "But whatever things were gain to me, those things I have counted as loss for the sake of Christ. More than that, I count all things to be loss in view of the surpassing value of knowing Christ Jesus my Lord, for whom I have suffered the loss of all things, and count them but rubbish so that I may gain Christ" (Phil. 3:7-8).

The key is knowing Christ.[54] He was willing to sacrifice everything to enter into that intimate relationship with Him. No sacrifice was too great, because Christ was everything to him. He was his treasure and his pearl of great price. But Paul didn't stop with the satisfaction of knowing he was going to heaven.

Shifting to his walk with the Lord, he writes, "[So that I] may be found in Him, not having a righteousness of my own derived from the Law, but that which is through faith in Christ, the righteousness which comes from God on the basis of faith" (Phil. 3:9).

Paul goes beyond speaking about his salvation to speak of his growth in holiness. Just as his long list of human credentials did not help him to be saved, he knows he would gain nothing by a personal legalistic effort to be holy. Like David, Paul opened his life to God so that the Lord would know his righteous living flowed from his relationship with Christ by faith and not from an external code. The righteousness Paul sought was the fruit of his worship, and worship was its goal.

His goal was "that I may know Him" (Phil. 3:10). Paul hungered and thirsted for intimacy with Him and to have his life conformed to the image of the risen Christ. Paul recognized that he wasn't there yet, but he made that his life pursuit. Maybe that is why he really wanted to move on from this life (Phil. 1:21-23). He knew that intimacy with the Lord would be unhindered after his death.

---

[54] *Gnōsis* in the Greek.

Our lives are often so different from Paul's. We enter into the door of salvation and become complacent and satisfied in our relationship with God. In contrast, the closer Abraham, Moses, and Paul grew to God, the more and more hungry for His presence they became. There are many other examples in the Scriptures of ordinary people like you and me, who did extraordinary things because they had an intimate relationship with the Master.

MISSING THE MARK

If intimacy with God and worship are not stressed in our lives and in our training of leaders, have we somehow missed the mark? The Jews certainly missed the mark. Paul bears witness of that when he says they had "a zeal for God, but not in accordance with knowledge"(Rom. 10:2). [55] This kept them from recognizing God's standard or His offer of righteousness. Therefore, they thought they could establish their own righteousness by works.

In one of the more sobering passages in Scripture, Jesus says, "Many will say to Me on that day, 'Lord, Lord, did we not prophesy in Your name, and in Your name cast out demons, and in Your name perform many miracles?' And then I will declare to them, 'I never knew you; depart from Me, you who practice lawlessness'" (Matt. 7:22-23). The emphasis is "in Your name." These people were doing good and apparently doing it to honor Jesus. They were not ignorant nor were they just sitting in the pew. However, they had missed the mark. They never really knew Jesus, but instead were focused on their own religious works. Of course, Jesus, being an omniscient God, knew who they were and that they had no relationship with Him.

SATISFACTION IN OUR LIVES COMES FROM
A SPIRITUAL COMPREHENSION OF JESUS.

The real focus of our walk with God is expressed in Jeremiah 9:23-24. "Thus says the LORD, 'Let not a wise man boast of his wisdom, and let not the mighty man boast of his might, let not a rich man boast of his riches; but let him who boasts boast of this, that he understands

---

[55] *Epignōsis* in the Greek. This is an even more intense word describing intimacy.

and knows Me, that I am the LORD who exercises lovingkindness, justice, and righteousness on earth; for I delight in these things,' declares the Lord." Satisfaction in our lives comes from a spiritual comprehension of the person of Jesus. As a result, we no longer trust in our strength but in His character. Such intimacy with Him helps us to become like Him as we reflect His character.

When cognitive knowledge becomes an end in itself, people tend to become arrogant. As Paul said, "Knowledge makes arrogant, but love edifies" (1 Cor. 8:1). He is not contrasting knowledge with love. He's saying that knowledge with a love for God and others will build others up. Knowledge without such love will lead to conceit. It is so easy to become fascinated with the study and teaching of Scripture that we lose sight of the real goal of intimacy with God. Paul warned Timothy about missing the mark in his ministry (1 Tim. 1: 5-6; 4:7; 6:11-12)

I have missed the mark so many times in my own life. I made a *decision* for Christ when I was 16. It was more an affirmation that Christ had died for me than anything else. When I truly came to know Him five years later, there was spiritual enlightenment and I changed, but my faith was still largely just intellectual.

While I was in graduate school, I discovered the importance of worship. However, I focused on the experience and equated worship with music. Over the years, I've discovered more and more the spiritual nature of worship by studying the Scriptures and reading the stories of great men of God.

I came to the mission field intending to focus on worship, but I finally began to experience the spiritual nature of worship a few years later when I started looking into the connection between intimacy with God, worship, and walking by the Spirit. One important key for me has been praying the Scriptures. I have read, meditated and asked God to apply the truths to me, giving me spiritual understanding. After having carefully studied Romans 6-8, I prayed through these chapters, verse-by-verse, every day for a month, hungering to live the reality of those passages.

The importance of the Scriptures in worship is the subject of the next chapter.

CONCLUSION

Worship is a complete act. At its core, it is the communion of our spirits with God's Spirit. However, it is not limited to one aspect of our beings, but will involve all that we are: Our spirits, our minds, our emotions, our wills, and our bodies. Above all, it is spiritual intimacy with God.

Worship is not just a ritual. It is possible to sing praises to God and to know a great deal about the Bible without ever really knowing God. It is also possible to have strong emotional feelings at certain times as we contemplate God without having a strong relationship with Him. It is impossible, however, to truly worship God without intimacy.

We saw from the examples of Moses and Paul that intimacy with God is progressive. Everyone who is saved has an introduction into His presence and *access* to communion with Him, but not everyone continues to seek Him and to *practice* worship.

We must never forget to keep the main thing the main thing: spiritual intimacy with God. We must drink deeply of the new wine of our relationship with Him to have the golden thread of worship integrated into our lives.

THE PARADIGM SHIFT

As love is more than a feeling, so is worship. It does not depend on our circumstances, but on our spiritual state. Worship is not the feeling of a sacred moment created by outward events but an inward, intimate spiritual walk with God.

THE SENSE OF THE SACRED	SPIRITUAL INTIMACY WITH GOD
1. OBJECTIVES: • To feel God's presence.	1. OBJECTIVES: • To have communion with God. • To be transformed by His presence.
2. MEANS: *The circumstances* • Through music. • Through sacred places. • Through religious moments.	2. MEANS: *A conscious choice to seek intimacy with Him.* • Through study. • Through prayer and meditation. • Through learning to fix our minds on the presence of the Holy Spirit in our lives.
3. RESULT: *Religious fulfillment*	3. RESULT: *Walking with God.*

WHERE TO START

1. **ASK GOD TO EXAMINE YOUR LIFE.** Do you have intimacy with God? Is your worship in spirit or is it more intellectual or emotional? Is intimacy the pursuit of your life? What is standing in the way of a deeper walk with God?

2. **TALK TO SOMEONE YOU KNOW WHO WALKS WITH GOD.** Find someone you feel has years of experience in his or her intimacy with God and ask the following questions. Explore any of these topics more in depth.

   • How long have you known the Lord?
   • How has your relationship with Him changed through the years?
   • What has most contributed to your growth in intimacy with Him?
   • What has been the biggest barrier to growing to know Him?
   • Describe your prayer life.
   • How do you commune with Him throughout the day?
   • How do you study and read the Bible?
   • What is worship to you?

3. **SEEK INTIMACY WITH GOD.** Spend some time reflecting on this chapter and your life. Ask God to draw you into spiritual intimacy with Him. Ask Him to open your spiritual eyes to see Him more clearly and to enjoy daily communion with Him. Pray that He would remove pride and other barriers to a deeper walk with Him. Tell God that you want the same intimacy with Him that Moses and Paul had.

4. **ASK GOD TO CREATE A HUNGER FOR INTIMACY WITH HIM.** Complacency is the Christian's greatest enemy. We can achieve a certain level of intimacy but then seek no more. Use Psalm 42 as the basis of your prayer, asking God to create the same longing for Him that the psalmist had.

DISCUSSION QUESTIONS

1. What is intimacy with God?

2. What is life?

3. How are worship and intimacy with God related?

4. How would you describe the spiritual side of humans?

5. What does the marriage metaphor teach us about intimacy with God?

6. Why is there a tendency to stress the cognitive knowledge of God rather than communion with Him?

7. Describe what spiritual intimacy is without referring to feelings.

8. What is friendship with God?

9. What kinds of barriers do we face in seeking intimacy with God?

10. How well can you identify with Moses and Abraham in their walks with God?

11. What did you learn from the life of Moses?

12. What did you see in Mary's praise that helped you understand worship?

13. What did you learn from your interview with a person who walks with God?

14. How have you grown in your communion with God?

15. What is standing in the way of your being more intimate with God?

16. How can we help each other grow in our walk with God?

17. How do you fit into the paradigm shift table?

Chapter 3

WHAT IS WORSHIP ANYWAY?

UNDERSTANDING WHAT HAPPENS WITHIN US THAT LEADS US TO WORSHIP

"But an hour is coming, and now is, when THE TRUE WOR-SHIPERS *shall* WORSHIP THE FATHER *in spirit and truth; for such people* THE FATHER SEEKS TO BE HIS WORSHIPERS*"* (John 4:23).

SEED TRUTH: WORSHIP IS A MIND-SET OF HONOR, FEAR, AND LOVE FOR GOD THAT OVERFLOWS IN PRAISE, MINISTRY, AND A TRANSFORMED LIFE. *An understanding of our internal attitudes that constitute true worship and its outward expression is essential to growth in our relationship with Him. Worshipers choose to fix their minds on God because they find satisfaction in His presence. Their intimacy expresses itself in their words and behaviors. People who are merely religious are often oblivious to God's presence until they are periodically reminded of Him during times of praise or prayer. They assume if they are performing the outward expressions of worship, they are indeed worshiping.*

I have a group of friends here in Brazil who have taught me more about worship than any book I have read. Two of them came from a very strict religious group. One was married to his work; another was an extremely violent man who drank heavily. And two of them were just regular guys. None of them had much formal education and all of them had family problems. Several worked together in a fruit stand, barely making enough to support themselves.

At the urging of the leader of their church, they took our leadership training classes every Tuesday night. The course itself is focused on preparing worshipers rather than scholars. Most of the material typically taught in seminary is included, but worship is integrated into every topic.

It was amazing to see how seriously they took each lesson. They seemed awed by everything they learned. They had a passion for Christ I had not seen in any other group. They were determined to become worshipers and were unconcerned that they had few material resources, talents, or abilities. What little they had, they offered completely to God.

They shared their faith with everyone they came across, whether it was the man changing their flat tire or the thieves holding them at gunpoint. The wife of the violent man had given up any hope of having a happy home, but with tears in her eyes, she shared how God had restored their home. The two religious guys are now full of the joy of the Lord. I have never seen a group that so freely shared what they had and demonstrated a genuine love for one another.

Why were they so involved in sharing their faith? What changed their marriages? How could people with so little give so much?

Simply, they had learned how to worship God, not as a religious form, but as a deep love and reverence from within their hearts. They gratefully gave themselves to God, and their ministry, generosity, and holy lives were outward expressions of that worship.

Up to this point, we have seen what worship is not, contrasting it with the divided religious life. In the previous chapter we looked at the spiritual nature of our intimacy with God. We are ready now to look at what happens within our spirits, leading us to true worship. What follows is a description of my thought process as I came to understand worship, concluding with a definition.

THE MARRIAGE METAPHOR

What is a marriage? It is commonly thought of as a legal arrangement between a man and a woman who have feelings for each other and make a commitment to live together. But perhaps there are as many definitions as there are couples.

Contrary to popular opinion, good communication, quality time together, the relative absence of conflicts, and a fulfilling sex life are not the cause of a loving relationship—they are the result. People confuse the cause and effect.

Bringing my wife flowers or helping with the housework is not the essence of my love for her, but the fruit of it. My love for her longs to express itself because of the joy I find in her. And each couple learns how to show their love in their own unique ways.

People often define marriage based on what motivated them to marry in the first place. Perhaps the most common reason for entering matrimony is the strong feelings of love couples have for each other. Often people believe that their partner will meet their need for affirmation. Others seek the security of the relationship, whether financial or emotional. Some marry for pleasure—whether it is for sexual gratification, companionship, or simply having a good time together. Some people get together because they want to have children or for purely pragmatic reasons such as having someone to provide a clean house, clean clothes, and a hot meal on the table.

A good marriage probably carries all those benefits. However love is not "you help me so much," or "you make me feel so good about myself." Rather, the source of a solid marriage is a commitment to join oneself to another person, to becoming one instead of remaining two. Individuality is willingly subordinated to becoming two in one. The resulting spiritual unity is characterized by faithfulness, honor, respect, trust, love, appreciation, and enjoyment.

In the same way, when we talk about worship, we could consider all the ways in which we are benefited. Worship produces peace and gives meaning to our lives. Worship transforms us into God's image. It brings us together as a body. Some people say they love going to church because they come away feeling so "light."

But none of these should be our motive for seeking God nor do they reflect the inner attitude that leads us to true worship. Instead of looking at what we receive, we need above all else to honor God, fear Him, and love Him. These three attitudes are the foundation of a worshipful life. This foundation is strengthened as we strive to know and understand God, unite ourselves with Him, and enjoy His presence—all with fear, awe, and reverence.

There is a strong tendency to try to deepen our oneness with God through the outward expressions of worship. We might try singing songs that are more relevant, more relational. We could shut our eyes tight and lift our hands to God and try to feel His presence. We could use a great sound system for our church and put together a great band. Although these acts may enhance our praise and even help focus our minds on God, in and of themselves, they are not worship.

In marriage, great relationship is the fruit of a commitment to love and find joy in one another, not the cause. In the same manner, praise and music are not the cause of worship, but the fruit of it. *Excellent praise is the fruit of honoring, fearing, and loving God.*

It is true that special times with the Lord can help us deepen our worship. We grow closer to Him when we join with other believers in praise. After all, God did create music. But singing to God, like good works and obedience, is the outward manifestation of a worshipful life-attitude. Worship starts in the heart.

THE OUTWARD EXPRESSION OF WORSHIP

IS WORSHIP INWARD OR OUTWARD?

Paul was swimming against the religious current of his day when he argued in favor of salvation by grace through faith. By saying, "For we maintain that a man is justified by faith apart from works of the Law" (Rom. 3:28), he was declaring that salvation was dependent on one's inner attitude and not on one's actions. The essence of salvation is purely inward as proven by Abraham's being justified apart from his works, the law, or circumcision (Romans 4).

Many have seen James as contradicting Paul, especially when he asked, "Was not Abraham our father justified by works when he offered up Isaac his son on the altar? You see that faith was working with his works, and as a result of the works, faith was perfected" (James 2:21-22). At first glance, it seems that he is saying it is both the inward faith and the external works that bring about salvation.

In general, most conservative scholars agree that the essence of salvation is the result of an inner attitude of repentance and faith.

Salvation *is* internal. However, James makes it clear that true internal faith will express itself outwardly through works.

As MacArthur points out, "James is not at odds with Paul…in 1:17-18, James affirmed that salvation is a gift bestowed according to the sovereign will of God. Now he is stressing the importance of faith's fruit—the righteous behavior that genuine faith always produces."[1]

The essence of salvation is genuine inward faith and the new birth. The reality of salvation expresses itself outwardly through our works, though this fruit will vary in quality and quantity from person-to-person. It is important for us to understand the relationship between the inner, heart attitudes of worship and its outward expression.

Some have maintained that the Greek word *proskunéo* means to bow down, thus associating worship with a physical act.

There is always a danger in defining a word using its etymology because word-use changes. As Kittel and Friedrich say, "….*proskyneῶoμ* is an ancient term for reverent adoration of the gods, which in the case of chthonic [infernal] deities would mean stooping to kiss the earth. The Greeks abandon the outward gesture but keep the term for the inner attitude. Later the word takes on a much more general sense expressing love and respect."[2]

Although it is mostly used in the New Testament to describe a physical act (Kittel and Friedrich call it a "concrete term"), Jesus gives *proskunéo* an inward meaning by saying that it is to be in spirit and truth (John 4:23). Paul puts it alongside the physical act of bowing down when he says that a convert, "will fall on his face and worship [*proskunéo*] God" (1 Cor. 14:25). This describes both the outward action as well as the inward attitude. Apparently, the outward expression of true worship should never be separated from the inward attitude of submission.

Other words for worship are *sébomai* and its equivalents. Vine tells us this word means, "to revere, stressing the feeling of awe or devotion."[3] This inward attitude is expected to be expressed outwardly in the life of a *godly* or *pious* person (see 1 Tim. 5:4).

[1] MacArthur, *Faith Works: The Gospel According to the Apostle*, p. 153.
[2] Kittel and Friedrich.
[3] Vine.

Quoting Isaiah 29:13, Jesus says, "This people honors Me with their lips, but their heart is far away from Me. But in vain do they worship [*sébomai*] Me, Teaching as doctrines the precepts of men" (Matt. 15:8-9). Again, it seems that what is expressed with our lips needs to flow from a worshiping heart that stands in awe of Him. Finally, *latreúō*, which is often translated *to serve*, probably emphasizes the external aspects of worship. In its original form, Kittel and Friedrich say, "The word is used literally for bodily service (e.g., workers on the land, or slaves), and figuratively for 'to cherish.'"[4] It is used in the Septuagint (O.T. in Greek) to describe cultic acts, especially of priests. In the New Testament, the word and its derivatives often carry the same outward sense (Rom. 1:25; Heb 8:5; 9:9; 10:2; 13:10).

Paul, however, definitely gives it an inward sense when he says, "For God, whom I serve [*latreúō*] in my spirit in the preaching of the gospel of His Son…" (Rom 1:9). His inward cherishing of God in his spirit led to the outward expression of worship, which was preaching the gospel (cf. 2 Tim. 1:3).

In a passage somewhat parallel with John 4:23, Paul says that we worship "in the Spirit of God" (Phil 3:3).[5] Since circumcision in this context is seen as spiritual rather than physical, there is no reason to assume that worshiping in the Spirit of God is anything but inward.

Also, in Romans 12:1, we are commanded to offer up our bodies, "which is your spiritual service of worship [*latreían*]."[6] Although it is obvious we are not putting our physical bodies on the altar, the sense of the passage is that there will be some sort of external evidence of worship. That is why this passage makes a prefect transition into the exhortation section of Romans.

---

[4] Kittel and Friedrich
[5] Although *pneuma* in both Phil. 3:3 and John 4:23 does not have a definite article and uses the dative case, it is probably best to see the Phil. 3:3 passage as referring to the Holy Spirit since it does not use the preposition en as in John 4:23 (locative sphere), and so it is probably instrumental (by the Spirit). In addition, it is followed by *theos* (God) in the genitive, defining whose Spirit it is.
[6] Generally, translators consider *logikos* to mean spiritual rather than physical worship. Some translate it, "intelligent" or "logical." Here, it is "spiritual."

All these passages confirm that true worship is internal and will always be accompanied by an outward expression of worship. As faith is the essence of salvation and will always be expressed through works, so worship is essentially inward but will always be manifested outwardly. It should be noted that the outward expressions of worship are not always praise and music, but might be acts of love and even evangelism.

We define legalism as an over-emphasis on the external expression of salvation to the point that works become the essence of salvation. Maybe when we emphasize the outward expressions of worship rather than its inward essence, we fall into the same trap.

WORSHIP IS MORE THAN ITS EXPRESSION.

A U.S. pastor once asked about the difficulties we faced in our ministry in Brazil. After hearing some of our stories, he asked how we weathered the storms without quitting, since many missionaries leave in the first couple of years on the field.

Without hesitating, I answered, "Worship!" If we had gone to Brazil for recognition, money, comfort, or pats on the back, we would have quit a long time ago. However, because worship has been our focus, we have stuck it out through some difficult times.

The pastor responded, "Stop right there. What do you mean by 'worship'?" He commented that worship had become a buzzword. When people ask, "How did you like the worship at our church?" they usually mean "What do you think of the music?"

Most discussion about worship today focuses on the style of our Sunday services. Signs in front of some churches indicate they have both contemporary and traditional meetings. Since people think of worship as an event rather than a life-attitude, the focus is on individual tastes in style rather than the essence of what happens in worship. The atmosphere created by the worship leaders takes precedence over the life-attitude of awe and reverence in the context of one's intimacy with God.

Sally Morgenthaler points out:

> Sadly, the source of David's power, a passionate worship relationship with God, is almost foreign to the contemporary born again experience. Many do not know the meaning of

longing after God as a deer longs for water (Ps. 42:1). We may long after exponential growth figures and five-thousand-seat sanctuaries, but if we are honest, not very many of us truly long after God. Rather, we tend to settle for God at a comfortable distance. The irony is we are now inviting the lost to replicate what is basically a very stunted relationship![7]

If our worship is limited to "holy" ceremonies in "holy" buildings, God does not delight in it, nor is He glorified. That leads to an important question: If we can't define worship by its outward expressions, what needs to happen inside our spirits for us to experience genuine worship?

WORSHIP AS A LIFE-ATTITUDE AND ITS EXPRESSION

Some time ago, I came to understand more clearly what actually happens within us as we develop as worshipers. I was teaching our leadership training material to a group of leaders from the interior. Although sincere, they had always focused on the outward expression of what the religious culture considers a holy life rather than on a walk with God. But after several months of looking at God's Word together, it seemed as if they were beginning to understand that true holiness flows from our hearts.

One day as I was waiting for class to begin, I began thinking and praying about a fresh way to express the importance of the inner life as the basis for a holy lifestyle. I tried to show them how their inner worldview, values, convictions, and attitudes affect the way they behave.

I drew this quickly on the blackboard:

LIFE-ATTITUDE   ⟶   **LIFESTYLE**
(Attitudes)   *(Actions)*

It then occurred to me that this is what distinguishes worship from religion. In religion, the source is not important, so long as the person performs the right rituals and obeys the right rules. Religion is not a life attitude; it is merely behavioral ethics and religious moments.

---

[7] Morgenthaler, p.36.

I wanted to show that a Christian lifestyle is not following a list of rules or traditions. All through history people have tried to mimic the dress, words, and habits of godly men without ever seeking to emulate their life-attitudes. Some leaders in our church in Brazil even imitate the accents and grammatical errors of American missionaries they have admired.

So I asked myself, "How does the Bible describe the expression of worship in the life of God's followers?" I discovered four outward manifestations of worship.

Praise

Praise is the most obvious expression of worship. The Psalms are full of declarations of the character of God, directed to Him and to His people.

> PRAISE IS THE MOST OBVIOUS
> EXPRESSION OF WORSHIP.

Praise in the Hebrew is *yahdah* – "to give thanks" or *halah* – "to praise, glory, boast or commend." Many of the Psalms were considered praise hymns.

The Greek word for praise is *eulogeo,* from which we get the word "eulogy," and it means "to speak well of." Praise, then, is a verbalization of respect, reverence, or admiration, but it is not limited to song.

The Portuguese word *louvor* can mean "to applaud, admire or approve."

In English, *praise* carries the idea of an expression of approval or a favorable evaluation, again, usually verbally.

In whatever language we examine, praise is always some sort of verbalization of those qualities in God that we admire, whether with songs, words, or gestures. Praising God can take on many forms. It can be directed at those around us, declaring who He is and what He has done. Testimonies and thanksgiving could be termed "horizontal," but praise can also be "vertical," as we address God, expressing our gratitude and awe of who He is. Both speaking *of* Him and *to* Him are praise.

We naturally praise what awes or excites us. We can't stop talking about that amazing finish to the football game or the spectacular scenery we saw on our vacation. A proud mother needs to control herself so she does not always tout the virtues of her children whom she loves.

Praise that comes from an inner worship glorifies God. As Piper says, "It is there spontaneously. It is not performed as a means to anything else. It is not consciously willed. It is not decided upon. It comes from deep within, from a place beneath the conscious will."[8]

When praise is performed as a ritual or duty, it is empty religion. Piper continues, "But when worship is reduced to disinterested duty, it ceases to be worship. For worship is a feast."[9]

Commenting on Psalm 45:1, MacArthur says, "The heart is so warmed by righteousness and love that, figuratively, it reaches the boiling point. Praise is the boiling over of a hot heart...As God warms the heart with righteousness and love, the resulting life of praise that boils over is the truest expression of worship."[10]

Service

Latrea and *leitourgeo* are two Greek words that are translated "worship," and they both convey the idea of offering or serving God or ministering to Him (see Luke 2:37; Rom. 12:1). They generally refer to the service and sacrifice rendered in the temple. It was supposed to be done as an outward expression of internal reverence for God.

I have read that *gottesdiest* is German for "God's service (to us) and our service to God."[11] The emphasis is on the expression of our reverence for God outwardly through our actions.

These same words may occasionally be applied to religion, but only when the action does not flow from true worship. Nothing is wrong with tradition and rituals as long as they are practiced as a result of a worshipful attitude and not an end in themselves.

[8] Piper, *Desiring God*, p. 91.
[9] *Ibid.* p. 98.
[10] MacArthur, *Ultimate Priority*, p.13.
[11] Morgenthaler, p. 46.

Evangelism

Although *latrea* and *leitourgeo* may be associated with temple worship, they sometimes refer to other outward manifestations of genuine worship that are outside of what we might typically think. For example, Paul describes his preaching of the gospel as *latreuo.* To him, evangelism was not merely a cold duty, but an expression of his worship to God (Rom. 1:9).

A holy life

Paul used *latreia* to describe the basis for a holy and acceptable life (Rom. 12:1). It is clear that the way we live should be a reflection of our inward worship.

Good works

Acts of service and good works, such as the offerings made to the Jerusalem church, are seen as an expression of a worship lifestyle (Rom. 5:27). These, too, if performed only as a duty, are empty and merely wood, hay, and stubble (1 Cor. 3:12).

MacArthur summarizes the relationship between worship and these activities when he says, "Praising God, doing good, and sharing with others [are] all legitimate, scriptural acts of worship. That draws into the concept of worship every activity and relationship of human living."[12]

GLORIFYING GOD AS A MANIFESTATION OF WORSHIP

So then, a worship lifestyle is expressed through praise, service, evangelism, a holy life, and good works that all flow from communion with God. I lumped all these acts together and refer to them as *glorifying God.*[13]

These acts glorify or shine forth the brightness or splendor of His character. Jesus asked that He would be glorified (John 17:1). The Father added nothing to His character, but Jesus was asking that the essence of who He is would shine forth to the world. By doing this, the Father, likewise, would be glorified.

---

[12] MacArthur, *Ultimate Priority,* p.16.
[13] The words *doxa* and *doxazo,* from which we derive the word *doxology,* translate the word "glorify" and mean "to shine forth."

Jesus also claimed that He glorified the Father through the works that He performed (John 17:4).

We are, likewise, told that the Father is glorified by our bearing much fruit (John 15:8), and we are admonished to do good works before men so they can see our good works and glorify God (Matt. 5:16).[14]

He is glorified because His character is being manifest, not mine.

When I am able to love someone, not with my own pumped up emotions, but with His unconditional love flowing through me, He is glorified. When I share my faith with others as a spontaneous act flowing from worship, He is glorified. When I resist temptation as the result of His character being imprinted in my soul through worship, He is glorified.

On the other hand, if I praise, evangelize, or try to live a holy life in my own strength, I am glorified because I am manifesting *my* character. Well, not really. I will inevitably fail in all of these endeavors and show myself to be a hypocrite. I would be exposing, not glorifying, myself.

So I added these new words to my drawing on the blackboard to look like this:

GLORIFYING GOD
Praise
Service
Ministry
A holy life
Good works

WORSHIP ⟶

THE INNER ATTITUDES THAT CONSTITUTE WORSHIP

It was about time to start the class, and since I was describing worship as an inward attitude, I asked myself, "What really is happening in our spirits when we worship? What values do I see in the life of David as he wrote the Psalms or in Paul's life as seen in the epistles?"

---

[14] It is interesting here that the New International Version translates *doxazo* as "praise."

ATTITUDES THAT PRODUCE WORSHIP
- HONORING GOD
- FEARING GOD
- LOVING GOD

I see three main attitudes woven together to produce worship within our spirits. There is no real chronological or hierarchical order to these words.

The first attitude we need is the desire to *honor God*.

I had been thinking of Piper's challenge to make God our treasure. The Greek word for honor, *timao,* can mean "to set a price or value on something" (Matt. 27:9), and it can mean, "to honor or revere someone."[15] In fact, in 1 Tim. 5:17, it is not easy to tell whether Paul is calling for financial support or for special respect for elders, or perhaps both. Either way, we are to value our leaders.

The word *worship* in English means "worthship" or "to give value and honor to someone." When we worship God, it means we treasure Him above all else. Nothing in this world is as precious as He is. That is why Jesus was constantly challenging the values of those following Him (see Luke 14:25-33). We cannot be disciples if we treasure anything more than Him.

The second value necessary for worship is *fearing God*. The Greek word, *eusebeia,*[16] is translated "godliness." Older translations use "piety." Although it is not generally thought of as a worship term, it expresses the essence of worship as an inner awe or fear of God, living one's life conscious of the presence of God. This naturally affects one's behavior.

The term "fear" captures the essence of what godliness is. There is a negative aspect that means flight, fright, or apprehension. Adam avoided God after the fall because he said, "I was afraid" (Gen. 3:10). This kind of fear causes us to recoil and avoid approaching a holy God because of His righteousness and awesome power. It can carry

---

[15] Bauer, et al.

[16] *Eu* – "well" or "good"; *sebeia* – "awe," is used several times in 1 and 2 Timothy to describe the quality of a leader. It was used to describe Cornelius who knew about God and had a profound respect and reverence for Him, even before he was saved (Acts 10:2).

the idea of a cowardly withdrawal, but a true reverent fear or godliness is an awe that draws us to Him.

In his allegory, *The Chronicles of Narnia,* C. S. Lewis's description of the lion, Aslan, who represents Christ, captures the essence of this fear.

> But as for Aslan himself, the Beavers and the children didn't know what to do or say when they saw him. People who have not been in Narnia sometimes think that a thing cannot be good and terrible at the same time. …For when [the children] tried to look at Aslan's face they just caught a glimpse of the golden mane and the great, royal, solemn, overwhelming eyes; and then they found they couldn't look at him and went all trembly.[17]

The children sensed many emotions that seemed almost contradictory. They were drawn to him, but were speechless in his presence.

As Tozer says, "I believe that the reverential fear of God mixed with love and fascination and astonishment and admiration and devotion is the most enjoyable state and the most purifying emotion the human soul can know."[18]

It should be noted that we usually emphasize a "godly" life in terms of behavior, but forget that those godly behaviors stem from an internal attitude of fear.

Fearing God means we tremble in His presence because we are keenly aware that we do not deserve to be there and, but for His grace, we would be destroyed by His awesome presence (Lam. 3:22).

The third and final value essential to worship is to *love God.*

In chapter two we talked about spiritual intimacy with God. It is impossible to have intimacy without love. Loving God is what makes worship a relationship rather than a duty. We could fear and honor God and not love Him, which would make our worship empty.

"Adoration" is often properly used as a synonym for worship, reflecting the notion that loving God is essential to worshiping Him. The Portuguese word for worship is *Adoração,* supporting the notion that loving Him is an integral part of worship.

---

[17] C. S. Lewis, *The Lion, the Witch, and the Wardrobe,* p.123.
[18] Tozer, *Worship,* pp. 30-31.

Fortunately, the word "adore" has passed from popular usage and is considered more formal. Maybe we can now reserve the word in reference to God to whom our adoration is due.

Do I love Him because I am merely grateful for what He has done for me? That would be a selfish relationship. I am, by the way, infinitely grateful for what He has done, and I tell Him often, but I don't love Him merely for what He has done for me.

Do I love Him because He has so many admirable characteristics? I certainly respect Him and am in awe of who He is, but a love relationship with God goes beyond admiration.

Loving God is finding our fulfillment and joy in His holy presence. It is He that we love, not just His character or what He does. When we love someone, we delight in just being close to that person.

My little drawing was getting bigger.

WORSHIP

Honor
Fear
Love

GLORIFYING GOD

Praise
Service
Ministry
A holy life
Good works

THE RESPONSE TO WORSHIP

But something in the diagram seemed to be missing. I continued to reflect on it for the next several months, but a nagging question kept coming up. Is it possible that we could have the right attitudes, but never act upon them? Could we worship in our spirits, and yet never be moved to do anything? What is needed for us to live outwardly our internal attitudes?

Then I remembered that the Greek word *proskuneo,* "worship," means to bow down before someone, indicating submission. That is why subjects bowed before the king, showing their submission to Him, placing their heads symbolically beneath his feet. That was the missing part. An attitude of submission is necessary for our inner worship to be seen in our daily lives.

SUBMISSION IS THE LINK THAT TRANSLATES OUR ATTITUDES INTO ACTIONS.

The temptation of Adam and Eve was a desire to be like God (Gen. 3:5). Since that time, all human beings have sought to be little gods. One of the fundamental statements in the Alcoholics Anonymous program is "The Bible says there is a God, and it isn't you."[19]

As we love, honor, and fear God, we respond by submitting ourselves to Him, giving to Him our divinity and claims to personal sovereignty, because we trust Him. Romans 12:1 is one of the key verses in this connection, "Therefore, I urge you, brethren, by the mercies of God, *to present your bodies a living and holy sacrifice*, acceptable to God, which is your spiritual service of worship" (emphasis added). That implies bowing in submission to God.

Ezra "*set his heart* to study the law of the Lord, and to practice it, and to teach His statutes and ordinances in Israel (Ezra 7:10, emphasis added). He offered His heart to God, placing his will, his thoughts, and his affections at God's feet so that he might truly be a man of the Word.

When we allow God to produce the essential attitudes within us, our response is to submit to Him, and the result is that we glorify God with our lives. Submission is the link that translates our attitudes into actions. The diagram was now complete:

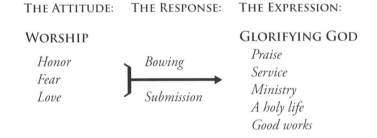

THE ATTITUDE: THE RESPONSE: THE EXPRESSION:

WORSHIP   GLORIFYING GOD

Honor   *Bowing*   *Praise*
Fear   *Service*
Love   *Submission*   *Ministry*
                                    A holy life
                                    Good works

---

[19] John Renesch, "Exploring the Better Future" <http://globaldialoguecenter.blogs.com/johnrenesch/2008/10/wall-street-cas.html>.

WHAT IS WORSHIP?

Having understood what worship is not, what is its spiritual nature, and the internal attitudes that lead to its outward expression, we are now able to discover a definition.

Worship is never really defined in the Bible. Like prayer and fasting, it is assumed the believer will understand it, by seeing it lived out in the lives of Bible personalities. Abraham, Moses, Joshua, David, Peter, Paul, and many other great men and women in the Bible were, above all else, worshipers. It has helped me to grow in my intimacy with Him by taking the words of these people in the Bible and making them my own.

The lives of men such as Jonathan Edwards, George Müller, and Brother Lawrence have impacted me as well. Their biographies relate their worshipful hearts.

ATTEMPTS TO DEFINE WORSHIP

We should never try to reinvent the wheel. Before we come to any conclusions about worship, we should look at what others have said to glean from their studies and their walk with God.

I have read a variety of books and listened to many people from diverse backgrounds with an open but discerning mind to try to understand how to develop as a worshiper. Of course, one of the difficulties in describing worship is that, although there are objective aspects to it, we all experience it differently. Here are some attempts by various authors to define worship.

Worship is honor and adoration directed to God.[20]

Worship is an active response to God whereby we declare His worth.[21]

[Worship is] the act and attitude of wholeheartedly giving ourselves to God, spirit, soul, and body. Worship is simply the expression of our love for God, which Jesus said should involve all our heart, mind, and physical strength (Mark 12:30).[22]

---

[20] MacArthur, *Ultimate Priority*, p.14.
[21] Ronald Allen and Gordon Borror, *Worship: Rediscovering the Missing Jewel*, p. 6.
[22] Gustafson in Morgenthaler, p. 47.

Worship celebrates God's saving deed in Jesus Christ.[23]

Worship is not only offering all that we are to a Holy God (spirit). It is an intentional response of praise, thanksgiving, and adoration to *The* God, the One revealed in the Word, made known and accessible to us in Jesus Christ and witnessed in our hearts through the Holy Spirit (truth).[24]

[Worship is] the total adoring response of man to the one Eternal God, self-revealed in time.[25]

The first essential condition for true worship is total submission. The second essential is that Christ alone should be glorified. We must meet these conditions, submitting ourselves absolutely, without reserve, to Jesus Christ as Lord.[26]

Worship involves both attitudes and actions. It is both a subjective experience and an objective activity. Worship is not an unexpressed feeling, nor is it an empty formality. True worship is balanced and involves the mind, the actions, and the will. It must be intelligent; it must reach deep within and be motivated by love; and it must lead to obedient actions that glorify God.[27]

Worship is the human response to the self-revelation of the triune God, which involves: (1) divine initiation in which God graciously reveals himself, his purposes, and his will; (2) a spiritual and personal relationship with God through Jesus Christ enabled by the ministry of the Holy Spirit; and (3) a response by the worshiper of joyful adoration, reverence, humility, submission, and obedience.[28]

[23] Webber in Morgenthaler, ibid.
[24] Morgenthaler, ibid.
[25] Underhill, in Wiersbe, p. 21.
[26] Carroll, p. 37.
[27] Wiersbe, p. 21.
[28] David Nelson, "Developing Practice of Worship" in Bateman, p. 149.

MY DESCRIPTION OF WORSHIP

One day, as I was discussing my reflection on worship with a friend, he challenged me to define worship in one sentence. After much time and growth, it came out like this:

> *Worship is a believer's choice to seek and enjoy constant spiritual fellowship with God by learning to see Him through His Word and growing in his fear, honor, and love for God, leading him to constantly offer his heart to God's guiding presence, resulting in his being transformed into Christ's image and overflowing into service.*

This is more of a description than a definition and contains these elements:

Its participants – believers
Its nature – a choice
Its motivation – to seek and enjoy fellowship with God
Its method – learning to see Him through His Word
Its results – growing in the fear and honor of God and in love for Him.
Its outcome – continual offering of oneself for God's presence and guidance, transformation into the image of Christ, and service to God

I describe it first as *a choice*. It is a conscious decision because, although the door to worship has been opened to all believers, there must be conscious effort and discipline to step through the door and move down the path toward greater intimacy with God. If that were not so, nor even possible, there would be no reason for approaching the subject. (See chapter 5.)

It is for *believers* because it is only through faith in Jesus Christ that we can have access to God's presence (John 14:6, Eph. 2:18). Although others may be sincere, all worship outside of Jesus Christ is empty and of no value.

We must choose to *seek* Him. Although He is the One who draws us into His presence (Rom. 3:11; Jer. 31:3), we still are responsible to seek Him with all our hearts. He is a rewarder of those who diligently seek Him (Heb 11:6).

The word *enjoy* is emphasized because worship is not a duty or a burden. Joy comes from finding pleasure in Him. (See chapter 9.)

The word *constant* shows that worship is not an event, but a life-attitude. It is not limited to certain religious moments.

Worship is *spiritual* because it goes beyond the intellectual or emotional dimension. (See chapter 2.)

It is *fellowship* because it is a relationship and not an activity.

Worship starts with *learning to see Him through His Word.* Worship flows from objective truth as God has revealed Himself in the Bible. By focusing on the Scriptures, we are not worshiping an image created in our own minds, but God, as He really is. (See chapter 4.)

His Word sharpens our minds so that we are able to see Him in every aspect of our lives. Seeing Him leads to worship and worship leads to beholding Him more clearly. (See Chapter 6.)

Beholding Him should lead us to *fear, honor, and love God.* These are the defining inner values.

Seeing Him requires a response of *offering our hearts* to Him. That means that we yield our emotions, thought, will, dreams, comfort, and motives to His guidance. We are "bowing" before Him in humble submission. (See Chapter 7.)

True worship is progressively *being transformed into His image* as we reflect on His character. (See Chapter 8.)

Finally, worship always precedes and is the foundation of *service.* As we worship, we are becoming one with God's mission and His purposes in service. (See Chapters 10 and 14.)

In this definition, we can see that holiness and service are the fruit of a deep love for God. I pray that with this understanding, we will avoid the checklist of personal merit, as Saul had, and the checklist for "clean living" as the Pharisees had, which are the lure of religion.

MOTIVES FOR WORSHIP

WRONG MOTIVES

Nothing is worse than doing the right thing for the wrong reason. God condemned those who performed with a wrong heart what He

Himself had prescribed (Isa. 1:11-20; 1 Sam. 15:22). When there is a problem at the source, the whole stream becomes polluted.

Some people seek to worship God out of duty, but their lives are unchanged. It is like the "believer who returns home for Sunday dinner with the singular satisfaction that he has worshiped God because he heard the choir and took good notes on a fine expository sermon,"[29] but then goes about his daily life oblivious to God's presence. If there is no impact on our lives, we have not worshiped.

Other people hope that worship will improve their position before God. Many activities such as Bible reading, prayer, fasting, praise, and church attendance can be motivated by the thought that, if we practice these things, God will love us more or will answer our prayers.

Some worship for personal benefit or to have an emotional experience. Much worship music today is more man-centered than God-centered. Such songs, consequently, could be interpreted wrongly and lead to a self-centered, self-serving view of worship. Although there is personal benefit in worship, worship, after all, is not about us.

THE RIGHT MOTIVATION FOR WORSHIP

We have seen that genuine worship flows from our inner attitudes of love, fear, and honor. If we want to grow in our intimacy with Him, we need to learn what produces those attitudes within us. They certainly are not willed into existence nor can they be pumped up from somewhere within. In our definition of worship we said that they come from "learning to see Him through His Word." That means we must study His Word, prayerfully, asking Him to open our eyes. Here is what stimulates the inner attitudes essential to worship.

What God has done

When we consider God's works as they are revealed in His Word and think of what He has done in our own lives, we are led to gratitude. We marvel at His awesome power in fear, and we see His love as He has made Himself known to us.

---

[29] Needham, p. 208.

The writers of many of the Psalms simply reiterate what God had done for Israel in the past and at the time of their writing, both corporately and individually. Reflecting on God's acts produces worship and serves as the basis of our praise.

"I will give thanks to the LORD with all my heart; I will tell of all Your wonders. I will be glad and exalt in You; I will sing praise to Your name, O Most High" (Ps. 9:1-2).

Who God is

God's person and His name lead us to marvel within our spirits at His greatness and to wonder at His love, which overflows into an outward expression that glorifies Him. Praise is much more powerful when it looks beyond what He has done to who He is. An understanding of His person elicits awe and wonder, leading to worship and drawing us into intimate fellowship with Him.

After hearing someone speak or seeing what someone has done, have you ever said, "I have to meet that person"? In the same way, we are drawn to know more and more of God's character as more of Him is made known to us. As God opens our eyes to His character, we are drawn to Him and hunger to know Him better. It is more than just an intellectual curiosity. We are drawn to fellowship with Him because we want to be like Him.

"Who…is comparable to the LORD?…Who is like You, O mighty LORD?" (Ps. 89:6, 8). "I am the first and the last, and there is no God besides Me" (Isa. 44:6).

THE HIGHEST FORM OF WORSHIP GOES BEYOND
BEING THANKFUL FOR WHAT HE HAS DONE AND
BEYOND ADMIRING HIM FOR WHO HE IS.
THE HIGHEST FORM OF WORSHIP IS
LOVING AND ENJOYING HIM.

God's love for us

There is no greater demonstration of love than His grace being poured out on undeserving, weak, rebellious enemies (see Rom. 5:6-10). To think that an infinite God would become flesh and die for us and rise again to give us a new life is unfathomable. That is why we are led to "exult in God through our Lord Jesus Christ" (Rom. 5:11). The highest form of worship goes beyond being thankful for what He has done and beyond admiring Him for who He is. The highest form of worship is loving and enjoying Him.

"You will make known to me the path of life; / In Your presence is fullness of joy; / In Your right hand there are pleasures forever" (Ps. 16:11).

THE GOAL OF WORSHIP

Perhaps foundational to having the right source for our worship is having the right goal in mind. Our ultimate goal in worship is to please Him and find our satisfaction in Him. Leviticus and Numbers describe the sacrifices of Old Testament worship as a ministry to the Lord. The result of the worship sacrifices is seen as an aroma pleasing to God. God is self-sufficient and does not need us, but at the same time, worship gives Him pleasure because it is a reflection of our relationship with Him.

Our goal is not to fulfill an obligation, derive any personal benefit, or improve our standing before Him. We want to please Him because we love Him and it is our pleasure to do so.

As Tozer writes, "We please Him most, not by frantically trying to make ourselves good, but by throwing ourselves into His arms with all our imperfections and believe that He understands everything—and loves us still."[30]

Although we cannot improve our position, we can always deepen our fellowship with God. That is our passion. The Scriptures say, "And without faith it is impossible to please Him, for he who comes to God must believe that He is, and that He is a rewarder of those who seek Him" (Heb. 11:6).

God promises us a reward for diligently seeking[31] Him (Heb 11:6). The reward is communion with Him. What we receive is not material benefits or a more comfortable life. In fact, the context indicates that saving faith often leads us to forfeit earthly pleasures in

---

[30] Tozer, *Worship,* p. 29.
[31] Paul uses an intense word for seeking God. *Ekzeteo* means, "to diligently search for or desire" something. In this case it is God, not a favorable position.

favor of a future hope. Faith places us in good standing with Him so we can worship Him. Commenting on this passage, MacArthur says, "For faith we receive forgiveness, a new heart, eternal life, joy, peace, love, heaven—everything! When we trust in Jesus Christ, we become mutual heirs with Him."[32]

The reward we receive is nothing more than He Himself. When we have Him, we are eternally satisfied with a much deeper pleasure than any temporal benefit can provide. "The Lord is my shepherd, / I shall not want" (Ps. 23:1). Intimacy with Him is all I need or want, because He Himself is my satisfaction.

THE RESULTS OF WORSHIP

In addition to the outward expressions that glorify God, worship will influence our lives as we respond in bowing before Him. When it is integrated into our lives, and our minds become fixed on God, we are transformed. As we grow in our intimacy with Him, His image is formed within our souls. Real worship is transforming. (See Chapter 8.)

WORSHIP WILL AFFECT OUR MINDS.

Our thoughts will be directed upward instead of inward. We will be at peace despite what goes on around us. Tozer writes, "As God dwells in your thoughts, you will be worshiping, and God will be accepting. He will be smelling the incense of your high intention even when the cares of life are intense and activity is all around you."[33]

Worship will bring about a renewing of our minds (Rom. 12:2).

WORSHIP WILL OFTEN AFFECT OUR EMOTIONS.

Deep feelings often result from worship, but feelings are never a measure or test of worship. It is easy to fall to either extreme. On the one hand, we may assume that worship is about feelings and if there are no deep emotions, we wrongly conclude we weren't worshiping. At the other extreme, we may avoid emotions altogether. But if there are no feelings, there isn't much of a relationship.

---

[32] MacArthur, *The MacArthur New Testament Commentary: Hebrews*, p. 310.
[33] Tozer, *Worship*, p. 127

"I delight to do Your will, O my God; / Your law is within my heart" (Ps. 40:8).

WORSHIP WILL CHANGE OUR VALUES, MOTIVES, AND ATTITUDES.

When worship is the golden thread of our lives, we become God-centered instead of need-centered or self-centered. Because worship *is* life, everything else becomes secondary. Our minds and hearts are fixed in the heavenly places, so our perspective is changed. Our only motive is to see God glorified and worshiped.

"One thing I have asked from the LORD, that I shall seek: / That I may dwell in the house of the LORD all the days of my life, / To behold the beauty of the LORD / and to meditate in His temple" (Ps. 27:4).

WORSHIP WILL TRANSFORM OUR ACTIONS.

Our words and actions will flow from our awe of God. Instead of being directed toward selfish ends, they will bring about His glory.

"For it is God who is at work in you both to will and to work for His good pleasure" (Phil. 2:13).

WORSHIP WILL MAKE OUR EVANGELISM MORE EFFECTIVE.

Instead of being forced and uneasy, our words will flow as praise. People will be drawn to the Christ they see in us. We will have a passion and a joy in seeing God transform rebels into worshipers.

The most effective evangelists here in Brazil are not the highly educated but those who have a passion to worship Christ. I have friends in what I call "the fruitful fruit stand." When Luis, the owner, was asked how he worshiped God selling fruit, he immediately replied that he marveled at the variety of fruits God had made to satisfy each customer's tastes. His love for the Lord is contagious, resulting in a number of people coming to know the Lord and those, in turn, going out to start new works. (See Chapters 11 and 14.)

"For God is my witness whom I serve in the preaching of the gospel…"(Rom. 1:8).

WORSHIP WILL AFFECT HOW WE INTERACT WITH OTHER BELIEVERS.

Because we will see God and learn at His feet, we will be eager to help others experience the same deeper walk with Him. We will be eager to learn from others to deepen our own spiritual walk. Since we are worshiping him for His love and mercy, that same love compels us to edify the worship lives of others. It is our passion to see God worshiped, as He should be. Sometimes we help others informally as the Lord sovereignly brings us into contact with others. At other times it is in a more organized fashion as we disciple those whom the Lord gives us. (See Chapters 10 and 15.)

"Holy Father, keep them in Your name, the name which You have given Me, that they may be one even as We are" (John 17:11).

WORSHIP WILL GIVE NEW MEANING TO OUR PRAISE.

Instead of catchy words and melodies, praise will flow out of the worship in our innermost beings. We will long to be with other believers to verbalize the worship that is inside us.

"I will bless the LORD at all times; / His praise shall continually be in my mouth. / My soul will make its boast in the LORD" (Ps. 34:1-2).

WORSHIP WILL CALL PEOPLE INTO SERVICE AND RAISE UP MORE LEADERS.

As more people are brought into the throne room, broken before God's holy presence and cleansed by a coal taken from the altar, more people will be saying, "Here am I, send me." (See Isa. 6:6-8.) Instead of being self-confident professionals, they will be active servants, spreading their passion for worship to the world. (See Chapter 14.)

WORSHIP WILL CHANGE OUR VIEW OF MISSIONS.

It will not be our goal to establish our denomination in other countries but to bring the nations together in worship. We do missions because we know that one day, people from every nation and all tribes and peoples and tongues will be standing before God's throne in worship (Rev. 5:9; 7:9; 14:6; 15:4). Missions is a passion to bring others to worship God.

One more thing: The nations will definitely enrich our own worship as we learn to strip away the cultural baggage of our wineskins. I have learned from my Brazilian brothers and sisters who are much more free in expressing their worship to God in praise. When we go beyond our own limitations and comfort zones, we will discover the richness of the new wine. It will become even more apparent to us that worship isn't in the form.

WORSHIP WILL CHANGE THE WAY WE DO CHURCH.

When we see the beauty of Christ's bride through the worship of the Bridegroom, we can no longer consider the church to be a building, a service, or an organization. If the golden thread is woven into our lives, we are truly His body. (See Chapter 10.)

"So that the manifold wisdom of God might now be made known through the church to the authorities in heavenly places" (Eph. 3:10).

HOW TO WORSHIP

Now that we have a notion of what it means to worship God, we can cultivate those inner attitudes within us. Although it is a life-attitude, there will be moments when we need to set apart time to minister to the Lord to help us learn to focus our minds on Him. Remember that the mind is not just the organ for rational thought. The mind, biblically, is the means by which we perceive, interpret, and evaluate the world around us. (See Chapter 8 for a more complete description of the mind.)

Madame Guyon said, "Through many years of habit your mind has acquired the ability to wander all over the world, just as it pleases."[34]

In order to worship, we must discipline our senses to perceive God in everything around us (Phil. 4:8). Instead of focusing our minds inward and allowing the mind to roam wherever it pleases, we must learn to direct our inner thoughts toward God. We should talk with God and enjoy intimate conversations with Him throughout the day. After all, we are seated with Him in the heavenly places (Eph. 2:6).

There are four basic steps in cultivating a worship life-attitude. Each will be developed in later chapters:

 1. *Believing:* Believing what God's Word declares about our position in Him and His presence in our lives (chapter

---

[34] Madame Guyon. *Experiencing the Depths of Jesus Christ,* p. 12.

4). Believing that if we seek Him, He will allow us to find Him.

2. *Beholding:* Training our minds to see God in everything and being in awe and wonder at who He is and what He has done, starting with His Word (chapter 6). We must purposely seek to cultivate fear, honor, and love as we behold Him so that our worship flows from the right source.

3. *Bowing:* Submitting ourselves to God in reverent fear, honor, and love, offering our lives to Him to be molded into His image (chapter 7).

4. *Becoming one:* Enjoying intimacy with God, finding pleasure in His presence so that His purposes become ours (chapters 1 and 10).

CONCLUSION

At the outset of this section and this chapter, we described worship this way:

> *Worship is a believer's choice to seek and enjoy constant spiritual fellowship with God by learning to see Him through His Word and growing in his fear, honor, and love for God, leading him to constantly offer his heart to God's guiding presence, resulting in his being transformed into Christ's image and overflowing into service.*

Worship is not just music or praise or a religious activity. It is the golden thread of our lives which, when woven into the fabric of our being, transforms us into the image of Christ. It consists of an inner attitude of fear, honor, and love as the basis for our spiritual intimacy with Him.

Praise, on the other hand, is the outward expression of the inward fellowship that we have with God. Worship's outward expression (glorifying God), in addition to praise, includes good works, service, ministry and a holy life. They are expressed as we respond to our inner attitudes by bowing before Him in submission.

We can cultivate a life of worship by learning to see Him through His Word so that it produces intimacy with Him within our spirits.

People live divided religious lives regarding worship because they fail to understand the difference between the inner attitudes and the outward expression of worship. It is not integrated into their lives because they see worship as an activity tacked on to an already busy life. That mentality comes from the idea that we are worshiping only when we are singing or praising God. We should not worship God as a religious duty nor for selfish personal benefit. Our goal should be to enjoy intimate fellowship with God and to allow His presence to transform our lives.

THE PARADIGM SHIFT

The divided life characterized by religious moments as contrasted with worship as a life attitude is similar to the topic of this chapter.

WORSHIP LIMITED TO PRAISE	PRAISE AS AN EXPRESSION OF WORSHIP
1. DEFINITIONS: Worship, praise, and music are seen as synonyms; they are done in a religious setting.	1. DEFINITIONS: • Worship is a life-attitude. • Praise is an outward expression of worship. • Music is only one of many ways to praise.
2. MEANS: Empty rituals: Worship is praise, which is music in a religious setting.	2. MEANS: The practice of the presence of God, the contemplation of His presence.
3. MOTIVES: • To feel fulfilled. • To fulfill an obligation. • To improve one's position before God.	3. MOTIVES: in response to • What God has done. • Who God is. • Because of His love for us.
4. RESULT: Temporary change.	4. RESULT: • Transformation of the mind, will, and emotions. • More effective ministry. • Unity with other believers.

WHERE TO START

1. **ASK GOD FOR AN UNDERSTANDING OF WORSHIP.** Everyone has a limited view of God and worship. Ask God to give you understanding of what it means to worship Him. Pray that as you read this book and do the exercises, God will open your eyes.

2. **ASK GOD TO TEACH YOU TO WORSHIP.** I have made it a practice to meditate on John 4:23 every day, telling God, "Since You are searching for worshipers, I want to be one of them. Teach me how to worship You in spirit and truth." I also read Romans 12:1-2 and ask Him to teach me how to offer my body as a living sacrifice. Write down those passages and ask God to make them a part of your life. Read through them prayerfully several times a day throughout this week. Ask Him to give you a hunger and thirst for His presence (Matt. 5:6).

3. **TELL GOD EVERY DAY THAT WANT HIM TO BE:**
   - Your treasure
   - Your refuge
   - Your joy
   - Your satisfaction
   - Your strength

4. **TRY DIFFERENT WAYS TO EXPRESS YOUR WORSHIP IN PRAISE.** Praise can be expressed by the position of our bodies, through song, and through words. Usually there is very little praise in our personal times with God, as we tend to focus on requests. Thank Him for all He has done. Move into a time of song, expressing your love for Him. Declare His character back to Him. Lift up your hands, kneel, or prostrate yourself in His presence. See if you can spend an hour in a focused time of praise.

DISCUSSION QUESTIONS

1. How would you define worship?

2. What is praise?

3. How does the marriage metaphor in this chapter relate to our definition of worship?

4. Why is it important to distinguish between the inward and the outward expressions of worship?

5. What is the role of music?

6. What are some of the differences between praise and worship? How are they related? Why is it important to distinguish between the two?

7. Why is it difficult for people to accept different forms in expressing praise?

8. How do you express your praise?

9. What does it mean to fear God? How can that be misunderstood?

10. What should be our motivation to become worshipers?

11. What has been the influence of worship on your life?

12. Name someone you feel is a worshiper. What do you see in his or her life?

13. What did you experience in trying new ways to praise God?

14. What is the most important truth that you learned from this chapter?

15. How has this chapter helped you to be a better worshiper?

Chapter 4

WORSHIP IS IN TRUTH

TRULY WORSHIPING THE ONE TRUE GOD

But an hour is coming, and now is, when the true worshipers shall WORSHIP THE FATHER IN *spirit and* TRUTH; *for such people the Father seeks to be His worshipers* (John 4:23).

SEED TRUTH: OUR WORSHIP MUST BE DIRECTED TO GOD AS HE IS REVEALED IN THE SCRIPTURES. *The higher and more accurate our concept of God, the greater our worship should be. Religious people tend to focus on the more humanly acceptable attributes of God and bow before an idol in the image of their liking. Their worship and knowledge of God is subjective. But to become a worshiper, one must worship Him in His fullness, seeking to understand and to believe who He is as revealed in the Bible. Worship cannot be separated from the objective truth of Scripture.*

One of my professors in graduate school, a Unitarian, described a meeting held in his house. The leader drew a circle on a chalkboard and invited everyone to share all his or her concepts of God with the group. As people called out different qualities of divinity, she wrote them on the board. When they had exhausted all the attributes that had come to mind, she said, as a Unitarian, she objected to certain ones, which she promptly erased. She asked if others had objections to any of the other characteristics of this divinity. The professor, of course, did not like the idea of a Creator God and that attribute was erased as well. When no one had any other objections, she declared, much as Aaron before the golden calf had, *"This is your god"* (Ex. 32:4, 8). She had reduced the God of the Universe to the least common denominator.

What idolatry! The class' god was not made of gold, silver, wood, or stone, but with ideas and words. Before we condemn others, however, what about our worship? Christians do the same thing when they ignore the totality of God's character. Do we worship Him for who He is, or do we ignore those qualities with which we are not comfortable? Is our worship flowing from the whole of God's Word? Are we constantly renewing our vision of Him through His Word?

We must recognize our limitations, but at the same time continually seek to know Him as He really is. Otherwise, we may fall into the same idolatry as the professor's discussion group, dishonoring God by not worshiping Him in His fullness.

THE MARRIAGE METAPHOR

People talk about "love at first sight." That, of course, is only infatuation. We can be attracted to someone by what we see, but we can have a mutual loving relationship only with people whom we know. *The more we know our spouses, the truer and deeper our relationship becomes.*

The problem with romantic love is that people tend to present false images of themselves, hiding their faults and ignoring the shortcomings of the other. "Love is blind," they say. Actually, infatuation is blind. Since this kind of love is not based on truth, it is easy to see why so many marriages fail. People think they love someone, only to discover much more beneath the facade they didn't realize was there

Before I even thought of dating my wife Lisa, she was a good friend. We got to know each other without any romantic intention. One day, after taking her to church with me, it suddenly dawned on me that I would like to develop a closer relationship with her. Soon after, Lisa wrote me a letter just as she left for a long family vacation, thanking me for taking her to church.

I pored over that letter many times, studying her words as I waited for her to return home so I could ask her out. I have the letter to this day. It is precious to me, because it is from the person I love most in this world. However, it is she whom I love, not the letter. It is valuable to me only because it came from her and helped me to know her.

We have been getting to know each other since 1980. The more we learn about each other, the deeper our love grows. Such a relationship is based on being truthful and accepting each other for who we are, including our weaknesses and failures.

So it is with our worship of God. If there is to be a relationship, it must be based on truth. Have you ever heard someone say, "Well, I don't think God is…" or "I don't believe God would…"? Do we dare think we can discover the fullness of God with our limited intellect, feelings, and opinions? That is why we need the Bible. *The more we know about God through His Word, the deeper and truer our worship relationship with Him should become.*

LIMITING FACTORS IN WORSHIP

OUR PERCEPTION OF GOD

One reason it is difficult to understand God and true worship is that we all have blinders, limiting our perception of Him. Remember the story of the three blind men trying to describe an elephant they can't see? One grabs the trunk and concludes that an elephant is like a hose. Another feels one of his legs and declares an elephant is like a tree. The third takes hold of his tail and is sure an elephant is like a rope.

All three are right, because each is describing the elephant based on his limited perception. At the same time, all are wrong because they are not aware of the whole elephant.

In trying to understand God, we are somewhat like those blind men. We have our personal and cultural barriers to seeing God in the plenitude of His character. We study the same Bible, but we do so through personal filters that limit what we perceive even when we apply proper Bible study methods.

For example, a person who was raised in an abusive home may have difficulty understanding the metaphor of God as our Father. A person brought up in a strict religious setting may not perceive the richness of God's love and grace. Someone born in the United States with the strong political and social emphasis on freedom may have difficulty seeing some aspects of God's sovereignty.

The variety of cultures, perceptions, and experiences is what gives the church its richness. Only the mature body of Christ with such diversity can "attain…to the measure of the stature which belongs to the fullness of Christ" (Eph. 4:13). Only through the unified body can we see the fullness of His character and worship Him as He truly is.

Our understanding of God is enriched through interaction within the body of Christ. No one has fully mastered the content of the Bible, but as we share with one another what we have learned, we see God more clearly and our worship is more "in truth."

OUR INABILITY TO DESCRIBE GOD

The blind men, attempting to describe the elephant, did what we all do when describing something unfamiliar. They compared it to something more familiar. The Bible also uses imperfect human language to describe the One who is perfect. Thus, the Holy Spirit describes God, using human qualities and even parts of the human body,[1] such as His hand, arm, feet, eyes, and mouth. Jesus took on human form, but these references to God the Father don't mean to suggest that He has a physical body, as the Mormons erroneously suppose. These figures of speech tell us of His blessing, strength, presence, etc.

At other times the Bible uses terms of human emotions such as joy, anger, regret, love, and compassion to help us understand God. Even those feelings are not the same as we experience, but they help us get an idea of what is in the heart of God.

By studying and meditating on His names and descriptions, we begin to understand what is beyond our experience. An admission that we don't fully understand Him puts us in awe of Him, and He is delighted to help us understand.

---

[1] Anthropomorphisms - God is really not like a human being, but human characteristics are attributed to Him in an attempt to describe Him in terms humans can understand.

OUR INABILITY TO COMPREHEND GOD

A. W. Tozer says, "The yearning to know what cannot be known, to comprehend the incomprehensible, to touch and taste the unapproachable, arises from the image of God in the nature of man. Deep calleth unto deep, and though polluted and land-locked by the mighty disaster theologians call the fall, the soul senses its original and longs to return to its source."[2]

One of the first steps to knowing God is to recognize our inability to know Him fully through our own resources. Paul writes, "For since in the wisdom of God the world through its wisdom did not come to know God, God was well-pleased through the foolishness of the message preached to save those who believe" (1 Cor. 1:21). Our resources are inadequate to achieve an understanding of Him.

UNDERSTANDING OF GOD COMES ONLY
BY HIS GRANTING IT.

Undoubtedly, Jesus' disciples were confused about the meaning of the parables and were disturbed that Jesus' teaching was not clearer to the multitudes. They questioned Him about it and He replied, "To you it has been granted to know the mysteries of the kingdom of heaven, but to them it has not been granted" (Matt.13:11).

This Scripture, along with many others, shows that the understanding of God comes only by His granting it. There is no room for any pride in our own ability to grasp who He is.

Furthermore, Jesus describes divine truth as a mystery. A mystery is something that was previously hidden but has now been made known. Paul says, "Yet we do speak wisdom among those who are mature; ...we speak God's wisdom in a mystery, the hidden wisdom which God predestined before the ages to our glory" (1 Cor. 2:6-7). This mystery is available only to the "mature" or those whom God has brought to a level of spiritual maturity and chosen to comprehend it. In this context, the mystery Paul describes is the gospel, but the principle applies to all mysteries God makes known through Christ.

---

[2] Tozer, *Worship,* p. 11.

Warren Wiersbe writes,

> True worship must always involve *mystery*. There are many things we can't explain but that we can experience. Mystery and humility go together, and there can be no real worship without humility. God reveals Himself but He rarely explains Himself. Christians don't live on explanations; they live on promises and on deepening relationships[3] (emphasis original).

That is why, quoting Isaiah, Paul says, "*Things which eye has not seen and ear has not heard, and which have not entered the heart of man, all that God has prepared for those who love Him*" (1 Cor. 2:9). This passage is not describing heaven, but the mystery of our relationship with God through the gospel. Our human senses will never enable us to figure out or discern His gospel or any other mystery. God wants to manifest Himself to us so we can enjoy more complete fellowship and worship, but it is apparent that the Corinthians were trusting in their own "fleshly" resources to understand God's mysteries. If we are humble and dependent on Him, He will open our eyes so that we are able to see what the prophets longed to see.

OUR LACK OF MATURITY

Another challenge to our understanding of God is our lack of experience in walking with God. We are all in the process of learning how to live in His presence. I have been studying worship for several decades and feel that I am only beginning to understand something about God and how to worship Him. The Bible is a dynamic book that interacts with life. We can study the same passage many times and continue to discover new truths. That is also what makes our worship dynamic.

Proverbs and Psalms are definitely not systematic books. They are more like mosaics, reflecting the pattern of life's experiences. Reading one chapter at different times will impact your life in a unique way each time. One day, when facing financial problems, certain verses seem to jump out at you. The next time you read the same chapter,

---

[3] Wiersbe, p. 25.

the biggest concern in your life might be a broken relationship, and other verses come alive.

So, the more we study the Scriptures and grow in our faith, the more complete our worship will be.

OUR LACK OF DISCIPLINE

My Greek teacher said that God does not honor scholarship, nor does He honor laziness. It is impossible to worship God when we do not put forth the effort to study His Word. In addition to study and meditation on the Word, we must discipline ourselves to spend time in God's presence and with other worshipers to grow in our intimacy with God.

WORSHIPING GOD IN TRUTH

UNDERSTANDING THE TRUTH

You worship that which you do not know; we worship that which we know; for salvation is from the Jews (John 4:22).

The Samaritan woman had asked Jesus about the place of worship. Jesus downplayed the importance of the place. As MacArthur points out, "The *where* of worship isn't really the issue; it's the *when, who, and how* that really count[4] (emphasis original).

As we have already noted, the Samaritans were known for their lively worship. Their worship, however, was not flowing from a correct understanding of God. There was no substance. Jesus said, "You worship that which you do not know" (John 4:22).

The Scriptures are foundational to real worship. The first thing we train our leaders in Brazil to do is to glean biblical truth about the character of God and to respond immediately in worship. Our minds need to be renewed constantly. Worship and Bible reading must be blended together. There are no shortcuts to becoming a worshiper. As God's Word becomes part of our being, we will be in awe of Him and humbly walk in worship.

Some claim to be seeking intimacy with God, but are unwilling to study the Scriptures. They not only downplay the importance of study, they even ridicule those who dedicate themselves to it.

---

[4] MacArthur, *Gospel According to Jesus,* p. 55.

Some people who had been participating in a hyper-charismatic church started attending our services. They accused me of being "only in the letter," or, as they saw it, studying the Word of God to the exclusion of relying on the Holy Spirit. They cited 2 Corinthians 3:6, "The letter kills, but the Spirit gives life." They interpreted the passage to mean, "Studying the written Word gives no life, so we must be open to the Spirit, whatever that might mean." But we know, of course that "the letter" refers to the law that only condemns and not to the study of the Word of God. The Holy Spirit speaks to us through the Word. As we study what He has already said, we can more clearly hear His voice.

The Bible is our worship manual. It tells us not only *who* to worship but *how* to worship.

A. W. Tozer writes,

> A right conception of God is basic not only to systematic theology but to practical Christian living as well. It is to worship what the foundation is to the temple; where it is inadequate or out of plumb the whole structure must sooner or later collapse. I believe there is scarcely an error in doctrine or a failure in applying Christian ethics that cannot be traced finally to imperfect and ignoble thought about God.[5]

The study of the Scriptures, however, is not an end in itself. Its goal is not primarily to acquire knowledge, but to develop a deeper love for God. The very act of study should be a worship experience. Ezra was worshiping when he "Set his heart to study the law of the Lord and to practice it, and to teach his statutes and ordinance in Israel" (Ezra 7:10). The term "set his heart," suggests an offering in worship to the Lord of his mind, will, and purpose so that he would understand the Bible.

Knowing about God provides the basis for knowing Him.

Richard Averbeck writes,

> I fear that we sometimes teach and practice *a way* of studying God's Word that, in fact, diminishes its effect in our lives and ministries by undermining our worship as his children

---

[5] Tozer, *The Knowledge of The Holy*, p. 3.

and our ministries as his servants....Our study needs to be a time and place where we "practice God's presence" while we are attending to his holy Word[6] (emphasis original).

Whenever I teach my seminary class on 1 Corinthians, I start by taking the students to 1 Corinthians 8:1, "Knowledge makes arrogant, but love edifies." It appears that Paul is criticizing knowledge and exalting love, but knowledge is not the problem. This is actually an ellipsis and could be translated "Knowledge *without love* makes arrogant, but *knowledge with* love edifies."

Love for God capsulizes the motive for study. If a person studies the Bible as a purely academic pursuit, he will become arrogant and actually destroy the faith of others. But, if like Ezra, he studies as an act of worship with a loving desire to edify others, he will be useful in God's service.

BELIEVING THE SCRIPTURES

Early in my language study in Brazil, I met some students from the university where I was working. In the course of our conversation, they found out I had taught biology in the U.S. and asked if that is why I had come to Brazil.

I told them that I had given up biology to teach the Bible. I asked them if that seemed strange, because in the U.S., most biologists reject the Bible. They replied that they found nothing unusual about what I was doing and added, "You will discover that we Brazilians all have a lot of faith."

People typically think of faith as a strong religious feeling or perhaps, positive or wishful thinking. The Greek words *pisteúō* and *pístis* can be translated, "to believe...belief, trust, faith," or "confidence." That means true faith is depositing all of our trust and confidence in God and His character and not in our own merit or abilities. The opposite of faith is not doubt, but self-sufficiency.

Faith is not a subjective feeling, but it is based upon the objective truth of Scripture. Abraham chose to trust in God's promises. "Against all hope," Abraham believed (Rom 4:18). He chose to trust what God had said rather than his circumstance.

---

[6] Averbeck, "Worshiping God in Spirit" in Bateman, pp. 102-103.

It is not enough to know what God has said if we don't believe it. Worshiping God in truth must flow from a conviction that God and His Word can be trusted. Hebrews 11:6 says, "And without faith it is impossible to please Him, for he who comes to God must believe that He is and that He is a rewarder of those who seek Him." Faith and worship are intertwined. Faith leads to worship and worship builds our faith.

RESPONDING TO THE SCRIPTURES

Hebrews 11 describes men who fully trusted the God they worshiped, and their faith resulted in actions.[7] Verse 6 states that faith is the basis of pleasing God or worshiping Him. Thus faith is a necessary element in our worship.

In one of the Indiana Jones films, Jones was searching for the Holy Grail. His instructions had led him into a cave. As he ran against the clock through the dark tunnel, he came to a huge abyss. His instructions told him to step out into open space to cross. He hesitated. Experience had told him that stepping out into thin air was suicide. Up to this point, the instructions had been true and were, in fact, his only hope. He believed what he had been told and acted upon it even though it seemed crazy to him.

I don't see worshiping God in faith as jumping into the dark, but as a casting of ourselves into the light. It is moving forward on what God has said. We can't hedge our bets. We must believe and seek life only in Him.

At an evangelism seminar some time ago, I invited a number of effective evangelists from several of our churches to give their testimonies of what God was doing through them. They shared how God was using them to bring people to the Lord through evangelistic Bible studies.

Afterward, a friend gave his impression of the conference.

Whether we like it or not, we have tended to divide the people of our churches into three groups: A, B, and C. When the highly trained and talented "A" group was lead-

---

[7] The term "*by faith*" is in an emphatic position in each passage and describes the basis for carrying out the actions of the worshipers.

ing things, nothing changed in our churches. When the "B" group took over, things still didn't change. Now I am seeing that the "C" people, the simple and uneducated, are moving out with the gospel. I am very optimistic about the future of our churches, because these guys are making it happen.

After he said that, I asked myself, *"Why?"*

For one thing, I believe that God wants to show us His strength in what is weak (1 Cor. 1:26-29; 2 Cor. 12:9-10). Jesus said, "I praise You, Father, Lord of heaven and earth, that You have hidden these things from the wise and intelligent and have revealed them to infants. Yes, Father, for this way was well-pleasing in Your sight" (Matt. 11:25-26).

But even more important, the actions of the "C" people gave evidence of real faith. We all have a tendency to trust in our training, experience, abilities, and hard work. These men had only the God they worshiped. Sometimes we trust in our own merit, as if, by our dedication, we deserve to be used by God. These men and women cast all their trust and hope on Him and acted on what they believed.

The last part of Hebrews 11:6 says, "…must believe that He is and that He is a rewarder of those who seek Him." Obviously, believing that "He is" is much more than an affirmation of His existence (cf. James 2:19); it is trust that He is exactly who the Bible says He is. His being a "rewarder of those who seek Him" means that our worship in faith has an incredible benefit.

John Piper gives a caution regarding this.

> Ordinarily faith would mean trust or confidence you put in someone who has given good evidence of his reliability and willingness and ability to provide what you need. But when Jesus Christ is the object of faith there is a twist. He himself is what we need. If we only trust Christ to give us gifts and not himself as the all-satisfying gift, then we do not trust him in a way that honors him as our treasure. We simply honor the gifts. *They* are what we want. Not him.[8]

---

[8] Piper, *Don't Waste Your Life*, p. 70.

God is a rewarder of those who worship Him in faith and the reward is intimacy with Him.

A BIBLICAL EXAMPLE

He read from the book of the law of God daily, from the first day to the last day. And they celebrated the feast seven days, and on the eighth day there was a solemn assembly according to the ordinance (Neh. 8:18).

The worst possible famine is a famine of the Word of God. The Lord sent just such a famine on Israel (Amos 8:11). During much of the captivity of the Jews, God was silent. But less than a week after completing the wall in Jerusalem, the Jewish people came together and asked Ezra to read to them the book of the law of Moses (Neh. 8:1).

When he opened the book, there was an immediate reaction. The people stood up (v.5). When he read the law, those who had been starving because of this great famine rejoiced and worshiped God. This, no doubt, was an act of reverence for the Word. However, the principal reason was their great anticipation of what was going to happen.

In American football, when a lightning-fast wide receiver gets behind the defenders and the quarterback heaves the ball down the sidelines, the fans stand up. In baseball, when there is a long fly ball into deep center field close to the wall, everybody stands up. When there is a fast break in basketball, everybody stands up. It is a natural reaction when something exciting is about to happen.

The people's reaction to the reading of the Word continued as Ezra praised God and the people prostrated themselves, raised their hands, and said "Amen" (v. 6). They physically expressed their awe and gratefulness to God for giving them His Word.

After their initial response, the people apparently stood for about six hours, listening attentively to the Word (v. 3). This probably involved not only translation, but also some interpretation of the texts because the people spoke only Aramaic and did not understand Hebrew too well. As they listened, they broke into small groups to make sure they understood what was being read (vv. 7-8).

Sensitive to the Word, the people were broken and they wept (v. 9). When we understand God's Word, we develop a sensitive heart, and our shortcomings become evident. That is why Jesus said, "Blessed are those who mourn" (Matt. 5:4). Grieving over our sin is an expression of our sorrow for having offended God.

Weeping, however, was not appropriate to this particular occasion, for this festival was to be a time of joy. The gathering was meant to strengthen them through the joy of the Lord (vv. 9-10). As instructed, the people celebrated their restoration with joy. They rejoiced because they understood and practiced the Word. Gladness was part of their celebration. Nehemiah 8:12 says, "And all the people went away to eat, to drink, to send portions and to celebrate a great festival, because they understood the words which had been made known to them." They understood the words, they were broken and restored, and they finally rejoiced in worship at what God had done.

An understanding of God's Word precedes worship. We usually start our worship services with music, but music is not the basis of our worship, the Bible is. It might be better, perhaps, to teach a passage of Scripture and then divide into small groups to make sure everyone understands. As a result, we would be able to come into God's presence to worship corporately in spirit and in truth.

WORSHIPING GOD FOR WHO HE IS

There are so many apparent paradoxes when we consider God's character because of our limited ability to understand Him. We are going to look at a few of those to stretch our understanding of God and understand Him more clearly. Don't just read through these. Stop after every section and ask Him to help you to understand spiritually what He has revealed in His Word. Worship Him for His greatness.

GOD IS NOT COMPLEX.

When people are difficult to get along with here in Brazil, we say they are "complicated," because they are so unpredictable in their responses. Not only are we human beings complicated in the sense that we are hard to get along with, but we are complicated because of the tensions within us, leading to indecisiveness.

For example, when we need to discipline one of our children, we wrestle with what the best course of action might be. We remember being a child and having done the same things. We may think that our parents never let us get away with that behavior. That could lead us to be more lenient or to take a hard line. Or maybe we never acted that way and can't understand what prompted that behavior in our child. We are tugged by feelings of righteousness, love, justice, compassion, indignation, and understanding. We are not consistent in how we respond because there are so many different sides to our personalities. Our moods change.

Human beings *are* complicated!

On the other hand, God is not complex in that way. He is deep and beyond our understanding, but He is not as complicated as we are. In an attempt to understand Him, we divide His character into attributes, but His qualities are not in conflict. We call this the unity of God. A. W. Tozer writes,

> The doctrine of the divine unity means not only that there is but one God; it means also that God is simple, uncomplex, one with Himself. The harmony of His being is the result not of a perfect balance of parts, but of the absence of parts. Between His attributes no contradiction can exist. He need not suspend one to exercise another, for in Him, all His attributes are one. All of God does all that God does. He does not divide Himself to perform a work, but works in the total unity of His being.[9]

Since God's character is not in conflict, neither should our worship be. Although there may be times when our praise is focused on certain aspects of His character, we cannot pick and choose which works and which qualities will be the exclusive object of our worship as though picking food from a menu. God said through the psalmist, "Lovingkindess and truth have met together; Righteousness and peace have kissed each other" (Ps. 85:10). No aspect of God's character is in conflict with another. God's attributes are in perfect harmony so that we can worship Him in His fullness. That is why

[9] Tozer, *Knowledge of the Holy,* p. 18.

the hymn writer called Him, "Merciful and Mighty, God in three persons, blessed Trinity."

Keith Green once wrote that he liked to discover passages of Scripture that challenge His concept of God. He knew that His view of God was imperfect and each new discovery of His character stretched him and opened his eyes to see the real God more clearly. Maybe that is why his music still speaks so clearly to us several years after his death.

For example, Revelation 15:3-4 has been put to music several times. The heavenly praise says, "Great and marvelous are Your works, O Lord God, the Almighty; Righteous and true are Your ways, King of the nations! Who will not fear, O Lord, and glorify Your name? For You alone are holy; For all the nations will come and worship before You, For Your righteous acts have been revealed."

It is often unnoticed that the marvelous works revealed in this passage are acts of judgment. If we study Psalms and the book of Revelation, we will find that God is praised for a wide variety of His attributes. Using these passages, our praise and worship become more complete. We are not really worshiping in the fullness of His character if our praise and thanksgiving do not include His justice.

GOD IS TRANSCENDENT AND IMMANENT.

Imagine your best friend is elected president of your country. The person with whom you have shared your darkest secrets and wildest dreams is occupying the highest office in the land. For the first time, you are given an audience with him. You go into his office, surrounded by security. You would undoubtedly not only be happy to see your friend, but, at the same time, you would be in awe of the position he now holds. After a few awkward moments, the conversation would begin to flow with ease and pleasure, though all the while you are conscious that he holds the most powerful office in the land.

That is much like our relationship with God. As Rick Warren puts it, "It's difficult to imagine how an intimate friendship is possible between an omnipotent, invisible, perfect God and a finite, sinful human being."[10] The human tendency is to emphasize either God's separation or His nearness and neglect the other. Either we fall

---

[10] Warren, *Purpose Driven Life,* p. 87.

into formalism, allowing fear to separate us from God or we become so informal and familiar that we lose our sense of awe.

A true worshiper learns to harmonize these two aspects of God. The worshiper draws near to God, like Moses, speaking face-to-face as one would a friend (Ex. 33:11), while at the same time he is trembling in awe at the presence of a Holy God.

> A TRUE WORSHIPER MARVELS THAT
> AN INTIMATE FRIENDSHIP IS POSSIBLE BETWEEN
> AN OMNIPOTENT, INVISIBLE, PERFECT GOD
> AND A FINITE, SINFUL HUMAN BEING.[11]

My wife was raised in the Catholic Church. When I first met her, I was impressed with her sense of God's holiness, while rejoicing in the intimacy of a relationship with the God of the universe. Perhaps the formalism of the Catholic liturgy instilled in her a sense that God was utterly separate from the world He created. But her newfound relationship with God caused her to rejoice in His friendship.

Theologians call the complete distinction and separation of God from His creation, "transcendence." The dictionary defines this as something "exceeding the usual limits or lying beyond the limits of ordinary experience."[12] God is certainly that.

Isaiah 55:9 says, "For as the heavens are higher than the earth, so are My ways higher than your ways, And My thoughts than your thoughts."

Tozer writes, "Forever God stands apart, in light unapproachable. He is as high above an archangel as above a caterpillar."[13]

What has made our access to Him possible? The author of Hebrews writes, "Therefore, brethren, since we have confidence to enter the holy place by the blood of Jesus, by a new and living way which He inaugurated for us through the veil, that is, His flesh, and since we have a great priest over the house of God, let us draw near…"(Heb. 10:19-22). Those words must have come as a total

---

[11] Ibid.
[12] Webster's New Collegiate Dictionary.
[13] Tozer, *Knowledge of The Holy*, p. 84.

shock to the Jews. They had a high view of the transcendence of God that was reinforced every time they entered the temple.

If I had been one of the High Priests that entered behind the veil, I would have been shaking in my boots. It was a once-a-year occasion on the Day of Atonement, but not without cleansing rituals and sacrifices. They had bells on the hems of their garments so those outside could hear if they were still alive. If the Lord should strike them dead, a rope tied around their waists enabled them to be pulled out from the presence of the Lord.

The author of Hebrews says they could enter with *confidence* into God's very presence. And not just the shadow of His presence, which was the temple, but into His very presence. That was a difficult concept for most Jews to understand, but God wants intimacy with us.

GOD IS LOVING AND JUST.

When we teach people about disciplining their children, it is often hard for them to understand they can spank their children without anger. For many people, if they are not angry, there is no reason to spank children, because anger is what demands justice while love leads us to be compassionate.

Humanly speaking, disciplining in love may seem contradictory. However, God both loves and disciplines, and there is no inner conflict within His character. The best illustration of this is the cross of Christ. There is no greater demonstration of holy wrath and justice, nor is there a greater demonstration of love, mercy, and compassion. That is why Paul described Christ, "whom God displayed publicly as a propitiation in His blood through faith" (Rom. 3:25). That shows His divine, holy justice. He also said, in the same verse, "This was [done] to demonstrate His righteousness, because in the forbearance of God He passed over the sins previously committed."

There is no tension in that verse. Both His justice and His love were fully expressed in the cross.

GOD IS HOLY.

John MacArthur commented in a message on Isaiah 6 that God's holiness was His "consummate attribute." Although God is love, the

Bible never says He is love, love, love, but it does say that He is "holy, holy, holy."[14]

God's holiness governs all that He is. For example, I once shared an office with one of the most intelligent men I have ever met. I cannot just think of God's intelligence as being a million times greater than this friend's. There is no comparison, because my friend gained his knowledge from observing the world around him (reading, talking, studying, researching, etc.). God, on the other hand, knows because He determines. He is holy in His knowledge, wisdom, and intelligence.

I love my family, but God's love is not just a million times greater. There is no comparison. I love, because He first loved me (1 John 4:19). God is holy in His love.

WORSHIPING GOD IN HIS FULLNESS

"For it was the Father's good pleasure for all the fullness to dwell in Him" (Col. 1:19).

"For of his fullness we have all received, and grace upon grace" (John 1:16).

"And he put all things in subjection under His feet, and gave Him as head over all things to the church, which is his body, the fullness of Him that fills all in all" (Eph. 1:22-23).

The word "fullness" implies the totality of God's character. Christ did not possess only certain attributes of deity or some divine powers. He was not a composite of different aspects of God. All the fullness of deity indwelt Him. That is why to know Jesus is to know the Father (John 14:9-10).

And God has chosen to do something amazing. He has made His fullness available to us. When we worship Him in His fullness, we understand that He has made us partakers of His fullness. He desires to form His character in us completely. Not only that, He chose to fill His church as a body with His fullness as a kind of second incarnation. Complete worship leads to complete transformation of the church and us into His image.

---

[14] From a message preached at Thomas Road Baptist Church, Lynchburg, VA. 1987.

FALSE WORSHIP: WHEN WORSHIP IS ABUSED

Worship in truth implies not only that worship is based upon a true concept, but also that it is done in the way God commanded it to be done. The New Testament does not give very much instruction about form except that it be done "properly and in an orderly manner" (1 Cor. 14:40). And there should be some sort of teaching or exhortation from the Word (1 Tim. 4:13). Prayer is to be a priority (1 Tim. 2), but there is no mention of music.

Although the Bible doesn't say much about forms, it does mention our attitude. We are told to approach Him with "reverence and awe" (Heb. 12:28). Our attitude is more important than the outward style. Most important in our New Testament instruction, worship must be through Jesus Christ (Heb. 10:19).

Worshiping God in truth is the opposite of false worship. The Old Testament is full of examples that illustrate that God must be approached in the manner He commanded.

If you were God and one of your leaders committed adultery, lied to cover it up, and ultimately killed a man to cover his crime, what would you do? If you were God and another of your leaders was impatient and worshiped with a wrong attitude, how would you handle it?

The Bible is such a fascinating book because God often does the opposite of what we think He would do. Of course, I am referring to David's sin with Bathsheba (1 Sam. 11) and Saul's failure to wait for Samuel (1 Sam. 13) as well as his failure to wipe out the Amalekites and king Agag as instructed (1 Sam. 15).

David was a man after God's heart (Acts 13:22). He knew how to worship God. In fact, the one thing he asked of the Lord and the one thing he sought was to dwell in the house of the Lord all the days of his life and to behold the beauty of the Lord (Ps. 27:4). David was far from a perfect man, but the Psalms just ooze with his passion to know and worship God.

God judges sin, and David paid a price for what he did. But God's judgment is much more severe against abuses of worship than any other sin. Consider the following examples.

AARON'S SONS (LEV. 10)

The first time Nadab and Abihu ministered before the Lord, they were struck down for their irreverence. It may seem like a little thing to us to offer "strange fire" before the Lord. We aren't even sure what that means. It seems, from the context, however, that they were celebrating this special day and had a little too much to drink and were careless (see vv. 8-10). The results were immediate and severe. In Portuguese, we say they were "carbonizados" or carbonized. I picture Nadab and Abihu as little piles of cinders.

Why did God do that? Because, "By those who come near Me I will be treated as holy, And before all the people I will be honored" (v.3).

THE SIN OF KORAH (NUM. 16)

Korah was partially right when he said, "All the congregation are holy, every one of them, and the LORD is in their midst" (v.3) If he were referring to those who were truly saved, he was right. God doesn't favor one person over another.

However, Korah erred in accusing Moses of exalting himself above the assembly. Moses didn't exalt himself, but God chose him to minister before Him. God gives us instructions on how we are to approach Him. He designated Moses and Aaron to perform certain important functions, separating them for that purpose.

Korah violated God's instructions on how He was to be worshiped, failing to treat God as holy. He thus failed to worship God in truth. They had "spurned the LORD" (v. 30).

UNHOLY ANGER (NUM. 20:1-13)

To provide water for the people of Israel, God had instructed Moses to speak to the rock. Moses, however, took it upon himself to call the people rebels and to hit the rock twice. Because of this, God did not permit him to enter the Promised Land, "Because you have not believed Me, to treat Me as holy in the sight of the sons of Israel" (v.12). Moses' actions were irreverent and he did not worship God in truth on that occasion.

DEADLY CURIOSITY (1 SAM. 6:19-20)

Because they were curious about what was in the ark and looked into the holy vessel, 70 men from Beth-shemesh were struck down. Their irreverence was fatal.

DAVID'S CARELESSNESS (2 SAM. 6)

David wanted to be close to God and that meant having the ark in his own backyard. He was careless in not following the specific instructions for moving the ark. It had been equipped with rings so it could be carried on poles (see Ex. 25:14). David and especially Uzzah should have known that.

Although it seems as though he was looking out for the ark's safety when the oxen stumbled, Uzzah's steadying of the ark was seen as inappropriate worship and he died on the spot (v. 7). He failed to treat God as holy.

UZZIAH'S PRESUMPTION (2 CHRON. 26)

Uzziah apparently thought he was such a good king that he could try his hand at being a priest and burn incense before the Lord. The priests tried to stop him, but it was too late. As a result, he became a leper until the day he died.

Because of this, the Bible says, "He acted corruptly, and he was unfaithful to the Lord his God" for entering the temple (v. 16). He did not treat God as holy.

Although there are many more examples in the Scriptures, clearly the way people worship is important to God. He is to be worshiped with reverence and according to His instructions. That applies to New Testament times, also, since God is to be worshiped "with reverence and awe; for our God is a consuming fire" (Heb. 12:28-29). Worship is very important to God.

THE TRUTH ABOUT GOD
AS REVEALED IN HIS NAMES

I have trouble remembering the names of some people here in Brazil because they often are quite creative in coming up with new ones. Sometimes a family will have eight kids with the only difference in their names being the first letter. Most names are chosen with no thought to their meaning. That wasn't true in Bible times. Names were very important.

People were named because of special circumstances surrounding their birth or because of certain personality qualities. When people were transformed by meeting the Lord, their names were often changed: Abram became Abraham, Jacob became Israel, and Simon became Peter. My favorite is Nabal, which means, "worthless" (1 Sam. 25:25). How would you like to go through life with a name like that? Unfortunately, he didn't live to see a transformation in his life.

God has chosen to reveal certain aspects of His character through His names. In John 17, as a kind of debriefing of Jesus before His crucifixion, Jesus said to the Father, "I have manifested Your name to the men whom You gave Me out of the world" (v.6).

Giving them the Father's "name" seems to be foundational to training His disciples. Surely it is more than just cognitive information about Him and a correct name that designates the God of the universe. David says, "Those who know Your name will put their trust in You" (Ps. 9:10). An intimate knowledge of His names leads us to a real faith in His character.

NAMES REVEALED TO ABRAHAM

As a result of his faith, Abraham had intimacy with the Lord; the Bible describes him as a friend of God (James 2:23). This verse implies that the friendship began when he was first saved and God imputed His righteousness into Abraham's life (Gen. 15:3). That was just the beginning of his journey, however.

El Elyon, "God Most High"

One of the first times Abraham was stretched in his growing trust in God was with the kidnapping of his nephew Lot (Gen. 14). Abram, later re-named Abraham, went out to rescue him with a small force of 318 men and defeated a superior army from four kingdoms. Other than Abram's dividing his forces and attacking at night, we know nothing about this amazing battle.

On his way back from this great God-given victory, Abram was reminded that it was not his own strength that won the battle. He was met by Melchizedek, the king of Salem (probably Jerusalem) who was a priest of "God Most High" or *El Elyon* (v. 18). This king and priest was likely one of the few remaining people in the post-flood world who continued genuine worship of the one true God.

The name *El Elyon* is based on *Elohim*, which emphasizes the power and sovereignty of the one true God. This is the Creator God who was powerful enough to give Abram the victory against impossible odds. Abram recognized this and addressed *El Elyon* in prayer, right after meeting Melchizedek.

Abraham didn't learn that lesson fully because he tried to help *El Elyon* keep his promise by having an adulterous relationship with Hagar. The Middle East is still paying the price of wars and death because of Abraham's lack of faith. Sarah, who had suggested this solution in the first place, suddenly turned on Hagar, forcing her to flee.

El Roi, "The One Who Sees"

An angel of the Lord appeared to Hagar during her flight and promised to bless her and her child. Her response was, "Thou art a God who sees" (*El Roi*. Gen. 16:13). She even called the place *Beer-lahai-roi* (v. 14) or "the well of the living One who sees me." Hagar, as well as Abraham, learned that God was not only omniscient, but also active and concerned for what happens to people. He is a living God who knows what is happening and acts.

El Shaddai, "The One Who Supplies and Satisfies"

In the next chapter, God reveals Himself by another name. He says, "I am God Almighty" (*El Shaddai*, Gen. 17:1). Although some feel the root word, "*Shad*" is related to the mountains or fields, emphasizing His power, others feel "*Shad*" is related to another Hebrew word for the woman's breast, and the latter meaning makes more sense in this context.

The mother's breast is everything to a newborn. The newborn child comes out of its mother's womb, suddenly exposed to a world of bacteria and viruses. The breast provides colostrum through the first feeding, which provides the protection from the invisible threats the child faces. Although nutritionists have tried to replicate the quality of mother's milk, there is nothing equal to its balance of nutrients for the baby's growth. When babies are agitated, they quickly fall asleep when they begin feeding. They want the comfort and security of being in their mother's arms.

As Stone puts it, "As connected with the word *breast*, the title *Shaddai* signifies one who nourishes, supplies, satisfies. Connected with the word for God, *El*, it then becomes 'One mighty to nourish, satisfy, supply.'"[15]

Abraham needed to learn that God was all-sufficient for him. God could provide *everything* Abraham needed and Abraham had to learn to rely on Him.

Psalm 91:1 shows these two aspects of God's character: "He who dwells in the shelter of the Most High (*El Elyon*) will abide in the shadow of the Almighty (*El Shaddai*)." There is the sheltered protection of the sovereign "*El Elyon*" and the tender mercy of the all-sufficient "*El Shaddai*."

God's Personal Name, *Yahweh*

We have already discussed the calling of Moses in Chapter 2, but it is important to look one more time at the importance of the name *Yahweh.*

When asked His name, God told Moses "I AM WHO I AM" or *Yahweh* (Ex. 3:14). This was the name of the Covenant. It is His personal name. It is a revelation of His faithful, unchanging, eternal existence.

Moses probably understood the significance of that name only after his initial confrontation with Pharaoh. God said, "I am the LORD [*Yahweh*]; and I appeared to Abraham, Isaac, and Jacob, as God Almighty [*El Shaddai*], but by My name, LORD [*Yahweh*], I did not make Myself known to them" (Ex. 6:2-3).

God continued to use various forms of this name to reveal Himself throughout the Old Testament.

---

[15] Nathan Stone, *Names of God*, p. 27.

Yaweh-rapha	"the LORD who heals you"	Exodus.15:26
Yaweh-nissi	"the LORD is my banner"	Exodus 17:15
Yaweh-m'qaddishkhem	"the LORD who sanctifies you"	Leviticus 20:7-8
Yaweh-shalom	"the LORD is peace"	Judges 6:24
Yaweh-sabaoth	"the LORD of hosts"	Isaiah 6:3
Yaweh-tsidkenu	"the LORD our righteousness"	Jeremiah 23:6

The most famous name involving Yahweh was actually the name that Abraham gave to a location. Abraham's intimacy with God finally bore fruit in an absolute trust in his God when he offered his son. Abraham trusted God's goodness and His ability to raise the dead, even if he had gone through with the sacrifice. Rather than stall, as I would have done, Abraham got up early to carry through God's orders to sacrifice his son (Gen. 22:3). Abraham had learned to believe and trust God. His intimacy with God led to faith, which led to obedience. A perfect triad. He called the name of the place where he almost sacrificed Isaac, "*Yahweh-Ireh*" or *Jehovah-Jireh* because "The Lord provided" the sacrifice in place of his son (Genesis 22:14).

THE BIBLE AS OUR WORSHIP MANUAL

I began to learn to worship God in truth when I began to see the Bible as my manual. This started after reading Madame Guyon's book, *Experiencing the Depths of Jesus Christ*. She writes,

> "Praying the Scripture" is a unique way of dealing with the Scripture; it involves both reading and prayer. Here is how you should begin. Turn to the Scripture; choose some passage that is simple and fairly practical. Next, come to the Lord. Come quietly and humbly. There, before Him, read a small portion of the passage of Scripture you have opened…You do not move from one passage to another, not until you have *sensed* the very heart of what you have read. You may then want to take that portion of Scripture that has touched you and turn it into prayer[16] (emphasis original).

It was at this point I began to see the connection between reading, studying, meditating, worship, and prayer. I had previously sepa-

[16] Guyon, p. 8

rated them as independent activities. By my combining them, the Scriptures became more alive and a part of my life.

Joseph Carroll reports a similar experience when he learned to pray the Scriptures during a prayer meeting with fellow missionaries in Sydney, Australia. He comments, "I knew then that I had been introduced to a priceless key, one that would introduce me to hitherto undreamed of heights of fellowship with my Lord."[17]

I first studied Romans 6 in 1991. I was intrigued because it made me see the whole Christian life in a different light. I went through the same passage two more times, studying in depth. Each time I was moved by what I studied, recognizing the importance of the truth being taught.

Nearly 10 years later, I studied Romans again. This time, I read through the passage every day, praying that each verse would be a reality in my life. As a result, my life was radically changed. It started with understanding the Scriptures, flowed into prayer, became worship, and resulted in transforming my life.

CONCLUSION

Just as a strong personal relationship is based on reality, the truth about someone, so our love and worship need to be based on the objective truth of Scripture. The Bible is both our manual of worship and its foundation. Faulty understanding of God as He has revealed Himself in the Scriptures will lead to defective worship.

Perhaps our church worship services should begin with the teaching of the Scriptures, and the rest of our time together should be an outflow of what we have learned.

Our goal should be to know and understand God more through the Bible, not as an end in itself, but to deepen our worship. It should be understood that there are many paradoxes in our understanding of Him, because of the limitations of our minds.

We tend to divide God's character into complex parts, which at times seem to contradict one another. However, it is useful to look at the various characteristics of God, if we are careful to see them as part of His whole being rather than independent aspects. The fact that we don't fully understand Him is evidence that He is God.

---

[17] Carroll, p. 17.

Despite our difficulty in understanding, God has revealed Himself to us through His names and through human language. As His character unfolds before us over time, we become more complete in our worship.

THE PARADIGM SHIFT

This paradigm shift is similar to the previous chapter's. There is considerable overlap when we talk of worshiping God in spirit and in truth. The two are inseparable. "In spirit" describes the subjective aspect of worship. We are certainly not trying to say that diligent study is not important. It is essential. However, we must never lose sight that the goal of our study, church attendance, prayers, and our very lives is to draw us into a deeper relationship with God. So much of our spiritual life can become mechanical and lifeless if it is not flowing from worship or with the goal of becoming worshipers. Keep in mind that worshiping God in truth is more than knowing about Him, but it is understanding truth that leads us into intimacy with Him.

KNOWING ABOUT GOD	KNOWING GOD
1. OBJECTIVES: • To acquire information about God • To teach others what we have learned	1. OBJECTIVES: • To be intimate with God • To worship Him more fully • To help others walk with Him
2. MEANS: • Through classes and seminars • Through personal study • Through the mind	2. MEANS: • Through study • Through prayer and meditation • Through fellowship with other worshipers • Through the mind and the spirit
3. RESULT: Arrogance (1 Cor. 8:1)	3. RESULT: • Loving obedience • Edification of others

WHERE TO START

1. **START LISTING THE ATTRIBUTES OF GOD AND USE THE LIST.** We obviously don't want to divide God into His attributes, but by listing them as we come across them in the Scriptures, we can make sure we are worshiping Him in His fullness. Use this list regularly in your worship.

2. **LIST GOD'S NAMES.** There are many names for God in the Scriptures. Look up the terms, "The God of….." or "The Father of……" to add to your list.

3. **ASK GOD TO GIVE YOU A COMPLETE VIEW OF HIM.** In the next chapter, we will talk about contemplating God. Ask Him to open your eyes to His oneness. Look at the attributes and names of God you have found as you have pored over your Bible. Place them before God in prayer, and worship Him for the completeness and oneness of His being.

4. **DEVELOP A PASSION FOR THE SCRIPTURES AS A MEANS OF WORSHIP.** In the first chapter, we challenged you to use Isaiah 40-46 as a means of worship. This is a different practice for many since they divide their quiet times into Bible reading and prayer. Psalm 119 is divided into 22 eight-verse units. Each day, for the next week, read three sections, praying after each verse that God would give you the same love and commitment to the Scriptures.

5. **OFFER YOUR HEART TO GOD.** Ezra placed His heart before God to seek Him (Ezra 7:10). All of his emotions, desires, will, and thoughts were at God's disposition. He did not worry about being balanced. He wanted to seek God with all that he was.

6. **INTERVIEW AT LEAST TWO UNBELIEVERS WHO BELIEVE THAT GOD EXISTS. ASK THEM:**
   - Who is God to you?
   - Do you believe He judges evil?
   - Are there times His actions contradict His character?
   - Does He know everything?
   - Does He influence everything?
   - How would you find out more about Him?

DISCUSSION QUESTIONS

1. What does it mean to worship God in truth?
2. What are some of the wrong ways to worship God?
3. How has God judged those who abused worship in the past?
4. What does the marriage metaphor teach us about worshiping God in truth?
5. Why are the Scriptures central to worship?
6. Based on your interview, what are some of the misconceptions people have about God?
7. What do we mean when we say that God is not complex?
8. Which attributes of God do you tend to emphasize?
9. Which attributes do you tend to neglect?
10. Describe your time praying through Psalm 119.
11. What is most striking to you about the names of God?
12. How have you grown in your knowledge of God through this chapter?
13. How has your worship developed recently?
14. How does God reveal Himself through His different names?
15. How can head knowledge get in the way of intimacy with God?
16. How does God reveal Himself through His various names?
17. Why is it important to know about God before we talk about intimacy with Him?
18. What are some of the attributes of God you have discovered?

Chapter 5

WORSHIP IS A CHOICE

MAKING A DELIBERATE CHOICE TO LIVE WORSHIP

Therefore, I URGE YOU, BRETHREN, *by the mercies of God, to present your bodies a living and holy sacrifice, acceptable to God, which is your spiritual service of worship. And do not be conformed to this world, but be transformed by the renewing of your mind, so that you may prove what the will of God is, that which is good and acceptable and perfect"* (Romans 12:1-2).

SEED TRUTH: WORSHIP IS A CHOICE THAT WE MAKE EACH MOMENT. *To develop our worship, we must discipline ourselves to have regular times of focused individual and corporate worship to train our minds on His presence. We then make a deliberate choice to be aware of God's presence in each moment and activity during the day. Religious people live their lives unaware of His presence except for designated times in which they remember God. To become effective worshipers, we must choose to integrate worship into everything we do.*

Years ago, I invited a colleague from work to a Bible study. He said he didn't have time. He seemed to have time for our softball league and our intramural football team. In fact, he had time for lots of activity, but not time to seek God.

Then a thought occurred to me: If I were to hand out $100 bills every time someone passed through the doors for a Bible study, people would suddenly have time to study the Bible. It is never really an issue of having the time. It has more to do with what is important to a person. We always have time for what is a priority for us. If it is valuable to us, we always make the time.

We always make choices based on what is most important in our lives. Sometimes, we make those choices because we know there will be personal benefits for us. Work is important, for example, because we get a paycheck. Other times, we make choices to avoid negative consequences. We pay our taxes so we aren't thrown in jail. Some things we have consciously determined to be "right," independent of any outside persuasion or pressure, such as helping someone in need.

We wrestle with some choices, considering all the pros and cons. Other decisions we make instinctively because our response is almost ingrained in us.

Seeking God does not come naturally. On the other hand, our natural tendency is to be religious, preferring rituals and rules while ignoring God's guidance. Being religious is the "default" setting in our thinking. It is automatic pilot. It is our habit and vice.

As Carroll points out, "You must therefore set your will to become a worshiper of Christ. You will never be a worshiper of Christ apart from a definite act of your will."[1]

The choice to be a worshiper is not a one-time decision. Each moment we can choose to walk by the Spirit or by the flesh. Spiritual growth requires spending increasingly more time depending on His guiding presence.

Religious activities can be done in the flesh, independent of God. Even ministry can be carried out apart from worship, although it is only wood, hay, and stubble when done so. In this chapter we will look at the moment-by-moment choice of integrating God's presence into our daily lives.

THE MARRIAGE METAPHOR

We often stress love as a choice rather than a feeling. The Bible never commands us to "*feel*" something because that is usually beyond our

---

[1] Carroll, p. 39.

control. We cannot negate or completely control our feelings, although we can affect some attitudes and actions that influence them. Feelings are not the foundation of a relationship, but if no feelings are involved, there is not much of a relationship. *Although we cannot control how we feel about our spouse at any given time, we can still make a conscious choice to love and to enjoy each other.*

When the Bible commands me to love my wife "just as Christ also loved the church and gave Himself up for her" (Eph. 5:25), I have a choice whether or not to obey. With obedience come benefits. Feelings are a benefit, but they fluctuate. The choice to love is a firm decision that results in security and consistency.

Worship, also, is a choice—a commitment and a spiritual discipline to find our joy in our relationship with God. Every moment of our lives we choose to walk either on the earthly or the spiritual plane (Col. 3:1). There are benefits, but we need to seek the joy of His presence whether or not we feel it or see any results. It's our highest calling. There will often be strong feelings when I choose to live in the spiritual realm, but those times will vary. While the emotions are not the essence of my worship, my walk with God should never be devoid of emotions. I cannot evaluate the quality of my relationship with Him, however, by something that ranges from "excited" to "less than enthusiastic." The deep joy of His presence in my life is much richer than any passing emotion.

CHOOSING TO BELIEVE

Understanding the difference between commands and declarations in the Scriptures is basic to understanding the Bible. Well-meaning speakers and authors sometimes admonish us to seek what is already declared to be true in the believer's life. We often ask God for what we already have.

For example, the Bible says that I am a saint (Eph. 1:1).[2] According to Scripture, I am a new person in Christ (2 Cor. 5:17). I am now a child of God (1 John 3:1). I am sealed with the Holy Spirit

---

[2] In this passage, Paul addresses all of the believers in Ephesus as "saints." Saints or *hágios* in the Greek is used some 60 times in the New Testament, generally referring to believers. Bauer et al. describe saints as a general term for Christians, describing them as consecrated to God.

(Eph. 1:14). I am freely and fully forgiven (Eph. 1:7). Many other similar declarations in the Bible tell me who I am in Christ. I am not called to try to be a new person or child of God, nor am I told to seek the Holy Spirit's presence in my life. When the Bible makes a declaration about who I am, my responsibility is to believe what He has already done.

On the other hand, when there is a command in the Bible, I need to obey. I am commanded to live consistently with my calling (Eph. 4:1) and to seek and pray for strengthening from the Spirit who already dwells within me (Eph. 3:16). I am commanded to be filled with the Spirit (Eph. 5:18) and to walk by the Spirit (Gal. 5:16) so that I am able to live who I am in Christ. There are many commands, even in the New Testament, that I have a choice to obey or not to obey.

The first three chapters of Ephesians tell us who we are individually and as a church "in Christ" (Eph. 1:1, 3, 6, 7, 9, 11, 13, etc.) and the last three chapters admonish us to *walk* according to who we are (Eph 4:1, 17; 5:1, 7, 15). In other words, this is what God has declared to be true; now believe that truth as you live your daily life. We must choose to act on the truth.

When Paul said, "Therefore, I urge you, brethren," he was not just giving a suggestion, but exhorting or appealing to the Romans to act.[3] The word translated *"urge"* is similar to the word used to describe the ministry of the Holy Spirit in our lives.[4] Paul says, "I am exhorting you to act" because worship doesn't happen automatically for Christians or because we walk into a church building. It is a choice.

Although we said in the introduction that true believers are worshipers, that means only that the door to worship has been opened to us. The Bible calls this having "access" (Rom. 5:1-2; Eph. 2:18; 3:12). Paul addresses this admonition to "brethren" because only believers can choose to worship God.

---

[3] Paul doesn't use an imperative to express this command, but instead declares, "I am exhorting you."

[4] *Parakaléo* (Greek) which means to come along side to help, comfort, counsel, and exhort. Since it is not an imperative and because Paul uses this word, it does not come across as an imposition, but it is nonetheless a strong urging to act.

One does not live a life of worship merely because the door to worship is open to him. Otherwise, Paul would not have urged people to seek to worship God in the way this passage describes.

CHOOSING TO MAKE GOD PREEMINENT

The dictionary defines "preeminence" as "having paramount rank, dignity, or importance."[5] "Prominence" means "readily noticeable; conspicuous."[6]

After describing Jesus as the Creator of the visible and invisible universe and declaring His eternity, His sovereignty, and His authority, Paul adds, "so that He Himself will come to have first place in everything" (Col. 1:18). He already had preeminence over the universe, but His resurrection made Him preeminent over the new creation.

One of the biggest barriers to worship is that we seek to make God "noticeable" by giving Him "First Place" in our lives, putting Him at the head of a long list of interests and priorities. However, His absolute preeminence implies that our relationship with Him and our worship of Him will govern every aspect of our lives and not just be prominent. Jesus Christ is not just a "religious side-interest." He is our one and only treasure.

Piper says,

If Christ is an all-satisfying treasure and promises to provide all our needs, even through famine and nakedness, then to live as though we had all the same values as the world would betray him...In other words, if we look like our lives are devoted to getting and maintaining things, we will look like the world and that will not make Christ look great. He will look like a religious side-interest that may be useful for escaping hell in the end, but doesn't make much difference in what we live and love here. He will not look like an all-satisfying treasure.[7]

[5] Webster's New Collegiate Dictionary (Merriam-Webster – 8th edition).
[6] Ibid.
[7] Piper, Don't Waste Your Life, pp. 107-108.

Our worship of God does not come from maintaining priorities, but by allowing our worship of Him to govern everything.

Is God preeminent or merely prominent in your life?

CHOOSING TO LIVE IN GOD'S PRESENCE

If you were a king, what would you want? More gold? A larger army? A larger territory? Not David. He said, "One thing I have asked from the LORD, that I shall seek: / That I may dwell in the house of the LORD all the days of my life, / To behold the beauty of the LORD, / And to meditate in His temple" (Ps. 27:4).

David responded to God's invitation and chose to seek God's presence. Psalm 27 continues, "When You said, 'Seek My face,' my heart said to You, 'Your face, O LORD, I shall seek'" (v.8). That was an act of David's will. His one passion was to behold God and it governed everything he did.

As Alexander Pope said, "One master passion in the breast / Like Aaron's serpent, swallows up the rest."[8]

CHOOSING GOD ABOVE THE EARTHLY

Paul wrote, "For to me, to live is Christ and to die is gain" (Phil. 1:21).

Commenting on this passage, Piper says,

So Paul's point is that life and death, for a Christian, are acts of worship—they exalt Christ and magnify Him and reveal and express His greatness—when they come from an inner experience of treasuring Christ as gain. Christ is praised in death by being prized above life. And Christ is most glorified in life when we are most satisfied in Him even before death.[9]

Paul's life was totally wrapped up in His relationship with God. Dying, although it represents the loss of everything in this life, represented gain to Paul, because after death he would be closer to Christ. As Manahan says, "Entrance into God's presence is a matter that consumes all that the worshiper is and does."[10]

[8] Quoted in Spurgeon, *The Treasury of David,* p. 9.
[9] Piper, *Dangerous Duty,* p. 27.
[10] Ronald Manahan, "The Worshiper's Approach to God" in Bateman, p. 72.

WORSHIP IS A CHOICE   145

Paul gave the key to living in the heavenlies. He said, "Be anxious for nothing, but in everything by prayer and supplication with thanksgiving let your requests be known to God. And the peace of God, which surpasses all comprehension, will guard your hearts and your minds in Christ Jesus" (Phil. 4:6-7).

Biblically, anxiety is not the same as stress. It means that our minds are filled with many thoughts and not necessarily worries. We all have directionless chatter filling our heads so that it becomes very difficult to hear God as we meditate on His Word.

Paul asks us to lay down at Jesus' feet all those issues we are so busy mulling around in our minds. He promises an incomprehensible peace that will protect our hearts and minds.

Incomprehensible peace means that in the midst of the difficulties and circumstances that normally stress people or cause them to lose their patience, worshipers will live in peace. Despite the storm around them, peace dwells within. This kind of peace is so foreign to human beings that it is beyond explanation.

That peace is what Horatio Spafford experienced. His four daughters had perished in a storm at sea. While traveling on the same route, he asked the captain of the ship to call him when they passed over the place where his family had gone down. The peace of the Lord flooded his spirit and he wrote,

When peace like a river attendeth my way,
When sorrows like sea billows roll;
Whatever my lot, Thou hast taught me to say,
"It is well with my soul." [11]

God wants us to leave these matters with Him so that our minds can dwell on "whatever is true, whatever is honorable, whatever is right, whatever is pure, whatever is lovely, whatever is of good repute" (Phil. 4:8). If these things fill our minds, certainly we are focusing on "the God of peace" (v. 9).

Paul's life exemplified that promise. He said, "The things you have learned and received and heard and seen in me, practice these things, and the God of peace shall be with you" (v.9).

---

[11] "It Is Well with My Soul," Joyful Noise Music Company, *Logos Hymnal.*

What had the Philippians seen in Paul's life? After casting out a demon from a young girl, he was unjustly accused of throwing the city into confusion; he was beaten with rods and thrown into prison (Acts 16:13-24). Paul did not lie awake at night tossing and turning because of the injustices he had suffered. His mind was fixed on God. Paul and Silas filled the prison cells with their praises and prayers.

If it had been merely a religious act, the other prisoners would have told them to be quiet so they could sleep. The reality of Christ in their lives, however, led the other prisoners to listen. They were so spellbound by the "peace of God which surpasses comprehension" (Phil. 4:7) in their lives, that they didn't even flee when their chains fell off and the cell doors opened.

Paul's secret was, "I can do all things through Him who strengthens me (Phil. 4:13). Paul's joy was in the Lord because His holy presence allowed him to be strong in his inner man and live above the circumstances.

CHOOSING TO HAVE A UNITED HEART

"Teach me Your way, O LORD; I will walk in Your truth; Unite my heart to fear Your name. I will give thanks to You, O Lord my God, with all my heart, And will glorify Your name forever" (Ps. 86:11-12).

Choosing to make God preeminent, choosing to believe, choosing to live in His presence, and choosing to live above the earthly—all boil down to having a heart that is united in its purpose to worship God.

What does it mean to have a "united heart"? In chapter 1, we commented that David was asking God to give him a single passion. He did not want to live a merely religious life, fulfilling his duty and having a thousand interests.

WHAT ARE HIS WAYS?

A person's "ways" are much more than what he does or says. It involves his or her inward drives and motivations. When we speak of God's ways, it involves His sovereign will or plans.

Kittel and Friedrich, editors of one of the leading theological dictionaries, define God's ways in this manner: "As regards the ways that God himself takes, the combination with [works] shows that [ways] may mean 'dealings' and that with [thoughts or will] (Isa. 55:8-9) the reference may be to 'purposes,' or 'plans.'"[12]

When a person seeks to know God's ways, he or she desires to know what is behind God's commands and actions. When we want to get closer to someone, we say, "I want to know what makes him tick." We want to get inside the person's head and find out what really motivates him or her.

Moses made the audacious request, "Now therefore, I pray You, if I have found favor in Your sight, let me know Your ways, that I may know You, so that I may find favor in Your sight" (Ex. 33:13; see the discussion of Moses in chapter 2).

Psalm 103:7 tells us God granted his request, "He made known His ways to Moses, / His acts to the sons of Israel." The people were content just to know what God did, while Moses wanted to see beyond what He did to see who He is.

Jesus told His disciples, "No longer do I call you slaves, for the slave does not know what his master is doing; but I have called you friends, for all things that I have heard from My Father I have made known to you" (John 15:15).

A slave simply obeys. He does not always know what his master is doing nor why. Jesus actually called His disciples, ourselves included, His friends.

Worshipers do not just observe what God does, but they see beyond His deeds into His character as revealed through His works.

WHAT IS THE HEART?

"Watch over your heart with all diligence, for from it flow the springs of life" (Prov. 4:23).

Most romantic songs include the word "heart" because it is considered the seat of our emotions in our culture. Biblically, the heart involves much more than that. Kittel defines the Hebrew word translated "heart" in the Old Testament this way: "The literal [the hearts] meaning is a) 'breast' and b) 'seat of physical vitality.' Figuratively the heart stands for courage (2 Chron. 17:6) in various expressions, for

[12] Kittel and Friedrich [Words in brackets are Greek words translated by the author.]

the seat of rational functions (Deut. 29:3), for the place of willing and planning (Jer. 23:20) and for the source of religious and ethical conduct (1 Sam. 12:20)."[13]

Kittel also shows us the broad usage of that term in the New Testament: "There is in the NT a rich usage of *kardía* for the seat of feelings, desires, and passions (e.g., joy, pain, love, desire, and lust), the seat of thought and understanding, the seat of the will, and the religious center."[14]

Biblically, therefore, we can conclude that the heart involves our whole inner being. To obey God "from the heart" (Rom. 6:17) means that our emotions, our will, our thoughts, and our inner desires are all directed toward obedience. When Ezra "set his heart to study the law of the Lord" (Ezra 7:10), he offered all these aspects of his heart before the Lord so he could understand God's Word.

When David asked God in Psalm 86 to "unite my heart to fear Your name" (v. 11), he was requesting God to grant that his whole inner being would be directed toward worship. To worship God from the heart is more than emotions, thoughts, and will. It is spiritual. Our hearts have been changed because they are now indwelt by God's Spirit. That means our whole inner being is different.

When God commanded the Jews to "love the Lord your God with all your heart and with all your soul and with all your might" (Deut. 6:5), He wasn't dissecting the inner man. Our thoughts, desires, and emotions are all focused on loving Him. We worship Him with our whole being.

If a person offers his heart to the Lord, he will not seek God selfishly, because his desires have been transformed. They are spiritual in nature, not self-serving. It is never wrong to desire to find joy and pleasure in God.

Piper correctly distinguishes between love and self-interest. He says, "Selfishness seeks its own private happiness at the expense of others. Love seeks happiness *in* the happiness of the beloved"[15] (emphasis original).

---

[13] *Ibid.*
[14] *Ibid.* Numbering and biblical references removed by the author to make easier reading.
[15] Piper, *Dangerous Duty,* p. 63.

If a person offers his heart to the Lord, he will not fall into emotionalism. God's Spirit will work through the believer's emotions so that they are spiritual and not superficial rushes. It is impossible to separate a transformed heart from transformed feelings.

Piper comments, "Minimizing the importance of transformed feelings makes Christian conversion less supernatural and less radical."[16] When we understand what it means to love God with all our heart, our worship will be balanced and complete.

If a person offers his heart to the Lord, he will not fall into cold intellectualism. Worship will involve his understanding, but it is more than an intellectual exercise. As we seek God from the heart, His thoughts become our thoughts.

Perhaps if we really understood what it means to worship God from a united heart, we would never be "unbalanced." Our worship would be complete, because His Spirit would be directing our hearts into real worship.

EXAMPLES OF SOME WHO CHOSE TO BE WORSHIPERS

MARTHA

Luke relates the well-known story of Martha and Mary's hosting Jesus in their home for lunch. The two sisters busily prepared the meal, but Mary was distracted. Soon, she was sitting at Jesus' feet and contemplating His words. Martha was "distracted" (lit. "pulled away") by her preparations and she asked Jesus to make her sister help her.

Jesus answered, "Martha, Martha, you are worried and bothered about so many things; but only one thing is necessary, for Mary has chosen the good part, which shall not be taken away" (Luke 10:38-42).

Although Martha loved Jesus, she was pulled away from His presence by her activities. We naturally tend to focus more on our work or ministry than on our intimacy with Christ. Martha was "worried and bothered" because she did not *choose* to sit at His feet.

---

[16] Piper, *Desiring God*, p. 89.

To be worried is to have a divided mind. She was not focused on Jesus. On the other hand, Mary made a conscious choice to sit at the Lord's feet.

Joseph Carroll has suggested that Mary's sensitivity to the moment when anointing Jesus and Martha's lack of faith when Jesus asked to roll away the stone were the result of the choices they had made in relation to worship.[17]

Some people believe the differences between the two women are a question of personalities. People excuse themselves because they think they are by nature "Marthas." Perhaps we all have a bit of Martha in us and it comes naturally. We become "Marys" by *choosing* the new wine and *choosing* to weave the golden thread of worship into our lives.

CHRISTIANS IN HISTORY

Usually, we attribute greatness to those who do notable things. In the Kingdom of God, great men have always placed worship ahead of ministry. Here are a few examples:

Hudson Taylor

"He was now an aged man; but, without fail, every morning just before dawn there would be the scratching of a match and the lighting of a candle, and Hudson Taylor would worship God. This was the key to his life. It was said that ever before the sun rose on China, Hudson Taylor was worshiping God."[18]

A. W. Tozer

Tozer once invited a man to pray with him. "If you ever want to pray with me, I'm at the lakeside every morning at five-thirty. Just make your way down and we can pray together." One day, the man "was so troubled that he made his way very early to the lakeside, about six o'clock, only to find God's servant prostrate upon the sand worshiping God."[19]

---

[17] See Carroll, pp. 28-30.
[18] *Ibid.* pp. 15-16.
[19] *Ibid.* p. 16.

George Müller

He described the deepening of his worship in this way.

> For the first four years [after my conversion], it was for a good part in great weakness; but in July 1829, now sixty-six years since, it came with me to an entire and full surrender of heart. I gave myself fully to the Lord. Honors, pleasures, money, my physical powers, my mental powers, all were laid down at the feet of Jesus, and I became a great lover of the Word of God. I found my all in God, and thus in all my trials of a temporal spiritual character, it has remained for sixty-six years.[20]

The door to worship had been opened four years earlier, and Müller finally learned to practice it. He worshiped God in truth, for his commitment was to the Word of God. He worshiped God in spirit, for he found his all in God. Most of all, he had a united heart, because nothing was more precious than his relationship with the Lord.

PERSONAL TESTIMONY

Developing a heart for worship has not been a one-step process for me, as it appears to have been for George Müller. I have had to make a series of choices.

I don't believe my heart was united when I came to Brazil. In deciding to become a missionary, I knew worship should be central. However, my heart was divided between my security, my comfort, my reputation, and the best use of my gifts and training. Not that it is wrong to think about those things, but it is a question of motivation and what is really most important. God was prominent, but not preeminent.

Even after I came to Brazil, I tried to keep my hand in science. I returned to the U.S. to teach an entomology course at Liberty University. I secured office space at the local university in Uberlândia and continued to do some research. Certainly there is nothing wrong with scientific studies, but I think my motivation was to maintain my security in my career and to maintain my reputation as a scientist.

---

[20] Quoted in James Gilchrist Lawson, *Deeper Experiences of Famous Christians*, pp. 244-245.

After being in Brazil about five years, I realized that my heart was divided. I made a conscious decision to stop my research and send the insect specimens back to the museums from which I had borrowed them. Although it was a hard decision, I felt free afterward.

A few years back, I made another conscious choice to put my life before the Lord and seek worship as never before. A crisis led me to place my whole missionary career as well before the Lord. I had not realized it, but my heart was divided between my ministry and worship.

I am convinced that the principal reason God sovereignly brought us to Brazil was to help unite my heart to Him, making me more of a worshiper. Not that everyone has to give up his or her career or become a missionary to be a worshiper, but in my case, moving to another country is what I needed to shift my values.

As Piper says, "It is true that God can be known and enjoyed in every legitimate vocation; but when he deploys you from one place to the next, he offers fresh and deeper drinking at the fountain of his fellowship. God seldom calls us to an easier life, but always calls us to know more of him and drink more deeply of his sustaining grace."[21]

CONCLUSION

People in the past had more focused minds than we do today. Perhaps it is because they did not have the distractions of modern media and had more time for study, reflection, writing, research—and worship. It seems as though our interests are more and more diverse in our busy, modern world, and all our activities squeeze out what is really important.

I used to like it when people looked at my life and said, "Where do you find the time?" It showed that I was busy and to be commended. That, however, is not a badge of honor with God. What honors Him is our secret times of worship that overflow into everything we do. The new wineskins that hold the new wine extend beyond the church walls and into our lives. Worship is part of everything we do. It should govern our goals in every area of life.

---

[21] Piper, *Don't Waste Your Life*, p. 178.

Most of us have chosen by default to emulate Martha, choosing doing over being. But Mary made a different choice, to sit at the Lord's feet and He commended her. Real worshipers have a one-track mind, putting their effort into developing their intimacy with Him. Does having such a one-track mind make one a religious fanatic? No! Fanaticism is a passion for rules, dogmas, programs, and religious activities. It is an emphasis on doing. But we can never be too dedicated to loving God and being in His presence. We make that choice daily. In fact, we confirm it every moment.

THE PARADIGM SHIFT

We have already discussed paradigm shifts. The difference here is worship as important or worship as essential. Is it prominent or preeminent?

GOD AS IMPORTANT	GOD AS PREEMINENT
1. OBJECTIVES: • To fulfill our religious obligations • To allow God to fulfill our needs • To fit God conveniently into our schedules	1. OBJECTIVES: • To find satisfaction in communion with God • To discover and fulfill His perfect will
2. MEANS: • Through religious moments	2. MEANS: • Through constantly choosing to be a worshiper
3. RESULT: • Non-submissive attitude • Shallow inner peace	3. RESULT: • Walking with God • Obedience • Peace

WHERE TO START

1. ASK GOD TO GIVE YOU AN UNDIVIDED HEART. We are so easily distracted. Only God can enable us to be single minded. That is why the psalmist asked for it. Spend some time in God's presence asking for it. Pray Psalm 86:11-12 for your life every day for one week.

2. TELL GOD YOU WANT TO BE LIKE MARY AND SIT AT HIS FEET. How much of your life is so filled with activities that you don't sit at His feet? It is your choice.

3. ASK GOD TO SHOW YOU THOSE AREAS STANDING IN THE WAY OF MAKING WORSHIP PREEMINENT. Allow Him to examine your life to show you what may be attracting your affections. What are the barriers to your intimacy with God? A relationship? An activity? Secret sin?

4. COUNT ALL THINGS LOSS TO GAIN CHRIST. It is impossible to have an undivided heart when you desire to determine your own destiny. Ask God to guide your life.

DISCUSSION QUESTIONS

1. Why do we say worship is a choice?

2. When do we make this choice?

3. Are all Christians worshipers? In what sense?

4. What can we learn from the marriage metaphor?

5. What is the difference between commitment and fanaticism?

6. How do we consciously choose to worship?

7. How did Jesus condemn the divided life?

8. What is the difference between God's being prominent and His being preeminent?

9. If we have jobs and responsibilities, how is it possible to live above the earthly?

10. What is the heart biblically?

11. What is the evidence that you have a heart for worship?

12. Why was David a man after God's own heart?

13. What stands in the way of your having an undivided heart?

14. What is religious hypocrisy?

15. How can you make worship preeminent in your life?

16. Where have you seen progress in your life as a worshiper?

17. What have you learned about worship through this chapter?

Chapter 6

WORSHIP STARTS WITH BEHOLDING GOD

TRAINING OUR EYES TO SEE GOD IN EVERYTHING

THEREFORE, *I urge you, brethren,* BY THE MERCIES OF GOD, *to present your bodies a living and holy sacrifice, acceptable to God, which is your spiritual service of worship. And do not be conformed to this world, but be transformed by the renewing of your mind, that you may prove what the will of God is, that which is good and acceptable and perfect"* (Romans 12:1-2).

SEED TRUTH: WORSHIPERS HAVE THEIR EYES TRAINED TO SEE GOD IN EVERYTHING. *Religious people are aware of God only in specified contexts during the week. Worshipers, on the other hand, are keenly aware of God's presence at all times, consciously placing Him before their eyes. Worship opens our eyes to the hand of God in the Bible, in nature, in other people, in the good we receive, and even in difficult situations. In the same way, seeing His hand in everything serves as a constant stimulus for worship.*

Speaking of Yuri Gagarin's historic first flight into space, Nikita Khruschev said, "Gagarin flew into space, but didn't see any God there." A Russian priest later said that if Gagarin didn't see God on earth, neither would he see him in the heavens. Someone else pointed out that if he had opened the hatch and broken the oxygen seal, he would have seen God rather suddenly.

The Russian priest was right. Major Gagarin did not see God, because he did not want to see Him. His eyes were trained to see and respond to the instruments of his spaceship, but he was blind to the Creator. The evidence was all around him as well as within him.

A young woman who had been struggling with depression for years approached me after a conference where I had spoken. She was drawn to what I had said about intimacy with God, and we talked about refocusing her mind to live in His presence. Her life was focused on doing, and she was very good and efficient in her ministry. However, the frustrations she felt made it obvious that what she was doing was not flowing from worship.

First, her lack of worship led her to see her own life through critical eyes. In her perception, God had given her tasks to do, but He was not sovereign over the problems that seemed to prevent her from completing those tasks. God was like a cruel boss who gave an assignment and didn't care about the challenges she faced. He just wanted to see the job done, and she was failing.

Further, she felt her shortcomings in ministry were the reason God did not give His approval. She should have been able to get things done, she thought. Obviously, she did not see herself sitting in the heavenlies with Christ.

Her lack of worship had led to a distorted view of God. Instead of being drawn into Christ as her refuge, her rock, her tower, and her shield, she had pulled away and viewed God as a distant tyrant. She did not understand that she already had God's approval and nothing she could do could make her more approved.

I gave her some worship exercises from the Scriptures, focusing on God's character and her position in Him. I also had her do some thankfulness exercises, worshiping God for what He had done. She had so much for which to be thankful and she knew that, intellectually.

When I visited with her and her husband a couple of months later, I found a different person. I could see there were still some struggles, but she was much more joyful. What struck me most was her comment, "I am seeing blessings where I never saw them before. They were always there."

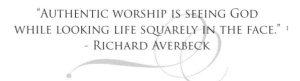

"AUTHENTIC WORSHIP IS SEEING GOD
WHILE LOOKING LIFE SQUARELY IN THE FACE." [1]
- RICHARD AVERBECK

In the previous chapter, we looked at Romans 12:1-2 and saw that worship is a choice. Obviously, it is God who opens our eyes, but we need to ask Him to open them so we can see Him. When we choose to seek worship, we begin to behold God. In this chapter we explore what it means to contemplate God so we can weave the golden thread of worship into the fabric of our beings.

THE MARRIAGE METAPHOR

Most of us can recall when we first fell in love. The world seemed different as we saw it through new eyes. Everything reminded us of that special person. As we move to a more mature love, we continue to see things in light of our relationship with our spouses.

I had been afraid of moving from the friendship stage to something more with Lisa. I didn't want to ruin a great friendship. I was a brand new Christian, and I enjoyed talking about the Lord with her more than anyone else. I asked her out, and through the course of the evening it became apparent that we both wanted to move our relationship to a deeper level. I was thrilled.

The next day, I went hiking with my family. Everything reminded me of Lisa. I could not stop thinking about her all that day. My friends became tired of hearing about her. My enthusiasm has not diminished after more than three decades, by the way. In fact it has grown. I have tried to learn, however, that others are not interested in hearing about it. However, she has become used to hearing from my students, "So, you are Lisa. I have heard so much about you."

When we are in love with the Lord, our whole outlook on life is changed. Everything reminds us of Him. It is not just an emotional high, but a new perspective on life since He is with us wherever we go.

---

[1] Averbeck, "Worshiping God in Truth" in Bateman, p. 131.

BEHOLDING GOD IN AWE

"Therefore, I urge you, brethren, by the mercies of God..." (Rom. 12:1).

As I was putting together the syllabus for a course on Romans, I came to the end of chapter 11, absolutely amazed at the final touch in God's great plan of redemption. I bowed my head in awe and worshiped God for His wisdom, mercy, love, and sovereignty.

As I finished the last verses in the chapter, I found that Paul, the human author of the passage, had done the same thing as his heart exploded in praise,

> Oh, the depths of the riches both of the wisdom and knowledge of God! How unsearchable are His judgments and unfathomable His ways! For WHO HAS KNOWN THE MIND OF THE LORD, OR WHO BECAME HIS COUNSELOR? Or WHO HAS FIRST GIVEN TO HIM THAT IT MIGHT BE PAID BACK TO HIM AGAIN? For from Him and through Him and to Him are all things. To Him be the glory forever. Amen (Rom. 11:33-36).

On the basis of this praise, he exhorts us in the next verse to worship God.

The "therefore" in 12:1 refers to the first 11 chapters of Romans, specifically to God's mercy and compassion poured out in our lives. Obviously, since Paul is exhorting us, worship is not something that comes automatically. We must consciously decide to respond. People try to pump up "worship" through music or words, but only seeing God as He has revealed Himself through Scripture can truly lead to worship.

There is an old saying that "familiarity breeds contempt." When we see or do something every day, it becomes routine. When I take Americans out on the Amazon River, they all "oooh" and "ahhh" at the wonders of our rainforest. The Brazilians who make the same trip several times a week are either sleeping or reading the paper.

However, a biologist could never be bored in the face of such a rich diversity of organisms. In that small stretch of river, there are probably scores of plants about which little is known. To those who see them every day, a tree is a tree. Those who live there see insects as pests and go for the Raid. However, in front of our eyes were probably scores of insects unknown to science. Besides that, there are fascinating birds, reptiles, fish, and mammals all over the place. It's all a matter of perspective.

Our contemplation of God should never become a ritual or routine. We need to look at the great truths of the Bible as though it were the first time we had ever seen them, because there is an unfathomable depth to every truth. We need to wonder at them.

I asked a friend of mine what she thought of God's grace. She looked at me blankly and said, "It is God's unmerited favor." She is right, but grace that is packed into a rote definition is no longer amazing.

Psalm 36:5-6 says, "Your lovingkindness, O LORD, extends to the heavens, / Your faithfulness reaches to the skies. / Your righteousness is like the mountains of God; / Your judgments are like a great deep."

I think I understand only a few centimeters of His lovingkindness and faithfulness. I have grasped a few grams of His righteousness. I have not gone very deep into His judgments. Surely I will spend eternity exploring just these four great aspects of His character. How could I not marvel!

Wiersbe writes, "Wonder is not a cheap amusement that brings a smile to your face. It is an encounter with reality, with God, which brings awe to your heart. You're overwhelmed with an emotion that is a mixture of gratitude, adoration, reverence, fear, and love. You're not looking for explanations; you're lost in the wonder of God."[2]

Of course, marveling and reflecting on God in our hearts must start with the objective knowledge of Him through studying the Scriptures. As Wiersbe says, "…wonder isn't born in ignorance: it is born of knowledge."[3] Bible study should be fresh and invigorating, a time of training our eyes to see Him.

As we explore the depths of His character through His Word, we begin to marvel at the creation that surrounds us. Everything begins to fascinate us as we see God all around us. That is why I like to be around new believers; they help me contemplate through fresh eyes what God has done.

---

[2] Wiersbe, p. 43.
[3] Ibid. p. 43.

BARRIERS TO BEHOLDING GOD

One Wednesday night at church I asked my prayer partner how he had seen God during the past week. He thought a minute and said He had not seen God in anything that week. It was obvious that he was neither worshiping nor praying.

Why aren't our minds always yielded to the Spirit? What keeps us from seeing God around us?

UNBELIEF

As with Nikita Khrushcev, unbelief completely closes our eyes. That is true not only for unbelievers, but a lack of faith in God will keep Christians from seeing God, too. Jesus said to Martha at Lazarus' tomb, "Did I not say to you, that if you believe, you will see the glory of God?" (John 11:40).

We say that seeing is believing, but here, Jesus says that believing will lead to seeing. Many people saw Lazarus come back to life, but did not see the glory of God. Like childish tattle-tales, they went to tell the Pharisees what had happened (John 11:46). Jesus had encouraged Martha to see what was about to happen through the eyes of faith.

FAMILIARITY

We close our eyes to God's presence when we think we already know all about God. We mentioned earlier that familiarity breeds contempt. Have you ever noticed that after memorizing a passage of Scripture, you tend to skip over it when reading because you already "know what it says"?

IMPURITY

Impure motives and thoughts will clutter up our inner voice and keep us from seeing God. Jesus said, "Blessed are the "pure in heart [internally pure] for they shall see God" (Matt. 5:8). That is not just for the future, but also for here and now. A. W. Tozer says, "God assures us in many ways that His worshiping people will be a puri-fied people, a people delighting in the spiritual disciplines of a life pleasing to God."[4]

---

[4] Tozer, *Whatever Happened to Worship?* p. 103.

PRIDE

Pride is a barrier to seeing God (James 4:6). When we trust in our own resources to solve our problems, we are not giving the Spirit liberty to work in our lives. We look to our own resources to determine the right course of action. That leads to anxiety and we fail to see God.

SEEKING GOD IN HUMAN STRENGTH

If we try to seek God in our strength, we will never succeed in that attempt. Tozer says, "I am a little irritated or grieved at the continuing hope of so many people that they will be able to grasp God—understand God, commune with God—through their intellectual capacities. When will they realize that if they could possibly 'discover' God with the intellect, they would be equal to God?"[5] If we seek with our own resources, we will never see Him.

ACTIVITY

Activities can get in the way of our intimacy with God. Packer writes, "…the irony is that modern Christians, preoccupied with maintaining religious practices in an irreligious world, have themselves allowed God to become remote."[6]

At times I have been so absorbed in the Lord's work that I lost sight of Him. Our churches can have meetings, committees, and programs, all of which have their place. However, in the midst of all we do, we may neglect worshiping God. As MacArthur says, "We have many activities and little worship. We are big on ministry and small on adoration. We are disastrously pragmatic. All we want to know about is what works. We want formulas and gimmicks, and somehow in the process, we leave out that to which God has called us."[7]

The parable of the Good Samaritan is directed at the religious leaders who were so busy with their religious activities that they did not have time to help others. Jesus' teaching was always clear that genuine worship would be manifested in the way we treat others.

---

[5] Ibid. p. 69.
[6] Packer, p. 6.
[7] MacArthur, *Ultimate Priority*, p.21.

At one of our church-planting conferences, a pastor from another denomination stood up and said he had finished first in his seminary class. After a number of years, he was involved in a very successful pastorate in a large church. Everyone spoke highly of him. Suddenly, he burst into sobs and cried out that he was empty inside. The ministry itself had crowded out his intimacy with God, and he was just going through the motions.

LACK OF DISCIPLINE

Finally, a lack of discipline in focusing our minds on God inhibits us from seeing Him. We are accustomed to allowing our thoughts to wander. We don't necessarily allow them to delve into sinful thoughts, but usually our musings are worthless. Our minds wander from our prayers, from our Bible reading, from the sermon, and from the music we are singing.

Paul admonishes, "Set your mind on the things above, not on the things that are on earth" (Col. 3:2). He also told us to let our minds dwell on "whatever is true, whatever is honorable, whatever is right, whatever is pure, whatever is lovely, whatever is of good repute" (Phil. 4:8).

Madame Guyon says, "The mind has a very strong tendency to stray away from the Lord."[8] That is why the Scriptures must be our focal point as we fix our minds on Him.

Gibbs gives an interesting observation about this mental discipline. He writes, "The goal of the worship experience is not to bring about an altered state of consciousness as a way for the devotees to detach themselves from the mundane experiences of daily life. It is not an escapist activity but an empowering one—the whole of life is infused with a sense of God's presence."[9]

The mind is the means by which we perceive the world around us. We process what we see, interpret it through our grid, and make moral judgments. To contemplate God, our minds need to be pure, disciplined, humble, and illuminated by Him.

---

[8] Guyon, p. 9.
[9] Eddie Gibbs, *ChurchNext: Quantum Changes in How We Do Ministry*, p. 129.

LEARNING TO BEHOLD GOD

Although our eyes are opened when we enter a relationship with Him, learning to behold Him is a process. We need to train our minds to see His presence where we were formerly blind.

THROUGH HIS WORD

The study of the Scriptures is no guarantee that we will see God. Jesus criticized the Jews for searching the Scriptures[10] and not recognizing that they "testify about Me" (John 5:39). Why didn't they recognize Jesus? It is because they chose not to (John 5:40) and they did not have His Word abiding in them (John 5:38). It is not just study, but meditating on the Word that causes it to abide in us.

Richard Foster says, "We desperately need to see who God is: to read about His self-disclosure to His ancient people Israel, to meditate on His attributes, to gaze upon the revelation of His nature in Jesus Christ. When we see the Lord of hosts 'high and lifted up,' ponder His infinite wisdom and knowledge, wonder at His unfathomable mercy and love, we cannot help but move into doxology."[11]

Paul echoed that thought when he said of the Jews, "Whenever Moses is read, a veil lies over their heart; but whenever a person turns to the Lord, the veil is taken away" (2 Cor. 3:15-16). He explained that it was because their "minds were hardened" (2 Cor. 3:14). The Jews, instead of seeing the glory of the Lord in the Pentateuch, saw only a list of rules.

The good news is that God has opened our eyes through Jesus Christ. Paul says, "But we all, with unveiled face, beholding as in a mirror the glory of the Lord, are being transformed into the same image from glory to glory, just as from the Lord, the Spirit" (2 Cor. 3:18).

We are "beholding as in a mirror" for we cannot see His glory directly because of our sin. The Word is like a mirror by which we see His glory indirectly. We are *unveiled* so that nothing is preventing us from seeing His glory through the Bible.

---

[10] The Greek can be translated either as an imperative (a command) or an indicative (a statement). In this context, it makes better sense to take it as a statement.

[11] Richard Foster, *Celebration of Discipline*, p. 139.

STUDY OF THE WORD IS ONLY THE STARTING POINT.
IT SERVES AS THE FOUNDATION FOR MEDITATION,
PRAYER, AND WORSHIP. IN FACT, MEDITATION IS
A MIXTURE OF PRAYER, WORSHIP, READING,
AND REFLECTION, ALL ROLLED INTO ONE.
IT IS ONLY WHEN THESE DISCIPLINES ARE BROUGHT
INTO PLAY THAT THE WORD BECOMES CLEAR TO US.

Describing meditation, Richard Foster writes, "If we hope to move beyond the superficialities of our culture—including our religious culture—we must be willing to go down into the recreating silences, into the inner world of contemplation."[12]

Joseph Carroll tells how he discovered the worship of God through the Scriptures, "by accident." He remembers a day of prayer he experienced in Australia where he was serving as a missionary.

> When it came my turn one afternoon, I was very tired and began to quote Psalm 19:1-3. ...Suddenly I was quickened by the Spirit of God and began to pour out my heart in prayer. I had not prayed like that all day. I had offered many prayers, but this was different. When I finished and the others were praying, I did a lot of thinking and waiting upon the Lord. What had I done? I had begun with these verses worshiping God from the Psalms; so the next time around I did the same thing, and the same thing happened. I was quickened by the Spirit of God, and there was that outpouring in intercession. I was borne along by the Spirit of God. I knew then that I had been introduced to a priceless key, one that would introduce me to hitherto undreamed of heights of fellowship with my Lord.[13]

Madame Guyon says, "In 'praying the Scripture' you are seeking to find the Lord in what you are reading, in the very words themselves. In this path, therefore, the content of the Scripture is the focal point of your attention. Your purpose is to take everything from the passage that unveils the Lord to you."[14]

---

[12] Foster, p. 13.
[13] Carroll, p. 17.
[14] Guyon, , p. 9.

Incredible as it may seem, some people lose sight of God in their Scripture reading. Training our minds to behold God starts with seeing Him afresh through meditation on His Word.

IN NATURE

The book of Job is the earliest book in the Bible and so could not reference any previously written Scriptures. As a result, Job and his friends regularly cited examples from nature to make their points. They were keenly aware that God showed His character through what was made, much as an artist reveals himself through his work.

Nature, however, is an incomplete revelation of God's character and, thus, inferior to the Scriptures. The world has been affected by the fall and no longer reveals its original perfection. Therefore, the world around us can never take the Scriptures' place as the foundation of our worship.

King Solomon wrote about nature. The Bible says of him, "He spoke of trees, from the cedar that is in Lebanon even to the hyssop that grows on the wall; he spoke also of animals and birds and creeping things and fish" (1 Kings 4:33). That would have been an interesting biology class. He undoubtedly demonstrated how different types of living creatures reflect the character of the Creator.

David commented, "When I consider Your heavens, the work of Your fingers, / The moon and the stars, which You have ordained, / What is man, that You take thought of him? (Ps. 8:3-4). It is easy to imagine the young shepherd contemplating the stars while he guarded his sheep at night. Although he did not have a telescope or any of the benefits of modern astronomy, he saw the awesome greatness of God through the brilliance of the heavenly bodies undiminished by light pollution. He worshiped God because he recognized how great He is and how small man is. Nature is a powerful reminder of that.

A. W. Tozer said, "These men, who were some of the holiest and godliest men of that ancient time, reveled in their writings that they were intensely in love with every natural beauty around them. But always they saw nature as the handiwork of an all-powerful, all-wise, glorious Creator."[15]

---

[15] Tozer, *Whatever Happened to Worship?* p. 43.

God told the Jews to write the Word on their doorposts (Deut 6:9) and to put tassels on their clothing (Num. 15:37-40) to serve as stimuli for worship and obedience. Nature is also a constant reminder of His greatness. The stars, clouds, birds, and trees make us think of His power and faithfulness even in the smallest of details. Of course, we could be like Yuri Gagarin, who very likely was oblivious to God's awesome presence all around him.

THROUGH OTHER BELIEVERS

The church is one of the most compelling evidences of the presence of God in the world today, or at least it should be. In chapter ten, we will explore the reality of the worshiping church. Suffice it here to say that the unity we are to experience because of the love of Christ in our lives causes even the spirit world to be in awe of God's wisdom (Eph. 3:10).

When we share with one another what we have learned through our contemplation of God, our lives are enriched. We see not only what God is doing in others, but we see Him in the way we relate to one another.

In describing spiritual gifts, Paul writes, "But to each one is given the manifestation of the Spirit for the common good" (1 Cor. 12:7). The Spirit's presence is made visible by our acts of edifying one another, and that serves as a stimulus for worship. The result of the proper use of spiritual gifts is that others benefit and the body is unified.[16]

Jesus asked us to perform our good deeds before men so that "they may see your good works, and glorify your Father who is in heaven" (Matt. 5:16). If our good works are done as a fruit of worship, they will stimulate others to worship God as well.

IN GOOD THINGS

"Every good thing given and every perfect gift is from above, coming down from the Father of lights, with whom there is no variation or shifting shadow" (James 1:17).

---

[16] *Sumphérō* means "to profit or help." Literally it means "to carry together." This word can mean that the purpose of spiritual gifts is for mutual benefit or for the unifying of the body. Both are certainly true. Perhaps that is why Paul chose this word.

In calling God the "Father of lights," James is acknowledging Him as the Creator of the heavenly bodies as David did. In contrast, however, God does not move around or change as the stars do. He is constant and faithful in providing all good things for our benefit. Our region of Brazil is probably the richest place in the world for tropical fruits. God blessed us with cupuaçu, biribá, bacurí, jambu, and açaí, just to name a few fruits unique to our region. He could have given the whole world just one type of fruit, but the variety of foods is for our pleasure. This rich variety of good things reflects His glory and stimulates us to worship Him.

Paul and Barnabas told the Gentiles, "He did not leave Himself without witness, in that He did good and gave you rains from heaven and fruitful seasons, satisfying your hearts with food and gladness" (Acts 14:17). God has revealed Himself to the world through His goodness in providing for all men, even though they don't deserve such blessings.

In Difficult Circumstances

> It is easy to see God in the good things, but the mark of a worshiper is that he sees God's sovereign purposes in the difficult times as well.

In chapter 7, we will look more in depth at suffering.

In Romans 5:2, Paul tells us, "we exult in hope of the glory of God." In other words, our expectation of contemplating the fullness of His glory in heaven is our hope and motivation to exalt Him in worship here and now. But that is not the only stimulus for worship.

He continues, "And not only this, but we also exult in our tribulation" (v. 3). It seems that difficulties and persecutions are motives for worship and trust in His sovereign purpose in allowing the hardships. We know He has something for us that goes beyond our temporal comfort and enjoyment. All things work together to conform us to His image and make us better worshipers (Rom. 8:28-29).

THE RESULT OF BEHOLDING GOD

One cannot see God without being changed. The Bible tells us what happens as a result of this "spiritual astonishment and wonder," as Tozer calls it.[17] Although there is fear and trembling at His presence, those who were drawn to God were radically changed.

Jacob met with God at the ford of Jabbok and was changed by the encounter. God changed his name to reflect his change in character (Gen. 32:22-32). Moses was transformed when he met God at the burning bush at Horeb (Ex. 3-4). Gideon was a coward until the Lord visited him (Judg. 6). Prophets were transformed and called into service when God appeared to them (Isa. 6 and Ezek. 2). In the New Testament, Paul was radically changed when Jesus appeared to Him (Acts 9).

Cowards were made bold. Swindlers became men of integrity. Liars began to proclaim the truth. Persecutors became the persecuted. God always calls people to ministry through their having seen Him, which resulted in worship. Salvation itself is a complete change of worship, where the idolater becomes a servant of the true God.

When we see God and wonder at who He is, it leads us to bow down to Him. Tozer says, "I will never bend my knees and say 'Holy, holy, holy' to that which I have been able to decipher and figure out in my own mind! That which I can explain will never bring me to the place of awe. It can never fill me with astonishment or wonder or admiration."[18]

There is one more inevitable result of contemplating God. When we see God for who He is, we see ourselves for who we are. A person may recoil at what he sees and draw back from God, or he can be drawn into His transforming presence.

When the Israelites saw God's presence manifested on the mountain, they did not want to approach God. They said to Moses, "Speak to us yourself and we will listen, but let not God speak to us, or we die" (Ex. 20:19). That fear, rightly placed, made them not want to approach God.

---

[17] Tozer, *Whatever Happened to Worship?* p. 85.
[18] Ibid.

Adam had the same reaction in the Garden, "I heard the sound of You in the garden, and I was afraid because I was naked; so I hid myself" (Gen. 3:10).

Peter said, "Go away from me, Lord, for I am a sinful man, O Lord!" (Luke 5:8).

After Manoah and his wife, Samson's parents, saw the presence of the Lord, Manoah said, "We shall surely die, for we have seen God" (Judges 13:22).

After seeing God on His throne, Isaiah cried out, "Woe is me, for I am ruined! Because I am a man of unclean lips, And I live among a people of unclean lips; For my eyes have seen the King, the LORD of hosts" (Isa. 6:5).

These passages clearly show the effect of contemplating God. We need to be prepared to have our deepest thoughts exposed in order to be cleansed. We need to be prepared to be broken before Him. Broken beyond repair. At that point, we can effectively offer ourselves to Him. Contemplation will inevitably lead us to bow ourselves before Him in humble submission. That is the next step in developing a life of worship and it is the subject of the next chapter.

PERSONAL TESTIMONY

When I was in high school, I was interested in the Bible and had "made a decision," but I didn't know the Lord and, of course, was not a worshiper. I lived a hypocritical double life, being at the bars on Saturday night and in church on Sunday morning. Toward the end of my sophomore year at Ohio State, God broke me through a series of circumstances, and I became truly God's. Everything that I valued and in which I put my trust was taken away from me. Not only did I change, but I was living in a different world. I saw God in everything, especially in the difficulties that led to my conversion.

My father was concerned at my new dedication to the Lord because he was afraid that my grades would slip. On the contrary, they got better. Although my biology professors failed to see God in what they were teaching, I did. I could honestly say, "I have more insight than all my teachers, / For Your testimonies are my meditation" (Ps. 119:99). They knew about the creation, but I knew the Creator. Every class was like a worship service.

Maybe what we call our "first love" is when we first have our eyes opened and see God all around us. It is all so new and different that we stand in awe. When we see other believers who don't share the same enthusiasm, our sense of wonder diminishes. I am so thankful that God has never let me lose my awe of Him.

CONCLUSION

Yuri Gagarin was the first person to see the earth from a "God's-eye" perspective. No one had seen the stars so clearly. He was an intelligent man with perfect eyesight, but, without faith, he could not see what the simplest believer contemplates every day, the glory of God.

A detective sees clues at a crime scene that you and I would find insignificant. A doctor sees symptoms that we pass over. A quarterback sees an open receiver while we are following the fake handoff. A biologist sees a new species of an insect when we see only a bug.

Just as men skilled in every profession have their eyes trained to see what the layman would miss, Christians need to have their eyes trained to see the glory of God in the world around them.

THE PARADIGM SHIFT

People have accused worshipers of being so heavenly minded they are no earthly good. The problem is that most people are so earthly minded, they are no heavenly good. It all depends on the perspective from which we see our surroundings.

SEEING GOD THROUGH THE WORLD'S EYES	SEEING THE WORLD THROUGH GOD'S EYES
1. STIMULUS: Religious reminders, such as worship services and prayer at meals	1. STIMULUS: • The Word • Nature • Other believers • Blessings • Difficulties
2. RESULT: Religious feelings	2. RESULT: Awe and wonder
3. FRUIT: Nothing lasting	3. FRUIT: More worship and peace

Where to Start

In and of ourselves, we will never seek God. He has to create the desire within us. He also has to open our eyes to be able to see Him. The Scriptures speak of our being drawn by Him rather than any meritorious effort of our own. The psalmist says, "Blessed is the man You choose, And cause to approach You, that he may dwell in Your courts" (Ps. 65:4 NKJV).

Therefore, seeking God is not something we can program. We can never say we "followed all the right steps" and it just didn't work, because there are no "right steps" besides prayerfully studying the Scriptures. Seeking God comes from within and is produced by God. The following exercises may provide a starting point in the Word.

1. CONTINUE LEARNING TO CONTEMPLATE GOD THROUGH HIS WORD. Continue going through Isaiah 47-53, worshiping God in the same manner as described in the first chapter of this section. This time, pray these passages every day this week:

    a. Ask God to open your eyes to behold His character in His Word (Ps. 119:18).

    b. Ask God to allow His Word to be implanted in your life (James 1:21).

    c. Make a commitment to walk according to what God shows you (Ps. 86:11).

2. LEARN TO CONTEMPLATE GOD'S CHARACTER IN NATURE. Spend a half hour worshiping God as you contemplate some aspect of His creation. Try to use parts of His creation to stimulate praise.

3. DEVELOP A THANKFUL HEART. Read Psalm 107. List ten reasons you are thankful, and thank Him for what He has shown
   you about Himself through each item on the list. Daily thank
   Him for these items.

4. BEGIN TO SEE GOD IN OTHERS. Ask God to enable you to see
   beyond the imperfections of others and contemplate His work
   in their lives.

5. WORSHIP HIM FOR HIS SOVEREIGNTY. This will allow you
   to see beyond the problems and trust Him for His higher
   purposes.

DISCUSSION QUESTIONS

1. What have you learned from worshiping God, using the Scriptures?

2. How has the marriage metaphor helped you understand worship?

3. Why is it so hard to focus our minds on worship?

4. What barriers do you face in contemplating God?

5. In what ways are you beginning to see God where you have not before?

6. How have you seen God's hand in the lives of others this week?

7. How do we see God's hand in His creation?

8. What is the relationship between thankfulness and worship?

9. How does worship change your perception of your surroundings?

10. How have you seen God's hand in the difficulties you have faced?

11. Why does contemplating God change your life?

12. Where do you stand in relation to the two paradigms?

Chapter 7

WORSHIP REQUIRES
SUBMISSION TO GOD

RESPONDING TO GOD'S PRESENCE
BY OFFERING OUR LIVES TO HIM

Therefore, I urge you, brethren, by the mercies of God, TO
PRESENT YOUR BODIES A LIVING AND HOLY SACRIFICE, AC-
CEPTABLE TO GOD, *which is your spiritual service of worship.
And do not be conformed to this world, but be transformed by
the renewing of your mind, so that you may prove what the
will of God is, that which is good and acceptable and perfect*
(Romans 12:1-2).

**SEED TRUTH: WORSHIPERS RESPOND TO GOD'S PRESENCE
BY OFFERING THEMSELVES TO HIM.** *Worship involves bowing
before God in surrender, giving up our rights, comfort, and personal
satisfaction as offerings to God. Religious people merely perform ritual
acts of worship while continuing to determine their own destiny, hoping
that God will make their lives easier. Intimacy with God usually comes
through suffering and persecution, as we learn to surrender ourselves.
When a worshiper offers himself to God, he bows before God in submission, saying that he is willing to pay a price through suffering in the hope
and joy of becoming more intimate with God.*

My kids roll their eyes when I talk about going to another Civil War
battlefield when we are in the U.S. One of our supporting churches

is close to Gettysburg, and I try to get there as often as I can. It is always moving to stand at the Confederate "high water mark" and look across the field where Pickett's charge was turned back. America's history hung in the balance at that spot.

The most moving scene in the movie *Gettysburg* is when the soldiers step out of the woods on Seminary Ridge and General Armistead says, "Virginians! Virginians! For your lands. For your homes. For your sweethearts. For your wives. For Virginia! Forward--March." [1]

How could those Confederate soldiers have walked across that open field to sure death? Were the causes of Confederate independence, the southern lifestyle, and the institution of slavery worth dying for? General Armistead himself led the charge and was cut down near one of the Union guns he had captured.

Are there any causes you are willing to die for? I don't know if I would be willing to give my life for any earthly cause. I probably will never know unless I am faced with the choice. But there is a cause to which I have given my life: Jesus Christ.

If we are going to drink of the new wine and not just be satisfied with new wineskins, we must give our lives to the pursuit of knowing Him. That requires sacrifice, dedication, and perseverance. But nothing is worth more than our intimacy with God. We will gladly sell everything we have to obtain this pearl of great price (Matt. 13:45).

We are willing to lose our relationship with our family and closest friends because intimacy with God is our greatest joy (Matt. 10:35-37).

With joy, we will be willing to take up our crosses to follow Him (Matt. 10:38).

We gladly lose our lives for His sake, because we know that we will gain real life through our relationship with Him (Matt. 10:39).

This chapter is about offering our lives to Him and being willing to pay the price to have the golden thread of worship woven into our lives.

[1] *Gettysburg,* Ronald F. Maxwell, New Line Cinema, 1993.

THE MARRIAGE METAPHOR

We must consider two aspects of the marriage metaphor that relate to this chapter. They are the concept of humble submission and the willingness to suffer. These two often go hand in hand.

We sometimes joke about a groom's taking on a ball and chain, portraying marriage as bondage. Such a caricature has a bit of truth to it. Although marriage is not supposed to be a burden, we are bound to our spouses because marriage is a surrender of individual rights. *My* money and *hers* become *our* money. *My* future and *hers* become *our* future.

This mutual subordination is a commitment to stick with each other regardless of what happens: "for better or for worse, in sickness and in health, for richer or poorer, till death do us part." It is a commitment to persevere through the good times and the bad. It is not about the blessings and benefits of marriage. It is about becoming one. And there is a cost.

I have heard that the Chinese word for "crisis" is made up of two characters, one representing problem and the other, opportunity. Every crisis we face in our marriages is both a problem and an opportunity for growth. The difficulties we face are like dynamite; they can do a great deal of good or they can destroy the relationship.

Every marriage relationship faces difficulties from within and without. Many people run from their problems instead of persevering and, as a result, have not experienced the richness of true and enduring love. There are many reasons for broken marriages, but often it is simply that one or the other did not count the cost before entering into the relationship. The price to preserve the bond was higher than he or she was willing to pay.

In our own experience, we have enjoyed God's blessing not only in preserving our marriage but also enriching it, because we both were willing to pay the price and persevere. For example, when our new church was starting, I became so absorbed in the ministry that I neglected my family. My wife persevered and remained loyal. Eventually, through a humbling experience in my own life, I began to change, and the change strengthened our relationship. It was not merely my willingness to change, but Lisa's sacrificial perseverance that preserved and deepened our marriage.

Our marriage was greatly enriched on two occasions when Lisa and I were separated for more than two weeks when she traveled to be with her parents because her mother was critically ill. Those difficult times strengthened our marriage. Although we were separated and in different hemispheres, we were together in spirit, and I suffered with her during the subsequent funeral.

In addition, we have had moments of crisis where we had to ask forgiveness for hurtful things. Rather than separating us, those moments drew us together. We have persevered and our marriage is stronger than ever.

How does this compare with our relationship with God? First, worship involves humble submission, a surrender of our rights to Him. We are giving up our individuality and personal comfort to become one with Him.

Second, God allows us to go through difficulties to build our character and to draw us closer to Him. Our worship is enriched through the difficulties we face. As Paul invited Timothy, so God invites us to "suffer hardship"[2] for Him and for the sake of the gospel.

WHAT IS SUBMISSION?

Submission to God is pictured in bowing before Him. The practice of physically bowing before God is not too common among Christians in North America, perhaps as a reaction against the ritual prayers of worshipers in other faiths. Bowing was practiced extensively, however, in Bible times to show submission to someone superior, such as Joseph's brothers bowing before him (Gen.44:14) and in recognition of God as the one true Sovereign Lord (Rom. 14:11; Phil 2:10).

Bowing, whether literally or metaphorically, is how we offer ourselves to God. It implies we are humbly submissive to His will and direction for our lives. Everything is subordinated to our relationship with Him.

Commenting on Romans 12:1, MacArthur says, "The living sacrifice we are to offer to the Lord who died for us is the willing-

---

[2] Paul twice invites Timothy to join with him in paying the price for the gospel (2 Tim 1:8 and 2:3). He uses the compound word, "*sunkakopathéō*" which is rather strong. *Sun* – together with someone. *Kako* – harm that is caused by evil intent. *Pathéō* – to suffer.

ness to surrender to Him all our hopes, plans, and everything that is precious to us, all that is humanly important to us, all that we find fulfilling. Like Paul, we should in that sense 'die daily' (1 Cor. 15:31), because for us 'to live is Christ' (Phil. 1:21)."[3]

Since the fall of Adam and Eve, who were enticed by a desire to be "like God," humans have attempted to usurp God's authority, refusing to submit to Him. Worship, then, can be seen as a surrender of any claim to personal deity we might think we have.

However, beholding God causes us to bow our hearts before Him, recognizing that He alone is Lord, even during times of suffering. It is not a one-time action, but a continuous, progressive attitude. We place our rights, our reputation, our comfort, our possessions, our relationships, our ministries, our time, and our lives at His disposal. This can be done only if we truly believe and trust Him.

PRESENTING OURSELVES TO GOD

…To present your bodies a living and holy sacrifice, acceptable to God, which is your spiritual service of worship.

The word used for presenting our bodies is the same word used for the Old Testament sacrifices, of placing an animal on the altar before the Lord. Some of those sacrifices were for sins while others represented communion between God and His children, like sharing a meal with someone you love. Whatever kinds of sacrifices were offered, they were always dead.

Our offerings, however, are to be *"living."* The problem with a living sacrifice, obviously, is it keeps crawling off the altar. That is why it is not a one-time action, but a moment-by-moment offering of our outward members, not for our own gratification, but for His satisfaction.[4]

Real offerings are voluntary, but not optional. After contemplating what God has done for us, we should desire to offer ourselves to Him. There is no other course of action or response. There should be no hesitation, but joy and peace at being able to make such an offering.

---

[3] MacArthur, NT *Commentary: Romans 9-16,* p. 146.
[4] Although Paul uses an aorist imperative in Romans 12:1, perhaps indicating a complete action, the fact that it is a *living* sacrifice indicates it is a constant action. It is possibly an ingressive aorist in which it could be translated, "Begin offering your bodies as a living sacrifice…"

Romans 6 tells us when a person becomes a believer, the inner man is offered to God, crucified with Christ, buried, and raised a new person. We live in the same bodies, however, that continue to have fleshly desires and cravings for gratification. As believers, we offer up our body's members as an act of worship to be used by Him (see Rom. 6:13).

Our offerings are to be *"holy,"* separate from the corrupt practices that surround us. Our goal is to reflect the character of God.

Our offering is to be *"acceptable to God,"* well pleasing to Him and, at the same time, very satisfying to us. We strive to live acceptably to Him. MacArthur writes, "A key adjective, often used in the New Testament to describe proper acts of worship, is the word *acceptable*. Every worshiper seeks to offer that which is acceptable"[5] (emphasis original).

Our offering is a *"spiritual service of worship."* This again reinforces the idea that worship is "in spirit" and should not be contingent upon outward circumstances. It must flow out of our inward communion with God. [6]

Bowing ourselves before God does not come naturally, but is a work of God in our lives. Spurgeon said, "Until divinely effectual grace shall work such worship in a man's heart, it is obnoxious to Him. He will worship God with robes, and incense, and flowers, and banners, but he will not consent to worship him in spirit and truth."[7]

One of the paradoxes of salvation is that it is a free gift (Eph. 2:8-9), while at the same time, it costs us our lives (Luke 9:24). It is free in that there is no merit on our part that has earned it. Nothing we can do, say, or seek deserves eternal life. However, it costs our lives because we are no longer our own. Our lives will never be the same; they will be radically transformed.

---

[5] MacArthur, *Ultimate Priority,* p.14.

[6] Some try to make the Greek word "logízomai" equivalent to "logic." While it is true that the logical response to what God has done is to offer ourselves, the word indicates that it is spiritual, rather than physical.

[7] C. H. Spurgeon, sermon, *"The Axe at the Root – A Testimony Against Puseyite Idolatry,"*

COUNTING THE COST

Now large crowds were going along with Him; and He turned and said to them, "If anyone comes to Me, and does not hate his own father and mother and wife and children and brothers and sisters, yes, and even his own life, he cannot be My disciple. Whoever does not carry his own cross and come after Me cannot be My disciple. For which one of you, when he wants to build a tower, does not first sit down and calculate the cost to see if he has enough to complete it? Otherwise, when he has laid a foundation, and is not able to finish, all who observe it begin to ridicule him, saying, 'This man began to build and was not able to finish.' Or what king, when he sets out to meet another king in battle, will not first sit down and consider whether he is strong enough with ten thousand men to encounter the one coming against him with twenty thousand? Or else, while the other is still far away, he sends a delegation and asks terms of peace. So then, none of you can be My disciple who does not give up all his own possessions" (Luke 14:25-33).

Jesus knew that most of the people following Him that day were not seriously interested in entering into a relationship with Him. He challenged them by saying that if they did not hold intimacy with Him as being infinitely more important than the most intimate of human relationships, they could not be His disciples.

Reflecting on the strong language Jesus uses, MacArthur asks a rhetorical question, "Why is the language so severe?" He answers, "Because He is eager to chase the uncommitted away and to draw true disciples to Himself."[8]

Jesus told them if intimacy with Him were not more important than suffering and even their own lives, they could not be His disciples. To take up one's cross means that one is willing to die. In other words, being close to Jesus is more important than life itself.

Some have tried to make this level of commitment optional by saying that this is a step beyond salvation called "discipleship," because it seems to contradict salvation as a free gift. However, Jesus

[8] MacArthur, *Gospel According to Jesus,* p. 201.

is discussing the attitude that a person has when he comes to Him. It is not a meritorious work to earn salvation.

MacArthur says,

> Thus in a sense we pay the ultimate price for salvation when our sinful self is nailed to a cross. It is a total abandonment of self-will, like the grain of wheat that falls to the ground and dies so that it can bear much fruit (cf. John 12:24). It is an exchange of all that we are for all that Christ is. And it denotes implicit obedience, full surrender to the lordship of Christ. Nothing less can qualify as saving faith.[9]

Sitting down implies that we take time to reflect on what is really important to us. Because of the high commitment Jesus requires, He asked those who wished to follow Him to consider the cost. Are we really willing to give up everything for intimacy with Him? Are we ready to say with Paul, "…I count all things to be loss in view of the surpassing value of knowing Christ Jesus my Lord, for whom I have suffered the loss of all things, and count them but rubbish so that I may gain Christ…"? (Phil. 3:8).

Jesus closes the passage saying that it is impossible to become His disciple if one does not give up[10] all his possessions. We won't necessarily give up everything, but there certainly needs to be a placing of everything at His disposal.

MacArthur says, "That consuming, selfless desire to give to God is the essence and heart of worship. It begins with giving first of ourselves, and then of our attitudes, and then of our possessions—until worship is a way of life."[11]

God does not promise an easy road, but it is the path to real joy and peace. It is not necessarily going to be a lifetime of suffering and hardships either. That is for Him to decide. However, we must be willing to place everything before Him, offering our bodies as a living sacrifice, not just once, but daily.

---

[9] Ibid., p.140.
[10] *Apotássō* in the Greek means to renounce or take leave of something. It can even mean to say farewell.
[11] MacArthur, *Ultimate Priority,* p.14.

SUFFERING AND PERSECUTION

I have never experienced physical persecution as so many of our brothers and sisters in various parts of the world have. However, I have experienced the hurt of being judged unfairly by my brothers in Christ. As David said, "For it is not an enemy who reproaches me, Then I could bear it; Nor is it one who hates me who has exalted himself against me, Then I could hide myself from him. But it is you, a man my equal, My companion and my familiar friend; We who had sweet fellowship together, Walked in the house of God in the throng" (Ps. 55:12-14).

When we started our first church in Belém, we did not want to start just another church, but a spiritual family that was committed to seeking intimacy with God through His Word. Since we did things a little differently, we were misunderstood and criticized severely by people within our own fellowship of churches. I lost some good friends during those years.

Some of it was because of my own insensitivity in how I described what was happening, because I was so enthusiastic about what God was doing among us. However, what happened was allowed by God to help change my life. Although there are still some who criticize us, most of that is behind us now. It was during those difficulties, however, that God taught us more about the gospel, the church, and worship than we could have learned any other way.

As mentioned in chapter 1, "godliness" is a very important word to me. I was teaching a class on First Timothy in 1994, which led to some big changes in our ministry. In his day, Timothy was facing a crisis and no doubt questioned his own leadership. Paul wrote to encourage him and described some of the characteristics of a leader.

Godliness is a key in this book. It is a translation of *eusebeia,* which we discussed in chapter 3. *Eu* means "good" and *sebeia* means "to be in awe or fear" of someone. It is a worship term, but it implies that those attitudes carry over into what we do. Paul told Timothy that he should discipline himself to strive for godliness (1 Tim. 4:7-8, 10). It is beneficial (1 Tim. 6:6) and is to be one of our key pursuits (1 Tim. 6:11). It seems the effectiveness of Timothy as a leader depended on his being godly.

Because Paul emphasized it, I started praying daily for godliness in my life. I sought out the characteristics of *godliness* in Proverbs and prayed that God would build them into my life. While preparing for the class, I studied a verse and said a prayer that changed my life. "And indeed, all who desire to live godly (*eusebeia*) in Christ Jesus will be persecuted" (2 Tim.3:12).

As I examined my life before God in the light of His Word, I found I wasn't anywhere near the biblical standard of *godliness*. I told God that the lack of persecution in my life was evidence that I was not *godly*.

In one of those rare moments, God's Spirit spoke to my heart so clearly, "Bruce, you didn't understand the verse. Study some more." I then realized that it doesn't say, "all those who are godly will be persecuted." It says, "All those *who desire to live godly* will be persecuted." Then I sensed God challenging me, "You have been praying for it, do you *really* want it?" Well, sure I did.

I didn't know what I was asking for. I was as ignorant as James and John (Matt. 20:20-28).

Almost immediately, I was blindsided. A young man whom I had been trying to help started spreading rumors about me. Another person turned one of my best friends and key disciples against me. A number of other problems arose, too. Everything hit at once.

At my lowest point, I was alone in my office and a tape of a Keith Green song, "Trials Turned to Gold," was playing. The words to the song described exactly what was in my heart, giving me a divine perspective on what I was going through. It was as if the song were written just for me.

By the end of the song, I was weeping and rejoicing before the Lord. I was seeing God's hand in all that happened and knew He was drawing me closer to Himself through it. I learned so much about worship through that experience. I learned how to offer my life to Him. It is not fatalism, but the sweet experience of seeing His loving hand in what seems so undesirable.

Piper wrote, "A life devoted to making much of Christ is costly."[12]

Our willingness to step out has led to the beginning of a church-planting movement that didn't seem possible a couple of years before. More importantly in the divine scheme of things, these difficulties

---

[12] Piper, *Don't Waste Your Life*, p. 63.

put me on a course that has deepened my worship of God. The times of greatest growth have been through the hard times.

Godliness and an intimacy with God do not come from taking the easy route. They can become real to us only on the narrow road of difficulties and suffering. It is obvious that the seven-fold praise of the martyred saints from the tribulation is unique to them because of the persecution and their redemption (Rev. 7:12-17). The Lord will be so precious to them and heaven so sweet because of what they went through.

WHAT IS SUFFERING?

Is it God's will for Christians to suffer? Like most Christians, I had unconsciously bought into the idea that God wants us to be happy and that things generally get better after you become a Christian. I had no idea that the Bible calls us to suffering to deepen our walk with God. After taking the plunge and allowing God to do His will in my life, I discovered so much in the Bible about suffering that I wondered how I could have missed it for so long.

Piper points out, "Suffering with Jesus on the Calvary road of love is not merely the *result* of magnifying Christ; it is also the *means*…His beauty shines most brightly when treasured above health and wealth and life itself."[13]

TYPES OF SUFFERING

Suffering can take a lot of forms. Many words are used to define the difficulties we face. Romans 8 describes suffering and its role in our lives. Each word builds progressively on the word before it.

Sufferings (v. 18)

Notice that Paul uses a plural form of the word. There are multiple sufferings of all different sorts. This word is usually associated with physical pain that comes on those who belong to Christ.[14] In the Scriptures it doesn't refer to the normal difficulties of this life, but is linked with what happens to us because of Christ.

---

[13] Ibid., p. 61.
[14] *Páthemā* from which we get the word "pathology." It means "that which is endured or befalls someone."

Tribulation (v. 35)

This word usually refers to difficult outward circumstances that befall someone.[15] It can be used for something as extreme as the great tribulation (Matt. 24:21) or as simple as the difficulties people face in their marriages (1 Cor. 7:28).

Distress (v. 35)

This word refers to the inner anguish caused by outer circumstances.[16]

Persecution (v. 35)

Generally, this describes religious persecution. It means to "run after." We might equate it to "being hounded."

Famine (v. 35)

This does not refer just to simple poverty, but to the hunger that results from losing one's means of support because of persecution.

Nakedness (v. 35)

The person has lost everything, including clothing and shelter, and is in deep need.

Peril (v. 35)

Threats of violence are made against those who follow Christ.

The Sword (v. 35)

This refers to a short sword. It is no longer just a threat of being killed, but the person has actually suffered the violent death of a martyr.

There are varying degrees of intensity in each type of suffering. This is reflected in the progressively stronger rhetorical questions that Paul asks –

"Who can be against us?" (v. 31).
"Who will bring a charge against God's elect?" (v. 33).

---

[15] *Thlipsis, which* means "pressure, oppression" or "affliction."
[16] *Stenochōría* literally means "narrowness" or "pressure caused by inner anguish."

"Who is the one who condemns?" (v. 34).

"Who will separate us from the love of Christ?" (v. 35).

The obvious answer is "No one."

We know that He is with us, but His presence becomes very real during the hard times. We may lose everything, but we will never lose the love of Christ, and He is all we really need.

Josef Tson is a Romanian pastor who suffered for the gospel and was exiled to the United States. He addressed my seminary class during missions week. He wrote the Greek word, *marturos* on the board. He said in his strong accent, "I don't know much Greek, but I do know this word." He explained that it meant to "bear witness" and soon became synonymous with giving one's life for that witness, giving rise to the modern word, "martyr."

He had left Romania on a four-day pass and ended up going to seminary for three years in England. While there, he studied this word and its historical context. He learned that the early Christians considered it an honor to die for the Lord. As they took Christians away, people would come out and say, "Take me, too. I am also a Christian." It became such an honor that the church fathers had to declare that martyrdom was not valid if it was sought.

The early Christians' willingness to pay a price for their faith led Josef Tson to return to Romania while it was still under the repressive communist regime. At first, he tried to walk a fine line and not rile the secret police who listened to his preaching. He then decided that he needed to please the Lord and not men. That is when he started paying a price and God started blessing his ministry.

He was regularly taken from his home and beaten. Tson said, "When the secret police officer threatened to kill me, to shoot me, I smiled and I said, 'Sir, don't you understand that when you kill me you send me to glory? You cannot threaten me with glory.' The more suffering, the more troubles, the greater the glory. So, why say, 'Stop this trouble'? Because the more [suffering], the greater the glory up there."

During one particularly harrowing session of interrogation, Tson told his inquisitors that spilling his blood would serve only to water the growth of the gospel of Jesus Christ. Part of the theology of suffering, he learned, was that tribulation is never an accident but is part of God's sovereign plan for building His church.

"I told the interrogator, 'You should know your supreme weapon is killing. My supreme weapon is dying,'" Tson said.

Now here is how it works, sir: You know that my sermons are on tape all over the country. When you shoot me or crush me, whichever way you choose, [you] only sprinkle my sermons with my blood. Everybody who has a tape of one of my sermons will pick it up and say, 'I had better listen again. This man died for what he preached.' Sir, my sermons will speak 10 times louder after you kill me and because you kill me. In fact, I will conquer this country for God because you killed me. Go on and do it." [17]

The officer was taken back by his boldness.

I was amazed at this man's story and sensed that he was a worshiper of God and walked with Him as few men I had ever met. I talked to him briefly after class and found that he had insights into the gospel that few Christians have. Suffering had molded this man. The few minutes I spent with him impacted me deeply.

Suffering can take many forms, from the difficulties and heartbreaks of living in this fallen world to persecution for loving Jesus Christ. The Bible usually speaks of the latter, although God uses them all to build our character and to help us to see Him more clearly.

Our natural tendency is to avoid difficulty, but in reality, our submissive worship of God is what gives our life meaning and joy independent of our outward circumstances.

Piper says, "Untold numbers of professing Christians waste their lives trying to escape the cost of love. They do not see that it is always worth it. More of God's glory can be seen and savored through suffering than through self-serving escape."

THE CERTAINTY OF SUFFERING

A slave is not greater than his master. If they persecuted Me, they will also persecute you (John 15:20).

---

[17] Jeff Robinson, "Romanian Josef Tson recounts God's Grace Amid Suffering."

Some suffering is because of sin or because of our own mistakes. Peter says, "Make sure that none of you suffers as a murderer, or thief, or evildoer, or a troublesome meddler…" (1 Pet. 4:15; cf. 2:20). Some suffering is just the result of living in a fallen world. However, the suffering that the Bible describes results from being Christians (1 Pet. 4:14,16) or doing what is right (1 Pet. 2:20; 3:14).

God permits our suffering so that we can become like Jesus. His Word has transformed our lives to the point that we no longer belong to the world system. The stark contrast between our lives and those in the world creates a tension. "I have given them Your word; and the world has hated them, because they are not of the world, even as I am not of the world" (John 17:14). To them it is strange that we don't run after the same things they do (1 Pet. 4:4).

Paul regularly warned the believers they would suffer. He wrote, "For indeed when we were with you, we kept telling you in advance that we were going to suffer affliction; and so it came to pass, as you know" (1 Thess. 3:4). He added that suffering should not discourage them because, "you yourselves know that we have been destined for this" (v. 3).[18]

After his first missionary journey, Paul went back to visit the churches he had founded, "encouraging them to continue in the faith, and saying, 'Through many tribulations we must enter the kingdom of God'" (Acts 14:22). In other words, expect suffering, because it is necessary for your spiritual growth. It should not come as a surprise (1 Pet. 4:12). It is part of God's plan and is not an accident, or unfair, or bad luck. A worshiper learns to see God's purpose and mercy in suffering and gains a completely different perspective.

THE PRIVILEGE OF SUFFERING

Jesus said in Matthew 5:10-12,

> Blessed are those who have been persecuted for the sake of righteousness, for theirs is the kingdom of heaven. Blessed are you when people insult you and persecute you, and falsely

---

[18] It is possible that Paul is saying that they, like the apostles, had been appointed for suffering? In light of what he said about the Thessalonians' suffering (1 Thess. 1:6, 2:14) and the fact that he was trying to encourage them, it seems best to take the "we" as referring to all Christians.

say all kinds of evil against you because of Me. Rejoice and be glad, for your reward in heaven is great; for in the same way they persecuted the prophets who were before you.

"Blessed" means to be happy because you have received a divine privilege. Serving the Lord is difficult when people say things against you falsely. You lose the divine perspective and start looking at the ignorance and evil of men. You try to defend yourself against the false attacks instead of rejoicing.

The apostles learned the importance of suffering and often quoted what Jesus had taught them (1 Pet. 3:14; James 1:2). Paul's statement in Philippians 1:29 is mind-blowing. "For to you it has been granted for Christ's sake, not only to believe in Him, but also to suffer for His sake." We like to think of God granting us heaven, not suffering.

The disciples took to heart Jesus' instruction about persecution. When they were accused falsely, they prayed, not for deliverance, but for strength to face what God had sovereignly brought their way (Acts 4:24-30). They addressed Him as a sovereign Lord.[19] They called Him the Creator of everything, emphasizing His absolute control over everything. As a matter of fact, persecution was prophesied (Acts 4:25-26). Even Jesus went through unfair persecution (v. 27). Why should we expect anything different? It all happened according to "whatever Your hand [sovereign] and Your purpose [sovereign] predestined to occur [sovereign]" (v. 28).

That is why in Acts 5, after being unfairly flogged, the disciples went out high-fiving each other, "rejoicing that they had been considered worthy to suffer shame for His name" (Acts 5:41). They considered it a privilege to suffer for Christ. Only worshipers can respond in that way.

Madame Guyon says, "As soon as anything comes to you in the form of suffering, at that very moment a natural resistance will well up somewhere inside you. When that moment comes, immediately

---

[19] Paul uses "Lord" not with the usual *Kúrios*, but with *Despótēs*, an absolute sovereign.

resign yourself to God. *Accept the matter*. In that moment give yourself up to Him as a sacrifice"[20] (emphasis original).

Piper wrote, "Whatever makes us more and more able to enjoy making much of God is a mercy. For there is no greater joy than joy in the greatness of God. And if we must suffer to see this and savor it most deeply, then suffering is a mercy."[21]

THE RESULT OF SUFFERING

Consider it all joy, my brethren, when you encounter various trials, knowing that the testing of your faith produces endurance. And let endurance have its perfect result, so that you may be perfect and complete, lacking in nothing (James 1:2-4).

It seems strange that James should tell us that suffering should be considered a motive for being joyful. Paul not only tells us we should rejoice in the hope of the future, but we also should rejoice in our current difficulties (Rom. 5:3). Jesus commands that we "rejoice and be glad" because of ill treatment (Matt. 5:12).

It is not the suffering itself that is the reason we are to rejoice, but the result that it produces within us. James explains that suffering produces *endurance*. The word means literally to "remain under,"[22] that is, we don't flee difficult circumstances (cf. Rom 5). We remain firm. But the development of perseverance is also not the reason we should rejoice. There is a much deeper cause.

James says that as a result of endurance, we will grow in becoming "perfect and complete, lacking in nothing" (James 1:4). Paul says that perseverance produces "proven character" (Rom. 5:4). That means our character is developed and shown to be genuine. The character of worship (faith, hope, and love) is strengthened through suffering.

Rick Warren says, "Pain is the fuel of passion—it energizes us with an intensity to change that we don't normally possess. C.S. Lewis said, 'Pain is God's megaphone.' It is God's way of arousing us from spiritual lethargy. Your problems are not punishment; they are wake up calls from a loving God."[23]

---

[20] Guyon, p. 38.
[21] Piper, *Don't Waste Your Life*, p. 62.
[22] *Hupoménō* in Greek.
[23] Warren, *Purpose Driven Life*, p. 98.

Piper writes,

> What a tragic waste when people turn away from the Calvary
> road of love and suffering. All the riches of the glory of God
> in Christ are on that road. All the sweetest fellowship with
> Jesus is there... Take up your cross and follow Jesus. On this
> road and this road alone, life is Christ and death is gain. Life
> on every other road is wasted.[24]

THE FRUIT OF SUFFERING

> *But even if you should suffer for the sake of righteousness, you
> are blessed. And do not fear their intimidation, and do not
> be troubled, but sanctify Christ as Lord in your hearts, always
> being ready to make a defense to every one who asks you to give
> an account for the hope that is in you, yet with gentleness and
> reverence* (1 Pet. 3:14-15).

Peter repeats the blessing on those who suffer with the same words
Jesus used in the Beatitudes. He tells them literally not to fear their
fear. In other words, they are not to fear the threats their persecutors
imagine will create fear in them, because it is what they dread. Instead
they are to fear or "sanctify" Christ as Lord in their hearts.

People who threaten us will be surprised that we are not intimi-
dated by their greatest fears. It is because our hope is not here, but in
Christ. This difference will lead to opportunities to explain to others
the hope that is in us.

On Christmas day, the "fruitful fruit stand" in Brazil usually has
its best day of business. The thieves know that, too, and were waiting for Luis and his wife Fátima one Christmas when they returned
home from work. As the thieves were cleaning them out, Fátima was
lovingly sharing her faith with the robbers. They finally put tape over
her mouth to shut her up.

I don't know what happened to the culprits, but I know seeds
were planted. Although being held at gunpoint shook them up, Luis
and Fátima's peace and joy were an incredible testimony.

When things are going well, it is easy to believe in God. It is
during our darkest moments that the light of Christ shines brightest

---

[24] Piper, *Don't Waste Your Life,* p. 76

in our lives. When we face difficulties, injustices, and even death with hope and joy, people can see a difference.

Speaking about the end times, Jesus said, "They will deliver you to the courts, and you will be flogged in the synagogues, and you will stand before governors and kings for My sake, as a testimony to them" (Mark 13:9). Such persecution will provide an opportunity to share the gospel with people who would not otherwise hear it.

Paul testified, "My imprisonment in the cause of Christ has become well known through the whole praetorian guard and to everyone else." He also added that his response has given "far more courage to speak the word of God" (Phil. 1:13-14). That is why Paul was so full of joy as he wrote the letter from prison.

Piper writes, "When we embrace with joy the cost of following Christ, his worth will shine in the world. The cost itself will become a means of making Christ look great."[25]

Why did the thief on the cross next to Jesus say, "Jesus, remember me when You come in Your kingdom!"? (Luke 23:42). He had been railing at Christ with the other thief earlier (Mark 15:32), but He saw the way Jesus was facing death, and his life was dramatically changed.

Why did the centurion who crucified Jesus with no remorse later say, "Truly this man was the Son of God!"? (Mark 15:39). He had seen hundreds of people die, but none died like Jesus. Instead of desperation, bitterness, and hatred, He showed love and peace.

How did Stephen's death impact Paul, when he said, "Lord, do not hold this sin against them" (Acts 7:60) as he was dying? It is hard to believe that Paul was not in some way shaken by the prayer Stephen offered.

How do you handle opposition? Do people see what you value most through the difficulties you face?

THE FRUIT OF SUBMITTING TO THE LORD

No story stirs the heart of Grace Brethren missionaries more than the story of a Philadelphia streetcar conductor who opened up the heart

---

[25] Ibid. p. 63.

of Africa for the gospel. James Gribble was a man with a passion for Christ who bowed before the Lord.

He wanted to be purified and used by the Lord. He was willing to pay the price. He wrote before going to Africa, "Oh God, purge me, and send me and put me always into the very thickest of the fight!"[26]

Disregarding his own life, he had a goal. He was willing to pay the price to serve the Lord. He also wrote, "My longings take me into a country where no missionary has ever been—and where none has ever wished to go."[27]

James Gribble knew that suffering was an important part of conforming him to the image of God. Once, he almost died of malaria. During his suffering he had an amazing encounter with the Lord. Although I am sure he would rather not have been sick, he recognized how God used this difficulty in his life. It gave him perseverance and a willingness to suffer further for the Lord.

He said, "And now, day by day, I know not where my path may lead—but I will follow on. I would not dwell on this illness, but I can never be too glad for this experience which brought me into such blessed fellowship with the Lord."[28]

The French government did not initially allow him into the region God had laid on his heart. He patiently waited for this approval during three years, camped with his team on a riverbank.

When he finally entered the targeted region, he served the Lord faithfully for two years before succumbing to a second bout of malaria. He gave his life in service to the Lord. Because of his sacrifice, there are more than 2,500 Grace Brethren churches in the Central African Republic. The gospel in that country has stood as a fortress against the southward advance of Islam in Africa. His sacrifice has borne much fruit.

What most impresses me is his perspective on suffering. James Gribble said, "God is not going to look us over for medals, degrees or diplomas, but for scars."

---

[26] Florence Gribble, *Undaunted Hope, the Life of James Gribble*, p. 36.
[27] Gribble, p. 7.
[28] Ibid. p. 38.

FAITH, HOPE, AND LOVE

It is important in the discussion of persecution and suffering to understand the centrality of character. To have character is to live consistently within God's principles despite the circumstances. The Bible calls this "wisdom" or the ability to act consistently with the Scriptures. Suffering is important in building character.

Character is more than do's or don'ts or what Piper calls "the avoidance ethic." As he says, "Avoiding fearful trouble and forbidden behaviors impresses almost no one. The avoidance ethic by itself is not commending or God-glorifying."[29]

What is glorifying to God is a life that reflects Christ's character. It is people who have bowed before the one true God instead of the modern gods of materialism, entertainment, comfort, and security. It is Christ's being "the pearl of great price" in our lives. Character has to do with what you most value and love.

Our goal in leadership training is to implant biblical culture and not just transplant biblical content. This means that values and character consistent with the Scriptures will become a part of the DNA of a person as he or she walks by the Spirit. Learned behaviors alone do not demonstrate character. Character has to flow from who one is.

It is important for a missionary to be able to observe cultural forms and cultural values and distinguish between them. The forms include dress, social customs, and language. These aspects are very apparent to a first-time visitor.

Cultural values explain why people behave as they do. We need to find out what each culture holds as its highest values. Some cultures place a much higher value on preserving relationships than on completing a task. One group may conclude that the other culture is uncaring or indifferent while the second group will label people from the other culture as unproductive and inefficient.

Every people group has a few core values that pervade its thinking.

For example, freedom is a very strong American value. Many have died to preserve it. It is in our veins. It even shapes how we preach the

---

[29] Piper, *Don't Waste Your Life*, p. 118.

gospel and how we do church. But not everyone in the world places such a high premium on freedom.

From an informal survey of friends who live in diverse parts of the world, I have found core values of honor, security, and happiness. These cultural lenses may create blind spots as we begin to be exposed to biblical truth.

Whatever the pervading cultural values, the gospel enters into conflict with many of these values and their resulting customs in virtually every part of the world. In many parts of the world, unfortunately, people retain their core cultural values when they become believers, so there is no change in their worldview. Consequently, in difficult times, they don't live consistently with what they now profess as Christians. That is why many "fall away" when faced with difficult times. There is no conviction and no willingness to pay the price.[30]

> WHEN A PERSON BECOMES A CHRISTIAN,
> LOVE BECOMES THE HIGHEST VALUE—
> LOVE FOR GOD AND LOVE FOR HIS FELLOW CHRISTIANS.
> LOVE AS A CORE VALUE IS
> THE ESSENCE OF CHRISTIAN CHARACTER.

The three core biblical values are *faith, hope, and love.* As we worship God in our walk through life, He desires to build these qualities into our beings (1 Cor. 13:13, Col. 1:4-5). These are the foundation of a God-honoring character and can be found only in a person who is a genuine worshiper.

Paul was thankful for the Thessalonians because they gave evidence of true conversion. Paul was aware of their "work of faith and labor of love and steadfastness of hope in our Lord Jesus Christ" (1 Thess. 1:3). The Word had powerfully transformed them (v. 5). Their example of character was making an impact around the world (vv. 7-8).

All this happened because they had become worshipers of God: "For they themselves report about us what kind of a reception we had

---

[30] When there is no change of values or worldview, there is no conversion. These people do not lose their salvation because they were never delivered out of the world system in which they lived (see 1 John 2:19).

with you, and how you turned to God from idols to serve a living and true God" (v. 9).

The Thessalonian church was a persecuted church, "Having received the word in much tribulation with the joy of the Holy Spirit" (v. 6). Their worship affected how they received the persecution, which in turn affected the way they worshiped God. Their character, their worship, their response, and the persecution were all interrelated. Their response to their circumstances showed that their core values had been transformed and their faith was real.

Persecution and difficulties not only strengthen our values, but also they show they are genuine.

HOPE, PERSEVERANCE, AND SUFFERING

The key value that helped the Thessalonians persevere was *hope*. There are numerous messages and books on faith and love, but very few about hope. It is similar to faith, but, instead of being directed toward the affirmations in the Scriptures, describing past or present realities, hope is a certainty of a better future based on the promises of Scripture.

A few years ago, Ohio State played Arizona State in the Rose Bowl. I hadn't seen the game, but I learned that OSU had scored the winning touchdown with 19 seconds left. I was now certain of the outcome. A few weeks later, I watched a videotape of the game. When Arizona State went ahead with less than two minutes left, I was not anxious, because I was certain of the final score. I knew my team was going to win even though I had not seen the final seconds tick off.

Reading the prophetic passages of the Bible is almost like being able to check the final scores on the Internet before seeing the game. The future the Bible talks about is just as certain as a past event.

Hope is a confident conviction of what God has declared about our future relationship with Him. This hope helps us persevere when difficulties come. Because we have *faith* in the Scriptures, we know the end of the story. Our *hope* in a better future is not just wishful thinking, but a certainty. We know Jesus will defeat His enemies and we will enjoy an unprecedented depth of worship in His presence for all eternity.

DEFINING HOPE

The Portuguese word for hope (esperança) is similar to the Hebrew word in that it carries the ideas of hope and expectant waiting. We know there will be a better future and we are expectantly waiting for it. Romans 8 gives one of the best definitions.

And not only this, but also we ourselves, having the first fruits of the Spirit, even we ourselves groan within ourselves, waiting eagerly for our adoption as sons, the redemption of our body. For in hope we have been saved, but hope that is seen is not hope; for who hopes for what he already sees? But if we hope for what we do not see, with perseverance we wait eagerly for it (Rom. 8:23-25).

First, the Spirit's presence in our lives is the first fruits of what we will ultimately receive. The joy and worship we now experience is just an appetizer for eternity.

Second, our groaning is not desperate, but rather a longing for His presence and the anticipation of perfect fellowship with Him.

Third, we are aware there is more, so we are "stretching out our necks,"[31] eagerly looking for that day when our bodies are redeemed and we are able to worship Him fully.

Fourth, hope produces perseverance and perseverance produces hope. I can put up with almost anything if I know that something better awaits me. By looking forward to being with God, my hope is not shaken by the ups and downs of this world.

I have run four marathons. Each time I reached the 20-mile point, my whole body cried out to stop. But I fixed my mind on the finish line and kept running. If there had been no finish line, I probably would have quit much sooner. My hope in receiving a cheap medal, a cheap shirt, a can of Coca-Cola, and finally being able to rest helped me persevere to the end.

Finally, hope fixes our minds on the ultimate purpose of suffering: to become more like Jesus. Romans 8:28 is ultimately a verse about hope.

---

[31] *Apokaradokía* in the Greek. This compound word means to stretch one's head out expectantly watching for something.

And we know that God causes all things to work together for good to those who love God, to those who are called according to His purpose. For whom He foreknew, He also predestined to become conformed to the image of His Son, so that He would be the firstborn among many brethren (Rom. 8:28-29).

The "good" in this verse is not my comfort or well being. Everything that happens to me is designed by God to make me like Jesus, and, therefore, everything will "work together for good." Jesus is the prototype among many brethren.[32] Someone said that God's ultimate purpose is to fill heaven with worshipers who are just like His Son.

HOPE AND WORSHIP

Hope is ultimately about worship. Some people seem to think that heaven is the ultimate resort where we will be sitting around drinking lemonades under the palm trees for eternity. However, instead of comfort, our hope is in our deepening worship of God now, and our perfect communion with Him in heaven.

This life is a preparation for eternity. If my joy and my goal are to worship God, to give Him pleasure, and to have fellowship with Him in this life, then eternity is going to be beyond my wildest expectations. Now, I can see only "in a mirror dimly, but then face to face" (1 Cor. 13:12). If, however, I do not long for true worship here, heaven will not be nearly so marvelous.

I can't wait for the day that Revelation 4 becomes a reality. In the previous chapters of Revelation, God promised rewards to the overcomers. They are the people who endured the difficulties of this life because of their faith, hope, and love. The 24 elders are representatives of the church. Put yourself in the place of one of those elders sitting on your throne before God. The scene is overwhelming because of the presence of the Triune God on His throne along with the crystal sea and the angels.

Suddenly, the four living creatures worship as they have from all eternity, singing the same song that Isaiah heard, *"Holy, Holy, Holy is the Lord God, The Almighty."*

---

[32] This is what being the firstborn among many brethren means.

Then it is going to dawn on us that the rewards we have received were for things God did through us. Everything *we* did in our strength will have been burned up (1 Cor. 3:15). The irony is that anything of value we do in this life is ultimately done by God through us as a result of worship.

At that point, we will deposit our rewards before Him, and say, "Lord, we don't deserve this because You alone are worthy to receive glory and honor and power. You did everything and made everything, including us and the good works for which you have rewarded us, for Your glory" (Rev. 4:11, author's paraphrase).

What a tremendous act of worship that will be! I can't wait. At that point we will truly be bowing before Him in every sense of the word.

Personal Testimony

When I was going through tough times, I questioned myself before the Lord. I asked myself what I had done to contribute to the problem. I was able to see the flesh in my life. I recognized my weaknesses and sins. I became more dependent on God because so much was out of my control. I couldn't even defend myself. Prayer became more important, and I cast myself upon the mercy of God.

Although those times were difficult, they were joyful. God's presence was real. I know I would not be where I am today spiritually if not for those times. God used them to shape me. I'm sure there are more such things to come because there are many areas God still needs to change in my life.

Persecution also opened new opportunities for ministry. People saw my reaction to the criticism and noted a difference in the way I responded. All this has been key in starting a new church-planting movement. Some people came to understand that our strategy was not so much a form or a different way of practicing Christianity, but a worship life-attitude. It is a Christianity that is a total submission of ourselves to worship and serve God. When someone is willing to pay the price for what he or she believes, then it becomes apparent that it is more than just a belief. It is a conviction.

CONCLUSION

I certainly don't want to give the impression that offering ourselves to God brings only suffering. It is not all suffering. In chapter 8, we will talk about the pleasure and joy involved in worship. However, when we offer ourselves to God, we must be ready and willing for Him to do as He pleases to develop us as worshipers. Sometimes it hurts. "Weeping may last for the night, But a shout of joy comes in the morning" (Ps. 30:5).

Paul said that persecution and difficulties happened to him and his companions "so that we would not trust in ourselves, but in God who raises the dead" (2 Cor. 1:9). Persecution has a way of weaning us from ourselves. We fall on our faces in humility and we worship the God on whom we depend.

Jesus asked His disciples if they were willing to pay the price to drink of the cup from which He was about to drink (Matt. 10:38-39). God is posing the same question to us.

Worship involves letting go of our rights and comfort and allowing God to work in our lives. To develop us as worshipers of the Lord, God must wean us away from ourselves and bring us into humble dependence upon Him. When you think you have made a sacrifice for God, you discover that it really wasn't a sacrifice. The benefits far outweigh anything we may have given up.

THE PARADIGM SHIFT

The biggest paradigm shift in this chapter is that, while we shouldn't seek persecution, we can definitely expect it. Our goal in life should never be the easy road. With the divine perspective of God's sovereignty, we learn to see His hand and worship Him in every circumstance. Difficulties and persecutions are God's instruments to change us. We need to allow Him to work in our lives as He sees fit.

SEEKING COMFORT	SEEKING GROWTH
1. FOCUS: This life	1. FOCUS: The next life
2. GOAL: Comfort and happiness that comes from this world	2. GOAL: Growth and intimacy with God while living in the world
3. RESULT: Complacency	3. RESULT: • Hope • Character • Worship

WHERE TO START

1. SEEK GODLINESS, WORSHIP, AND INTIMACY WITH GOD.
    We should never seek persecution or difficulties. We need to
    be willing, however, to allow God to do what He sees best in
    transforming our lives.

2. EXAMINE YOUR LIFE. List five unfortunate or tragic events that
    have shaped your life. Can you now see God's sovereign hand
    in allowing what happened so He could shape your character?
    Spend some time meditating on this and thanking Him for His
    sovereign plan for your life.

3. READ THE STORY OF JOSEPH (Gen 37-45). How do you see the
    sovereignty of God in this story? How would you have reacted?
    Why did Joseph keep a good attitude and not complain or take
    revenge? Ask God to give you the same peace and wisdom.

4. LOOK FOR GOD'S HAND IN EVERYTHING. It is easy to become
    upset over little things. We need to look for God's hand in ev-
    erything, including the things that don't seem to go right. Make
    a conscious effort this week to see God's hand in everything that
    does not go as you would have liked.

5. PRAY THROUGH THE GREAT WORSHIP PASSAGES OF THE BOOK
    OF REVELATION. Often we focus on prophetic details and miss
    the moments of intense worship by various groups in Revelation.
    *   Start by meditating on Christ's character (Rev. 1:12-18).
        Praise Him for His holiness.
    *   Place all your works before Him and declare His worth to
        Him (Rev. 4:11).
    *   Use the words of Rev. 5:9-14 to praise Him.
    *   Worship Him, using Rev. 7:10-12. Notice that those who
        suffered the most worshiped Him most intensely.

6. OFFER YOURSELF TO HIM. Pray, "God, I want to be a worshiper
    and walk with You. I am willing to pay the price to do that.
    Open my eyes to see what You are doing and allow me to be
    conformed to the image of Christ."

DISCUSSION QUESTIONS

1. How do we offer ourselves to God? What do we offer? How?

2. What does the Bible mean by suffering?

3. How does suffering produce spiritual growth? Give an example from your life.

4. How does suffering lead to worship?

5. Why are faith, hope, and love core values of the Christian life?

6. What is hope?

7. How does hope relate to perseverance?

8. What did Jesus teach about suffering?

9. How should we handle criticism in light of this chapter?

10. What are some of the positive results of suffering?

11. What is godliness?

12. Why do we tend to avoid suffering?

13. What is the most important truth you learned from this chapter?

Chapter 8

WORSHIP TRANSFORMS OUR LIVES

FORMING CHRIST'S CHARACTER IN US THROUGH WORSHIP

Therefore, I urge you, brethren, by the mercies of God, to present your bodies a living and holy sacrifice, acceptable to God, which is your spiritual service of worship. AND DO NOT BE CONFORMED TO THIS WORLD, BUT BE TRANSFORMED BY THE RENEWING OF YOUR MIND, *so that you may prove what the will of God is, that which is good and acceptable and perfect* (Romans 12:1-2).

SEED TRUTH: WORSHIP CONFORMS US TO THE IMAGE OF GOD. *Religious moments make people feel good, but do not have a lasting effect on daily living. As we reflect on God's character and respond to Him in surrender, His image is formed in us. We become like Him as certain aspects of His character are etched into our souls. When worship is woven into our lives, the fabric of our being will reflect God's glory.*

When people strive to become Christ-like, their first tendency is to make a list of the "shoulds" and "should nots" or as Piper calls it the "avoidance ethic." We tend to look at the outward manifestation of a holy life instead of its inward cause.

At a youth camp in Brazil, a 16 year-old girl kept following me around, asking, "Pastor, is it wrong for a Christian girl to use ear rings? Pastor, is it a sin to wear pants? Pastor, is it wrong to talk to a guy about this or that?" She must have asked twenty questions, trying to figure out all of the "do's" and "don'ts."

Trying to define the limits is fairly typical of teenagers. As one person put it, they are really asking, "How much of the world can I enjoy without ruining my testimony or offending God?" Those are not the kinds of questions a worshiper will ask. A worshiper will ask, "How can I know God more intimately and how can I glorify Him the most?"

I finally told her she had a wrong view of what it means to live a holy life. She was trying to come up with a list of rules. Following rules is not the same as being transformed.

Her view of holiness is precisely what Jesus preached against. When asked why His disciples didn't fast regularly, Jesus replied that the time was not appropriate. He further emphasized that we can't put new wine in old wineskins. You cannot mix the legalism and religious rituals of the Pharisees with a worship life-attitude. Legalism kills the spiritual life of those striving to walk with God and never truly changes a person's life.

However, the Scriptures constantly exhort us to live holy lives. For example, Peter says, "As obedient children, do not be conformed to the former lusts which were yours in your ignorance, but like the Holy One who called you, be holy yourselves also in all your behavior; because it is written, 'You shall be holy for I am holy'" (1 Pet. 1:14-16).

This passage stresses obeying, rejecting ungodly desires, and maintaining holy behavior. The tendency is to codify a holy, obedient lifestyle and look to one's own moral fortitude to maintain the manmade standard. Such legalism leads to frustration, hypocrisy, and arrogance. Paul makes it clear that legalism may look and sound rigorous, but is, "of no value against fleshly indulgence" (Col. 2:23).

THE HOLINESS OR DISTINCTLY DIFFERENT LIFE THAT PETER AND THE OTHER NEW TESTAMENT AUTHORS ADVOCATE IS AN OVERFLOW OF A LIFE TRANSFORMED PROGRESSIVELY INTO THE IMAGE OF CHRIST BY WALKING IN THE LIGHT OF GOD'S GRACE. IT IS NOT THE RESULT OF HUMAN EFFORT.

Here in Brazil, the idea of walking in grace is very hard for people to grasp. The very word "grace" in popular usage means an earned favor. One group teaches that God punishes sins seven times more severely after baptism, especially when the "sin" is women cutting their hair or using makeup. Another group gives a 50-page book of rules and regulations, governing everything from how wide women's belts can be to how to take a shower so as not to be found naked if the Lord should return, based on a wrong interpretation of Revelation 16:15. Holiness is considered the means by which a person comes to deserve God's blessing.

Of course, American Christians think we know better. Our "freedom" mind-set makes us quick to embrace grace and a life of freedom from the law. However, I don't think Americans have fared any better in the pursuit of holiness. There is still a subtle, unwritten code of conduct among many Americans who are concerned about living a life pleasing to God. At the same time, others have an almost Gnostic view of the Christian life and God's grace that leads them to believe that as long as they have the truth and have "made a decision," their behavior doesn't really matter.

Is it possible to live a life of freedom and grace and, at the same time, live a holy, sanctified life? It seems as if the two are incompatible. People tend to fall into legalism or license, neither of which glorifies God. So how can we live a truly holy life?

The key is seeing holiness as flowing from worship. It is not my trying in my own strength to live up to some standard, nor is it throwing out all restraints and living as I please. If we are truly worshiping God, His character will be formed in our lives.

Averbeck comments, "It is the Holy Spirit's work to sanctify us as individuals and communities of believers, and…one of the most powerfully transforming processes through which he does this is worship. In fact, it all really starts and ends with worship. Worship shapes and motivates the whole sanctification process…."[1]

This chapter is about the transforming influence of worship. As Foster said, "If worship does not change us, it has not been worship. To stand before the Holy One of eternity is to change…If

[1] Averbeck, "Worshiping in Spirit" in Bateman, p. 104.

worship does not propel us into greater obedience, it has not been worship."[2]

THE MARRIAGE METAPHOR

They say that married people start to look and act alike after they have been married awhile. It is easy to know what the other is thinking and we can almost complete each other's sentences. When we are first married, we bring together two different family cultures. We have different tastes in entertainment, vacations, decorating, etc. We have different values in friendships and the use of money and time.

However, *through the deepening of the marriage the two develop their own culture as they take on each other's tastes and values.* They acquire some of the characteristics of the other through shared experiences and just being together. They influence each other. That can be negative or positive, depending on whether they take on the desirable or undesirable qualities of their spouse.

For example, Lisa and I differed in our view of the use of the telephone when we were first married. She picked up the phone to call a friend in another city to chat. I was horrified, because in my family, long distance calls were only to take care of business when absolutely necessary. Through time, Lisa has become more discerning in her use of the telephone and I have learned how to use phone calls to reach out to others. We have tried to take on the positive aspects of each other's values and character.

The marriage metaphor begins to break down when we realize that the transformation that takes place through our relationship with God is a one-way street. The deeper our communion with Him, the more we become like Him. Of course, He never becomes like us. *We become more like God through the deepening of our worship as His character is formed in us.*

A PERSONAL TESTIMONY

As I started preparing leadership-training material, I was challenged by some of the leaders of our mission to think about what *seeds*

---

[2] Foster, p. 148.

should be planted in the lives of leaders, and how those seeds should be *watered* to overflow into a *fruitful* life.

After much reflection, it seemed that the most important seed to plant in the "soil" of Brazilian leaders is the understanding of God's character, watering it with worship and expecting the fruit of God's image to be formed in their lives.

I asked myself, "If I worship a God of love, would I become more loving? If I worship the Father of mercies, would I be more merciful? Would worshiping God for His holiness make me more holy?" I thought of passages such as "We love, because He first loved us" (1 John 4:19), which seem to indicate that our ability to love comes from our understanding of His love for us.

I did not expect my own life to be transformed so drastically as I put the training material together. As a teacher, I didn't want to ask my students to do something that I wasn't doing, so I did the exercises. My wife noticed changes in my life almost immediately.

During a visit to the U.S., I was worshiping through the book of Job, reflecting specifically on the sovereignty of God. I was asked by a Latin American friend to give a lecture on culture at a prison. When we got there, the prison guard refused to let me enter even though the proper paper work had been submitted some time before.

Although I insisted that he go in and teach the class, my friend refused to enter without me, saying that Latin Americans would never neglect a friend like that. We ended up wandering around a mall for a few hours while an accompanying professor finished teaching his class. When we returned from the trip, my friend commented that most "gringos" would have been very upset about losing eight hours of their time for nothing. I probably would have been, too, if I had not been so focused on God's sovereignty and so in tune with His purposes.

That same week, my wife noticed that I was very patient with an inconvenience that normally would have upset me. It wasn't that I was consciously trying to be more patient. My goal wasn't to change my behavior, but simply to grow in my intimacy with God. Worshiping God for His sovereignty allowed me to see things through His eyes and be more patient. My newfound patience was an overflow.

HOW WORSHIP TRANSFORMS:
BEHOLDING CHRIST

And do not be conformed to this world, but be transformed by the renewing of your mind (Rom. 12:2).

The world is constantly trying to slip us into its mold and make us something we are not. We have already become new creatures in Christ. When we sin, we are not demonstrating who we really are, but we are actually going against our new character.

To be conformed[3] means to be molded into something we are not. As MacArthur points out, it "refers to an outward expression that does not reflect what is within. ...It also carries the idea of being transitory, impermanent, and unstable."[4] It seems some of the Romans were passively allowing the world to influence their thinking and now he is telling them to stop[5] allowing the world to force them to behave contrary to their true nature.

When our daughter Maria was younger, she had a number of dolls. One time, her older brother nudged me and said, "Dad, look at this." He pushed in the nose of one of her dolls and its face was distorted, which made for a good laugh. However, as soon as he took his finger off its nose, the face went back to its original shape. He forced the doll's face to take on a form contrary to its nature.

The world is trying to do the same thing to us—to force us to be what we are not. When we come into a relationship with Christ, a real change takes place so we are no longer sinners, but are now saints. Although we still live in our earthly bodies and are subject to temptations, our inner man has already been transformed so we are no longer slaves to sin (see Rom. 6:7, 11, 14, 17, 20; 8:12). Yet the whole system around us is trying to convince us otherwise and to force us to behave contrary to our new identity in Christ.

Worship helps us clearly see who we are, strengthening our inner man to act consistently with our new life in Christ. Presenting ourselves to Him renews our minds and thus transforms our actions. Wiersbe says, "Our lives are being changed either by pressure from

---

[3] *Suschēmatízō* in the Greek from which we get the word *scheme*.
[4] MacArthur, *The MacArthur New Testament Commentary: Galatians*, p.149.
[5] The present passive imperative with *mē* demands that an action already in progress cease. It is passive, indicating they are commanded to stop allowing this to happen.

without (conforming) or by power from within (transforming). The difference is—worship."[6]

Transform is from a Greek word that is the basis for the term metamorphosis.[7]

In my first entomology class, my professor told us that people tend to focus on the outward changes of metamorphosis. He pointed out that this process is really a change of purpose. The caterpillar's purpose is to eat, and its design reflects this. The butterfly's goal is reproduction and its wings and beauty serve to fulfill this purpose.

The transformation that worship brings about in our lives is really a shift in our purpose, a change in our values or mind-set. As we focus on pleasing God, our character is changed to reflect that change in purpose. God changes our lives from inside out through the power of His Spirit working within us.

Morgenthaler writes, "A true encounter with God leaves us with a lot more than good feelings. It leaves us with changed hearts and calls us to changed lives. Very simply, to experience God's presence is to be transformed from the inside out."[8]

The command *to be transformed* implies that God is doing it. Since it is a passive command, it might be better understood as, "be being constantly transformed."[9] We are commanded to allow Him to transform us into His image through worship by consciously rejecting the world and by renewing our minds.

MacArthur says,

> …we are commanded to allow ourselves to be changed outwardly into conformity to our redeemed inner natures…Although we are to aspire to this outward change, it can be accomplished only by the Holy Spirit working in us, by our being "filled with the Spirit" (Eph. 5:18). The Holy Spirit achieves this transformation by the renewing of the mind, an essential and repeated New Testament theme. The outward transformation is effected by an inner change in the

---

[6] Wiersbe, p. 30.
[7] *Metamorphóō*
[8] Morgenthaler, p. 52
[9] The verb is a present passive imperative. Such commands mean that we are actively and constantly to allow God to do this work in our lives.

mind, and the Spirit's means of transforming our minds is
the Word.[10]

TRANSFORMATION IS PROGRESSIVE.

*But we all, with unveiled face, beholding as in a mirror the glory
of the Lord, are being transformed into the same image from
glory to glory, just as from the Lord, the Spirit"* (2 Cor. 3:18).

In chapter 6, we talked about "beholding as in a mirror," because
we cannot see His glory directly. The mirror, in this context, refers
to God's Word. As believers, we are "unveiled" so there is nothing to
keep us from seeing His glory.

Paul uses the same Greek word that is translated "transformed"
in Romans 12:2. In this passage, He says even more directly that it
is the contemplating of God that transforms us. The Jews of Paul's
day would read the Law of Moses and could not see the glory of
the Lord (2 Cor. 3:15). Instead they saw only rules and regulations.
When someone turns to God, the veil that keeps him from seeing
God is removed and he can be transformed by God's presence (2
Cor. 3:16).

This change into His image that is brought about by God, more
specifically the Holy Spirit, is progressive and continuous.[11] Although
it is not a command here as in Romans 12, that does not mean we
are uninvolved. Our role is to seek to behold God in worship and
to allow the Holy Spirit to do His transforming work in our lives.
In other words, we are to get out of His way and stop trying to help
Him by our fleshly efforts.

Wouldn't it be great if we could approach His presence and be
instantly and permanently transformed? Unfortunately, that is not
a reality. Perhaps God knows that if we were changed so quickly,
we might cease to depend on Him and no longer seek to grow in
worship. But there is a progression "from glory to glory." We are, in
a sense, transformed the moment we enter into a relationship with
Christ. That is why it says "from glory." It is only a starting point but

---

[10] MacArthur, *NT Commentary: Galatians,* pp.150-151.
[11] This is a present passive imperative in Romans and a present passive indicative in
2 Cor. In other words, "You are being continually transformed."

doesn't stop there. It continues to progress to what is more and more glorious as we grow as worshipers.

What could be more glorious than being transformed into Christ's image? Being more like Him allows us to enjoy deeper communion with Him. His ultimate goal for us in worship is to make us like Him so we can enjoy fellowship with Him more fully.

As Madame Guyon says, "Jesus Christ actually makes an imprint of Himself upon your soul. Each time He comes to you, He leaves a new and different impression of His nature upon you."[12]

TRANSFORMATION INVOLVES OUR MINDS.

When we say someone has a "great mind," we are generally talking about a person's ability to process and assimilate information. Some people are scholars and have the ability to research minute details with great precision. Others are great thinkers or philosophers, having the ability to see beyond the superficial and to understand underlying principles.

But this is not what the mind is biblically.

The Bible uses two Greek words that give us insight into what is indeed this renewing of the mind.

The Mind and Our Worldview

The first word[13] is used in Rom. 12:2 and describes our physical and intellectual perception, but also includes the ability to arrive at moral judgments.

Vine says it is the seat of reflective consciousness, comprising the faculties of perception and understanding, and those of feeling, judging, and determining.[14] Kittel and Friedrich say it is the, "'mind' or 'disposition' in the sense of inner orientation or moral attitude."[15]

Today, we might describe the biblical concept of "mind" as worldview. It is the filter through which we see and interpret and respond to the world around us. It includes our inner values, which govern our actions. It is not so much a question of intelligence, because

---

[12] Guyon, p. 41.
[13] *Noús*
[14] Vine, p. 69.
[15] Kittel and Friedrich, p. 637.

some of the brightest scientists I know have a very poor perception of the world around them and as a result make foolish decisions. The problem is not their mental capacity, but their worldview.

Before someone enters into a relationship with the Lord, he has a worldview that may be shaped by religion, atheism, materialism, or a number of other philosophies or ideas. His worldview shapes his values, his actions, and his whole outlook on life, answering questions like, "Why am I here?" or "Why do bad things happen?" It will determine how he behaves.

Paul says that the *soulish* or natural man is incapable of discerning spiritual truth (1 Cor. 2:14). He says that those who are *spiritual* (truly converted) have "the mind[16] of Christ" (1 Cor. 2:16), enabling them to perceive things from God's perspective. They have a divine worldview.

Those truly born again have a new mind that is being shaped by Scripture and guided by the Spirit. Even the most simple, uneducated people often have incredible perception and are able to see things that others cannot. It is not just a matter of memorizing Scripture either, although that certainly may be a part of it. Filling their heads with biblical facts will not bring about change. However, memorizing Scriptures as a means of humbly meditating through worship will transform our *minds* so that we begin to see the world as God sees it. A transformed mind will bring our thoughts into a spiritual realm.

Although we have received a new mind, it needs to be renewed constantly because it is continually being bombarded with unbiblical concepts and values (Rom. 12:2). Paul admonishes us not to be anxious, but to pray (Phil. 4:6). The anxious mind[17] is one that keeps replaying ideas over and over, trying to figure things out and find solutions. His promise in the next verse is that God will guard our *minds* and hearts and thoughts in Christ Jesus.

The Mind and Our Mind-set

The other word for *mind* has more to do with a person's mind-set, his way of thinking or aspirations.[18] It might be thought of as someone's

---

[16] Paul again uses *Noús* to describe one of the changes that happens when we become Christians.

[17] As in Rom. 12:2 and 1 Cor. 2:18, Paul uses *Noús* in Phil. 4:7.

[18] *Phrónēma* in the Greek.

goals or desires. We say that people may have a "one-track mind." We mean they are focused on what is most important to them. This is the word most used in Romans 8 and it expresses the mind-set of a person, not just his passing thoughts. Those whose mind-set is on the flesh are dead spiritually and those whose mind-set is on the Spirit are alive spiritually (Rom. 8:6). Salvation changes our mind-set, but it is strengthened and renewed through worship.

The transformation of the *mind* as it is used in this sense also takes place through faith in God's Word. As we study what God has said in the context of worship and prayer, what we profess becomes an inner conviction. His goals become our goals. This is obviously a process.

Neil Anderson writes, "Renewing our minds does not come naturally; there is no automatic 'delete button' that erases past programming."[19] As we progressively become worshipers, both our mind-set and our worldview are transformed to conform to His.

Fixing the mind on the flesh or on the Spirit reprograms our minds to be in conformity to Christ.

An inner conversation is constantly taking place inside us. We are continually perceiving, interpreting, and evaluating everything around us and talking to ourselves about it. The mind of the person who does not know Jesus will frequently have a wrong perception or interpretation of the world in which he lives. The Bible describes this as the mind set on the flesh (Rom. 8:5). The inner conversation may lead that person to make seemingly good decisions, but inevitably those decisions are made with wrong attitudes and no consideration of God's will.

On the other hand, the believer who has a mind actively yielded to the Holy Spirit in worship will perceive and evaluate from God's perspective. Paul says, "But he who is spiritual appraises all things, yet he himself is appraised by no one" (1 Cor. 2:15). The inner conversation will be with God and wise decisions will result. What the believer does will not always make sense to those who don't know the Lord.

---

[19] Neil Anderson, *Who I Am in Christ*, p. 11.

BECOMING WHAT WE WORSHIP

In our city here in Brazil, there is a huge idolatrous procession in October. It seems that most evangelical churches preach on Psalm 115 that weekend. The passage includes a great description of the impotence of an image, but the most striking phrase is verse 8, which describes the result of such worship. It says, "Those who make them [idols] will become like them, Everyone who trusts in them."

A person who makes an idol is creating his own object of worship. Those who trust in such an object will become equally impotent and spiritually lifeless. As a general rule, the worshiper takes on the characteristics of whatever is being worshiped.

E.H. Hengstenberg says, "Every one is just what his God is; whoever serves the Omnipotent is omnipotent with him; whoever exalts feebleness, in stupid delusion, to be his god, is feeble along with that god."[20]

BIBLICAL PROFESSIONS BECOME SPIRITUAL CONVICTIONS,
BUT THEY BECOME PART OF OUR CHARACTER
ONLY THROUGH WORSHIP.

God Delights to See Himself in Us.

Another passage that demonstrates the transforming power of worship is Jeremiah 9:23-24.

> "Let not a wise man boast of his wisdom, and let not the mighty man boast of his might, let not a rich man boast of his riches; but let him who boasts boast of this, that he understands and knows Me, that I am the Lord who exercises lovingkindness, justice, and righteousness on earth; for I delight in these things," declares the Lord.

When I talk with men, it seems they are often jockeying to show their importance through their education, their sports prowess, their position, or their wealth. We have all heard the talk. "I have my doctorate from Harvard." "I was offered a six figure income by IBM."

---

[20] Hengstenberg, cited in Spurgeon, *The Treasury of David.* Vol. 2, p. 61.

"I'm vice-president of management." "I hit three home runs in one game last week."

However, as servants of God, our renewed minds no longer base our importance on these types of accomplishments. This passage makes it clear that these or any other achievements have nothing to do with who I am. Unless you are Michael Jordan, there will always be a better athlete than you. Unless you are Albert Einstein, there is always someone smarter. Unless you are Bill Gates, it is probable there are many people richer than you. By the same token, many people are poorer, less intelligent, less popular, and less talented than you. None of them is more or less important than you because of what they have or do.

Would you like to leave your mark on this world? Then know and understand God. Our real identity comes from intimacy with God. That should be our boast. It is not just knowing about Him. That could be another one of those fleshly pride things, and I have seen the "I-know-more-about-the-Bible-than-you-do" attitude. It is all about knowing God intimately. It is all about worship. That is our identity.

But notice the transition in this passage. He delights in seeing His qualities in us. He summarizes His character as loving, righteous, and just. That is what He wants us to be.

God Will Make Us Like Him.

If our goal is to be pleasing to Him and be like Him, it is frustrating to recognize that we are not manifesting His character, as we should. John comments:

> Beloved, now we are children of God, and it has not appeared as yet what we shall be. We know that when He appears, we will be like Him, because we will see Him just as He is. And everyone who has this hope fixed on Him purifies himself, just as He is pure (1 John 3:2-3).

When we became believers, we became children of God, indicating that some aspects of the image of God that were lost in the fall have been restored to us. We know, however, that the complete restoration of that image will happen only "when He appears." At that time, "we will be like Him."

Why will we be like Him? It is "because we shall see Him just as He is." Perceiving, knowing, understanding, and worshiping God will transform us fully into His image.

WHAT WORSHIP TRANSFORMS: CHRIST'S CHARACTER IN US

We have shown that our inner man and our position radically changed the moment we entered into a relationship with God. On the other hand, our bodies are the same as before. Our minds are still in the process of being renewed. That must mean that worship progressively transforms our minds as the result of the change in our inner man.

Here are a number of qualities of God and exercises that we use to see God's image formed in a person's soul.

WORSHIPING GOD FOR HIS FAITHFULNESS

When we worship God for His faithfulness, it will lead us to trust Him.

God is faithful and trustworthy when He speaks. Although in today's society it is considered intolerant to believe in absolute truth, God has chosen to make that absolute truth known through His Word.

What would happen if we really believed in what God says? If I really believed the Bible, how would I feel about myself? What would I do differently if I were truly convinced of what the Scriptures say? What would I stop doing?

Our problem is that we trust more in our own evaluation than we do in God's. Instead of seeking His mind, we judge God when we try to decide if what He said in His Word is really best for our lives.

God challenged Job's response to Him by saying, "Will you really annul My judgment? Will you condemn Me that you may be justified?" (Job 40:8). How often we do the same, putting ourselves in the judgment seat to evaluate whether God is really telling the truth or not? We do it whenever we disobey God's Word. We are like Abraham who thought he needed to lie to protect himself (Gen. 12:10-20; 20:1-17). Or we are like Moses who doubted that God's power could work through him to save Israel (Ex. 4:13; 5:22-23).

Believing God is not just professing truth. Faith is not merely a positive attitude or wishful thinking that enables us to get what we want. It is a choice to believe what God has already declared to be true. Neil Anderson says, "Faith is the biblical response to truth, and believing the truth is a choice…Faith doesn't *create* reality; faith *responds* to reality"[21] (author's emphasis).

The following table is a summary of David's description of God's Word in Psalm 19. It helps us look at the Hebrew parallelisms and reflect on the awesomeness of His Word.

VERSE	DESCRIPTION OF THE WORD	CHARACTERISTIC OF THE WORD	IMPACT OF THE WORD
v. 7	LAW *His will or teaching.*	PERFECT *Complete.*	RESTORES YOUR SOUL *It transforms your interior.*
v. 7	TESTIMONY *A witness to who He is. Warnings.*	SURE *Faithful, deserving of our trust.*	MAKES THE SIMPLE WISE *Teaches us how to live.*
v. 8	PRECEPTS *Principles to govern our lives.*	RIGHT *Correct.*	REJOICE THE HEART *Produces joy and peace.*
v. 8	COMMANDMENT *Divine orders.*	PURE *Clear, well defined.*	ENLIGHTEN THE EYES *Helps us understand and interpret things.*

[21] Neil Anderson, *The Bondage Breaker*, p. 191.

VERSE	DESCRIPTION OF THE WORD	CHARACTERISTIC OF THE WORD	IMPACT OF THE WORD
v. 9	**FEAR** *That which promotes worship.*	**CLEAN** *Pure and undefiled* **ENDURES FOREVER** *Eternally applicable.*	**PRODUCES FEAR** *Instills worship* **MAKE CLEAN** *Makes us ceremonially clean.* **ENDURES FOREVER** *Produces eternal life*
v. 9	**JUDGMENTS** *His judicial decisions.*	**TRUE** *Correcting.*	**MAKE RIGHTEOUS** *The correction of His judgments makes us righteous.*

The Scriptures are more valuable than the finest gold (v. 10).
The Scriptures give more pleasure than the sweetest honey (v. 10).
When we worship a faithful God, we trust in His faithful Word and live according to it.

Exercises:

1. Write down a passage that is an example of each aspect of His Word (laws, testimonies, precepts, etc.). Thank Him one by one for each precious gift to you.
2. Ask God to open your eyes to see each characteristic of His Word (perfect, sure, right, etc.).
3. Pray that God would use the Word to impact your life as He said (Enlighten your eyes, give you wisdom, etc.).
4. Tell God you want to value His Word as gold and find pleasure in it as honey.

WORSHIPING GOD FOR HIS SOVEREIGNTY

When we worship God for His sovereignty, we will trust in His plan and control over the circumstances of our lives, leading to peace.

What would happen if I truly believed in God's sovereignty, seeing everything that happens as within His plan? How would it affect my character? How would I view life if I had the mind-set that God is in complete control of everything? Would I have more peace? Would I become so passive that I would become ineffective?

After studying the sovereignty of God, a friend began worshiping Him for His authority and power. He could not stop talking about God's sovereignty. I was puzzled at his enthusiasm until later in the conversation when he told me his life story.

His biological mother had tried to abort him twice with medicine. After he was born, she was walking down a pier to pitch him in the river, when a pastor's wife met her. The birth mother gave the baby to this woman, and she and her husband raised him. He realized, as never before, that God had sovereignly led him into a godly home, sparing him for a purpose.

He shared what he had learned about God with a couple of friends. Not long afterward, they came back to tell my friend a story of their own. Their boat ran out of gas on the way to take fruit to market. What could have ruined the whole day became a praise time as the men looked at the situation through God's sovereign eyes. At the last minute, God sent someone along who gave them the fuel they needed to make it to the market in time to sell their fruit.

We have already examined one of the most well-known and often misunderstood passages in Scripture, Romans 8:28. "And we know that God causes all things to work together for good to those who love God, to those who are called according to His purpose." This verse is often interpreted to mean that everything is going to come out okay and the good guy is going to win in the final reel.

The key to understanding this passage correctly is to know what the "good" is. It does not mean that everything is going to have a happy ending, turn out how I want it to, or leave me richer or more comfortable in the end. The "good" is related to God's calling and purpose for my life.

He expresses that purpose in verse 29. "For whom He foreknew, He also predestined to become conformed to the image of His Son." His purpose is clear.[22] His goal is to conform us to His image. He wants us to be like Jesus, and He has predestined us for that.

When we worship a sovereign God, we live in peace because we know He is in control, coordinating all the circumstances in our lives to conform us to His image.

Exercises:

1. Read the life of Joseph (Gen. 37-46), considering God's sovereign hand in his life.
2. List three negative experiences that positively shaped your character.
3. List three positive experiences over which you had no control, but which shaped the direction of your life.
4. Spend some time worshiping God for His sovereignty, asking Him to enable you to see His hand at work in your life.

WORSHIPING GOD FOR HIS HOLINESS

When we worship God for His holiness, we become more holy.

A friend of mine said that we who profess justification by grace through faith often end up encouraging sanctification by works. He is right. Instead of exhorting people to be "fixing [their] eyes upon Jesus, the author and perfecter of faith" (Heb. 12:2), we unwittingly lead people to focus on rules, drawing on their own resources to try to please God. That leads to legalism, pride, hypocrisy, and frustration.

Worshiping a holy God is the key to becoming holy, as we have already seen. Note another illustration from Isaiah 6. "In the year of king Uzziah's death, I saw the Lord..." (v. 1). Isaiah had the rare privilege of seeing God on His throne where His glory filled the

---

[22] Whether you believe foreknowledge is just knowing ahead of time what people are going to decide or believe that it is determinative in election, His purpose is to conform the lives of His elect to the image of His Son. *Foreknowledge* translates the Greek Word *prógnōsis* that has led some to conclude that God is merely predicting what man will do and basing His election on what He foresees. However, that ignores the fact that God's knowledge is not based on observation, but on His sovereign control. It is best to interpret this as God predetermining a relationship with someone.

temple. God demonstrated His sovereign control during a moment of national crisis. In that context, Isaiah heard the seraphims' three-fold declaration of God's holiness. It is not only a reference to the Trinity (Holy is the Father, Holy is the Son, Holy is the Spirit), but it is also an emphasis on God's supreme attribute.

God is holy, separate, distinct, and set apart in all His characteristics—His love, His wisdom, His justice, His knowledge, His mercy—everything is distinct and infinitely higher than anything we humans know.

"Then I said, 'Woe is me, for I am ruined!'" (Isa. 6:5). There is nothing like a vision of God's holiness to show us what we really are. Isaiah had pronounced numerous "woes" on the Jews in the previous chapter. Now he was condemning himself.

"He touched my mouth with [a burning coal from the altar] and said, 'Behold, this has touched your lips; and your iniquity is taken away and your sin is forgiven'" (v. 7). God purified Isaiah through the burning coal, which represents His holiness and transforming power. The divine fire touched the very part of Isaiah that was identified as sinful. It was, however, the vision of God's holiness that purified Isaiah, preparing Isaiah to be God's messenger. Of course, the natural response to God's call was availability and that is why Isaiah said, "Here am I. Send me!" (v. 8).

Exercises:

1. Read the following passages: Numbers 16; Leviticus 10:1-3; 2 Samuel 6:1-8; 2 Chronicles 26:16-21.
2. Using Isaiah 6, worship God for His holiness, asking Him to shine a light on those areas in your life that are displeasing to Him.
3. Ask God to cleanse you and make you fit for service.

Worshiping God for His Love

When we worship God for His love, we become more merciful and loving.

Is it really possible to love our enemies? Isn't it hard enough to love our spouses? If we were to receive God's love and mercy fully, would we, in turn, be more loving and merciful?

I have a friend from another country who is a follower of the Lord Jesus Christ. He is a diligent, hard worker, and I knew that where he worked, the employees tried to do as little as possible. I suspected they would resent his diligence and that a *foreigner* was showing them up.

When I asked him about it, he admitted he had been criticized and resented by his fellow workers. I asked him how he dealt with that. He smiled humbly and said, "Oh, I overcame it with the love of Christ."

He explained that his wife would regularly make pies and cakes for him to share with his fellow workers. As a result, they now accept him. He overcame evil with good and glorified God.

He had the same problem with a neighbor who resented a *foreigner* moving in across the street. He smiled again and said, "I also won her over with the love of Christ."

That is not normal. No one would naturally do that. The only way to explain it is, "We love, because He first loved us" (1 John 4:19). My friend is a worshiper of the Lord Jesus Christ, and the character of Jesus showed in the way he treated others.

To understand this principle, consider the parable of the unmerciful servant (Matt. 18:21-35). Verses 34 and 35 are difficult. They seem to say that the king has reneged on his promise to forgive the debt. The servant was handed over to the torturers (a heavy word) until the debt could be paid (never). The last verse applies the parable to God who will not forgive those who do not forgive. Some people do not forgive others, because they have never embraced the forgiveness that God offers.

The best way to understand this parable, perhaps, is to recognize that the servant asked for more time, but was offered a complete cancellation of the debt. His subsequent actions are difficult to explain. Perhaps he was still thinking he had been granted only an extension of time to pay his debt. Maybe he thought he deserved to be forgiven. It is also possible that he never really understood the magnitude of the forgiveness that had been offered. Whatever was in his heart, we know that the king's offer was never really understood or embraced by the man.

The point of the parable is that the forgiven will be forgiving. Those who have received mercy will be merciful. The loved will be loving. If we are worshiping a loving, merciful God who has forgiven us, it is only natural for us to be patient and forgiving of others. In practice, that is not so easy. We forget what God has done for us. We start believing we are pretty good people and somehow we deserve what He has done for us. At that point, we become impatient and harsh with others who don't treat us as we think we deserve to be treated.

The remedy for such behavior is to worship God, remembering what has happened. Peter said that the one who is not growing, "is blind or short-sighted, having forgotten his purification from his former sins" (2 Pet. 1:9).

By nature, I am not a very patient person but my wife is. She is very friendly and often, when out visiting, she doesn't make it back promptly. If I become irritated or impatient when she is late, I remember how patient she has been with me. She has put up with much more from me than I have from her. But more importantly, God has shown me so much patience. He has been so loving and patient with me all these years. It is truly amazing.

If we ever stop being amazed that God could save us, we are in deep trouble. We should all sing with Wesley,

And can it be that I should gain
An int'rest in the Savior's blood?
Died He for me, who caused His pain?
For me, who Him to death pursued?
Amazing love! How can it be
That Thou, my God, shouldst die for me?[23]

When worship leads us to be amazed at the love, mercy, and patience God has poured out on us, we will be more compassionate toward others.

Exercises:

1. Read through Isaiah 53, worshiping God for what He has done for you.
2. Reflect on the changes God has made in your life by His grace. Thank Him for saving you.

---

[23] Charles Wesley, copyright ©1986 by WORD MUSIC. All Rights Reserved. Used by Permission.

The Result of Transforming Worship: Glorifying God

In chapter 3, I mentioned that glorifying God means that we shine forth His character. When His character is formed in us, His qualities become manifest to those around us. We are not adding anything to Him by what we do. Depending on our heart attitude, our actions can either glorify ourselves or glorify Him. Consider the following passages:

> 2 Chronicles 5:13 - "In unison when the trumpeters and the singers were to make themselves heard with one voice to praise and to *glorify* the Lord...then the house of the Lord, was filled with a cloud." Here glorifying God is seen as praise. They declared His character with their voices. God manifested His glory in the temple.

> Matthew 5:16 - "Let your light shine before men in such a way that they may see your good works, and *glorify* your Father who is in heaven." Allow all your actions to reflect God's character.

> Romans 15:6 - "...that with one accord you may with one voice *glorify* the god and Father of our Lord Jesus Christ." Be unified to reflect the character of God.

> 1 Corinthians 6:20 - "For you have been bought with a price: therefore *glorify* God in your body." Your sexual actions should reflect God's character.

> 1 Corinthians 10:31 - "Whether, then, you eat or drink or whatever you do, do all to the *glory* of God." Use your freedom in such a way that it reflects God's character.

> 1 Peter 2:12 - "Keep your behavior excellent among the Gentiles, so that in the thing in which they slander you as evildoers, they may because of your good deeds, as they observe them, *glorify* God in the day of visitation." Handle your criticisms in such a way as to reflect God's character.

These passages give us a picture of what it means to glorify God. When our minds and hearts are transformed through worship, our outward actions will glorify God. Our praise, ministry, good works, and holy living should always flow from our inner attitudes of worship. These diagrams from chapter 3 illustrate the transformation that results from worship:

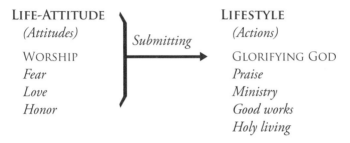

LIFE-ATTITUDE
(Attitudes)

WORSHIP
Fear
Love
Honor

Submitting

LIFESTYLE
(Actions)

GLORIFYING GOD
Praise
Ministry
Good works
Holy living

Here is a brief outline of the basic truths related to the transformation that comes from being filled with the Spirit.

KNOWING YOUR POSITION

> *For in Him all the fullness of Deity dwells in bodily form, and in Him you have been made complete, and He is the head over all rule and authority* (Gal. 2:9-10).

We saw earlier that many Christians spend their time seeking what they have already been given. We are complete *in Christ.* Nothing we can do or not do will make God love us more or less. People fast, pray, read their Bibles, go to church, and even try to worship in an effort to earn God's favor instead of growing in their relationship with Him. If there is something I do that will make God love or bless me more, then salvation is no longer by grace.

Ephesians is about who we are in Christ and then walking according to that position. Paul knew that giving the Ephesians the facts would not be enough. He knew those truths needed to be assimilated into the Ephesians' lives spiritually through prayer and worship.

He prayed for a "spirit [spiritual state or condition] of wisdom and revelation" through intimacy with God (Eph 1:17). Study of the

Word is very important to provide the basis of our knowledge, but only intimacy with God will give us true, spiritual understanding and open the eyes of our heart (Eph 1:18).

In Ephesians 3, Paul prayed that his readers would be "strengthened with power through His Spirit in the inner man" (v. 16). That spiritual strengthening would help them to comprehend the magnitude of the church (v.18),[24] and the greatness of Christ's love (v. 19). How can we ever understand something that "surpasses knowledge"? (v. 19). Only when God opens our eyes can we understand the incomprehensible.

FIXING YOUR EYES ON JESUS CHRIST

Let us run with endurance the race that is set before us, fixing our eyes on Jesus, the author and perfecter of faith" (Heb. 12:1-2).

I was an offensive guard on our high school football team, and I still remember the coaches telling the running backs, "If you look at your feet or the ground, that is where you will go. Keep your eyes on the end zone."

In Romans 7:14-25, Paul describes the frustration he felt when trying to please God through obeying the Law in his own strength. Notice how Paul's eyes were focused on sin and the law in this passage instead of on Christ and walking by the Spirit. Legalism takes our eyes off Jesus and focuses on our sin. When we look at our feet stumbling in sin, we will fall.

Jesus is our standard. He is "the firstborn among many brethren" or the prototype (Rom. 8:29). We are to be conformed to His image (1 Cor. 3:18; Col 3:10, 1 John 3:2). Following the principle "What Would Jesus Do?" could lead us to focus on the externals and could become a form of legalism. Maybe we should ask, "What would Jesus want us to be?" Worship takes our focus off our own abilities and fixes our eyes on Jesus.

DEVELOPING INTIMACY WITH GOD

[You] have put on the new self who is being renewed to a true knowledge according to the image of the One who created him (Col. 3:10).

---

[24] See chapter 10 for a complete discussion of Eph. 3:18 as referring to the church.

As we emphasized in chapter 2, worship and intimacy with God are twin strands that make up the golden threads that blend into one. It is impossible to worship God without developing intimacy with Him, and it is impossible to have intimacy with God without first worshiping Him. The third strand is walking by His Spirit.

WALKING BY THE SPIRIT

But I say, walk by the Spirit, and you will not carry out the desire of the flesh (Gal. 5:16).

Although it may be hard to conceive, this verse affirms that it is impossible to sin when we are walking by the Spirit.[25] The problem is that we spend very few of our days walking by the Spirit.[26] That is why we sin so often.

We are usually not aware of walking by the flesh until something provokes us. Let's say someone cuts us off in traffic and we become angry. The carelessness of the other driver did not necessarily lead us to walk by the flesh. We were already walking by the flesh, but this only became apparent when something that didn't please us led to a fleshly response.

On the other hand, when we are driving by the Spirit, we will see others and our circumstances through God's perspective and therefore react very differently.

Worship brings intimacy that leads to walking by the Spirit. The three are inseparably part of the golden thread. When we know what it means to walk by the Spirit, it becomes obvious that it flows from intimacy with God and worship. Walking by the Spirit is the third strand in the golden thread, that, when woven together with worship and intimacy, makes a strong cord. Worship is the foundation for the other two strands. Our intimacy with Him develops as we learn to worship. As we learn to commune with Him, we will learn how to walk by His Spirit.

---

[25] Paul used a subjunctive emphatic negation (*ou mē* with the subjunctive). This is the strongest way grammatically to express an impossibility.

[26] I am avoiding the term "walking *in* the flesh or Spirit," because Paul makes it very clear that if we are "in the flesh" (*en sarki*—locative sphere), we do not know the Lord (Rom. 8:9). Nor are we "according to the flesh" (*kata sárka*—norm or standard), because that also signifies an unsaved person (Rom. 8:13). It is better to use the biblical terminology "by the Spirit" (*pneumati*—instrumental agency). Every true believer is "in the Spirit" and "walks according to the Spirit," but not every Christian walks "by the Spirit." That is a conscious choice that only believers can make on a moment-by-moment basis.

We mentioned earlier that the Bible contains both declarations and commands. Our response to declarations should be to believe and conduct our lives in light of our conviction of their truthfulness. Our response to commands is to obey. The Bible also contains promises that God will fulfill, either during our lives or when we are with Him in heaven. Our response to them should simply be to believe.

The promises related to the Spirit's presence in our lives are that He will guide me into all truth (John 14:26; 16:13), He will be with me when I witness (John 16:8-11), He will help me (John 14:16), He will assist me in praying (Rom. 8:26), and He will never leave me (John 14:16).

God has declared that I am regenerated by His Spirit (Titus 3:5), indwelt by His Spirit (Rom. 8:9), sealed by His Spirit (Eph. 1:13), and baptized with His Spirit (1 Cor. 12:13). These truths have already been fulfilled in me! These are true no matter what I may feel at any given time. Each promise should lead me to great rejoicing and praise.

There are four commands related to the Holy Spirit. Two are negative and are related. I am not to grieve (Eph. 4:30) or quench the Spirit (1 Thess. 5:19). The two positive flipsides are that I am to walk by the Spirit (Gal. 5:16) and be filled with the Spirit (Eph. 5:18).

Walking and being filled with the Spirit are not mysterious concepts. They simply mean that I willingly ask Him to guide me, yielding my thoughts and actions to His direction as I commune with Him in worship. He does not seize control[27] of my thoughts or force me to do anything. He works in conjunction with my mind as I consciously yield to Him.

MacArthur writes,

> The life walked by the Spirit is the Christlike life, the saturation of a believer's thoughts with the truth, love, and glory of His Lord and the desire to be like Him in every way. It is to live in continual consciousness of His presence and will, letting "the word *of* Christ richly dwell within you" (Col. 3:16). Life walked by the Spirit is life patterned after the teaching and example of the Lord Jesus Christ.[28]

[27] I am also avoiding the term "control of the Holy Spirit" because it does not adequately express the biblical teaching of His role in our lives. See chapter 13.
[28] MacArthur, *NT Commentary; Galatians,* p. 154.

BEING DISCIPLINED TO WORSHIP

So then, my beloved, just as you have always obeyed, not only in my presence only, but now much more in my absence, work out your salvation with fear and trembling; for it is God who is at work in you, both to will and to work for His good pleasure (Phil. 2:12-13).

To speak of personal discipline may appear to be a contradiction to much of what has been said so far. It may seem that we are advocating human effort or works.

The Philippians obeyed God, whether Paul was watching or not. It flowed from a transformed life. It was the result of their love for God. Still, Paul told them to work out their salvation.[29]

That does not imply a works salvation, but is a command to strive to grow in sanctification continually. Salvation, in this passage, does not refer to justification, but to sanctification. This distinction is very important. The Philippians were to do it with fear and trembling or, in other words, with a worship mind-set. It is not supposed to be a fleshly striving.

Paul reminds them it is really God through His Spirit who does the transforming, changing our wills and our actions to conform to His.

MacArthur says,

> Although Bible study, prayer, worship, witnessing and certain behavior standards are commanded of believers and are essential to faithful Christian living, spirituality cannot be measured by how often or how intensely we are involved in such things. To use them as measures of spirituality is to become entrapped in legalism, whose only significance is the outward, the visible, the humanly measurable.[30]

The spiritual disciplines are not to be pursued to merit God's favor or to display our spirituality. As Foster says, "The Disciplines allow us to place ourselves before God so that He can transform us."[31]

---

[29] *Katergázomai* in the Greek means "to bring about, produce or create." It is a present imperative, showing that it is to be done continually.

[30] MacArthur, *Galatians*, p. 152.

[31] Foster, p. 6.

"Self-Control" is one aspect of the fruit of the Spirit (Gal. 5:23). It means that we are strengthened by His presence to say no to those activities that stifle our worship. It takes an act of the will on our part to deny the flesh so that nothing stands in the way of our worship.

CONCLUSION

A transformed life does not come from following a list of rules, no matter how biblical the standard might be. Our flesh is hostile toward God. It will not and cannot be subjected to God (Rom. 8:7). If we try to live a holy life through our will power, we end up weakening ourselves spiritually, strengthening the flesh, and suffering defeat.

True transformation happens as we begin truly to believe what He has done for us and that we are seated with Him in the heavenly places right now. Our minds become filled with the Spirit's presence and, at that moment, it becomes impossible for us even to think of fulfilling the desires of the flesh. More importantly, His character is formed in us.

We become distracted so easily. We put our minds on autopilot and we lose our focus on His presence. Sometimes we dwell on a specific sin instead of on our position in Him. As we grow, we fix our minds more and more on whatever is true, honorable, right, pure, lovely, of good repute, excellent, and worthy of praise (Phil. 4:8) and less on the things of the world. It is not that we are not conscious of this world, but we are now seeing it through God's eyes, because our minds are transformed by worship. Our perceptions and affections have changed. When we are distracted and stumble, our fellowship is more and more quickly restored as we give ourselves to worship again.

Jesus invited us to throw off the tiresome burden of legalism and walk in the freedom of the Spirit. He said, "Come to Me, all who are weary and heavy-laden, and I will give you rest. Take My yoke upon you and learn from Me, for I am gentle and humble in heart, and you will find rest for your souls. For My yoke is easy and My burden is light" (Matt. 11:28-30).

PARADIGM SHIFT

When people opt for rules and self-help techniques in order to live a holy life, they may very well fall into hypocrisy. Behavior modification can never be pleasing to God. Only a transformation that comes from real worship can truly bring about a lasting change.

BEHAVIOR MODIFICATION	LIFE TRANSFORMATION
1. OBJECTIVES: • A change in behavior • Careful definition of necessary qualities for a sanctified life	1. OBJECTIVES: • A change in attitudes and values that leads to a different lifestyle • Cultivation of spiritual attitudes that lead to a sanctified life
2. METHODS: • Rules • Attending religious functions and giving offerings • Disciplining the flesh	2. METHODS: • Worship • Exhortation on a personal level • Walking by the Spirit
3. CHARACTERISTICS: • Emphasis on external actions. • Guilt • A low standard of holiness but with the appearance of being rigorous	3. CHARACTERISTICS: • Emphasis on internal attitudes. • Freedom with responsibility • A high standard of holiness because it involves thoughts and attitudes
4. RESULTS: • Concern for other people's behavior • Hypocrisy (to try to hide that one is not living up to the standard) • A guilty conscience • Pride	4. RESULTS: • Concern with your own attitudes and actions before God • Transparency with others to be helped and help others to live a life pleasing to God • Joy and freedom • Humility

WHERE TO START

1. PRAY THROUGH THIS LIST OF PROMISES. One of the keys to living a holy life is to know who you are in Christ. You may know these truths intellectually, but worship makes them become convictions. Knowing your position is also essential. Pray over each truth and lie, asking God to help you believe what He has already declared.[1]

THE TRUTH	THE LIES
1. I am accepted by God unconditionally (Rom. 15:7).	1. I would be more accepted by God if I read my Bible more, if I were more faithful, if…
2. I am a son or daughter of God (John 1:12).	2. I am a son or daughter of the world. I am trying to change.
3. I am friend of God (John 15:15).	3. God sees me as a servant.
4. I am one spirit with the Lord (1 Cor. 6:17).	4. I am distant from God.
5. I have access to God (Eph. 2:17-18).	5. Those who are more spiritual than I am have access to God.
6. I am a saint (Eph. 1:1).	6. I am a sinner.
7. All my sins are forgiven (Eph. 1:7).	7. There are still sins hanging over my head.
8. I am complete in Christ (Col. 2:10).	8. There is a lot still lacking in my life.
9. I am free from all condemnation (Rom. 8:1).	9. I still feel guilty.

[1] Adapted from Anderson, *Who I Am in Christ.*

THE TRUTH	THE LIES
10. Nothing can separate me from the love of Christ (Rom. 8:38-39).	10. I feel distant from the love of God.
11. I am a citizen of heaven (Phil. 3:20).	11. I feel very much at home in this world.
12. I am the salt of the earth and the light of the world (Matt. 5:13-14).	12. Nobody would know I am a believer if I didn't tell him or her.
13. I am seated with Christ in the heavenly places (Eph. 2:6).	13. My attention is given to my job, my family, my studies, my belongings, and my friends.
14. I am God's co-laborer (2 Cor. 6:1-2).	14. Money is all I can contribute to God's work.

2. ASK GOD TO EXAMINE YOUR LIFE. David asked, "Who can discern his errors? Acquit me of hidden faults" (Ps. 19:12). Attitudes are the hardest to root out. Ask Him to show you areas that need to be changed. Thank Him for each one He shows you.

3. START ALLOWING GOD TO TRANSFORM YOU. After identifying the aspects of your character that do not reflect the character of Christ, think of the qualities of God that need to be a part of your life, or at least need to be believed. For example, if you have problems forgiving others or are impatient with them, you may want to focus on His love and mercy. If you are impatient when things go wrong, you need to believe that He is sovereign. Record that quality in your notebook, and worship Him every day for that aspect of His character. You may want to find a verse that describes Him in that way as a basis for your worship.

DISCUSSION QUESTIONS

1. What does it mean to live a holy life?

2. How does one develop a holy life?

3. What can we learn from the marriage metaphor?

4. How does worship change our lives?

5. Why is it impossible for rules and laws to purify our lives?

6. How does beholding God make us more aware of our sinfulness?

7. How did worshiping God for His sovereignty affect your life?

8. How did worshiping God for His love change you?

9. What impact did worshiping God for His faithfulness have on your life?

10. How can worship make us more forgiving?

11. Where do you see your life in the paradigm table?

12. What does it mean to walk by the Spirit?

13. How do we know if we are walking by the Spirit or by the flesh?

14. What was important for you in comparing the declarations of truth with the lies we believe?

15. How have you become more holy through worship recently?

Chapter 9

DELIGHTING IN GOD THROUGH WORSHIP

WORSHIP IS FINDING TRUE SATISFACTION IN INTIMACY WITH GOD

Therefore, I urge you, brethren, by the mercies of God, to present your bodies a living and holy sacrifice, acceptable to God, which is your spiritual service of worship. And do not be conformed to this world, but be transformed by the renewing of your mind, so THAT YOU MAY PROVE WHAT THE WILL OF GOD IS, THAT WHICH IS GOOD AND ACCEPTABLE AND PERFECT (Romans 12:1-2).

SEED TRUTH: WORSHIPERS ENJOY GOD'S PRESENCE. *Religious people seek the warm feelings that come from singing and performing rituals. Worshipers find real satisfaction in their relationship with God and pleasing Him. Worship, although not selfishly motivated, brings true joy and peace through becoming one with God. When the golden thread of worship is woven into our lives, we become united with Him to the point that His pleasure becomes ours.*

It is a pleasure to watch players like Michael Jordan who excel and seem to be having fun playing their sport. John Elway made football look like fun. I could name a few soccer players here in Brazil who are like that as well. Whatever the sport, you get the sense that some of those athletes would play, with or without the pay and the cheering fans. They delight in the game.

But as they approach retirement, many professional athletes say they no longer enjoy the game. They used to. They used to find pleasure in suiting up and going out on the playing field. Now that they are hanging up their cleats, they say it just isn't fun anymore. Maybe they played for the applause and recognition, and now they are being criticized because they aren't quite as good as they used to be. Many played for the money, but now younger players are getting the big contracts. Maybe they still love the game, but injury and age have taken their toll, and their bodies can't quite do what they used to do. The sport they once enjoyed has now become a burden. What used to be exciting has now become professional responsibility.

Have we come to view worship in the same way? Is it an obligation, a responsibility, or a duty? Do you seek and enjoy God's presence the same as when you first believed? Time with Him should not be a burden. It is a privilege. It is a delight and a pleasure. Worship is enjoying God.

When I first heard about John Piper's concept of the "Christian hedonist," it sounded like a self-centered modern theology. However, Piper used an example from E. J. Carnell that made the concept come alive for me. "Suppose a husband asks his wife if he must kiss her good night. Her answer is, 'You must, but not that kind of a must.' What she means is this: 'Unless a spontaneous affection for my person motivates you, your overtures are stripped of all moral value.'"[1]

Piper explains, "In other words, if there is no pleasure in the kiss, the duty of kissing has not been done. Delight in her person, expressed in the kiss, is part of the duty, not a by-product of it."[2]

Some people view the Christian life as though God commanded, "Thou shalt not have fun." Or "If it is fun, don't do it." They look upon God as if He were some sort of cosmic killjoy. We used to call those who hold such views "the frozen chosen."

On the other hand, the Christian life is not like the frivolous "Fun in the Son" philosophy that allows us to do whatever we want as long as it does not involve sinful acts or ruin our testimony. For many, their joy is here in this world and they have lost the pilgrim mentality.

---

[1] Edward Carnell, *Christian Commitment* (New York: Macmillan, 1967), 160-161. Quoted in Piper, *Dangerous Duty*, p. 14.
[2] Piper, Ibid.

Neither of these two attitudes is a result of worship.

When we allow worship to transform us, we soon discover that God's will is not restrictive and boring, but "good and acceptable and perfect" (Rom. 12:2). There is no greater peace, joy, or pleasure than becoming one with God. The goal of this chapter is to help us see that real joy is found in worship.

THE MARRIAGE METAPHOR

My wife does many things for me: She brings me coffee when I am writing; she brings me food when I am hungry; she is patient with me; and she gives me clean clothes. I am grateful and thank her often, but I don't love her for what she does for me—I love *her*.

Lisa has many admirable characteristics: She is loving, generous, caring, thoughtful, and patient. *However, I love my wife and find joy in her person, not her attributes or what she does for me.*

Nothing is selfish about the joy of love. Love between couples is a decision in which each chooses to subordinate his or her individualism and personal satisfaction to the relationship. It is and isn't a sacrifice. We give up everything, our individual happiness and pleasure, but in return there is incredible enjoyment of each other. My goal is to make my wife happy and thus, my joy becomes integrally tied to hers. We are pleased to please each other.

As a worshiper, I love God and find joy in my relationship with Him. Although I admire His attributes and I am grateful for what He has done for me, my love for Him goes beyond that. I meditate on who He is and what He has done, and I express gratitude constantly. I stand in awe of Him and express that in praise. However, my ultimate pleasure is when God is well pleased. Of course He delights in pleasing me with His presence as well.

One aspect of worship, then, is God and I enjoying each other's company.

SEEKING GOD ALONE

FINDING REFUGE IN GOD

During our leadership training, the students are to interview people who have addictions. On one occasion, every person interviewed commented that they did not constantly practice their habit, but when facing a difficulty, they fled to their addiction for escape.

A few years back, I was saddened by some events and found myself tracking down my wife just to hold her. I was seeking refuge in her. Then a friend of mine nearly lost his wife in a car accident. I realized Lisa could easily be taken away from me, and then where would I find refuge? I realized my wife was not to be my refuge.

At that time, I was praying through the Psalms and the words, "refuge," "shield," "fortress," "rock," "hiding place," and "tower" stood out to me. I began to worship God for being my refuge, much as a young child seeks the warmth and security of his or her mother's lap.

Certain sinful behaviors may become our refuge. People can escape into drinking, drugs, or the fantasy world of pornography when facing a difficult situation. Of course, we rightfully condemn these behaviors. However, it is easy to make other things our refuge when we are stressed, tired, or overwhelmed. Television, the Internet, sports, our spouses, video games, sleep, or any number of activities can be our escape. There may be nothing overtly sinful in any of these things, but they become so when they are our refuge.

What is your escape? When you find the answer to that question, tell God that you want Him to be your refuge. I encourage you to read through the Psalms and mark the words that are related to our security in God. Whenever you find one, stop to worship Him as your only true refuge. Our refuge should be in His Kingdom.[3]

Jesus commanded us to "seek first His kingdom and His righteousness, and all these things will be added to you" (Matt. 6:33). He is not asking us to seek a physical location called His kingdom, but rather His rule in our lives. We are to seek the King. When we seek His righteousness, we are seeking His perfect character. We are seeking intimacy with Him.

MacArthur writes,

> The person who truly *seeks for God* is like David, who declared,
> "I have set the Lord continually before me" (Ps. 16:8). Such

---

[3] A simple way to understand the kingdom of God is to think of it as wherever He rules. There is the messianic kingdom, of course, but what is in mind here is the rule of God in our lives.

a person seeks first the kingdom of God and His righteousness (Matt.6:33). God becomes the focus of everything, the source of everything, the beginning and end of everything. To truly seek for God is to respect and adore His sovereign majesty and to feed on the truth of His Word. It is to obey His commandments, to speak to Him in prayer, to live consciously in His presence with a desire to please Him. No one can do such things naturally, but only by the Spirit of God working through him. The natural inclination of men is to "seek after their own interest" (Phil.2:21).[4]

One of the biggest paradoxes in Christianity is whether we actually seek God or whether He draws us (Jer. 31:3; John 6:44; 12:32).[5] The Bible is clear that both are true. He graciously draws us to Himself and yet we are responsible to seek Him.

Spurgeon said, "Jesus likewise states that gospel worship is to be of a kind that does not result from the man himself merely, but comes from God. This is implied in the sentence, 'The father seeketh such to worship Him' as if no true worship would come from any man unless God sought it."[6]

Greek grammar is much richer than English. Commands can take on many forms. It is possible for commands to be passive and continuous. The fact that these are passive commands in the Greek shows the paradox.[7] It is passive in that God does the filling or strengthening; He makes it happen. But it is a command in that we are responsible to obey. By obeying, we put ourselves in a position for God to work in our lives. The willingness and desire come from Him, but we obey.

Although their writings are somewhat attractive, the mystics represent an extreme position in this paradox, almost ignoring our role in seeking God. They say, "The contemplation of the perfect

---

[4] MacArthur, *NT Commentary. Romans 1-8*, p. 185.
[5] These passages are probably all referring to God drawing us to salvation, but it is also true that He draws us into a closer relationship with Him.
[6] Spurgeon, sermon: "The Axe at the Root—A Testimony Against Puseyite Idolatry," 1866.
[7] For example, Eph. 5:18 commands us to "be being continually filled." 2 Tim. 2:1 commands us to "be being continually strengthened" (literal translations).

244 Worship, the Golden Thread

Christian consists in a total abandonment of the self to the will and operation of God in the soul. The soul has to rid itself of all efforts to act virtuously, to form thoughts and desires, or even to repel temptations."[8]

"Passive surrender to God is taught to the almost total exclusion of human volition and action."[9]

The mystic's viewpoint[10] was born in a time when asceticism or self-discipline was rampant in the church, and some people even submitted themselves to torture in an attempt to mortify the flesh. This self-denial represents the other extreme in which human effort is emphasized.

Madame Guyon, a well-known French mystic, spent time in a convent and submitted to self-affliction to rid herself of sin. She, however, found that her time in the convent was not effective in developing her walk with God. In rejecting this path, she overemphasized passively waiting on God.

There was another movement that was born out of the German reformation know as "Pietism." This movement was an attempt to bring a balanced approach to Christianity. Spener, the movement's founder, "called the church to a life of piety, to a faith that not only used the mind, but touched the heart and inspired the hands as well."[11]

Which viewpoint is right in leading us to worship? Is it God who draws us or do we seek Him? The answer is both: We need to give ourselves to seeking God while at the same time allowing Him to draw us fully. This means that we are to be practicing faithfully the spiritual disciplines in the power of the Spirit, humbly asking Him to draw us, and committing ourselves to respond to that call. We need to be listening for His voice in the Scriptures and to be quiet before Him in prayer. Seeking God in worship is both very active and very passive.

---

[8] J. D. Douglas, Philip W. Comfort, and Donald Mitchell, editors, "Miguel de Molinos," *Who's Who in Christian History.*
[9] MacArthur, *NT Commentary: Galatians,* p. 153.
[10] The movement is known as "Quietism".
[11] Douglas et al. "Philipp Jakob Spener,"*Who's Who.*

PLEASING GOD

What Pleasing God Means

Worship is to be the source of all our pleasure and delight. As C. S. Lewis said, "We are far too easily pleased,"[12] settling for something less than the joy of worship. If our pleasure is not in God, we are not worshiping Him. That is our one and only pursuit: to worship and enjoy God.

Pleasure can conjure up many different images in our mind. It could mean something that makes us feel good, relaxed, or comfortable. Sounds, sights, smells, and physical sensations can be pleasurable.

Emotional pleasure may also make us smile, laugh, or just leave us content or satisfied. Doing something for someone or receiving a special gesture of kindness may be very pleasing to us.

Is it possible that there is a *spiritual pleasure* we can experience? Some people seek ecstatic or emotional religious experiences, which might be confused with spiritual delight in God's presence. A subtle pride might also slip into someone's life because he feels he has somehow earned God's approval. Instead of being spiritual pleasure, it is merely religious pride. It goes much deeper than a good feeling.

The Bible describes *spiritual pleasures* as joy. This is an important biblical theme related to those who walk with God. A number of words in the Bible are used to describe joy or pleasure. One word speaks of "good pleasure," something that is pleasing or satisfying to God as He brings about His will, especially in saving His people (Luke 12:32; 1 Cor 1:21; Col. 1:19).[13]

✝ A second word describes something as being pleasing or pleasant in a favorable relationship (John 8:29; 1 John 3:22).[14] This can refer to sexual pleasure as well (Matt. 14:6). There is a worshipful joy in God's presence, a festive rejoicing (Rev. 19:7; Luke 1:44; Mt 5:12; 1 Pet. 1:6,8).[15] Another key word for joy has the same root as the Greek word for grace. This rejoicing is one aspect of the fruit of the

---

[12] C. S. Lewis, *The Weight of Glory and Other Addresses*, (Minneapolis: Macmillan, 1949), pp.1, 2. Quoted in Piper, *Dangerous Duty*, p. 23.
[13] *Eudokēsis or eudokéō*
[14] *Arestós*
[15] *Agallíasis*

Spirit (Gal. 5:22) and comes from faith (Phil. 1:25) and accompanies salvation (Acts 8:8, 39; 13:52)[16]

Spiritual pleasure then, is deep, inner satisfaction, contentment, peace, and joy that will be manifest in our emotions.

Think of the God of the universe. What makes God smile? What would give Him pleasure or a sense of satisfaction? Can we even attribute such a quality to God?

The Bible attributes joy, pleasure, and rejoicing to God Himself. Just as God can be grieved and angered by what is evil, He is pleased with what is consistent with His character.

What pleases God? Here are some Scriptures that tell what delights Him.

1. God is pleased to make known His gospel to the simple (1 Cor. 1:21).
2. God is pleased to give us His kingdom (Luke 12:32).
3. God is pleased when He sees His character formed in people (Jer. 9:23-24).
4. God is pleased with praise and thanksgiving (Ps. 69:30-31).
5. God delights in our prayers (Prov. 115:8).
6. God delights in His people (Ps. 149:4).
7. God delights in those who are faithful and honest (Prov. 12:22).
8. God is pleased when we dwell together in unity (Ps. 133:1).

It is logical that if some things please Him, there are also things that do not please God:

1. Those who are in the flesh (Rom. 8:8).
2. Empty rituals and sacrifices (Heb. 10:6-8).
3. Those who do not exercise faith (Heb. 11:6).

Most of all, God is pleased with His Son.

1. It pleased the Lord for the fullness of deity to dwell in His Son (Col. 1:19).
2. He was pleased at His baptism (Matt. 3:17).

---

[16] *Chará*

3. He was pleased at His transfiguration (Matt. 17:5).
4. He was even pleased with His Son's death
   (Isa. 53:10 KJV).

To summarize these verses, what most pleases God is to see His character in the lives of His people. He delights in His Son, so only those who have humble faith and are "in Him" can truly please Him.

In light of these passages, let's think once again about the meaning of pleasure or joy, especially focusing on His *grace*. For all of my Christian life, I have had a somewhat cold, technical view of God's grace. I understood it to be His unmerited favor poured out on undeserving sinners, cleansing them from their sins and bringing them into the family of God. That is certainly true.

However, grace is more than that. When we focus on the word *favor* as we have just defined it, we begin to see that God has chosen to delight in His elect. Kittel groups the Greek word for grace (*cháris*) into the same category with the word for joy (*chará*). [17] This means that God has *spiritual pleasure* in His people.

Considering all the Greek words for joy or pleasure as they relate to God, it becomes even more apparent that He is pleased and even delighted to save us and have a relationship with us. Referring to God being "well-pleased" in 1 Cor. 1:21, Kittel and Friedrich say, "Of the various words for election, this one brings out most strongly the emotional side, i.e., God's love for the one whom he chooses." [18]

Why do I *enjoy* being with my friends? It is usually because of some quality that draws me to them. Maybe something one of my kids has done makes me very pleased with him or her. But why was God pleased to reveal His Son in me? (Gal. 1:15-16). Simply because He chose to rejoice over me. Nothing in me could bring Him pleasure, but He decided to delight in me! That is grace!

How then should I respond? Since He has delighted in me, I should, in turn, have *spiritual pleasure* in Him. However, my delight in Him is not unfounded. "We love [Him], because He first loved us" (1 John 4:19). He chose to love me because He wanted to. There is no greater pleasure than knowing this.

---

[17] Kittel and Friedrich.
[18] Ibid.

Seeking Pleasure

Many objects or activities seem to be sources of endless pleasure apart from God. We can selfishly seek satisfaction in a number of overtly sinful activities and become enslaved to them (Titus 3:3). We might put leisure, work, or family ahead of God, thinking that real pleasure comes from them (2 Tim. 3:4). We might even seek the approval of others to find fulfillment in the applause that rightfully belongs to God (Gal. 1:10). If someone's joy is in people, things, or activities, he is not a worshiper—religious, maybe—but not a worshiper.

Paul said, "We also have as our ambition, whether at home or absent, to be pleasing to Him" (2 Cor. 5:9). That is the goal of all worshipers. That should be our pursuit and our passion—our lives.

Paul also challenged Timothy to lay aside his personal comfort and make it a priority to be pleasing to the Lord. He said, "Suffer hardship with me, as a good soldier of Christ Jesus. No soldier in active service entangles himself in the affairs of everyday life, so that he may please the one who enlisted him as a soldier" (2 Tim. 2:3-4). We need to keep free from distractions and focus on our overall goal of pleasing God.

We may want to please our boss so that he gives us a raise or doesn't fire us. There is fear of punishment. However, pleasing God goes deeper than that. Our whole pursuit is to give Him pleasure, not because we are striving for His approval or some benefit. Our pleasure is inseparably tied to His.

If we live this truth, everything becomes an outflow of worship. "Whatever you do, do your work heartily, as for the Lord rather than for men" (Col. 3:23). Work, then, becomes an expression of worship, because we are no longer working for a paycheck or a pat on the back, but to give God pleasure. Work becomes a joy.

Finding Pleasure in God Alone

> *Delight yourself in the Lord; and He will give you the desires of your heart"* (Ps. 37:4).

One false religion in Brazil is constantly promising material benefits with some new gimmick. One week they sell a flaming hammer so you can pound it and get what you want. The next week they put a throne in front of the church so you can go get from God what is rightfully yours. The next week it is the "prayer of the 318" (based on Abraham's going out with 318 men to rescue Lot) that will get back everything you have lost. They have sold trumpets, breastplates, gavels, hammers, brooms, anointing oil, salt, crosses, rings—you name it. All of it with the promise of prosperity.

Peter described these groups as "springs without water…speaking out arrogant words of vanity they entice by fleshly desires, by sensuality…promising them freedom while they themselves are slaves of corruption" (2 Pet. 2:17-19).

Certainly God would not honor those who seek to please Him in exchange for material blessings. Those who are enticed by promises of prosperity find themselves enslaved to materialism. They do not delight themselves in God, but in this world.

Describing a true motivation for seeking God, Piper says, "In the end the heart longs not for any of God's good gifts, but for God Himself. To see Him and know Him and be in His presence is the soul's final feast. Beyond this there is no quest."[19]

"To delight" is an intense term that can mean to revel or indulge oneself until totally satisfied. It is a word used of an animal that has gorged itself and lies back, completely content.

Imagine yourself before God, "feasting on His presence" in worship. Rather than getting "full" and slowing down, you only become "hungrier" as you are drawn to Him. You seek Him with greater intensity because there is such joy in pleasing Him. The cycle continually expands. The more you please Him, the more satisfied you become and you desire only to please Him more.

At this point, the desire of your heart will not be a new car, a better job, or a new house. None of that will satisfy. They are trinkets that glitter, but for the one who is delighting in the Lord, they don't even catch the eye. Your satisfaction is in God alone. You no longer *need* anything else.

[19] Piper, *Desiring God*, p. 87

SATISFACTION IN JESUS

TRUE SATISFACTION

As the deer pants for the water brooks, So my soul pants for
You, O God. My soul thirsts for God, for the living God (Ps.
42:1-2).

If you have ever been thirsty in the desert, you know what an obses-
sive longing means. My brother and I once were caught in the New
Mexico mountains during a drought, far from water. I remember
hiking out of a valley and getting into his car to drive 20 miles on a
dirt road to a ranger's station. Our minds were focused on water the
whole way.

There is no greater physiological drive than thirst. David compares it to his driving desire for intimacy with the living God.

In several passages, God invites us to have our thirst satisfied in
Him (Isa. 55:1-2; John 4:14; 7:37-38). Jesus uses the water metaphor
to show that only God can satisfy our deepest longings.

Jesus also called Himself the "bread of life" (John 6:35). In the
same verse He promised, "He who comes to Me will not hunger,
and he who believes in Me will never thirst." Real satisfaction is not
found in material goods, fame, or religion. Only Jesus can fill and
satisfy us.

Jesus offered the Samaritan woman real satisfaction so that she
would "never thirst" but would have an internal source of everlasting
joy (John 4:14).

The disciples had gone into town for food. When they returned,
Jesus said, "I have food to eat that you do not know about" (John
4:32). He was saying that He knew what satisfies more than food.
He explained, "My food is to do the will of Him who sent Me and
to accomplish His work" (v. 34). Jesus' real satisfaction was not in
eating, but in pleasing His Father.

A PERSONAL TESTIMONY

I discovered the real meaning of fasting when I was facing a rather
unpleasant situation and decided to fast. I believed God would
somehow solve my problem if I abstained from eating, as if that
would put me in a better position to be heard. Part way through,

however, I found that it was not in solving my problem that I would have peace, but in His presence. My outward circumstances became meaningless in comparison to His holy presence. I realized that all I needed was God. I was so full of joy when I went to church that night. It was so appropriate that we sang Michael W. Smith's song, "Breathe" which speaks of our deep need and desire for Him. Our praise fit with what God was teaching me and the worship that was in my heart.

DAVID'S DELIGHT

David discovered that the only true satisfaction he could have is in God. That is why he said, "I have no good besides You" (Ps. 16:2). His kingdom, his wealth, his army, his wives, his fame—none gave him the satisfaction that he found in God. That is why he said later in the same Psalm, "In Your presence is fullness of joy; / In Your right hand there are pleasures forever" (v. 11).

Can you sense that David and God enjoyed each other? David's relentless pursuit was the pleasure of being with God. From God's standpoint, David was a man after His own heart (1 Sam. 13:14). This means that David's heart was of the same standard as God's.[20] That is what Paul meant when he said, "The one who joins himself to the Lord is one spirit with Him" (1 Cor. 6:17).

SALVATION'S JOY

Have you ever noticed in the book of Acts the immediate impact on people's lives when they came to know the Lord? There was always joy and rejoicing (see Acts 8:8; 8:39; 13:52; 16:34). When a person comes to know God, his or her life does not become dull or boring. For the first time that person experiences real pleasure in fellowship with God.

Joy is not giddiness. It does not mean we don't take the Christian life seriously. Nor does it mean we always have a smile on our face. However, if we really understand what Christ has done for us and who we are in Him, we can experience the joy of being set free, even during difficulties.

---

[20] *Katá* means that it is according to the norm. David's heart became like God's heart.

Too many Christians beat themselves up over their sin and feel they are not worthy to be joyful. They strive to regain God's favor instead of resting in what He has already done.

FEARING GOD

We need to keep our attitudes balanced. Some people become focused on friendship with God to the point that they lose their sense of awe of God. Informality can become irreverence. On the other hand, the greatness of God leads others to recoil and hide behind formalism.

That won't really happen to true worshipers. As we noted in chapters 2 and 3, worship involves fear. But there are two kinds of fear: a kind of cowardly fear that leads us to withdraw and an awesome fascination with God that draws us toward Him.

Tozer writes, "This fear of God was more than a natural apprehension of danger; it was non-rational dread, an acute feeling of personal insufficiency in the presence of God the Almighty."[21]

This reaction of ungodly fear can be seen in the parable of the talents. The unfaithful servant said, "'Master, I knew you to be a hard man, reaping where you did not sow and gathering where you scattered no seed. And I was afraid, and went away and hid your talent in the ground. See, you have what is yours'" (Matt. 25:24-25). Although he claimed to know about his master, he did not know him intimately. In fact, he accused Him of being unjust and hard. This created a fear that caused him to distance himself from his master and as a result he did not act.

When He commissioned His servants, God often said, "Fear not," a formula He uses some 75 times. He does not want His servants to flee.

On the other hand, godly fear will draw us to the Lord. "Reverence" and "respect" don't fully capture the whole essence of the word. Those words can communicate a cold, respectful distance. Even in the rabbinic writings there is a sense of love and intimacy when speaking of fear. Tozer called it "astonished reverence" and "reverential fear of God mixed with love and fascination and astonishment and admiration and devotion."[22] There is no dread.

---

[21] Tozer, *The Knowledge of the Holy*, p. 85.
[22] Tozer, *Whatever Happened to Worship?*, p. 30.

Using a concordance, check how the word "fear" is used in the Bible. Proverbs alone has 18 references to godly fear, considering it the foundation of a godly life.[23]

David's fear of God did not lead him to back away from God, In fact, he invited God into the most intimate recesses of his being, "Examine me, O LORD, and try me; Test my mind and my heart" (Ps. 26:2). He could say this because, "Your lovingkindness is before my eyes" (v. 3). In other words, whatever David did or wherever he went, he saw God's presence and it affected how he lived. David was a worshiper.

CONCLUSION

A life of worship doesn't seem very exciting to those who have not tasted the pleasure of intimacy with Him. However, worship is the path to the greatest satisfaction that exists. We are drawn to seek Him with all our heart because we desire to experience oneness with Him. As insignificant creatures, we are drawn to fellowship with the awesome Creator of the universe. We find true pleasure and fulfillment in communion with Him as He delights in us.

It is so easy to be distracted and satisfied with something less than what God has for us. We are too easily satisfied with things that give only a temporary happiness and leave us feeling empty. Although all Christians have been given access to His presence, some often seek fulfillment in other areas, thinking they will find joy somewhere else.

When we give ourselves to Him, becoming one spirit with Him, we are transformed into His image. It is only when the golden thread of worship is woven into our lives that we truly discover His will is "good and acceptable and perfect" (Rom. 12:2), and we experience true joy and fulfillment.

---

[23] Wisdom is moral rather than intellectual in the book of Proverbs. It has to do with the ability to live a godly life by applying biblical principles. It might be better thought of as "godliness."

THE PARADIGM SHIFT

There must be a real paradigm shift in our thinking about the purpose and result of worship if we are to move beyond a religious experience to true communion with God. That will change our understanding and experience of real pleasure and where we find.

Many Christians still find their greatest joy in this world while being careful not to do anything that is overtly sinful. The true worshiper is by no means a solemn stick in the mud, nor does he isolate himself from all that God intended for him to enjoy. His real joy, however, is in doing everything in God's presence.

SEEKING PLEASURE WITHIN RELIGIOUS LIMITS	SEEKING PLEASURE IN GOD
1. GOAL: Enjoy this world to the maximum	1. GOAL: Enjoy God to the maximum
2. ACTIVITIES: • Sports • Entertainment • Work • Social interaction	2. ACTIVITIES: • Sports • Entertainment • Work • Social interaction
3. LIMITS: • The law • Whatever causes a bad testimony	3. LIMITS: • Whatever interferes with worship • Whatever displeases God
4. RESULTS: • Temporal satisfaction • Hypocrisy	4. RESULTS: • Real joy in God • A holy life

Where to Start

Everyone's experience is different. If you were to take a trip through time and talk to all the great men of God, they would probably give you different descriptions of their walk with God. When I want to challenge myself to grow in my intimacy with Him, I like to read biographies of the great men of God or their writings. Here are some characteristics of those who walk with God.

1. **Dissatisfaction with the status quo.** Complacency is the Christian's greatest enemy. We get in a groove, put it on automatic pilot, and cruise. That is why people like religious rituals. They know what is coming and it fits into their routine. Compare your life to the lives of Abraham, Moses, and Paul. As people, they really weren't different from you. Lay your life before God and allow Him to create a stirring within your soul.

2. **Understanding their priorities.** We who are vocational Christian workers (who are commonly said to be "full time" in the ministry) know how easy it is to let our activities choke out our walk with God. We can easily use the excuse that we are working for God. I have heard appalling statistics of how little pastors pray. Sometimes I think I was more disciplined in seeking God as a biology professor than I have been as a missionary. Thankfully that has changed in the last few years.

3. **Practicing spiritual disciplines.** We will talk more about spiritual disciplines in a later chapter. They are not religious duties, but spiritual practices that put one in a position to hear from God. They are done with a humble, receptive attitude. Intimacy with God doesn't come instantly or by "tarrying." It comes through actively seeking to be in God's presence through prayer, fasting, meditation, and study. It also comes through putting oneself in contact with godly men and women, helping each other in this pursuit.

4. **Persistence.** Seeking God is not something you do, expecting to arrive at maturity quickly. There are frustrating times and

times of dryness. Madame Guyon says, "When you have learned to come to the Lord with this attitude, you will not be upset if the Lord withdraws Himself from you. The times of spiritual dryness will be the same to you as the times of spiritual abundance. You will treat them both the same. Why? Because you will have learned to love God just because you love Him, not because of His gifts, *nor even for His precious presence.*"[1] Of course God never withdraws Himself, but there certainly are times when we may not sense His presence. At those times, we must continue to seek Him.

5. FINDING SATISFACTION IN GOD. People often think that seeking God is a burden and a solemn task. The real quality of a powerful walk with God is simply enjoying His presence. Sit in silence before Him, just love Him, and allow Him to love you back. Tell Him you want to enjoy Him forever. Meditate on Psalm 16:9-11, praying that it would be real in your life.

---

[1] Guyon, p. 24.

Discussion Questions

1. In what way are we to seek pleasure in the presence of God?
2. What can we learn from the marriage metaphor?
3. What does it mean to please God?
4. What is the difference between selfish pleasure-seeking and spiritual pleasure in God?
5. What does it mean to fear God?
6. Why do we tend to seek refuge in people or things rather than God?
7. What does it mean to seek God?
8. What did you learn from the two paradigms?
9. Where do you find pleasure apart from God?
10. How can we seek satisfaction in God without being selfish?

Chapter 10

BECOMING THE BODY OF CHRIST THROUGH WORSHIP

WORSHIP BRINGS US INTO A PROPER RELATIONSHIP WITH THE CHURCH.

For through the grace given to me I say to everyone among you not to think more highly of himself than he ought to think; but to think so as to have sound judgment, as God has allotted to each a measure of faith. FOR JUST AS WE HAVE MANY MEMBERS IN ONE BODY AND THE MEMBERS DO NOT HAVE THE SAME FUNCTION... (Romans 12:3-4).

SEED TRUTH: WORSHIP DRAWS US TOGETHER WITH OTHER WORSHIPERS IN SPIRITUAL COMMUNITIES. *An individual can be very isolated and solitary during religious moments, even in group settings. However, genuine worship gives us a humble perspective of ourselves, drawing us into an interdependent relationship with the rest of the* body of Christ. *We lose our individualism through worship. The golden thread of worship not only ties us to God, but also binds us intimately to other worshipers.*

When I first arrived in Brazil, I was eager to start doing something for the Lord. Since I wanted to teach, but didn't know Portuguese yet, I offered an English Bible study at our language school. A number of young professionals who were already believers started coming. We became good friends and I was eager to learn from them about the church and Christianity in Brazil.

I asked them about their concept of the church and how it functioned. They said they really didn't have a church per se. As they described it to me, it seemed more like a very good parachurch organization, but not really a church. They had some small groups, teachings in larger groups, and discipleship, but never was there any talk about worship. One of their meetings I attended had a good Bible study, but no group prayers, interaction, or singing. It was more like a lecture followed by a social time.

Wanting to explore the group more to learn from them, I gave a study on worship to see how they would respond. Nothing was said about music or forms, just some of the basic concepts that we have developed in this book. One of the key leaders said that worship was an interesting concept, but they didn't feel the need to practice it. Although they were studying the Word and reaching out, it seemed to me that something was really missing.

I wrote to the American missionary who had started the group and suggested we explore the idea of putting together a culturally relevant church for this group. I shared with him my concept of the church, such as it was at the time. He replied:

"Let me give you the bottom line first, Bruce....What you see Carlos, Magrão, Giba and the ones involved in *is* an organized church already. It is believers living in community (not in congregation) with one another; using their gifts & resources to help one another grow to look like Christ & reveal Him to their lost friends and families."

Years later, I re-read the letter from that missionary. He was right in that my thinking of organization and my paradigm of the church were probably more like a congregation than a community. His letter led me to meditate even more on what a church is. Since that time, God has taken me through a number of paradigm shifts to help me see the church, His bride, more clearly.

CONGREGATION OR COMMUNITY?

DEFINITIONS

A "congregation," by my definition, is a group of Christians who gather periodically to sing songs and listen to a message. Organizational structure holds the group together and provides the context for the relationships. It would not really be appropriate to call this a "body" because there is no interdependence or functioning together for a common goal. Maintaining the organization and its physical structure consumes most of the time and resources of the group.

On the other hand, a "community" is held together by relationships, and the structure flows out of that. All the participants have made a mutual commitment to join their hearts together in worship, to edify one another, and to work together to reach the lost. There is an interdependence such that through their unity, they manifest the fullness of Christ (Eph 1:23; 3:19; 4:13). It would be correct to call this group a "body" because they have a commitment to one another and work together, having different functions, but they are one in spirit, mind, and purpose.

Until a few years ago, I saw the church as a congregation. I had not come to see what the body was all about because I had an individualistic mind-set. Through starting a church and helping a number of other men plant new churches, I have seen more and more clearly what God intended for the church. It also helped that I taught ecclesiology (the theological study of the church) for a number of years in a local seminary. But what really advanced my understanding of the body was putting together a study on the book of Ephesians.

Being a missionary has opened eyes to the beauty of Christ's bride. Coming into another culture has helped me strip away my cultural biases and look at the church from a different perspective and see its essence more fully.

However, thinking back to the group I met when I first arrived in Brazil, the question still remains: Can you truly develop a spiritual community without a focus on worship? Members of a club develop some sense of camaraderie around their interests, but it is not a spiritual community. People can get together and sing hymns, but that doesn't make it a spiritual community. Churches can rally around evangelism, discipleship, missions, social outreach, etc., *but if worship is not the golden thread that ties the group together, it is* not really *a spiritual community.*

Tozer defines the purpose of the church in this manner:

> I believe a local church exists to do corporately what each
> Christian believer should be doing individually – and that is
> to worship God. It is to show forth the excellencies of Him
> who has called us out of darkness into His marvelous light.
> It is to reflect the glories of Christ ever shining upon us
> through the ministries of the Holy Spirit.[1]

The church is not just a parenthesis between two kingdoms. It is
God's master creation. God chose to fill the church with His fullness
(Eph. 1:22-23). That means the church is the second incarnation of
Christ. A church that worships individually and corporately has dis-
covered the key to fulfilling His purpose for His bride. Corporately,
as a worshiping body, we are to reflect the fullness of His glory.

Commenting on this passage, Julien says, "Imagine if you can:
He who has been exalted above all principalities and powers has
chosen to express His fullness in the Church! This must mean that
the Church, too, is exalted above all other things...."[2]

This chapter is about how worship brings people together into
spiritual communities.

A WORSHIPING COMMUNITY DEALS WITH SIN
SO THE PERSON WHO STUMBLED CAN BE RESTORED
AND BROUGHT BACK INTO FELLOWSHIP.

EXAMPLES

One night I received a disturbing call. A woman immediately
identified herself as a student of mine, but not a member of any
of our churches. She would not give me her name. She confessed
that she was involved in an adulterous affair and that my class on 1
Corinthians 7 had spoken to her.

I asked her if she could talk to one of the leaders of her church
to get help.

[1] Tozer, *Whatever Happened to Worship?*, pp.93-94.
[2] Tom Julien, *Studies in Ephesians*, p. 30.

"No way," she said. "I have seen others try that and their life becomes a hell. I would never live it down and I could never be involved in any kind of activity or ministry ever again. They would never forget it."

Not long after this phone conversation, I was teaching on the difference between a congregation and a community. I was discussing the paradigm shifts necessary to live worship.

A woman came up afterward and said, "If I were part of a congregation, I would be living in another city right now."

She also had become involved in an adulterous affair a few months earlier. Instead of the church alienating her, its loving concern and prayer surrounded her. The community's actions broke her. Instead of piling self-righteous guilt upon her, they allowed the Holy Spirit to convict her and change her life.

She knew if her spiritual family had not responded the way it did, she would have walked away from everything in defeat, shame, and bitterness. God was glorified and her marriage and life were restored. Years later, she is happily married and has children. She is very active in the community and serving the Lord with her husband.

The other woman from the phone conversation? Well, the last I heard, she had left her husband, abandoned the church, and was involved in another affair.

Congregations tend to shoot at their wounded. Their focus is to maintain order and purity in the structure. Of course, evil within a community is devastating and we should never tolerate evil (see 1 Cor. 5). A worshiping community, however, deals with sin so the true believer who stumbled can be restored and brought back into fellowship.

THE MARRIAGE METAPHOR

Many people think of a Christian marriage as two Christians who live legally under the same roof with the blessing of the church.

God's ideal for marriage is stated in Genesis 2:24, "For this reason a man shall leave his father and his mother, and be joined to his wife; and they shall become one flesh."

Commenting on this passage, Jesus said, "So they are no longer two, but one flesh" (Matt. 19:6). He described this oneness as being such that the separation of the two would cause serious harm to both parties.

In fact, one aspect of the image of God that was created in humans was oneness. The Hebrew word for God, *Elohim*, implies a plurality within the one true God. Genesis 1:27 records that He created male *and* female in His image, implying that they shared the same unity that exists in the Trinity.

So what happened to this oneness? At the fall, both the man and the woman became individualistic. The "*desire*" of the woman (Gen. 3:16) became one of wanting to control her husband and the "*rule*" of the husband became domineering. Chauvinism and feminism were born at the fall.

However, Christ came to restore our oneness, starting with the marriage relationship. There are to be no more individual rights, but everything is subordinated to the relationship. My honor becomes our honor. Her pain is our pain. We are one.

The lack of oneness in marriage manifests itself in different ways. A missionary friend told me it was difficult when he and his wife visit supporting churches because he receives most of the attention. His wife resents her less visible role and becomes jealous of the focus on him.

If they were truly one, that kind of competition would not exist. If I am pushed to the forefront, my wife feels as if she is being honored. If someone compliments Lisa, it is no different than complimenting me. I take that back. I actually enjoy it more when people speak well of my wife, just as she takes it harder than I do when someone speaks evil of me.

Paul, also commenting on the Genesis passage, said, "This mystery is great; but I am speaking with reference to Christ and the church" (Eph. 5:32). What if that oneness were not limited to marriage? What if it could be experienced on the level of the church? What if everyone stopped thinking about his or her own rights, benefits, comfort, and preferences? What if our mutual commitment led us to subordinate all these things to the group?

Our life at home is the real test. If the golden thread of worship is woven into my "private" life, I will not only be one with my wife, but also with my brothers and sisters in Christ.

WORSHIP MAKES THE DIFFERENCE

For just as we have many members in one body and all the members do not have the same function, we, who are many, are one body in Christ, and individually members one of another (Rom. 12:4-5).

The way communities restore the sinning saint is only one way the church manifests itself. This passage describes what makes a church a community: It is a body rather than a group of people.

It is highly significant that Paul preceded his discussion on the body in Romans by teaching on worship and the transformation it produces. Without worship, Christianity is just another dead religion. Worship draws us into communities because it transforms our whole mentality toward each other by going against our fleshly individualism.

We usually think of the flesh[3] as sensuality. The church usually disciplines what are considered sins of the flesh (immorality, drunkenness, etc.). However, the essence of the flesh is self-centeredness, including individualism. Many churches cater to the individualistic lifestyle of our day by allowing people to slip in right before the service and make a quick exit afterward without any call to commitment. Although it is not wrong to be culturally relevant, to be conscious of the presence of unbelievers, and to speak to the needs of the people, seeker-driven churches and needs-driven ministries tend to encourage individualism at the expense of community.

When Paul lists the "*deeds of the* flesh" in Galatians 5:19-21, eight of the fifteen are directly related to our relationship with others. The other deeds, which we would normally consider "fleshly," include false religions, immorality and drunkenness. It seems that the flesh will manifest itself mostly as we relate with one another.

In a congregation, people come into the pews, sing some songs, hear a message, cordially greet each other, and go home. In this context, there is not much opportunity to provoke a fleshly response in each other, except maybe in the parking lot as we are jockeying to leave.

When a spiritual community is formed, we have found that the relationships are so close that it is easy for fleshly attitudes to come

---

[3] *Sárx* in the Greek.

into play. Even small differences can cause major upheaval, creating a ripple effect shaking the whole foundation of the community. For this reason, the group needs to be rooted in worship, and to break its fleshly individualism. Foster describes what happens as "a divine melting of our separateness." [4]

When there is a community mind-set, people are bonded together through worship and they delight in being together. David expressed his pleasure in Psalm 16:3: "As for the saints who are in the earth, They are the majestic ones in whom is all my delight."

WORSHIP'S ESSENTIAL QUALITY: HUMILITY

For through the grace given to me, I say to every man among you not to think more highly of himself than he ought to think; but to think so as to have sound judgment, as God has allotted to each a measure of faith (Rom. 12:3).

Paul, immediately after expounding the essence of worship and before talking about the body, exhorted the people to be humble.

MAN IN RELATION TO GOD

Worship is key in producing a unified community because worship produces humility by focusing our minds on God rather than ourselves. The closer our relationship to God, the more we have a proper perspective on our lives, especially in relation to other believers. Worship drives egotism from our lives. It is impossible to bow down before God, offering our lives to Him, while maintaining a lofty view of ourselves.

Egotism can be expressed in two ways: One is to take ourselves too seriously and give ourselves undue importance. The other is to minimize our gifts and importance to the body. Both are self-centered, because they focus on us instead of the glory of God and His church. Either way, we are comparing ourselves to others and focusing on who we are, rather than on Him.

Worship always gives us a proper perspective of ourselves. Psalm 8 is a good summary of how worship humbles us so we can really live community. If we don't start with humility, we can never live the reality of the church.

[4] Foster, p.143.

God's Greatness

> *"O LORD, our Lord, How majestic is Your name in all the earth, Who have displayed Your splendor above the heavens! From the mouth of infants and nursing babes You have established strength, Because of Your adversaries, To make the enemy and the revengeful cease"* (Ps. 8:1-2).

Anyone who has lain on his back and looked into the vastness of space has had a small glimpse of the infinite power of the Creator. It is amazing to think that He even knows how many stars there are and has given names to each one (Ps. 147:4; Isa. 40:26).

What David saw in looking at the night sky was God's majestic splendor. He saw greatness, but at the same time, meditating on His power, he recognized that God delighted in displaying that strength through the weakest of beings. He is able to wipe out the strongest adversary with the weakest child.

Man's Insignificance

> *"When I consider Your heavens, the work of Your fingers, The moon and the stars, which You have ordained; What is man, that You take thought of him, And the son of man that You care for him?"* (Ps. 8:3-4).

As David continued to contemplate the stars God had created and placed in order, he gained a perspective of how small, helpless, and insignificant he was before God's greatness. To think that God created all this with His "fingers"! In other words, such a vast task was effortless for God.

What is there about man that would cause such a great God to stoop down to care for Him? The two thoughts of verse 4 are parallel.[5] There is really no reason the Creator of this great universe should even think about a piece of cosmic dust like us. It is amazing that we could even think that the world should revolve around us. But we do.

Man's Significance

> *Yet You have made him a little lower than God, And You crown him with glory and majesty! You make him to rule over the*

---

[5] This is a Hebrew parallelism typical of poetic literature. Man = Son of man; Take thought of = Be concerned about or care for.

works of Your hands; You have put all things under his feet, All sheep and oxen, And also the beasts of the field, The birds of the heavens, and the fish of the sea, Whatever passes through the paths of the seas (Ps. 8:5-8).

Even though we are so insignificant and unworthy of consideration, God has made us temporarily a little lower than the angels in the created order of the universe.[6] Our current position is a result of the fall. However, He has destined us to be rewarded with glory and majesty, two of His attributes He will bestow upon us. He has also destined us to have full rule over His creation, including His angels.

Although man's destiny was lost at the fall, Christ came to restore our future (Heb. 2:10). Creation is not subject to us as it should be at this point, but through Christ, it will be restored. David, in this Psalm, is amazed and astounded that such a great and powerful God would restore authority to us through His grace and mercy.

God wants us to focus on the fact that it is by His grace that we have this destiny and position. If it had any merit, we would have room for boasting (Eph. 2:8-9; 1 Cor. 1:27-31). That God has stooped down and elevated us should create in us humility.

God's Greatness Repeated

"O LORD, our Lord, How majestic is Your name in all the earth!" (Ps. 8:9).

After reflecting on what God did, David is even more amazed at God and finishes with this praise. Take a minute from your reading and praise Him for His greatness and for our restoration by His unmerited favor.

JESUS TEACHES ABOUT HUMILITY

Jesus taught His disciples two truths that just didn't seem to sink in. The first was His crucifixion and resurrection. The idea that the Messiah would have to suffer before He reigned was outside their messianic paradigm. The second teaching beyond their grasp was the importance

---

[6] The Hebrew uses Elohim while the LXX uses *ángelos*, as quoted in Hebrews 2:7. It seems best to understand this as God temporarily making man inferior to the angels.

of humility. Their difficulty in understanding humility was probably one of the reasons they couldn't imagine a suffering Messiah.

Jesus' first extensive teaching recorded in the New Testament starts with, "Blessed are the poor in spirit, for theirs is the kingdom of heaven" (Matt. 5:3). The word Jesus used for "poor" means *humble* as in being, "miserable, beggarly, impotent."[7]

MacArthur points out:

> The word commonly used for ordinary poverty was *peni-chros,* and was used of the widow Jesus saw giving an offering in the Temple. ...She had very little, but she did have "two small copper coins" (Luke 21:2). She was poor but not a beggar. One who is *penichrós* poor has at least some meager resources. One who is *ptōchós* poor, however, is completely dependent on others for sustenance. He has absolutely no means of self-support. [8]

Recognizing our helpless condition is not only the first step toward humility, it is also the first step toward salvation. That is why Jesus added, "...for theirs is the kingdom of heaven." The reason this attitude is so crucial is that, without it, we will never see our need for Christ; we will never be able to enter into a right relationship with the body of Christ, and we can never be a worshiper.

As Jesus and His disciples descended from the Mount of Transfiguration, they met the other nine who were having trouble casting out a demon. Their inability to cast out the demon and the fact that Jesus had taken James, John, and Peter up on the mountain with Him undoubtedly sparked the discussion as to which of them was the greatest (Mark 9:33-34). They finally asked Jesus to settle the question and He answered by bringing a child or toddler among them (Matt. 18:2).

He told them in no uncertain terms that to change or be converted one must become like that little child. Which quality did the disciples lack? Humility. Here, Jesus used another term that describes the lowering of oneself as a mountain is leveled.[9] It means

---

[7] Bauer et al.
[8] MacArthur, *The MacArthur New Testament Commentary; Matthew 1-7,* p.145.
[9] Tapeinóō in *the Greek.*

to think lowly. How is a child humble? It has to do with the child's simple, unassuming trust. Humility is dependence, in contrast to self-sufficiency.

This lesson apparently didn't sink in because soon after, the mother of John and James asked Jesus to give the best thrones to her sons (Matt. 20:20-23). She and the sons obviously were thinking of the twelve thrones Jesus had promised after the talk with the rich young ruler (Matt. 19:28). They wanted to have first dibs on the best seats. The other disciples were upset because John and James made their request ahead of them (Matt. 19:24).

Once more, Jesus told them the standard for leadership was the inverse of the world's standards. It was not about power, influence, and privilege, but about love and service. He finished by pointing to Himself as an example of real humility, "just as the Son of man did not come to be served, but to serve, and to give His life a ransom for many" (Matt. 20:28).

Jesus then provided a very practical demonstration of humility. Here He was, the most important man to ever walk the face of the earth, going to the most important event in history. He had a whole crowd following Him, but two beggars on the side of the road cried out. Everyone told them to be quiet, because they were unimportant. However, Jesus stopped and said to them, "What do you want Me to do for you?" (Matt. 20:32).

It should have been pretty obvious what they wanted. However, Jesus' words were those of a servant. The Greatest One was willing to serve the lowliest. The fact that He healed them is secondary. He demonstrated what it means to be a leader and a servant.

His example still didn't sink in to the disciples. At the last supper, they were still arguing about who was the greatest (Luke 22:24). That must have hurt Jesus deeply, but He patiently repeated the same lesson.

Jesus was preparing His disciples to be worshipers and to be part of His body. That could happen only if they were truly humble. It is obvious from the example of the disciples that people can never produce humility in themselves.

MacArthur says,

> Humility is not a necessary human work to make us worthy, but a necessary divine work to make us see that we *are*

unworthy and cannot change our condition without God. That is why monasticism, asceticism, physical self-denial, mutilation and other such self-efforts are so foolish and futile. They feed pride rather than subdue it, because they are works of the flesh. [10]

When the Holy Spirit came upon the disciples, it was another story. At that point, they were transformed into humble worshipers. That is why the church came together so quickly and powerfully.

THE HOLY SPIRIT AND HUMILITY

And do not get drunk with wine, for that is dissipation, but be filled with the Spirit, speaking to one another in psalms and hymns and spiritual songs, singing and making melody with your heart to the Lord; always giving thanks for all things in the name of our Lord Jesus Christ to God, even the Father; and be subject to one another in the fear of Christ (Eph. 5:18-21).

The command to be filled with the Spirit was always confusing to me. I used to liken it to filling the gas tank in my car. Did the Holy Spirit somehow leak out of me during the week so that I had to go back to church to fill up again? It didn't make sense.

The word that Paul used in Ephesians 5:18 is not the word typically used for filling a water jar. It means to penetrate or permeate everything, as did the sound at Pentecost (Acts 2:2) and the fragrance that Mary used to anoint Jesus (John 12:3).

It follows that I could be fully indwelt by the Holy Spirit at all times, but without His presence permeating my being so I would be under His guidance. Paul illustrated the idea with the example of wine. When wine goes through the stomach wall and into the bloodstream, it permeates and influences the entire body.

Worship and being filled with the Spirit are integrally related. When we fix our mind on things above and things of the Spirit, we are worshiping. When our minds are distracted to fleshly things, we are no longer worshiping.

---

[10] MacArthur, *Matthew*, p. 149.

MacArthur, describing the Eph. 5:18 passage, writes:

> The continuous aspect of being *filled* ("be being kept filled") involves day-by-day, moment-by-moment submission to the Spirit's control. The passive aspect indicates that it is not something we do but that we allow to be done in us. The filling is entirely the work of the Spirit Himself, but He works only through our willing submission. The present aspect of the command indicates that we cannot rely on a past filling nor live in expectation of future filling.[11]

In Ephesians 5:19-21 Paul tells us the results of being filled with His Spirit.[12] The first has to do with our conversation. The Word of God and "spiritual songs" will be on our lips, and praise will flow from our mouths.

The second and third results of being filled deal with what is in our hearts. Praise will flow through our veins in an attitude of worship.

The fourth concerns our attitude. A person filled with the Spirit will be "always giving thanks" rather than complaining.

The fifth result of being filled with the Spirit is mutual submission, which is only possible when we are humble. This is foundational in being the church.

Jim Petersen says, "The Holy Spirit is the source of life for God's people. Without Him there is nothing. With Him, every believer becomes an essential, contributing part of the whole. There are to be no bleachers—no place to just sit and watch."[13]

For the next chapter-and-a-half, Paul tells how being filled with the Spirit will play out in our relationships with one another, starting with marriage. When the golden thread of worship is woven into our lives, it will affect our marriages, our families, our employer-employee relationships, and, most of all, our relationships within the church.

[11] MacArthur, *The MacArthur New Testament Commentary; Ephesians,* p. 249.
[12] Paul uses five present tense result participles to show the continuous fruit of being filled with the Spirit.
[13] Jim Petersen, *Church Without Walls*, p.171.

HUMILITY AND THE BODY

Therefore if there is any encouragement in Christ, if there is any consolation of love, if there is any fellowship of the Spirit, if any affection and compassion, make my joy complete by being of the same mind, maintaining the same love, united in spirit, intent on one purpose. Do nothing from selfishness or empty conceit, but with humility of mind regard one another as more important than yourselves; do not merely look out for your own personal interests, but also for the interests of others. Have this attitude in yourselves which was also in Christ Jesus (Phil. 2:1-5).

Paul was suffering in prison while the Philippians were fighting among themselves about questions similar to those of the disciples. Paul even called attention to two women who were faithful servants of the Lord, but were having trouble getting along (Phil. 4:2-3).

The first statements in Philippians 2 are not conditional, but are presumed realities within the church. There *is* comfort and encouragement among believers. The Holy Spirit placed it there. There *is* compassion and consolation within the love of the church. There *is* real fellowship between believers. There *is* heartfelt compassion for one another.

Those qualities exist and are at our disposal as a body. God has done His part in giving the qualities to the church.

Paul's joy is directly related to God's good pleasure. Nothing pleases God more than a holy unity among His people (Ps. 133). God wants us to love each other deeply. Paul's joy would be complete only if those attributes that God had given to the church were visible through their relationships.

That unity is described as "being of the same mind" (Phil. 2:2), which means the group has a common vision; they share a love for the Lord and for each other, and they are intent on one purpose.

The quality that is most intriguing is "united in spirit" (2:2), which literally means the souls are being joined together.[14] It is reminiscent of David's soul being knit to Jonathan's (1 Sam. 18:1). This unity is possible because each of us is "one spirit with the [Lord]" (1 Cor. 6:17). Uniting ourselves to the Lord unites us to one another.

---

[14] *Súmpsuchos* in the Greek. *Sum* – together; *psuchos* – soul.

Lack of humility is the barrier to this kind of unity. Paul defined humility as getting rid of all selfishness or excessive ambition. We are to have humility of mind or a lowly mind-set (Phil. 2:3).[15] It is not a false humility that says, "I am really undeserving." It is not personally degrading yourself, nor is it an inferiority complex.

Paul defines humility as regarding others as more important than ourselves and looking out for the interest of others before our own. We should think of the group first. At that point, we have a community mind-set.

Then Paul gives the key to everything: "Have this attitude in yourselves which was also in Christ Jesus" (Phil. 2:5). The word for attitude is the same as for the mind,[16] though different from the one used in Romans 12:2 and 1 Cor. 2:16. Here it emphasizes the mind-set of Jesus.

This completes the connection. Through worship we become like Christ, having our mind-sets transformed to think like He does. Instead of the normal human self-preservation model, we consider the needs of others above our personal comfort.

Jesus did not hold on to His privileges as God, which included the comfort of heaven. Without emptying Himself of His deity, He voluntarily became a servant. His servant attitude led Him to become absolutely obedient to the Father, although He is co-equal to Him. His obedience led to His death and ultimately to His exaltation (see Phil. 2:6-11).

Only when we are filled with the Spirit and worshiping will we experience true humility. Losing our individuality, we are drawn into the body of Christ. Then, we will be willing to give up our comfort and find real satisfaction in His presence in the body of Christ, the church.

A Personal Testimony

How am I personally doing in that area? Brazilians are by nature some of the friendliest people I have ever met. I can see my fleshly, private, individualistic attitudes exposed in this culture.

---

[15] *Tapeinophrosunē* in the Greek.
[16] *Phroneō* in the Greek.

Soon after we arrived in Brazil, the new President seized all the money in the banks in an effort to curb runaway inflation. This left us for almost a week without any money. Since our rent was due, I went several times to explain to the man at the rental agency why we were late with our rent. He was so understanding. He knew that things were in chaos economically and was patient.

After a week we were still flat broke, and so I returned to the rental agency again to explain that I had nothing, not even enough to buy formula for Maria who was only four months old. He was very kind and said not to worry about it.

That night, some missionary friends invited us for dinner. When we returned home, the man from the rental agency was waiting. He had brought his kids across town by bus to give us formula for Maria. How humbling!

I have no doubt God brought me to Brazil to expose my wrong thinking and make me more into His image. My Brazilian brothers and sisters have been an example, teaching me what it means to be humble, generous, forgiving, and patient. It seems as though the less they have, the more generous they are. When you visit them, they give you the very best.

WORSHIP AND UNITY

Jesus, in His priestly prayer in John 17, laid out some high standards as He reviewed His ministry before the Father. One of the intriguing aspects is oneness or unity: "Holy Father, keep them in Your name, the name which You have given Me, that they may be one even as We are" (John 17:11).

Jesus prayed that the unity of His church would reflect the unity of the Father and the Son. Maybe our lack of unity is the reason people have trouble understanding the Trinity. Such unity, however, cannot be an impossible ideal or Jesus would not have prayed for it.

JESUS PRAYED THAT THE UNITY OF HIS CHURCH
WOULD REFLECT THE UNITY OF THE FATHER AND THE SON.

One aspect of our being created in the image of God is oneness. The word for God, *Elohim,* reflects plurality. The Scriptures say, "And God [Elohim] created man in His own image, in the image of God, He created him; male and female He created them" (Gen. 1:27). Adam and Eve had the oneness of the Trinity. It was obviously lost in the fall, when selfishness crept in. However, Jesus came to restore us to the pre-fall state, and one aspect of this restoration is oneness.

Obviously, we cannot create this kind of unity. The key is in Jesus' prayer to "keep them in Your name, the name which You have given Me…" (John 17:11). "The name" is not just an epithet to designate His person, but a reflection of His very nature. To be kept in His name implies that we are worshiping Him, and His character is being formed in us. That brings us full circle to the image of God being formed in us in terms of His oneness. Thus, only worshipers can experience that kind of unity.

THE MYSTERY OF THE CHURCH

Nothing can compare to the church. That is why the Bible uses metaphors to describe it. Some people invent metaphors, describing the church as a business, a club, or a hospital, but such comparisons do more harm than good. On the other hand, the living metaphors (body, bride, flock, living stones, etc.) that the Bible uses give us a better understanding of the life of the church.

The Bible also describes the church as a "mystery," something that was hidden, but has now been revealed in Christ. This revelation is so marvelous that it is only through God's opening our eyes that we can begin to understand the glory of the church.

The fact that the church is beyond our understanding should give us a sense of awe. Wiersbe says, "When we lose the wonder of the church, then what we do as a part of the congregation will be boring and routine."[17]

Ephesians 2 and 3 speak of the mystery of the church (Eph. 3:4). After using several metaphors to describe the church, Paul prays for spiritual understanding of the church.

---

[17] Wiersbe, p. 89.

Next he prays for the spiritual strengthening of the inner man so Christ will "dwell" or be at home "in [our] hearts" (Eph. 3:17).[18] At this point we will "be able to comprehend with all the saints what is the breadth and length and heighth and depth" (Eph. 3:18).

Although the Greek does not supply an object to these dimensions, the NIV inserts "love." This initially seems logical, since "love" is mentioned in verses 17 and 19. However, such an interpretation ignores the larger context of the passage, which is the church.

Eadie catalogs ten different interpretations of this passage, but affirms that the most probable reference is to the church. He says these dimensions refer to the temple metaphor in chapter 2, which is a description of the church.[19]

We have seen how the previous language of the prayer is molded by such an allusion; that the invigoration of the inner man, the indwelling of Christ, and the substructure in love, have all distinct reference to the glorious spiritual edifice. This idea was present, and so present to the apostle's imagination that he feels no need to make mention of it.[20]

LOVE CAN BE UNDERSTOOD ONLY WHEN WE ARE ABLE TO SEE THE CHURCH THROUGH SPIRITUAL EYES.

Paul does pray for our understanding of love in verse 19, but this is distinct from the request in verse 18.[21] This love "surpasses knowledge." If our understanding of love should surpass knowledge, it can happen only if God opens our eyes to comprehend the church. Love can be understood only when we are able to see the church through spiritual eyes.

God opens our eyes to the mystery of the church through worship. Worship leads us to understand the church, and the church fulfills its ultimate purpose in worship.

---

[18] *Katoikéō* – To reside and settle down.
[19] John Eadie, *Commentary on the Epistle of Paul to the Ephesians,* pp. 258-262.
[20] Eadie, p. 261.
[21] The *kaí* is not epexegetical, but a conjunction. He is making two distinct requests that are joined by the *kaí*.

THE BODY METAPHOR

Almost all the metaphors for the church are used to describe Israel as well. Both Israel and the church are flocks, people, families, vines, brides, etc., but only the church is described as a body. Perhaps it is because only the human body can represent both the organic unity and the diversity that exists in the church.

UNITY IN DIVERSITY

"For the body is not one member, but many" (1 Cor. 12:14). Although this passage is specifically referring to the diversity of gifts, there is still unity in the diversity.

Early in my Christian life, I was involved in a church that was racially and culturally diverse. Our pastor had a vision for reaching out to internationals and there were people from all walks of life and virtually all continents meeting together as one body. This diversity brought an incredible richness to our body life and strength into our corporate worship.

A student of mine from another denomination has been planting a church in an unusual location here in Belém. If you go in one direction, there are mansions and well-to-do families. In another direction, there is the middle class. In a third direction you come to very simple homes. The church's building is right at a convergence point of these three different cultures, and he was reaching out to them all.

A missionary commented to him that he was going to have to choose his target group, because this group could not "worship" together. He suggested that the church might even have to go to separate services to reach these diverse groups.

It is not easy for a heterogeneous group to meet together and feel they have much in common. People tend to segregate to be with people who are most like them.

However, if people who would not naturally get along together could be united in one body, it would be an incredible manifestation of the power of God. It is unfortunate that Sunday morning is the most segregated time of the week in the U.S. There should be more of a cultural mixing, not to be politically correct, but to express the richness of the body of Christ. We are missing out because we are not experiencing the richness of a diverse corporate worship time.

That is why Paul made such a big deal about the breaking down of the separation between the Jews and the Gentiles in Ephesians 2:11-14. How could natural enemies be made into "one"? Only as God brings together transformed individuals into one body of worshipers. Unity, despite the diversity, is a demonstration of the power of God. Three amazing things happen: Unbelievers recognize the members of the body as true disciples (John 13:34-35), people come to see that the Father sent the Son (John 17:21), and the spiritual world sits up and takes notice (Eph. 3:10).

Paul explains how all of this relates to worship. "…and have put on the new self who is being renewed to a true knowledge according to the image of the One who created him—a renewal in which there is no distinction between Greek and Jews, circumcised and uncircumcised, barbarian, Scythian, slave and freeman, but Christ is all, and in all" (Col. 3:10-11).

As our new man is being renewed, we become more intimate[22] with Him, we are more and more transformed into His image. This breaks down all the barriers, whether they are racial (Jew or Gentile), religious (circumcised or uncircumcised), cultural (barbarian or Scythian), or class (slave or free). The differences between us become unimportant because we have all been transformed. Outward differences still exist, but the presence of the Holy Spirit allows the diversity to become an asset instead of a hindrance to unity.

Diversity in Unity

"But now there are many members, but one body" (1 Cor. 12:20). This verse goes beyond accepting the difference and leads us into true oneness. There is no room for an inferiority complex ("Because I am not an eye, I am not a part of the body," v. 16), or for arrogance ("The eye cannot say to the hand, 'I have no need of you,'" v. 21).

Paul said, in reference to marriage, "No one ever hated his own flesh, but nourishes and cherishes it, just as Christ also does the church" (Eph. 5:29). That does not apply just to my wife, but to the whole body of Christ. Hurting my brother is hurting myself.

The Great Commandment says we are to love the Lord "with all your heart, and with all your soul, and with all your mind" (Matt.

---

[22] *Epígnōsis in the Greek.*

22:37). Jesus is describing worship. Worship is the Great Command and the Great Commission. It is not singing hymns, but an internal love relationship that involves one's emotions, volition, intellect, affection—everything. Then, and only then, can we obey the second part to "love your neighbor as yourself" (v.39).

John, in his first epistle, repeatedly emphasizes the link between worship and love within the body of Christ:

> The one who says he is in the Light [says he has fellowship with God or is a worshiper] and yet hates his brother is in the darkness until now (1 John 2:9).

> But whoever has the world's goods, and sees his brother in need and closes his heart against him, how does the love of God [love for God: worship] abide in him? (1 John 3:17).

> The one who does not love does not know [intimacy—worship] God for God is love (1 John 4:8).

> If anyone loves the world, the love of the Father [love for the Father or worship] is not in him (1 John 2:15).

Consider this:

> "No one has seen God at any time; if we love one another, God abides in us, and His love is perfected in us" (1 John 4:12).

God doesn't abide in us *because* we love, but love is the evidence that God abides in us. In other words, love is the evidence that we are worshipers.

Where does unity in the body come from? Worship.

THE UNITY FACTOR

> "But speaking the truth in love, we are to grow up in all aspects into Him who is the head, even Christ, from whom the whole body, being fitted and held together by what every joint supplies, according to the proper working of each individual part, causes the growth of the body for the building up of itself in love" (Eph. 4:15-16)

Paul describes a mature church as one that has attained to the "unity of the faith, and of the knowledge of the Son of God" (Eph. 4:13).

"The faith" does not refer to our trust in God, but rather to the objective content of the Christian faith or doctrine.[23] In other words, a mature church is one that knows what it believes, worshiping God in truth. But it also says that the body is united in "the knowledge of the Son of God." This refers to intimacy with Jesus Christ or worshiping God in spirit.

But the church is more than a group of individuals who have been drawn together because of a common belief and practice. It is a spiritual union that springs out of worship. Christ is the head that coordinates this body.

Using the body metaphor, Paul describes believers as being "fitted and held together by what every joint supplies" (v. 16). That describes an incredible unity and harmony[24] among its members. "Every joint supplies" refers to the ligaments and tendons. Applying this to the church, we would be just a collection of disjointed bones if it were not for the ligaments that hold the bones together. Furthermore, we would not be able to move if it weren't for the tendons that connect the muscles to the bones. They are what hold us together as a physical body, but what do these tendons and ligaments represent in the church, the body of Christ?

The clue is in the next part of the verse. Paul speaks of "the proper working"[25] of each of the members in reference to the Holy Spirit's action in our lives. So it is the "in-working"(lit.) of the Holy Spirit in each individual's life that acts as the ligaments and tendons to tie us together as a body, coordinated by our head, Christ.

The Holy Spirit's working in each member of the body not only draws us together, but also works together so there is mutual edification that builds up the body. All this is in the context of love.

This is possible only through worship. Worship as a life-attitude in each individual allows the Holy Spirit to draw us together into the body.

---

[23] The definite article means it is the content of what is believed rather than the faith itself.

[24] *Sunarmologéō* in the Greek. It is intensified with a suffix that means together (*sun*). We get the word "harmony" from the second part of the word.

[25] The Greek word he uses is *enérgeia* from which we get the word "energy." It is used several times in Ephesians (1:19, 3:7,3:20) and can be translated as God's "in working," usually through the Holy Spirit.

THE TEMPLE METAPHOR

Having been built upon the foundation of the apostles and prophets, Christ Jesus Himself being the corner stone, in whom the whole building, being fit together is growing into a holy temple in the Lord; in whom you also are being built together into a dwelling of God in the Spirit (Eph. 2:20-22).

I like to ask students who are studying 1 Corinthians, "What is the difference between 1 Corinthians. 3:16 and 6:19?" Both passages refer to our being a temple of the Holy Spirit. Despite the warnings to be prepared with an answer, many still miss the question on the test.

The answer is that the latter reference is to the Holy Spirit's indwelling each individual believer. The former refers to His corporate indwelling of the church. For some, it is difficult to grasp the fact that the Spirit not only inhabits each person's life, but He also indwells the church.

Perhaps it is because of our individualism that we tend to emphasize the personal indwelling rather than the Spirit's corporate presence. He not only dwells in us, He also dwells among us collectively, and His presence is manifested in ways that are impossible to experience individually. Christianity is to be experienced in community. He describes the church body, not the individual, as "the fullness of Him who fills all in all" (Eph. 1:23).

THE BARRIERS

I enjoy leading groups of Americans in a corporate time of worship when they come to Brazil, because I get to do it in my native language. However, one of the frustrations comes in finding songs in English that talk about the community in the presence of God. Most American Christian music is intensely personal with little thought of a unified worship. Often in worship services you can see it on the faces of people that each of them is having an intense personal encounter with God, but they are not together in His presence. We have the same Holy Spirit drawing us together, but often our individualism stands in the way of experiencing genuine corporate worship.

But what would happen if the whole body, in union, would come into His presence? What if, instead of singing about *my* being here to worship, *my* bowing down, *my* praise, and saying that He is *my* God—what if we instead sang about *our* worship, *our* bowing down, *our* praise, and acknowledging God as *our* God? What if we sang about *our* longing for righteousness, and righteousness being the air *we* breathe?

Maybe we would still close our eyes, but we might be holding hands or have our arms around each other.

> IT IS NOT ABOUT WHAT WE DO WITH OUR BODIES
> [WHEN WE SING] OR THE WORDS OF THE SONGS,
> BUT WHAT IS IN OUR HEARTS. ARE OUR MINDS AND
> HEARTS JOINED TOGETHER IN WORSHIP?

Do we have a corporate mind-set?

On the positive side, many of the newer songs are more personal and more directed toward God. However, songwriters, how about creating more songs, not in the first person singular, but in the first person plural? Don't think about leading individuals into worship, but consider how to bring the body into God's presence.

Perhaps one hindrance to corporate worship is our passivity. We listen to preaching and we listen to "special music," but we are largely uninvolved. Luther tried to emphasize the priesthood of all believers by writing hymns in the language of the people in a style they could relate to. Contemporary services today are trying to do the same thing.

However, a big problem is the lack of interaction within the body during the services because we are focused on the platform rather than on each other and God. Perhaps we have not used our imagination in how to express praise corporately outside of singing together. In many creative ways, a group of individual worshipers can lock arms and stand before God as one.

PERSONAL EXPERIENCES

A number of years ago, I visited Uruguay with a few Brazilian friends. The pastor of a church there related that his mentor, an American missionary, had asked him to describe his church. After he explained their style of meetings, his mentor commented that surely, if an American visitor who knew Spanish would come to his church service, he would feel very much at home.

Then he asked the stinging question: "However, do you think the national Uruguayans who come to your services feel at home?"

In other words, instead of taking biblical principles and applying them to the Uruguayan culture, his services were just a transplanted copy of the North American/European model translated into the language of the people.

Since that time, the pastor has really tried to make the church more culturally relevant, and I was eager to see what they did differently in Uruguay. When the service began, the pastor led the group standing in the corner of the room, and our chairs were in semi-circles radiating from that point. People seemed at ease and passed the maté up and down the rows.[26] It seemed pretty much cultural in its form.

After lunch, I asked a friend to walk around the park across the street. We noticed small groups of Uruguayans huddled around small campfires with guitars and drums. They were standing in very tight circles, laughing, singing, and drinking maté.

When we got back to church, I noticed that the believers were standing in a tight group in a circle singing praises, sharing, laughing, and drinking maté. They were much more spontaneous, open and free in expressing their love for God in this setting than they had been during the service when sitting in chairs.

APPLYING WHAT WE'VE LEARNED

Not long after returning from Uruguay, I went with a friend to central Brazil to teach church-planting principles. There were a number of tense moments as we presented a paradigm for the church that was quite different from the concepts firmly held by many evangelicals. Some listened with much suspicion, which made for a stressful day.

When we wrapped things up in the afternoon, we announced that the evening session would be a corporate time in God's presence. We had no idea what we were going to do. I collapsed into my bed, drained and empty.

---

[26] *Maté* is an herb that people from the southern part of South America drink. A gourd is filled with the herb and hot water is poured over it and it is drunk through a slotted metal straw. It is present at every social event, especially in Uruguay.

At dinner, my friend and I stared at each other, trying to figure out what was going to happen. We prayed and then the ideas started flowing. We set up the chairs in concentric circles, placing our chairs in the innermost circle. I got the idea from seeing how Brazilians sit at parties, pass the guitar around, and sing.

We used Isaiah 6 as our model and worshiped progressively through the passage, mixing teaching, sharing, and prayer. I taught five times, but never more than 10 minutes at a time. In between the teachings, they read passages of Scripture individually and shared in smaller groups what they learned. There was a time of corporate sharing and confession of sins. We knelt, we stood, we held hands, we hugged, and we lifted our hands. We sang, and there were times of spontaneous, verbal expression of praise.

At the end of the time, not one person came up to me to express appreciation for what had happened because it wasn't about the leaders of the meeting. We were all awestruck with God's presence in our midst because it was a corporate time. We knew we had met God—together. The impact was tremendous.

That is why Paul described the ideal of corporate worship and edification in 1 Corinthians 14:25. He said that if any unbeliever were present, he would "fall on his face and worship God, declaring that God is certainly among you." His conversion is described as an act of worship and it was the presence of God in their midst that led him to that point.

What the Church Is

After looking at these metaphors, we have a pretty good idea about what the church is. In the first chapter, we talked about the typical model for religion using this diagram:

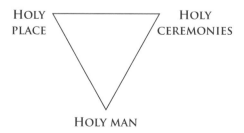

Whatever religion it might be, these are the necessary elements. Catholics have cathedrals, masses, and priests. Protestants have church buildings, services, and pastors. Muslims have mosques, prayers and imams.

We define the body of Christ by relationships, however, not structure. We have seen that worship is the basis of our relationship with God. It also influences our relationship with others and our impact on those who don't yet know the Lord.

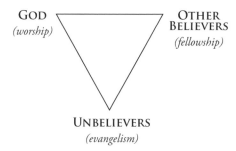

Relationships are what set Christianity apart from mere religion. We need to be careful that our faith does not slip into religion because we fail to live out worship in our relationships.

CONCLUSION

Although worship starts with a personal encounter with God, we are naturally drawn to other worshipers by the mutual presence of the Holy Spirit. Worship leads to unity, and unity stimulates more worship.

Worship is the glue that holds the church together and makes its members a body. Corporate structures, constitutions, creeds, organization, and statements of faith can never come close to stimulating the unity the Holy Spirit has already created among us (Eph. 4:3). We are more than just a body working together. As a body of believers, we are a temple where God dwells, enthroned on the praises of His people (Ps. 22:3). His presence in each individual and in the midst of the group should be obvious to anyone who participates.

The golden thread of worship not only ties us to God, but also ties us intimately to one another, making us one with God and with each other. Corporate worship leads us all to drink new wine from the same chalice.

THE PARADIGM SHIFT

We chose to call our local church "Comunidade Vida" or "Community of Life." Our goal was not to form a congregation, but a living community of believers. This paradigm shift is probably the most difficult to grasp because it is dependent on the other paradigm shifts mentioned in this section as well as the next section of this book. Certain aspects of this paradigm will be discussed in the next section.

FIRM CONGREGATIONS	LIVING COMMUNITIES
1. EVANGELISM: Objective: To grow in the number of church members.	1. EVANGELISM: Objective: To lead people into a worship relationship with Jesus Christ.
2. DISCIPLESHIP: Objective: To involve the person in the church.	2. DISCIPLESHIP: Objective: To develop intimacy with God through worship, drawing the person into the church.
3. UNITY: • Emphasis on meetings and services. • Activities inside the church building. • Organizational unity • Cordiality between members. • Programs ---> Relationships. • Limits of the group well defined: Who is saved, who is not saved. Who is a member and who is not a member.	3. UNITY: • Emphasis on relationships. • More activities are outside the building than inside. • Spiritual unity. • Love for one another for mutual edification. • Relationships --> Programs • Vague limits – several levels of involvement in the group. Who is moving toward Christ and who is not.

FIRM CONGREGATIONS	LIVING COMMUNITIES
4. WORSHIP: • Worship limited to praise services. • People attend - passive.	4. WORSHIP: • Worship daily as a life-attitude. • People are actively participating in celebrations.
5. SANCTIFICATION: • Spirituality defined by behavior. • Emphasis on external works. • Sins hidden in shame. • The sinner is punished and ostracized.	5. SANCTIFICATION: • Spirituality defined by attitudes. • Emphasis on the interior. • Transparency concerning sins and problems. • The sinner is exhorted, loved, and healed.

WHERE TO START

1. **EXAMINE YOUR ATTITUDE.** We are taught to be individualistic since we were born. Where do you see that attitude in your life? How can you develop a community mind-set? Ask God to change your mind-set.

2. **EXAMINE THE SCRIPTURES.** Look at Acts 2:42-47. Pray that your church would reflect the qualities of the first century church. Pray for your spiritual leaders. Ask God to use you to be an instrument of weaving worship into the fabric of your church. Pray that you can bring unity and be a catalyst for the church to begin functioning as a body. Remember, you can never bring this about in the flesh by arguing or criticizing, but rather by being an example and encouragement.

3. **PRAY.** Pick out ten people from your church and pray intensely that God would open their eyes spiritually to learn to worship Him. You will be surprised at how prayer bonds you to people.

Discussion Questions

1. What is the church?

2. In what ways is the church like a body?

3. What can we learn about the church from the marriage metaphor?

4. What is individualism and how do we see it demonstrated?

5. How is corporate worship different from personal worship?

6. In what ways does worship unite the church?

7. How do worship and unity relate to the temple metaphor?

8. How did this chapter help shape your view of the church?

9. How have you seen the "holy man, holy place, and holy ceremonies" model applied?

10. What are the differences between a body and a congregation?

11. How do you see individualism in your own life?

12. How can you help unify your church more through worship?

Part Two

WORSHIP AS THE GOLDEN THREAD OF MINISTRY

Part Two Introduction

WORSHIP
AS THE
GOLDEN THREAD
OF MINISTRY

Please, don't stop reading if you think this section is only for those "in the ministry." The Bible does not make the "clergy/layman" distinction. That is another man-made dichotomy where the "clergy" are "in the ministry" and are usually paid professionals who have some sort of theological degree. The "laymen" of the church, who are not "in the ministry," are there to support the ministry of the clergy.

Such a dichotomy is as foreign to the New Testament as dividing our lives between worship and secular life. Every person who worships the Lord Jesus Christ is in full-time ministry. Some have jobs to support their ministries, while others rely on income from their ministries. As a matter of fact, a worshiper's job is part of his or her worship and ministry. Rick Warren says, "A 'non-serving Christian' is a contradiction in terms."[1]

> OUR MISSION—THE MISSION OF THE CHURCH—IS NOT
> EVANGELISM, DISCIPLESHIP, OR MISSIONS.
> OUR MISSION IS WORSHIP.

The first section of this book laid the foundation for what follows. The principal reason I wrote this book was to show how ministry should

---

[1] Warren, _The Purpose Driven Life_, p. 229.

flow from worship. Our mission and the mission of the church are not evangelism, discipleship, or missions. Our mission is worship. And that worship will always result in being called to serve Him. As Wiersbe says, "If in our worship we have sensed the holiness and glory of God, and if we have felt the joy of sins forgiven, then we are ready to go out and serve Him, no matter how difficult the task."[2]

Whatever the Lord has called you to do will include elements of evangelism, discipleship, corporate worship, and leadership development to a greater or lesser extent. Every believer is called to be involved in these areas, and worship is the golden thread that gives our ministry continuity, keeping us focused on God and not the "work."

BEING VERSUS DOING

One of the great tragedies of our time, particularly in the United States, is that we focus on *doing* rather than *being*. I am probably the foremost offender since I know of the priority of worship. Foster says, "Service as a substitute for worship is idolatry."[3]

Worship does not just affect our lives and ministries. It *is* our life and ministry. We will not be effective if we neglect it, nor will God be honored. Our great ideas and strategies will not result in eternal fruit.

A. W. Tozer writes,

We all should be willing to work for the Lord, but it is a matter of grace on God's part. I am of the opinion that we should not be concerned about working for God until we have learned the meaning and the delight of worshiping Him. A worshiper can work with eternal quality in his work. But a worker who does not worship is only piling up wood, hay and stubble for the time when God sets the world on fire.[4]

In addition to emphasizing doing rather than being, there are problems in leadership training. Seminary or Bible Institute education

---

[2] Wiersbe, *Real Worship*, p. 78.
[3] Foster, *Celebration of Discipline*, p. 140.
[4] Tozer, *Whatever Happened to Worship?*, p. 12.

is often divided into another artificial dichotomy of the theoretical (theological) and practical. The two are taught as disjointed truths. Not only are theology and practice not integrated, but methods often contradict the theology that is taught. This is most evident in evangelism. Our soteriology (the study of salvation) should determine our evangelistic methods. Unfortunately, most people ignore or even change their theology to match their methodology. Perhaps this is because we have not tied biblical theology and evangelism together with the golden thread of worship.

For example, I have observed the evangelistic methods of some Christians who have studied missiology, cross-cultural ministry, and theology. They often use tracts written in the United States with verses taken out of context and pressure people into making a decision. It is as if they never made the connection between biblical theology and daily life. It is as though they never made the connection between biblical theology and their methods.

The terminology used by most American gospel tracts presumes the reader already has a biblical worldview. Many use verses unrelated to the gospel, such as Revelation 3:20, to justify a decision to "ask Jesus into your heart."[5] They use Romans 3:23 and 6:23, which certainly affirm the sinfulness of man, but merely leading someone to acknowledge their sinfulness is not the same as bringing them to repentance. Faith is often presented using Romans 10:9 in such a way that it means just agreeing with the historical facts of Jesus' death and resurrection. These methods may lead people to make "decisions," but they do not produce worshipers.

Although many leaders know what the Bible says, they continue to promote tracts that are inconsistent with it. An understanding of worship takes the deepest theology and applies it to our lives. If we understand that the motivation and goal of evangelism is not "decisions," but worship, our methods will reflect it.

I had been a missionary for about 11 years before I woke up to the need for my ministry to flow out of worship. I had known the truth theoretically and it had been my goal, but something was missing. I began a prayerful study of what it means to walk by the

[5] This passage is an invitation to the self-sufficient Laodicean church to invite Jesus into their midst, not an invitation to an individual.

Spirit. As I sought to live its reality, I was humbled and transformed. A year and a half later, I incorporated the worship principles I had learned into leadership training and I began to see major changes in my life and ministry.

In the first section, we defined worship as a life-attitude, stressing the importance of the inward values that result in outwardly glorifying God. This is represented on the left side of the diagram below. Our ministries, as we shall describe in this section, comprise the right side.

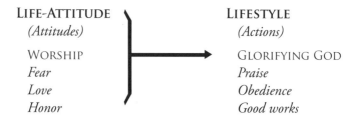

LIFE-ATTITUDE   LIFESTYLE
(Attitudes)   *(Actions)*

WORSHIP   GLORIFYING GOD
Fear   *Praise*
Love   *Obedience*
Honor   *Good works*

We can summarize the diagram like this: As Christ's character is formed in us through a worship life-attitude, it flows into a lifestyle that manifests His character to those around us, and He is glorified in our lives.

Is it possible to minister and not glorify God? It sure is. I can attest to that in my own life. Ministry at times has been done from a sense of duty or to show my own character and draw attention to myself rather than to God.

In 1 Corinthians 13, Paul uses hyperboles, including speaking "with the tongues of men and of angels" to describe an eloquent speaker. He said, "[If I do all kinds of ministry and good works, but] do not have love… I have become a noisy gong. …I am nothing…. it profits me nothing" (vv. 1-3).

Loving God and loving others should be the root of all of our good works, praise and ministry. Unfortunately, often it is not.

WEAVING WORSHIP INTO THE "ACT" STRATEGY

To outline how worship should be woven into the ministry, let's look at what one mission agency calls the "ACT (Apostolic Church-planting Team) strategy." This strategy was elaborated by various missionaries under the leadership of Dave Guiles, the executive director of Grace Brethren International Missions, Winona Lake, Indiana.

By *Apostolic* we mean that we should have the same mind-set as the apostle Paul. Like him, our goal is to lay the foundation for a church-planting movement rather than establishing ourselves as pastors and leaders. We are essentially working ourselves out of a job and looking to the next generation to carry on.

Church planting is our goal. Although parachurch organizations meet specific needs, I believe the real long-term impact of evangelism and discipleship is best achieved through establishing churches. God did not give His great commission to individuals, but to the church. And the churches we plant should be worshiping communities that are reproducing themselves.

We believe the biblical model for church planting is a *Team* effort. Jesus sent out the disciples in pairs rather than as individuals. Paul always surrounded himself with a team. A team that plants churches is already a model for the church they are starting. Such unity is possible only when the members of the team have a passion for worship.

Although it is not the purpose of this section to elaborate details about the ACT strategy, the steps of the strategy form a good outline to show how worship is to be integrated into every aspect of ministry.

THE CHURCH IS BORN AS PEOPLE COMMIT THEMSELVES
TO HELPING ONE ANOTHER GROW IN THEIR WORSHIP AND
TO REACHING OUT TO FIND OTHER WORSHIPERS.

The essence of our strategy begins with finding spiritually sensitive people (potential worshipers) within the area we are trying to reach and starting evangelistic studies with them. As they come to the Lord, they are taught how to walk with God and are brought together with other worshipers. The church develops from the relationships within the group.

In traditional church planting, a location is selected and facilities rented, and people are invited and encouraged to become involved in the church's programs. The sermons are often evangelistic, presenting the gospel during the weekly service. When evangelism is done out in the community, it is usually done by mass distribution of invitations. This method is most effective if there is a Christian tradition in the area, because it is rare for people with no religious background to respond to invitations and come to meetings. Discipleship and small groups, if they exist, are often not a high priority and are focused on integrating people into the church culture rather than helping them walk with God.

Programs, meetings, and organization hold many churches together. If the relationships among the people or even their relationship with God should grow cold, the structure remains. Worship is not essential to their function as a body, but it is merely part of its program.

On the other hand, a New Testament church stands or falls on the relationship among its people, which is based upon their worship. We must ask, "Is the church held together by the organization or by the Holy Spirit? Is the church an organization or an organism?" If worship is what unites the people, the latter will be true.

The outline of this section is based on the seven steps of the ACT strategy.

1. CONTACT DISCOVERY: Finding those whom God is calling to be worshipers
2. PROCESS EVANGELISM: Transforming people into worshipers
3. DISCIPLESHIP: Developing a worship life-attitude
4. SPIRITUAL COMMUNITY: Stimulating one another to worship
5. LEADERSHIP DEVELOPMENT: Calling people to service and training them through worship
6. CORPORATE WORSHIP: Expressing corporate worship

7. ORGANIZATION: Facilitating continuation and expansion of worship

We will look at the first three steps in separate chapters. The fifth step, leadership training, will also be treated separately. Spiritual families, celebration as a body, and the development of structure will be treated together in the final chapter.

CONCLUSION

As my wife and I were about to embark on a second honeymoon to celebrate our twenty-fifth wedding anniversary, we had lunch with a pastor friend. We talked about the way God had transformed our marriage from pretty good to wonderful. He asked Lisa what changes she saw in me.

She said, "Bruce has always been focused on ministry. He gives 110 percent to serving the Lord. He still works hard, but now he is more God-centered than ministry-centered." Although I realize I am still often self-centered, I'm gratified that her evaluation is increasingly true. And it's amazing how the ministry has been more effective as a result.

This is my prayer for you, the reader of this book. I don't want anyone, including me, to appear before God and see that all our fleshly efforts were just piling up wood, hay, and stubble for a celestial bonfire, as Tozer described it. Instead, I want to worship Jesus, casting down my crown at His feet, saying, "You are worthy of this, God. Because you have created all things, both me and the works that flowed from my worship, I cast my crown before You. And because of Your will they were created. You are worthy, Oh, God" (author's paraphrase of Rev 4:10-11). As Piper says, "The opposite of wasting your life is living life by a single God-exalting, soul-satisfying passion."[6]

May God richly bless you as you continue to weave worship into your ministry, having already saturated your life with His presence.

---

[6] Piper, *Don't Waste Your Life*, p. 43.

Chapter 11

DISCOVERING
POTENTIAL
WORSHIPERS

WORSHIP AND CONTACT DISCOVERY

But an hour is coming, and now is, when the true worshipers
will *worship the Father in spirit and truth; for such people* THE
FATHER SEEKS TO BE HIS WORSHIPERS (John 4:23).

SEED TRUTH: GOD IS SEEKING WORSHIPERS. *Many people
are searching for a religion that will give them inner peace or a solution
to their problems. They are not seeking a worship relationship with God.
However, God has planted in the hearts of a few a dormant desire to
worship Him. As evangelists, our goal is to discover these potential worshipers by exposing Jesus Christ to them through the Bible and through
our own lives.*

THE GOSPEL BLIMP

Although it dates back to 1960, the parody *The Gospel Blimp*[1] is just
as relevant today as when it was written. The story involves a group
of Christians with a desire to reach their city for Christ. It started in
a discussion during a barbecue about how to reach George's neighbor
with the gospel. Someone suggested they put verses on the airplanes
that flew by. They decided airplanes passed too quickly for the verses

---

[1] Joseph Bayly, *The Gospel Blimp.*

to be read, but a blimp would give the neighbor a better chance to read them.

The idea escalated into a full-scale campaign called "International Gospel Blimps, Inc." They bought a blimp that hovered over the city, blaring sermons and gospel music, and throwing gospel tracts to the people below.

George later dropped out of the "I.G.B.I" group and started hanging around with his lost neighbor. His friends in the I.G.B.I. figured he was backsliding because, instead of being involved in "evangelism," he was associating with lost people.

After several months, George hosted another barbecue for his I.G.B.I. friends and his lost neighbor. At first, his friends were offended that George had invited an unbeliever to this Christian social event. They became excited, however, when the neighbor announced he had become a follower of the Lord Jesus.

They asked which verse, preaching, or tract had "won" him. He said that those things were irritating and had little effect on him. What changed him were the lives of George and his wife. He said, "Why, they've been Christ Himself to us. I'd never met anyone before to whom Jesus was real."

The "Gospel Blimp" group left, amazed that something so simple had brought those people to the Lord. They concluded that God works in mysterious ways. They still didn't get it—that living a life that glorifies Christ and sharing it through relationships is the key to reaching others for Christ. To them, evangelism is a church program.

The author's analysis is the best part of the book. He observes,

> Today we have perfected various technical means of presenting the Christian message. We are hitting a mass market with the mass gospel media. But in the process, we have often passed our personal responsibility on to blimps and loud speakers and impersonal organizations. But technical, organizational means have one enormous lack: a human heart.[2]

He continues,

> Jesus Christ didn't commit the gospel to an advertising agency; He commissioned disciples. And He didn't com-

---

[2] Ibid. pp. 77-78.

mand them to put up signs and pass out tracts; He said that they would be His witnesses. Those first disciples were lights set on the town lampstands of Christian morality and Christian love, shining in the darkness of a hostile pagan culture, or the twilight of the hostile religious culture, which was more difficult. No message in the sky could match the witness of their holy lives and works of love.[3]

That story effectively illustrates what contact discovery is all about. It was not the proclamation of the gospel through impersonal means with preaching and an invitation that brought the man into a relationship with the Lord. It was the gradual exposure of Jesus Christ through the life and words of George. "Gospel Blimps" might draw some people. However, the potential worshiper in this story was drawn to salvation by the life of a worshiper.

"MAKING A DECISION" OR WORSHIP?

I became interested in Latin American missions because of how easy it is to strike up a conversation about spiritual matters with the people of that region. There is certainly no need for "Gospel Blimps." During my graduate studies I traveled to Mexico, Guatemala, Colombia, and Peru. Although I was chasing insects, I had opportunities to talk with several individuals about Jesus Christ, and people seemed genuinely interested in talking about spiritual matters. This openness, however, does not necessarily make evangelism any easier.

Most Americans who visit Brazil comment that it is wide open to the gospel. Visitors mistake this candidness for receptivity. It soon becomes apparent, however, that some are just trying to please a new friend or are simply looking for another religious experience rather than seeking an intimate relationship with the Lord of the universe.

Having lived here since 1990, I wouldn't trade being a missionary in Brazil for anything. I still like not having to beat around the bush about the gospel or going through a long process of building bridges to open up spiritual conversations. However, I have learned to discern which people are looking for a religion or an improvement in their circumstances and those who are seeking to know and worship Jesus Christ.

---

[3] Ibid. pp. 78-79.

Once, we were doing door-to-door interviews in a poorer section of Belém, looking for people interested in studying the Bible. We met a young mother who had been attending a church for two years, praying for a change in her alcoholic husband.

When I asked her if she was interested in studying the Bible, she said she was not able to because she was committed to going to church every night to participate in a "campaign." This involved putting her prayer request with $10 in an urn. If her name were drawn, she would have the privilege to go up front for special prayer from the "pastor."

I asked her if, after two years of attending church, she thought God would accept her as she was at the moment, if she were to die. She didn't think so. I asked her what she lacked. She said she needed to "accept Jesus."

My friends who were accompanying me were pleased with what seemed to be a good answer. Then I asked her what it meant to "accept Jesus." She said it meant to begin giving tithes and joining the church.

In reality, she was looking for a religion that would meet her temporal needs, and nothing more.

OUR GOAL AS EVANGELISTS IS NOT TO GET PEOPLE TO "MAKE A DECISION" OR "ACCEPT JESUS," BUT TO BRING PEOPLE INTO A WORSHIP RELATIONSHIP WITH GOD.

Whether you find many "open" hearts, as in Brazil, or many "closed" hearts, as in Uruguay, it is an overwhelming task to find those whom God is calling to be worshipers.

What then is a contact in evangelism? How do we recognize contacts? What can we do to find them? What do we do when we find them? In this chapter, we look at these questions by examining the seed (the message that attracts potential worshipers), the soil (potential worshipers) and the sower (worshipers who are telling others about Christ). When the seed, the sower, and the soil are all connected in a vital way, there will be fruit (new worshipers).

We will start tying the golden thread of worship into the ministry with the very first step: "contact discovery" or, perhaps more aptly named, "worshiper discovery."

THE MARRIAGE METAPHOR

Although "courtship" in many circles is an outdated term, it better than "dating" to describe *the process of selecting a lifelong mate.* A young man who is courting a young woman is trying to discern whether she is suitable as a mate and at the same time demonstrate that he would make a good husband.

That works well if both are being "real" with each other. In this stage, you get what you sow. A woman who tries to draw attention by her sensuality may not find the man who would be best for her. A man who tries to impress a woman with his quick wit may end up with a woman that has very different priorities from his. The best way to attract a godly mate is to be godly. If, during courtship, a genuine, open friendship develops, there is a good chance for a solid, long-term relationship.

When I first met Lisa, I really had no intentions of dating her, because I was already dating someone else and so was she. This gave us the freedom to get to know each other as friends without trying to impress the other. Although we both were pretty immature in our Christian lives, as our friendship developed, we were drawn to each other by a mutual hunger to know God.

Contact discovery is similar to courtship. It is a time of discovery, as the new contact learns about Jesus. The person gradually comes to know and understand the reality of who Jesus is. The seeds are beginning to be sown for a lifelong relationship with Him.

If a person entices people to go church by talking about its music, programs, and activities rather than Jesus, his contacts will be religious people who may start going to church and yet might never come to know Jesus.

On the other hand, if the person sharing his faith is a worshiper whose life reflects the glory of God, he will draw prospective worshipers to study the Bible with him. As the inquirer discovers the truth about Jesus, a strong, intimate relationship with the Lord will develop.

Contact discovery, then, is the process by which we discover the people who are interested in becoming eternal worshipers.

Sowing

The Parable of the Sower

We are all familiar with the parable of the sower (Matt. 13:1-23; Mark 4:1-20; Luke 8:4-15). Several interpretations miss the main point. Christ is teaching principally about evangelism in preparation for sending out His disciples for the first time. He shows them that when they faithfully sow the seed, they will get various responses, represented by different soil types. On the surface, however, the soils all look the same, so it is necessary for them to sow broadly to find the good soil.

The soil on the side of the road has been compacted. The sower didn't foolishly sow in the middle of the road, but roads then, like in most parts of the world, were vaguely defined. There are places near paths where the soil is harder and unreceptive to the seed, because it has been compacted by people constantly walking over it. However, it looks the same as the rest of the field after it has been tilled at planting time. Matthew says the person represented by this soil type doesn't comprehend the "seed" or the Word. That person will never become a worshiper because his heart is hardened to the truth.

The rocky ground is actually shallow soil. Any good farmer will take the rocks out of his field. In certain parts of the field, however, the bedrock lies close to the surface and the soil has no depth. In the springtime, when there is a lot of rain, the seed will germinate and start to grow. However, the roots don't go deep and when the summer sun comes out, the plants dry up and die.

The person represented by this type of soil has a superficial understanding and a superficial response. No person who has become a worshiper will be concerned about what others think when he is persecuted, because he fears God. Nevertheless, the shallow soil looks the same as the good soil. In fact, it may initially look better because it has more minerals and humidity in the spring.

The thorny soil also looks good after plowing. Many weeds have huge root systems for over-wintering while others lie dormant as seeds. These weeds often have a head start on the planted crops and eventually choke them out.

Some people think the person represented by this soil type is a true Christian who is unfruitful, since the plant doesn't die. I believe there is no such thing as an unfruitful Christian. While we don't all produce the fruit we should, all believers bear some fruit. A true worshiper of the Lord Jesus Christ will not allow his relationship with God to be choked out by the things of this world.

The thorny soil represents a person who seemingly repents and believes, but his treasure is still in this world. There may be an initial excitement, but it gradually fades. He may become a member of the church and even continue to attend, or he may gradually drift away. Someone has noted, "For every person who falls away from the Lord, hundreds drift." They drift because they never knew the joy of a relationship with the Lord.

The good soil is what we are looking for. We cannot change the nature of the soil or persuade people to become good soil. We cannot even recognize them until we have sown the seed in their lives and waited for it to grow. Our responsibility is to sow the seed, water it, and wait patiently for the Word to bear fruit, producing worshipers. Most of the time, according to the Scriptures, our seed falls in soil that is unproductive. We will not find potential worshipers among the superficial, hardened, and worried.

For the good soil, however, life begins with comprehension. Matt. 13:23 says the man pictured as good soil hears the Word and understands it.[4] Here in Brazil, religion is so ingrained in people's minds, it takes months for them to grasp the grace of God. All religion, including most Brazilian Pentecostalism, is based on a merit system (tithes, prayers, sacrifices, works, etc.). Understanding faith, repentance, and the significance of what Jesus did on the cross does not come easily. In the next chapter we will discuss the comprehension process.

The old saying, "You reap what you sow," is true in evangelism. In this chapter we emphasize sowing and in the next, harvesting, as we look at contact discovery and the process of evangelism, respectively.

---

[4] The Greek word (*suníēmi*) for understanding is not merely an intellectual grasp of the facts, but has to do with a putting together of the big picture or comprehension.

AN EXAMPLE OF SOWING

One of the most moving stories I have ever heard about evangelism is one simply called "George Street." Rev. Dave Smethurst tells the story of meeting people in his travels—people from Australia, London, India, and the Caribbean who had started down the road toward salvation as a result of a tract they had received from "a strange, little elderly man" on George Street in Sydney, Australia.

Eventually, he managed to track down this man who had a worldwide impact by simply sowing a portion of the gospel message. Smethurst and a friend went to see the elderly man and gave this report of their meeting:

> The London preacher sat there and told him of all these accounts from the previous three years. This little man sat with tears running down his cheeks. He told them his story. "I was a rating on an Australian warship. I was living a reprobate life. In a crisis I really hit the wall. One of my colleagues, to whom I gave literal hell, was there to help me. He led me to Jesus and the change in my life was night to day in 24 hours. I was so grateful to God; I promised God that I would share Jesus in a simple witness with at least 10 people a day. As God me strength I did that. Sometimes I was ill and couldn't do it, but I made up for the days I missed it at other times. I wasn't paranoid about it. I have done this for over 40 years. In my retirement years, the best place was on St. George Street where I saw hundreds of people a day. I got lots of rejections, but a lot of people courteously took the tract. In 40 years of doing this, I have never heard of one single person coming to Jesus until today.[5]

Although gospel tracts are not often the ideal way of sowing, this man did what he thought best. He had faithfully sown the Word for 40 years and never harvested any fruit. The point is he sowed although he never harvested. That does not mean he was not successful. His sowing was motivated by a grateful and worshipful heart for what God had done for him. That is why he persevered even though he didn't see any fruit at the time.

[5] Dave Smethurst, "I Got Off at George Street." This story can be found at www.baptistboard.com.

CONTACT DISCOVERY

When I first wrote the term in Portuguese, my friend who was correcting the document said, "In Brazil, we say, 'making contacts,' not 'discovering contacts.'" That may have been your initial reaction as well. However, there is a distinction between the two phrases. The Bible teaches that most people will never submit their lives to God, and no amount of effort on our part will convince them to do so. Therefore, our focus should be to discover the people in whom the Spirit of God is working.

We need to find those who are interested in the Bible. It is the "calling out" of the "bride." It is about discovering potential worshipers.

As Rick Warren says, "Our job as church leaders, like experienced surfers, is to recognize a wave of God's Spirit and ride it. It is not our responsibility to *make* waves but to recognize how God is working in the world and join Him in the endeavor."[6]

When we first went to Brazil as short-term missionaries, we visited Bill Burk, who lives two hours by boat from Belém. I had heard about "Amazon Bill," as he is affectionately called in Grace Brethren circles, and I was nervous about meeting him. Bill blew me away. We sat down to visit and he opened his Bible to Acts 13. The part I remember most was Acts 13:48: "And when the Gentiles heard this, they began rejoicing and glorifying the Word of the Lord; and as many as had been appointed to eternal life believed." Bill said:

> When I went out on the river, I would pray every day that God would show me His elect. The only way to identify the elect is by their interest in the Word of God. His Word is the only seed that God has promised to bless. If I would see a man on the shore, I would pull up and introduce myself. If you win the man, you win the whole family. I would hand him a book of Proverbs and say, 'Friend, this book was written 3,000 years ago, but if you read it, it is like it was written yesterday. Read it, and I'll be back to get your opinion in a week.' If, when I returned, he was more interested in the horsepower of my outboard motor, I would

---

[6] Rick Warren, *The Purpose Driven Church*, p. 14.

move on. However, if he apologized for getting the booklet dirty from reading it so much, I would think that maybe I had found one of the elect. I would then set up a study for the first chapter of the book of Mark. As long as he read the study before I came, I would continue studying with him.

Whether one believes in election or not, I'm sure we can all agree that no one can create a work of the Holy Spirit. But we can discover where He is working and enter into His work. We need to discover potential worshipers and not just those interested in a religion. If we sow the seed of the Word right from the start, potential worshipers will become evident. If we talk about religious activities, we will reap religious church attendees.

This first stage of sowing is crucial in every stage of ministry.

We want to lay the correct foundation; therefore, we must pay close attention to our message right from the start. It will influence how we do evangelism, discipleship, leadership training, and how we worship as a body.

SOWING AS AN OVERFLOW OF WORSHIP

Not only is the sower a worshiper, but the very act of sowing is an expression of worship.

Paul, the Worshiping Sower

Paul saw his proclamation of the Gospel as an act of worship. He wrote, "For God, whom I serve in my spirit in the preaching of the gospel of His Son, is my witness as to how unceasingly I make mention of you" (Rom. 1:9).

We usually equate serving with working. However, Paul used the word "serve" in the sense of ministering to the Lord in worship.[7] We call our Sunday gatherings "worship services" based on the same idea, seeing it as ministering to the Lord. By using a present tense verb ("whom I serve"), he showed that serving God was not a part-time activity, but a continuous state of having his mind fixed on God.

Paul told us that the life-attitude was within him. He said it was "in my spirit." Worship is more than an emotional experience or an

---

[7] The Greek Word *"latreúō"* is used of performing an act of worship.

intellectual activity. It is a spiritual experience and not just something external. Paul worshiped God in spirit and truth.

In addition, Paul describes himself as "ministering as a priest the gospel of God, so that my offering of the Gentiles may become acceptable, sanctified by the Holy Spirit" (Rom. 15:16).

Nelson, commenting on this passage, points out, "Paul…employs common liturgical language… not to refer to congregational worship but to the proclamation of the gospel and the conversion of the Gentiles to faith in Jesus Christ. It is difficult not to conclude that Paul sees evangelism in some sense as an act of worship itself."[8]

For our purposes in this chapter, the most important question is *how* Paul worshiped. He said he worshiped God "in the preaching of the gospel of His Son" (Rom. 1:9). By proclaiming the good news of Jesus Christ, he was worshiping, expressing his love for God, and glorifying Him.

The Sowing Psalmist

Psalm 96:1-4 is another example of the close link between worship, praise, and evangelism.

> *Sing to the LORD a new song;*
> *Sing to the LORD, all the earth.*
> *Sing to the LORD, bless His name;*
> *Proclaim good tidings of His salvation from day to day.*
> *Tell of His glory among the nations,*
> *His wonderful deeds among all the peoples.*
> *For great is the LORD, and greatly to be praised;*
> *He is to be feared above all gods.*

The first three commands for us to "sing" and the fourth telling us to "bless" are all directed toward God. The first command tells of the content. A "new song" is a new and fresh experience with God, perhaps speaking of a new life. Worshipers always have a new song to sing because they are constantly discovering different aspects of God and marveling at what He has done.

The second command tells us that everyone should be worshiping God. The general calling of unbelievers to begin to worship God is the same as calling them to salvation.

---

[8] Nelson in Bateman, p.155.

The third command simply tells us to sing.

The fourth command is a command to praise (bless)[9] His name or to extol His character.

In the third verse there is a subtle, but important shift. Instead of being exhorted to join in God-directed praise, the people are told to tell other people about Him. This transition is not a strong contrast, but a natural overflow of our praise into evangelism. We are told to tell of the gospel and God's glory. The wonderful deeds we are to proclaim are marvelous things that make us stand in awe of Him.

The evangelism described in this Psalm is new, fresh, and exciting. David is genuinely excited about who God is and what He has done in his life. Many years later, John and Peter said, "we cannot stop speaking about what we have seen and heard" (Acts 4:20), because they were astounded at what God had done for them.

It was hard for most Jews to think about being a blessing to the nations as God had promised Abraham he would be. They preferred to think that it was a national blessing just for them. Psalm 46, however, speaks of proclaiming God's greatness and His salvation among the peoples and nations of the world.

Missions, as evangelism, is also the fruit of worship. When we behold the greatness of God, we can no longer be narrow, nationalistic, or denominational. God is much too big to limit Him to any group.

As Piper says, "All of history is moving toward one great goal, the white-hot worship of God and his Son among all the peoples of the earth. Missions is not the goal. It is the means. And for that reason it is the second greatest human activity in the world."[10]

At times, when I am around some of my relatives, I am determined *not* to talk about the Lord. I know that in my youthful enthusiasm I had said more than they wanted to hear, and now I want to be more sensitive to the moment. However, it doesn't take long for something about the Lord to come out of my mouth. Jesus is my life. It is almost impossible to have an extended conversation without there being something related to Him. Everything is related to Him. Talking about Jesus is not an obligation I feel, nor is it a desire to convince other people to believe as I do. It's simply the overflow of my heart.

[9] *Eulogéō* means to speak well of or praise.
[10] John Piper, *Let the Nations be Glad!* p. 15.

As Wiersbe says, "When you look upon preaching and evangelism as acts of spiritual worship, it certainly makes a difference in your ministry. For one thing, it helps to purify your motives. The minister who preaches or who seeks to win the lost simply because this is God's commandment is going to operate from a feeling of guilt; and this is not the highest motive for service."[11]

THE SOWER

Many people visit cemeteries on the day of the dead here in Brazil. A friend noticed at the entrance to a cemetery a man handing out gospel tracts, taking advantage of the opportunity. When my friend approached him, he discovered the man knew nothing of the gospel; he had merely been hired by a local church to pass out the tracts.

It is essential that the message we share (the "seed") focuses on Jesus as He is presented in the Scriptures. It is also essential that the seed-bearers have been impacted by the message themselves. The sower must not only have the right message, but his sowing also needs to be the overflow of his love for the Lord and his love for others. The very life of the sower is in the seed and it must have life in it or else it will not germinate.

As Piper says, "A heart for the glory of God and heart of mercy for the nations make a Christ-like missionary."[12]

THE LIFE OF THE SOWER

Every *good tree bears good fruit; but the bad tree bears bad fruit. A good tree cannot produce bad fruit, nor can a bad tree produce good fruit* (Matt. 7:17-18).[13]

The sower will inevitably reproduce himself through the seed he sows. That is why Jesus warned us in this passage to watch out for false teachers. We must examine who is sowing and what they are sowing into our lives.

---

[11] Wiersbe, p.121
[12] Piper, *Let the Nations Be Glad!* p. 30.
[13] Jesus used *agathós* (good) to describe the quality of the tree and used *kalós* (good) to describe the usefulness of the fruit. This analogy suggests that the excellent quality of a person's transformed life will produce useful fruit.

The story is told of a missionary who spent months talking with an older gentleman who was helping him with the language. They spent hours talking about the Bible and spiritual matters. Finally, the missionary asked him if he wanted to become a Christian. The old man replied that he would if he could ever see an example of one. Saddened, the missionary realized that his own life had not been light or salt. The presence of the Holy Spirit had not been apparent to his tutor.

The life of the messenger needs to match the message. That can happen only if the messenger is a worshiper. As Neil Cole says, "People don't respond to cold facts; they are moved by passionate people who have a testimony of the difference Christ has made."[14]

THE IMPACT OF BARNABAS' LIFE

Then when he arrived and witnessed the grace of God, he rejoiced and began to encourage them all with resolute heart to remain true to the Lord; for he was a good man, and full of the Holy Spirit and of faith. And considerable numbers were brought to the Lord (Acts 11:23).

Barnabas, or the "son of encouragement," came to Antioch and did what he was known for. He encouraged them[15] to persevere in the Lord. The fact that considerable numbers came to know the Lord speaks of his fruitfulness.

Why was Barnabas fruitful? First, he was "a good man." That speaks of his character. The reason his character was excellent is that he was "full of the Holy Spirit." The reason he was full of the Holy Spirit is that he was "full of faith."

Obviously, Barnabas talked about Jesus, but it seems that his life loudly confirmed his message. He was a worshiper.

THE IMPACT OF PAUL'S LIFE

But thanks be to God, who always leads us in His triumph in Christ, and manifests through us the sweet aroma of the knowledge of Him in every place. For we are a fragrance of Christ to

---

[14] Neil Cole, *Cultivating a Life for God*, p. 4.
[15] *Parakaleō* – To exhort, encourage or urge.

God among those who are being saved and among those who are perishing (2 Corinthians 2:14-15).

You are our letter, written in our hearts, known and read by all men; …and are not like Moses, who used to put a veil over his face so that the sons of Israel might not look intently at the end of what is fading away (2 Corinthians 3:2, 13).

But we all, with unveiled face, beholding as in a mirror the glory of the Lord, are being transformed into the same image from glory to glory, just as from the Lord, the Spirit (2 Corinthians 3:18).

Paul interrupted his discourse on the struggles in his ministry to move to a more positive note. He used three metaphors to characterize his ministry.

The first metaphor is that of a "triumphant" parade (2:14), characteristic of the conquering Roman generals. This image is also used in Revelation 19 as Christ leads the triumph at His return. Certainly, things looked bleak during parts of Paul's ministry. However, he knew and lived the reality of the ultimate victory in Christ. That is one of the reasons Paul was able to "use great boldness in" his speech (3:12). He knew he was destined to be a participant in a victory parade.

Second, Paul compared his life to a "sweet aroma" and "a fragrance." These are terms related to Old Testament sacrifices. He describes his life and ministry as a sacrifice that permeated everything so no one could escape the "fragrance of Christ." It is like the perfume that Mary used to anoint Jesus. Its smell filled the room.

Finally, he compares his life and ministry to "Moses, who used to put a veil over his face" (see Exodus 34). The Scriptures say, "the skin of his face shone because of his speaking with Him" (Ex 34:29). Literally, the Shekinah glory of the Lord was shining from Moses' face because of his fellowship with God. Paul said that he himself was not covering that glory, but openly manifesting it through his life and speech. Spending time in the presence of God worshiping showed on his face.

As we contemplate His glory in fellowship with Him through His Word, we become conformed to the image of His glory. Not only do people hear of the Lord Jesus Christ through our words, but they also see Him in our lives as His image is formed in us.

What about our lives? Does it show that we have been in His presence? Evangelism is not something that should be a chore. It should flow out of our lives. Peter and John said, "we cannot stop speaking what we have seen and heard" (Acts 4:20). Their lives were so full of Christ that testifying about Him was as natural as breathing.

We held an informal graduation ceremony in our new church plant for the three graduates of our Bible Institute while I was the director. Nonato from Marituba was one of the graduates. He commented to me afterward that he was amazed that our little church had five preachers. He said his larger church depended exclusively on his preaching. Although our church was heavily criticized because we were "different," he wanted to resign his pastorate and become part of our group.

I suggested that would only lead to more criticism. I urged him to branch out to start a new church. He took me seriously and asked me to look at a place he was considering for a new work.

After meeting some of his contacts, he asked, "Will you teach me your methods so I can start a church like yours?"

I told him, "Nonato, it is not about methods. It is about intimacy with God. You are a faithful pastor, but you don't have intimacy with God." After thinking about that for a week, he asked me to teach him how to have intimacy with God.

His church plant is doing better than anything I have started. He has learned that growth doesn't come from trying to grow a church, but from being light. It comes from being a worshiper. Light attracts light.

Training Timothy to Have Impact

Paul wanted Timothy to be an excellent servant of the Lord Jesus Christ (1 Tim. 4:6). To be that, Timothy needed to be a godly man.[16] To be godly is to fear God or be in awe of Him. Timothy was probably about 35 or 40, and in his culture, no one under 40 years of age was respected as a leader.

Instead of ministry credentials or an ecclesiastical position, Paul told Timothy that godliness reflected in his lifestyle would give him

---

[16] *Eusébeia* – see chapter 2 for an explanation of worship as it relates to godliness.

credibility as a leader. The way he lived needed, above all, to proclaim the glory of God. Paul said, "Let no one look down on your youthfulness, but rather in speech, conduct, love, faith and purity, show yourself an example of those who believe" (1 Tim 4:12). He further admonished Timothy to "Pay close attention to yourself and to your teaching; persevere in these things, for as you do this you will insure salvation both for yourself and for those who hear you" (1 Tim. 4:16).

Not only did Timothy, as a sower, need to pay attention to the seeds he sowed in others' lives, but he was also to evaluate his own life. It is so easy for someone in the ministry to lose sight of the importance of spending time at the feet of the Lord in worship or in quietness before Him.

Piper writes, "It is possible to be distracted from God in trying to serve God. Martha-like, we neglect the one thing needful, and soon begin to present God as busy and fretful."[17]

I traveled one day with Nonato to São Paulo. We looked at each other and smiled as the flight attendant gave instructions about the mask that would automatically drop from above our heads in the event of decompression. We were both reminded of the illustration I use to show the importance of a constant seeking of intimacy with God by those who are evangelizing.

The attendant said that people traveling with small children should put the mask over their own face first and then help their children. The natural tendency for a mother or father would be to care for the children first. However, if the adult should pass out, the child would be unable to help himself or his parent. On the other hand, in the unlikely event that the child would pass out, his or her parent could easily put the mask on and the child would soon revive.

Nonato and I both remembered 1 Timothy 4:16 and the importance of "putting the mask on your own life first." If a leader is not first of all a worshiper, he will not be able to help others effectively. He becomes, in effect, the blind leading the blind.

---

[17] Piper, *Let the Nations Be Glad!* p. 13.

THE SEED: JESUS CHRIST

The sower sows the word (Mark 4:14).

The seed is the Word of God, not our arguments and illustrations. More specifically, it is what the Bible says about the person of Jesus, God incarnate who deserves our worship. Upon meeting the Ethiopian eunuch, "Philip opened his mouth, and beginning from this Scripture he preached Jesus to him" (Acts 8:35). Philip boldly shared the Bible as it flowed from his life. He focused on Jesus. If our goal is to find worshipers of Jesus Christ, we need to share Jesus as the seed. Obviously, the way the seed is packaged will differ in every culture, but Jesus as the essence of the message is cross-cultural.

Sweet corn is not popular in Brazil, so I was excited to come across some seeds that are adapted to our equatorial photoperiod.[18] I cleaned a spot in my yard and heavily fertilized it before planting my seeds. I was disappointed to find they had been on the shelf too long and no longer had any life in them.

When we sow the seed, it must have life, and that life is the sower's relationship with God. He may have the right message and share it with the right person, but if there is no spiritual life, it is doubtful anything will happen. That is why the seed is not just the message, but the life of the sower also.

The three-fold witness in which the seed is always presented can be summarized as "Jesus in your mouth (your message), Jesus in your life (your lifestyle), and Jesus in your community (your relationships). Look at Acts 4 as an illustration.

JESUS IN YOUR MOUTH

> *And there is salvation in no one else; for there is no other name under heaven that has been given among* men *by which we must be saved* (Acts 4:12).

Why did Jesus tell His disciples not to tell anyone who He was (Matt 16:20)? There are probably two reasons. First, they didn't have the right message. They knew Jesus was the Messiah, but they didn't realize why He had to die. That is why Peter, after his great confession, turned

---

[18] Corn begins to tassle based on the length of daylight. When planted near the equator, temperate corn will grow only a foot tall before it begins to form ears.

around and rebuked Jesus for saying He was going to die (Matt. 16:22).

Jesus is the message we must sow to find potential worshipers. We need to present the object of our worship so people can worship Him in spirit and truth.

In the Acts 4:12 passage, Peter boldly proclaims Jesus as the only means to becoming a worshiper.

JESUS IN YOUR LIFE

Now as they observed the confidence of Peter and John and understood that they were uneducated and untrained men, they were amazed, and began to recognize them as having been with Jesus (Acts 4:13).

The second reason Jesus told them not to tell anyone is that the disciples' lives did not reflect their Savior's life. They were not yet worshipers in the New Testament sense, nor were they filled with the Spirit. They were only potential worshipers.

Peter had been ready to take on the Roman army single handedly, and said he was willing to die for Jesus. But when his courage was tested, he was cut down by a teen-age slave girl. Now, in the power of the Holy Spirit, he boldly proclaims the gospel to the religious leaders (Acts 4). The message was, "*You* crucified Him, *but* God raised Him" (Acts 4:10).

It wasn't, however, the message that struck them, but the lives of the messenger. The sowers, more than the seed, impressed the leaders. The first thing they noticed was their "confidence." They had boldness, fearlessness, and outspokenness that were uncharacteristic of men of their type. They were "uneducated and untrained." Although the word "laymen" is somewhat derogatory, that is what they were to the religious leaders. "Layman" means anyone who does not belong to the official group.

There was no earthly reason these men should have suddenly become courageous and confident. Something had to have happened. That is why the religious leaders were "amazed," and wondered at how this could have happened. They also noticed they had "been with Jesus." Luke puts these two facts together. Grammatically, there is no link between the ideas, probably because the religious leaders didn't make the connection between the change in these men and the fact that they had spent time with the Master.

The spiritual life of the messenger is essential, but God, in His sovereignty, uses undeserving vessels. We are never the worshipers we should be. God is so good that He works even through people we would never consider worthy.

There are exceptions to the rule that the person's life is as important as the message. Considering the results, the most successful evangelist of all time was Jonah. It is possible that an entire city of more than a half million people repented at his preaching. He did not preach as an overflow of worship; however. He was rebellious, and certainly didn't love the people to whom he was ministering. Yet God worked through him despite his lack of worship, because, in His mercy, God chose to. On the other hand, Jeremiah and Isaiah didn't have too much fruit for their efforts, but they were certainly worshipers of the Lord.

Generally speaking, however, if evangelism is a religious duty, it will be weak and ineffective. If it is seen as a technique, it will not produce real converts.

One of our members was a violent man before becoming a worshiper. He lived in an interior town called Capitão Poço. One day, he found his grandmother crying at home. She was upset because someone had broken one of the images in the Catholic Church. He decided to go after the local Assembly of God, single handedly breaking in and busting up everything he could get his hands on.

A few years later, he was transformed into a worshiper. When he returned to town, he went to the church and apologized for his actions. His life transformation has been so dramatic that there are now evangelistic Bible studies all over Capitão Poço as well as the start of a new church.

This can be likened to the impact of the man possessed by "Legion." After delivering him from the demons, Jesus told him, "Go home to your people and report to them what great things the Lord has done for you, and how He had mercy on you" (Mark 5:19). Imagine the impact of that man's changed life. There is evidence that churches popped up in that area soon after Jesus died.

JESUS IN YOUR COMMUNITY

And the congregation of those who believed were of one heart and soul; and not one of them claimed that anything belonging to him was his own, but all things were common property to them all (Acts 4:32).

....the people held them in high esteem. And all the more believers in the Lord, multitudes of men and women, were constantly added to their number (Acts 5:13-14).

We often underestimate the church as an effective witness. I am not referring to evangelistic programs, but to the relationships among members. Jesus said, "By this all men will know that you are My disciples, if you have love for one another (John 13:35). He also prayed, "That they may be perfected in unity, so that the world may know that You sent Me and loved them, even as You have loved Me" (John 17:23).

We cannot express our love for God fully without considering our relationships with other believers. We are often so individualistic that we think of our personal testimonies much more than the corporate witness of the church. *Jesus made it clear that the reality of our becoming worshipers will be reflected in the way we treat each other in the body.* That is a sobering thought.

THE SOIL: POTENTIAL WORSHIPERS

I believe God places a desire to worship into the hearts of certain people long before they believe. I remember wondering about God and my purpose for living when I was three years old. Early in my life, I realized I was not a worshiper. I knew there was something missing in my life, even while attending church as a child and Bible studies as a high school student. I longed to find fulfillment in worship, although I searched for it in many different areas.

I know many of you would say that before entering into a relationship with Christ, worship was the farthest thing from your mind. Maybe all you could think about was the next party. But deep down there was a deep longing for fulfillment. You weren't aware yet that peace and intimacy with God were the only answers. You may have turned your back on religion, rejecting the ritualistic formalism that some call worship, but deep down you were searching for real worship.

Some religious folks are also potential worshipers, but are in a different category. They go to church and sing the hymns. However, there is something missing in their lives. When the religious man finds Christ, the door is opened for real worship. How could he have missed it all those years? Let's look at a few examples of individuals who had worship in their hearts and proved themselves to be the good soil.

THE ETHIOPIAN EUNUCH

> So he got up *and went*; and there *was an Ethiopian eunuch, a court official of Candace, queen of the Ethiopians, who was in charge of all her treasure; and he had come to Jerusalem to worship* (Acts 8:27).

We don't know much about the eunuch beyond what is written here. If he were physically a *eunuch,* he would have been excluded from becoming a proselyte or entering the temple. We do know that he was a high official with great responsibility.

Some have hypothesized that the churches that arose in Ethiopia soon after may have been a result of this man's testimony. It is certainly possible, because of such a man transformed by the gospel.

Why did he go up to Jerusalem? He was drawn there to worship.[19] In his seeking of intimacy with God, he purchased a copy of the book of Isaiah, hoping that in the Holy Scriptures he might find what he was seeking. God sent Philip to him to present Jesus Christ as the only path to true worship.

Philip did not give him the "plan of salvation," but presented to him the person of salvation, Jesus Christ (Acts 8:35). When a person is drawn to become a worshiper and has been introduced to the object of that worship, the means of conversion is relatively simple. The Ethiopian entered into a relationship with God and he wanted to be baptized! As a result, he "went on his way rejoicing" (v. 39).

---

[19] *Proskuneō* Since this is a future participle, it should be taken as indicating his purpose. It does not indicate that he actually worshiped, but that was why he went to Jerusalem.

LYDIA

It was Paul's custom to go to synagogues when arriving at a new city. Besides following his conviction that the gospel should be declared to the Jews first, he also found it to be the best place to discover potential worshipers among the Jews, proselytes, and interested Gentiles. When Paul went to Philippi, he went to a Jewish "place of prayer" (Acts 16:13), which was typically along a riverbank. Lydia, although not yet a believer, was described as "a worshiper of God"[20] (v. 14).

Luke reports, "the Lord opened her heart to respond to the things spoken by Paul" (v. 14). She had been prepared. Paul sowed, but it was God's Spirit who opened her eyes. Paul did not make a contact; he merely discovered one.

CORNELIUS

Cornelius obviously had an impact and told others about his interest in God long before Peter arrived. The Scriptures indicate that not only was he "a devout man, and one who feared God," but that also extended to his household (Acts 10:2). His servants and one of his soldiers testified that he was "a righteous and God-fearing man" (Acts 10:11). Cornelius' life enabled him to assemble a large group of people to hear Peter when he arrived (v. 24).

We mistakenly think of unbelievers as all bad and disinterested in the things of God. We also tend to draw a distinct line between the saved and the unsaved. God knows those who are His (2 Tim. 2:19), but it is not always easy for us to see. As we study with people, we see definite signs that God is calling them to be worshipers by the way they respond to the Word and its impact on their lives even before they give their lives to Christ.

HOW TO FIND THE GOOD SOIL

The most obvious way to find the good soil is to sow generously. If you never sow, you will never find out what grows. One of the main points of the parable of the sower is that the different types of soils

---

[20] *Sébomai* - A present adjectival participle, describing her. It refers to a worshiper or God-fearer. It is also a technical term used for Gentiles who accepted the God of Israel as the one true God, but did not keep the whole Jewish law (see Bauer et al.).

are not readily distinguishable. It is only when the seed is sown and starts to grow that its nature becomes apparent.

I asked the most effective evangelists in our movement here in Brazil how they recognize potential worshipers after they have sown the seed. This is what they said.

First, potential worshipers have an interest in the Word in addition to their scheduled times for Bible studies. People who are interested only in religion consider small group meetings, celebrations, or individual studies with the evangelist as religious moments, and even something that might bring a blessing or luck to their home. This "soil" type will rarely read their Bibles during the other six days.

In Acts 13:7, the proconsul of Paphos, Sergius Paulus, was described as "a man of intelligence" That means he was understanding and perceptive.[21] He summoned Paul and Barnabas because he "sought to hear the word of God."[22] This was more than casual curiosity, but a determined seeking to understand. So much so that he was not dissuaded by the false magician, Elymas, who was struck blind by the Lord (vv. 8-11). However, what amazed Sergius Paulus and left him in awe was, "the teaching of the Lord" (v. 12).

Second, potential worshipers soon understand the connection between their lives and the Scriptures. Those interested in becoming religious are curious to learn facts about the Bible, but don't relate what they are learning to everyday life. Bible study is more of an academic study or religious activity than a new perspective on life. The Pharisees were the quintessential example of this dichotomy. How many times did Jesus ask, "Have you never read?"

I have seen several situations where people become interested in studying the Bible when they discover how it directly applies to their marriages. It is powerful to see the Lord change a relationship as people begin relating the Scriptures to their daily lives even before they become believers.

Third, potential worshipers have a deeper insight into the Scriptures. I have learned so much from the questions and insights of

---

[21] *Sunetós* is akin to *suníēmi* and means to be able to put ideas together. I believe that for believers, it is the spiritual perception that allows us to see the relationship between spiritual truths.

[22] *Epizētéō* - To seek zealously, investigate or desire.

those who have not yet entered into a relationship with Christ. They begin tying various passages together, seeing the relationship between the ideas. On the other hand, it seems as though even the most simple, biblical concepts are so hard for religious people to grasp, and it isn't because of a lack of intelligence. (See 1 Corinthians 2:14.)

My wife Lisa was talking with a brilliant Chinese graduate student about Christ and gave him a Bible. After reading it, he made the observation, "We scientists write detailed, long papers to state a very simple truth. Jesus, however, in a few simple words spoke volumes."

Fourth, the lives of potential worshipers begin to change. No one has to tell them to quit doing this or start doing that. Certain activities start losing their appeal even before the person gives His life to Christ. Before becoming a worshiper, he or she begins to find pleasure in the things of God rather than the things of the world.

One of my friends had been studying for about a year with a man who is very popular in his town and writes all the music for Carnaval, the Brazilian equivalent of Mardi Gras. He has only been to church once and is not yet a believer, but he has already lost his interest in this immoral festival that was so much a part of his life before.

Finally, potential worshipers begin talking about Jesus to others even before entering into a relationship with Him. It may seem strange, but people get excited about what God is teaching them, and they share it with others before they themselves are saved. It is obviously not a religious duty, but a reflection that God is already watering the seeds of worship in their lives.

HARVESTING

Do you not say, "There are yet four months, and then comes the harvest"? Behold, I say to you, lift up you eyes and look on the fields, that they are white for harvest. Already he who reaps is receiving wages and is gathering fruit for life eternal so that he who sows and he who reaps may rejoice together. For in this case the saying is true, "One sows and another reaps." I sent you to reap that for which you have not labored; others have labored and you have entered into their labor (John 4:35-58).

Sowing Is Not Harvesting

Two of the most labor-intensive moments in farming are sowing and harvesting. Of course the plowing, cultivation, spraying, and fertilizing also require a great deal of effort, but they are usually not as urgent, nor is the timing as critical as with planting and harvesting.

Evangelism is traditionally seen as a brief presentation of the plan of salvation with an invitation to "accept Christ."[23] However, when we consider the agriculture metaphors that Jesus frequently used, it becomes clear that evangelism cannot be reduced to a brief conversation. The sowing and harvesting metaphors can be compared to evangelism.

The initial contact is sowing, and the harvest is when the person finally gives his or her life to the Lord. There is an investment of time and energy on the part of the sower to create conditions for the seed to sprout, grow, and eventually produce fruit.

After talking with the Samaritan woman about the real nature of worship, Jesus told her who He really was ("I am"). In shock, the woman went back to the city and made the bold statement, "Come, see a man who told me all the things that I have done."[24]

Before, she had slunk out of the city at noon to avoid contact with the other women, but now she boldly calls attention to herself and to her sin.

The disciples were more interested in eating lunch and getting away from this despised Samaritan territory as fast as possible. However, Jesus had a different perspective. He said, "My food is to do the will of Him who sent Me and to accomplish His work" (John 4:34). In other words, pleasing His Father gave Him more satisfaction than physical food.

Jesus then quoted a proverb, "There are yet four months, and then comes the harvest (v. 35)." This saying carries the idea of waiting until later, putting off a responsibility. We might say today, "Don't worry, there's plenty of time. We can do it later." Evangelism is a priority, but we have a way of placing it on the back burner and getting on to *more important* tasks related to our ministries.

---

[23] "Accepting Christ" is one of the many non-biblical terms used to describe someone's conversion.
[24] The relative pronoun is probably a qualitative pronoun indicating the kind of things she has done. It can carry the idea of the degree of things that she has done as well.

Then Jesus added, "Behold, I say to you, lift up you eyes and look[25] on the fields, that they are white for harvest." Jesus was declaring that the specific moment to harvest had arrived and they must not delay. There was an urgency to respond quickly.

Jesus explained, "Already he who reaps is receiving wages and is gathering fruit for life eternal; so that he who sows and he who reaps may rejoice together. For in this case the saying is true, 'One sows and another reaps.' I sent you to reap that for which you have not labored; others have labored and you have entered into their labor (vv. 36-38)."

The word used for "labor" in this passage means to work to the point of being weary, a striving or struggle. The "others" are probably the Old Testament prophets who strived and struggled but never saw the harvest in which the disciples are about to become involved. This could also be a reference to John the Baptist who also preached nearby. The Samaritans were prepared by the woman's own testimony, too. Obviously, the Spirit of God had also been working in their hearts before the disciples arrived. That explains the large and almost instantaneous response to Jesus' preaching.

THERE NEEDS TO BE A GREAT DEAL OF SOWING BEFORE
THERE CAN BE HARVESTING.

Jesus said, "in this case," to describe the specific circumstances related to the Samaritans. He is not applying the principle broadly to every culture. Some cultures, because of their Christian background, may be more ready than a Muslim country, for example. In most cases, there needs to be a great deal of sowing before there can be harvesting. The Samaritans in this story had been prepared to be "harvested" because someone else had sown the seeds.

Jesus implied that the hard work is sowing, not harvesting. Sowing is hard work because there is not an immediate return for the effort. It requires patience and perseverance.

---

[25] *Theásasthe* ("look") is an aorist ingressive imperative: "Start looking!" The idea is to begin looking beyond what they might perceive with physical eyes, but to see their circumstances with spiritual eyes.

Harvesting is the fun part. When I harvested my grandparents' cherries, I was pleased to see the baskets fill up, and more than a few made their way into my mouth. Instant results and instant rewards. Almost all the evangelistic programs and tracts used today are geared toward harvesting. We equate evangelism with harvesting rather than sowing. People who are good at sowing but not at harvesting often become discouraged because they never seem to be able to "close the deal."

A HUGE HARVEST

Peter's preaching on the day of Pentecost is seen as a justification for mass evangelistic campaigns. There may be moments when the Lord prepares a people for such a time. Most certainly, God prepared this group, sowing truth into their lives in preparation for the Spirit's conviction.

The men were potential worshipers, described as "devout men from every nation under heaven" (Acts 2:5). Although many were there as a religious duty, many others were there because they desired to worship God. However, they had no access to His presence because of their sins. They could not go into the Holy of Holies, but could only marvel outside the sanctuary.

Notice how Peter addressed the group: "Men of Judea and all you who live in Jerusalem…" (v. 14). These were men, well versed in the Scriptures, who were devoted to seeking God in Jerusalem.

Peter continued, "This is what was spoken of through the prophet Joel" (v.16), He explained what they were seeing by referring to a passage of Scripture familiar to them. The noise and the speaking in other languages were evidence that God was giving His Spirit to every member of the church.

"Jesus the Nazarene, a man attested to you by God with miracles and wonders and signs which God performed through Him in your midst, just as you yourselves know" (v. 22). Peter did not have to read anything about Jesus' life, miracles, or teachings. They all had personally heard Him and seen what He did.

"This man…you nailed to a cross by the hands of godless men and put Him to death" (v. 23). They did not need to see a film or read a medical description of what happened to Jesus and how much He suffered. They had been eyewitnesses of the horrors of the cross less than two months before and it had dramatically impacted their lives. Then came the startling new information: "But God raised Him up again" (v. 24). Peter repeated this truth in verse 32, testifying that he, along with the other apostles, was an eyewitness of this important event. However, he mentioned that this should not come as a great surprise to them, because the prophets attested to the resurrection. Peter cited Psalm 16 as evidence that it was in God's plan to raise Him; hence Jesus deserved to be worshiped as their Messiah.

Were these Jews prepared? They sure were! These men were "devout" or God-fearing (v. 5).[26] They were potential worshipers and had come to Jerusalem to worship, as they knew how. The Spirit took Peter's words, their previous knowledge of the Scriptures and their personal experience with Jesus and put it all together until "they were *pierced* to the heart," and they asked, "Brethren, what shall we do?" (v. 37). Peter did not need to give an invitation; they invited themselves—without reservations. When they understood who Jesus was and how He fit into the prophecies they already knew, they needed little instruction on how to respond.

The result was the beginning of a church in which "Everyone kept feeling a sense of awe (v. 43) and were continually "praising God" (v.47). It was a worshiping church.

A HARVEST AMONG GENTILES

Although God had prepared many Jews, He had also prepared Gentiles to understand the message about Jesus.

Because of his Jewish upbringing, Peter was hesitant to go to the house of a potential worshiper named Cornelius. He was "a devout man and one who feared God" (Acts 10:2). Those terms indicate he had a certain awe of God[27] and a continuous awareness of His

---

[26] *Eulabēs* (*eu-* well; *labēs* from *lambánō*, which means to grasp). This person has grasped the deep truths of Scripture by God's grace. It is a worship term that parallels *eusébeia*. It is used of Simeon in Luke 2:25 and of the way we are to worship God in Heb. 12:28.

[27] *Eusebēs* – This term is translated godly when referring to believers. It indicates that a person lives in awe of God.

presence[28] even though he was not yet a believer. The word translated "devout" was often used by Jews to refer to Gentiles who respectfully listened to the Scriptures in the synagogues, but had not become proselytes. However, the addition of the phrase "and feared God" indicates there was a different attitude. He prayed regularly and God even heard his prayers as an unbeliever (Acts 10:2, 4). Even his servants testified of his character (Acts 10:22).

God had prepared Cornelius and his family. It is likely that he became aware of God through hearing the Scriptures read in the synagogue and had heard testimonies from those who knew God. Most importantly, he was aware of Jesus.

Peter knew God had prepared their hearts. He said,

> You yourselves know the thing which took place throughout all Judea, starting from Galilee, after the baptism which John proclaimed. You know of Jesus of Nazareth, how God anointed Him with the Holy Spirit and with power, and how He went about doing good and healing all who were oppressed by the devil, for God was with Him (Acts 10:38-39).

As with the Jews on the day of Pentecost, the seeds of worship had been sown before Peter arrived. There was a combination of the objective knowledge of Jesus and the Scriptures and there was the more subjective spiritual awe of the one true God placed within their hearts.

It seems that those who are prepared for the harvest already have a reverential fear of God. They are hungry to know how to worship Him.

Most Gentiles, however, had no notion of God whatsoever. In Paul's second recorded message (Act 17), he does not emphasize Jesus, but the nature and character of God. This is the only message recorded in the Bible addressed to a group of people who are utterly unprepared for the gospel. They had no idea of the God of the Old Testament and certainly had never heard of Jesus. Paul recognized they were idolaters with a non-biblical worldview (Act 17:16).

---

[28] *Phobéō* - Luke uses a present substantival participle to indicate that he was continually aware of His presence and as a result was reverent.

Paul's sermon was a cram course on the character of God. In His presentation of the true God they should be worshiping, he implied that God was the Creator (v. 24), omnipresent (v. 24), sufficient in Himself (v. 25), sovereign (v. 26), immanent (v. 27), holy (v. 29), merciful (v. 30), and just (v. 31). In closing, Paul mentions the resurrection, although he never mentions the name of Jesus.

It would seem necessary, before becoming a believer, to have a notion of who one is supposed to worship. Paul was not just giving the Athenians a list of important facts about God. He gave them spiritual truth so they would see they were not worshiping as they should. They were worshiping idols and they needed to discover whom and how to worship.

Paul even told them the reason for their existence: "That they would seek God, if perhaps they might grope for Him and find Him, though He is not far from each one of us" (Acts 17:27). God is seeking potential worshipers who will grope until they find Him. Paul knew such a presentation would not appeal to the masses who were looking for a philosophy or a religion, but it would draw those who were being called by God. As the Scripture says, some sneered, some wanted to hear more, and some joined him and believed (Acts 17:32-34).

Is Brazil Ready for Harvest?

My experience in Brazil indicates that almost everyone needs to have the Word sown in their lives when we first meet them. But, they are not ready to be harvested immediately. People have very little exposure to the biblical Jesus or to biblical truth, for that matter. Their concepts of God are more influenced by spiritism, Catholic myths, superstitions, soap operas, and movies than by the Bible. People are not prepared to embrace the gospel, but instead need to be prepared for the gospel through His Word.

As I was writing this chapter, I ran into a U.S. missionary from a charismatic group. A visiting friend from the United States asked about the great revival in Brazil he had heard about. I was pleasantly surprised by the missionary's answer. He said the evangelical churches are filling up with people who are in some way changing their religious practices, but lives are not being changed. He understood revival as I do, a transformation of lives that impacts society.

The evangelical church in Brazil is like a river a mile wide, but only an inch deep. Unfortunately, instead of flowing with living water, that centimeter of water is polluted with empty ritual.

IS THE UNITED STATES READY FOR HARVEST?

There was a time when Americans were well educated in the Bible. A half-century ago, most people had an understanding of biblical concepts and terminology, even though they did not necessarily embrace Christ. These teachings were part of the public school curriculum and many people attended church. That is long past. Americans, as a whole, are not "white for the harvest."

Several evangelism tools still used today presume that people already understand sin, faith, repentance (if mentioned), grace, eternal life, and Jesus Himself. In reality, we need to approach most people much as Paul addressed the Athenians, starting from square one and seeing evangelism as a process.

Many parts of the evangelical world are in desperate need of materials and methods that are geared toward sowing the seed that produces worshipers, rather than harvesting techniques that fill our churches with religious people.

WHAT WE DO IN BRAZIL

One of the key values of our strategy is "Life over methods." We emphasize that any method or skill is only as good as your worship relationship with Christ. Nothing should be done mechanically or as a religious chore, but as an overflow of our worship.

We use the "Seven Signs" from the Gospel of John, noting the significance of the seven miracles Jesus performed in the first eleven chapers. The beloved apostle had spent almost 60 years telling people about Jesus. He said he could fill the whole world with books telling all that Jesus did. However, he chose his favorite seven stories that best illustrate Jesus' deity and the faith response to Him that is necessary for eternal life (John 20:30-31). As we go through these signs, one-by-one, the lights start going on as those who continue to study the Bible with us begin to grasp who Jesus is and what faith is.

Also, people like the stories. Most people can relate to a story from the life of Jesus more than one of the doctrinal passage in Paul's epistles.

We either hand out printed copies of the signs door-to-door and follow up with interviews after the third sign, or we make personal contact with friends, neighbors, or relatives, inviting them to study with us. We have found it to be most effective when there is already some sort of relationship with the person. That makes sense in that people are able to see the changes in our lives, recognizing the power of the Word to transform people.

While I was writing this chapter, I spent some time with Pedro Borges in Campinas. Pedro was known in the Brazilian church as a great "soul winner." He had been using well-known "soul-winning" techniques that had been translated into Portuguese. Although his church grew in numbers, the people did not mature spiritually. Consequently, Pedro left the ministry discouraged.

When Pedro later went to Campinas to start a church, he went with a "fruit-bearing" mentality regarding the process of evangelism. The first nine people were baptized while I was with him. Pedro read 2 Corinthians 5:17 afterward and said he had always wondered why his "soul-winning" techniques never led to changed lives as described in that verse. Now, he was so joyful to see the fruit of changed lives that God has borne through his life.

Some of the evangelism groups in our churches have recognized a difference between sowing and harvesting. As a result, some people make the initial contact, doing the first studies, and then pass off the potential worshiper to someone who is more of a harvester.

This has several benefits. It obviously takes advantage of a person's giftedness. It has the added advantage of exposing people to different parts of the body of Christ so they don't get too tied to one individual. Most importantly, when someone comes to the Lord, it is a group victory and not the result of one individual's work.

Since our emphasis is on worship, we start our evangelism training by stressing the worship life of the sower. Our goal is to present Jesus to as many people as possible with the certainty that some of the seed will fall on good soil.

CONCLUSION

For a rebel to become a worshiper, three elements need to be present: The seed, the sower, and the soil. To produce worshipers, the seed needs to emphasize Jesus Christ as He is revealed in the Bible. The sower needs to be a worshiper himself. He cannot do evangelism as a task, and he cannot reproduce what he himself is not. Finally, the soil needs to be receptive, potential worshipers. We can make "converts" by telling them the facts, but only God can give the comprehension necessary for someone to become a worshiper.

As we begin the process of building Christ's church, we search for those whom God is calling to be part of the body. We could even call the initial step of "contact discovery" the "calling out of His bride."

Whom is God calling? He is seeking and calling worshipers, not religious people. If we sow religious seeds, we will reap religious "believers" who never grow. If we sow the seeds of worship because the golden thread has been woven into our lives as sowers, then potential worshipers will be drawn to us and our community.

Paradigm Shifts

As I have informally surveyed people who know the Lord, I have found that the majority of them came into a relationship with God through sustained exposure to the Scriptures from a friend or relative who is living the reality of a changed life. They may have made a "decision" through some method, but there may have been years of preparation by fruit bearers. The most effective evangelists are often not considered great "soul winners." They often don't even realize the great impact they have had in directing non-believers towards God. They are worshipers.

SOUL WINNING	FRUIT BEARING
1. Objectives: • To convince the sinner • A decision • To add members to the church	1. Objectives: • To discover potential worshipers • A process that leads to the new birth • To bring people into a relationship with God
2. Methods: • Based on a methodology • A quick presentation • An explanation • Not transferable—evangelist needs the personality of a salesperson • Convert needs follow-up—a more detailed explanation of what has happened. • Marketing	2. Methods: • Based on the spiritual life of the evangelist • A process of discovery of biblical truth • A biblical study • Transferable—any person can participate, even new converts • It leads naturally to discipleship • Sow the Word

SOUL WINNING	FRUIT BEARING
3. THE MESSAGE: • The mechanism of salvation • An explanation of repentance, faith, and grace	3. THE MESSAGE: • The person of salvation, Jesus • Discovery of repentance, faith, and grace through Jesus' life
4. THEOLOGY: A belief in the persuasiveness of man to lead people to make a decision	4. THEOLOGY: A belief in the sovereignty of God in salvation and human responsibility

A second paradigm shift is how to define a potential contact. With the traditional view of evangelism, which stresses the importance of a "decision" rather than worship, people often feel pressured into "accepting Christ" by the threat of hell or the promise of heaven. We distinguish between those contacts who are seeking fire insurance and those who are potential worshipers being drawn into a relationship with God.

SEEKING FIRE INSURANCE	SEEKING GOD
1. GOAL: To go to heaven, which is for our eternal personal benefit	1. GOAL: To please God, not any personal benefit
2. MEANS: A decision—a belief in the death of Jesus Christ	2. MEANS: The death of our old self through Jesus Christ
3. RESULT: A religious life with little or no change	3. RESULT: A transformed life. A worship lifestyle

WHERE TO START

1. **ASK GOD TO ALLOW HIS CHARACTER TO SHINE THROUGH YOUR LIFE.** Make sure you are sowing the worship of Jesus Christ through the way you live your life.

2. **ASK GOD TO SHOW YOU WHETHER YOUR STRENGTH IS SOWING OR HARVESTING.** Don't expect some revelation about your giftedness. God makes it known through your doing it. Every Christian should be aware of casual contacts throughout the day, but some people are effective at going up to someone cold turkey and talking about Jesus. Just try it. Ask some friends or relatives to start studying the Bible with you and see what happens.

3. **EXAMINE YOUR EVANGELISTIC METHODS.**
   a. Do you use religious words that might attract religious people and repel potential worshipers?
   b. Do you emphasize the life, character, death, burial, and resurrection of Jesus?
   c. Is there a draw to worship?
   d. Do you emphasize Jesus or the plan of salvation?
   e. Do you think of evangelism as a process or an event?
   f. Do you have tools for sowing and harvesting?

DISCUSSION QUESTIONS

1. Why do we call it "contact discovery" instead of "making contacts"?

2. What is the difference between planting and harvesting?

3. Why is there a tendency to stress the reaping instead of sowing?

4. Who do you know that is effective at sowing? Why is he or she good at it?

5. Do you feel you are better at sowing or harvesting? Explain.

6. How is evangelism a form of worship?

7. Why is it important that a sower be a worshiper?

8. What are potential worshipers? How do you recognize them?

9. In your salvation, do you think you were drawn to worship? Explain.

10. What is the most important truth you learned from this chapter?

11. What is your evaluation of the evangelistic tools you have used?

12. What will you do differently now when you talk to people about Jesus?

Chapter 12

WORSHIP
AND
EVANGELISM

HELPING PEOPLE BECOME
TRUE WORSHIPERS OF GOD

For they themselves report about us what kind of a reception we had with you, and how YOU TURNED TO GOD FROM IDOLS *to serve a living and true God* (1 Thessalonians 1:9).

SEED TRUTH: EVANGELISM IS A PROCESS THAT LEADS TO CONVERSION, WHICH CHANGES THE OBJECT OF A PERSON'S WORSHIP. *There is a process through which God opens the eyes of people, leading them to surrender their personal deity, depend on Jesus Christ, and become worshipers of Him. Religious people make decisions so they can go to heaven, but often continue to worship the same things they always have. An effective evangelist plants biblical seeds that, falling on good soil, will lead to the new birth and the integration of worship throughout the person's life.*

One of my favorite places to visit is Monkey Island. It got its name, not from being inhabited by monkeys, but because the original owner's nickname was "Macaco" or "Monkey." All of the houses are on stilts in the jungle. A generator that runs for a few hours in the evening provides the only electricity.

However interesting the surroundings and lifestyle might be, the attraction is the people. They are open to the Word of God and quickly apply it. I don't have to watch the clock when I am teaching the Bible, because they are hungry to learn. They don't have much, but they are the most hospitable people in the world. When I visit, I know they will fill me up with all the shrimp and açaí[1] I can handle.

A few years back we took a group of teenagers from the United States out to this island. Our goal was to teach them something about cross-cultural evangelism and church planting. As usual, the Monkey Island people rolled out the red carpet.

One day, I was out with a group of them going door-to-door by boat (more like dock-to-dock) to find people interested in studying the Bible. After several visits, we were talking about the gospel with a couple and I asked a girl to give her testimony. She said, among other things, "All you have to do is ask Jesus to come into your heart."

When we were waiting in the boat after the visit, I said, "Sarah, I have a confession to make. I didn't exactly translate what you said. I changed your testimony." I explained to her I didn't feel that what she said was truly part of the gospel. For example, I asked her where in the Bible we were told to invite Jesus into our hearts.

She said, "Yeah, I've always wondered about that. But that is what I have always been told."

Suddenly, the American teenagers seemed very interested in hearing what in fact the gospel is, biblically. I think they were more open at that point because they had spent three weeks in Brazil already trying to talk about Jesus with people whose worldview was different from their own.

I can still remember another girl looking at me and asking, "So what is the gospel, anyhow?" After I explained what the book of Romans had to say, her mouth was hanging open and she said, "We have never heard that."

The Heart of the Gospel

Ever since I was in seminary, I have been studying and restudying to make sure I understand the gospel, so I can truly say with Paul,

---

[1] Açaí (pronounced ah-sah-ee) is a purple pulp from the fruit of a palm tree. It is high in energy and is almost a staple for many people.

"For I am not ashamed of the gospel, for it is the power of God for salvation to everyone who believes" (Rom. 1:16). I want to know and be convicted of the message and its power to transform lives. What is the message that turns rebels into worshipers?

I have been trained in, and have used, virtually every evangelism method around, but something about them hasn't seemed right to me. The message of salvation by grace through faith in Christ's death and resurrection seemed simple enough. However, in trying to simplify it and make it more acceptable, some of those methods downplayed the need for repentance and its impact on one's life. Consequently, some of the gospel's power to transform people into worshipers has been lost. Maybe something was lost when we "put the cookies on the bottom shelf" to make it easier to accept. Maybe more time was needed for people to really come to grips with the message and finally bow down before the God of the universe who became flesh and died for our sins.

With the different ideas and methods floating around in my head, I was confused for some time. It has since become clear to me, however, that the gospel is all about worship. That puts everything in perspective for me.

Harold Best expresses the essence of salvation, saying:

> There can only be one call to worship, and this comes at conversion, when in complete repentance we admit to worshiping falsely, trapped by the inversion and enslaved to false gods before whom we have been dying sacrifices. This call to true worship comes but once, not every Sunday, in spite of the repeated calls to worship that begin most liturgies and orders of worship.[2]

The previous chapter dealt with "contact discovery" and finding potential worshipers. This chapter treats the process of evangelism through which we help lead those potential worshipers into a worship relationship with Jesus Christ through the death of the old rebel and the new birth of a worshiper.

Some people may object to saying evangelism is a process, because it seems to imply a person is 10 percent saved today, 30

---

[2]Harold Best, *Music Through the Eyes of Faith*, p.147.

percent next week, etc. But, I am not saying *justification* is a process. There is a moment when a person passes from death to life (John 5:24), becoming a new person in Christ (2 Cor. 5:17) because of the death of the old man and the birth of the new (Rom. 6:5). The *calling*, however, is often a long process during which the Holy Spirit opens the eyes of a person as he discovers the truth in the Bible. The evangelization process is completed when the potential worshiper actually has the door opened to begin a worship relationship.

THE MARRIAGE METAPHOR

Courtship is followed by engagement. There is usually not a drastic transition from a dating relationship into engagement, if a solid friendship is developing. I don't think it is common for a man to catch a woman by surprise, getting down on one knee with a diamond ring in his hand and asking her to marry him. They have usually had some long talks about future plans.

After engagement, however, the couple get to know each other better and begin taking steps toward a lifetime commitment. They still may back out if their deeper understanding of each other seems to reveal that the relationship might not work. However, if both are convinced they have a genuine love for each other and are ready to make a commitment, the two become one when the vows are made and the relationship is consummated.

Imagine, however, a much different scenario. Would you be concerned for a couple that met each other at a park on a Friday afternoon and decided to get married the very next day? A quick presentation of the gospel, followed by an invitation to "accept Christ" might be compared to such a quick wedding. And a decision to follow Christ has much greater consequences than even the choice of a marriage partner.

The process of evangelism is much like the engagement period. The person has decided he wants to pursue intimacy with the Lord, but has not entered into a worship relationship with Him, yet. He is learning, reflecting, and even growing closer to God. One day, the person passes from death to life and is transformed into a worshiper, becoming one with the Lord.

Stretching the metaphor further, many people spend enormous amounts of money and energy on a one-hour wedding ceremony and very little energy on laying a firm foundation for the relationship that follows. The result is a strained or stagnant relationship that started with a huge bang, but fizzled out. This is comparable to the emphasis that is placed on the plan of salvation while slighting the person of salvation, the Lord Jesus Christ.

I was asked to marry some friends here in Brazil. In our last meeting before the wedding, I asked each of them how they planned to serve God together as a couple. He said he wanted to work with the praise band and she said she wanted to teach Sunday School to the older kids at church.

I looked at them and said, "Is that it?"

The bride-to-be burst out sobbing as her future husband and I looked on in shock. She said she had felt called to be a missionary as a teenager. She felt now as though she was abandoning her dreams so that she could marry him.

We spent the rest of the afternoon dealing with all the implications of their marriage and serving the Lord. I knew the heart of each of them and their hunger to be worshipers. That time together was extremely important in building their relationship in preparation for the marriage. The subsequent marriage ceremony was what made the marriage official, but the relationship had been the focus of our time together.

Salvation is much the same. The actual "decision" is relatively easy when the person knows and is drawn to a worship relationship with Jesus Christ through the process of evangelism. There will be no doubt about His love and grace. Our sinfulness becomes obvious, leading to repentance. As we see Him for who He is, the meaning and application of Christ's death on the cross become apparent. The "plan of salvation" at this point becomes believing on the Lord Jesus Christ.

THE SEED THAT GROWS

And He was saying, "The kingdom of God is like a man who casts seed upon the soil; *and goes to bed at night and gets up by day, and the seed sprouts up and grows—how, he himself does not know. The soil produces crops by itself; first the blade, then the head, then the mature grain in the head. But when the crop permits, he immediately puts in the sickle, because the harvest has come"* (Mark 4:26-29).

One commentator, who believes as I do that evangelism is a process, said that the parable of the sower teaches the need to prepare the soil. I agree that the "good soil" needs to be prepared. It can be fallow and hardened on the surface after years of neglect. A person's culture and worldview can make even the good soil resistant at first.

The point of the parable of the sower, however, is not preparation of the soil. No amount of preparation can change one soil type to another type. I suppose that extensive aeration could make the soil beside the path less compact. Herbicides could eliminate the thorns and we could even blast the bedrock out and haul in additional topsoil. Jesus is teaching, however, that people differ and they will have different responses to the Word. The good soil describes those whom God has prepared.

The parable of the seed that grows appears only in Mark (4:26-29) and is often neglected, because it does not fit into the traditional paradigms of evangelism. People aren't sure what to do with it. It is, in fact, an expansion of the parable of the sower, describing what happens when the seed falls into good soil.

SOWING THE SEED

The parable begins much the same way as that of the soils, "The kingdom of God is like a man who casts seeds upon the soil." The sower then "goes to bed at night and gets up by day," indicating both the passing of time and his confidence in God. God never sleeps or slumbers (Ps. 121:4), but the sower, trusting in the seed that he has planted, rests easy.

A friend described his first experience in planting beans as a child. He could hardly wait to get up the next day to harvest the new crop. Although disappointed that nothing grew the first day, he sprang out of bed the second day, hoping to see results. Again, nothing. On the third day, sure something was wrong, he dug up the seeds to see what was happening. Of course, he destroyed the plants and never did get a crop.

In contrast, the confident farmer waits patiently in this parable, because he knows that "the seed sprouts up and grows—how, he himself does not know."

THE PROCESS

I studied plant physiology in college and learned about what initiated the mitotic processes within the endocarp and how the stored energy was released to begin the germination process. We even did experiments to show geotropism and phototropism.

I doubt most farmers even remember what the pericarp and endocarp are. Despite all the advanced information and modern technology, the simple fact that corn seed produces corn is an ageless truth. Everyone knows it doesn't happen overnight either.

Although in the next chapter we will explain a few aspects of what happens, not even the most brilliant theologian can explain how the gospel transforms rebels into worshipers. Jesus described the Spirit's work as being like the wind, "You hear the sound of it, but do not know where it comes from and where it is going" (John 3:8).

Jesus said, "The soil produces crops by itself."[3] This means the farmer does not directly influence the process. Notice the process: "First the blade, then the head, then the mature [complete] grain in the head." Jesus is obviously describing something that takes time to complete.

Some have suggested this process could be describing Christian growth, but the context indicates otherwise. The harvest is the conversion of the person, and so the growth of the plant represents the process leading up to the moment a person is regenerated. Jesus said, "When the crop permits, he immediately puts in the sickle, because the harvest has come." The time for the harvest is here. The mysterious power of the seed itself to produce a crop is emphasized to demonstrate the ability of the gospel to change lives.

THE HARVEST

When I worked on a farm, an older gentleman taught me about farming. One day, we were looking over a field of soybeans that to me

---

[3] Jesus uses the Greek word "*autómatos*" from which we get the word "automatic." Jesus puts it in an emphatic position in the phrase to emphasize this fact.

looked dry and ready for harvest. I asked him when they were going to harvest it. He reached down and took a pod and started chewing on a soybean. Raw soybeans are not exactly a delicacy. He spit out the seed and said it would be at least another week. He said that from the texture, he knew the moisture content was too high. If the beans were harvested then, they would either become moldy or the farmer would have to spend money to have them dried. A wise farmer knows when to harvest.

We cannot play the role of the Holy Spirit in bringing someone to conversion. Our role is to proclaim God's Word so God can use it to bring someone to Himself. Paul was very clear that he did not want to make the message more appealing somehow by adding or taking away from it with "persuasive words." He did so in order that their "faith would not rest on the wisdom of men, but on the power of God" (1 Cor 2:4-5). This "power" does not refer to miracles, but to the power of the living Word to transform rebels into worshipers. If it is our convincing arguments that lead people to "make decisions," they will more than likely be merely religious and not become worshipers.

Because of the pressure to have a "harvest of souls" and show the results or fruit of our ministry, we tend to cut short the process of repentance. A person needs to understand his own sinfulness and who Jesus is. God let Paul sit for three days to ponder the words, "I am Jesus whom you are persecuting" (Acts 9:5). A wise evangelist will trust in the seed and be patient for the results as the Spirit works in the life of potential worshipers.

Only one time I "led someone to the Lord" after my first contact with her. I had given a seminar in a public school on sex and the Bible. This girl seemed to be broken because of her immoral lifestyle. As we talked afterward, she appeared repentant, so I led her in prayer to give her life to the Lord. Since she seemed so ready, my usual principle of first studying the Bible with an interested person seemed unnecessary.

Wasn't this a perfect example of how to do evangelism? There was a message from the Word, the person was convicted of sin, and a prayer of faith followed it. This young girl, however, showed no further interest in the Bible when we visited her a couple days later. Did we shortcut the process of repentance? Probably. Would she have been truly converted later had we started a Bible study with her? I don't know.

A SUMMARY

The farmer in Mark 4 trusted that the seed would bear fruit. However, there are many ways to apply this and other parables, and Jesus' intention was for us to meditate on them. That is why He said, "He who has ears to hear, let him hear" (Mark 4:9).

Reflect again on these four principles that can be applied to evangelism:

1. **THE WISE FARMER IS PATIENT, TRUSTING IN THE POWER OF THE SEED.** As we said, this parable is an elaboration of the good soil from the parable of the sower. In it, the process and the passage of time are emphasized. The progress is "first the blade, then the head, then the mature grain in the head." People do not become worshipers overnight.

2. **THE WISE FARMER DOESN'T NEED TO UNDERSTAND EVERYTHING.** The farmer doesn't understand the entire process, but he knows it takes time. All the farmer needs to know is what conditions are necessary for a certain seed type to germinate so that he does not plant it too early or too late. A person does not need to have a seminary education to plant the seeds that germinate into fruitful worshipers.

3. **A WISE FARMER WILL KNOW WHEN IT IS TIME TO HARVEST.** A good farmer will never harvest before its time. Mark 4:34 says, "But when the crop permits, he immediately puts in the sickle, because the harvest has come." Often we are in a hurry to see "results" and we end up giving birth prematurely. Maybe that is why so many Christians have to be on "life support" for most of their lives. Maybe that is why so many Christians are not worshiping as they should.

4. **THE WORSHIPING FARMER SOWS LIVING SEED.** Every farmer knows you get what you sow (Gal. 6:7). If we sow a religious lifestyle, we will reap religious people. If we sow the living word, we will reap worshipers. That is why it is essential

for the sower himself to be a worshiper. Worshipers reproduce worshipers.

To this point we have discussed the need for patience in the process of evangelism. The seed (the message of the gospel), the process of growth (understanding the gospel), and the harvest (conversion) will serve as the outline for this chapter.

THE SEED: THE GOSPEL

In the previous chapter, we defined the seed for contact discovery as the person of Jesus. Our focus was on sowing Jesus through our words, our lives, and our community relationships. Here, we are going to look a little more closely at the message about Jesus so we can understand the process leading up to the harvest.

THE NEED FOR THE GOSPEL

Why is sowing necessary before there can be a harvest? Only when we understand the bad news of mankind can we better grasp the process that leads up to conversion.

God's Purpose for Mankind

Chapter 2 points out that the most important result of our being made in God's image is our capacity to have fellowship with God. Without a will, a transcendent mind, and a spiritual nature, humans would be no different from the animals He created.

The bottom line: God wants us to have a vibrant worship relationship with Him. Although all of creation (Psalm 98:7-9) and angels (Heb. 1:6) worship Him, the spiritual union between God and man is different because of His image in our lives. That is why Adam was not included in the "Hall of Faith" in Hebrews 11. His worship of God, in its original perfection, was not a matter of faith because He saw God.

The second important implication of God's image in us is the spiritual union made possible between human beings. The unity of the Trinity is reflected in Adam and Eve's perfect fellowship with one another. The Bible says, "...in the image of God He created him; male and female He created them" (Gen. 1:27). This will be important to bear in mind when we examine the impact of worship on spiritual community

The Loss of Life and Worship

God created perfect circumstances for Adam and Eve, but that was ruined by sin. Everyone now has a broken relationship with his Creator because of the fall. Man's basic problem is a lack of worship and spiritual life and thus, human beings are not fulfilling the purpose for which they were created. Adam and Eve were expelled from the garden, isolated from the presence of God. They were cut off from the intimacy of worship, and their lives no longer glorified God.

The advent of the law through Moses only emphasized that there was no longer direct access to God. The veil in the Tabernacle, separating the Holy of Holies, was a vivid reminder that their worship did not bring them into intimacy with Him. Their rebellious, disobedience self-sufficient individualism was shown to be utterly sinful by the law.

Ryan asks the rhetorical question, "What happened in the fall? We forgot how to worship. We forgot how to put God first. In our redemption, we learn to put the right things first again, and when we worship, we celebrate the fact that God has enabled us to do that. And we do it with joy."[4]

What is the Gospel?

What is the gospel? It is the good news that, through Jesus, human beings can be restored to their original purpose to have a worship relationship with God. The saints of the Old Testament believed a rudimentary gospel before Jesus' time as a basis for their salvation. Prophecies prepared people to receive the gospel. The law itself is a preview of Christ's sacrifice on the cross and His impact in the lives of those who believe in Him. It is the righteous standard of the law that shows our utter sinfulness and the impossibility of salvation through human merit.

This gospel, however, came to light fully only in New Testament times. It is Jesus. He is the good news. The Old Testament points

---

[4] Ryan, p. 33.

forward to Him and the New Testament points back to Him. The gospel involves what Jesus said and what He did. It emphasizes His deity and His humanity. But most of all, it focuses on His death and resurrection as fulfillment of the Old Testament prophecies and the impact of those facts on our lives today (1 Cor. 15:1-4).

The gospel is all about Jesus and about becoming a worshiper of Him. You cannot worship what you do not know nor submit to someone whom you have never met.

Jesus made it clear that He came to restore worship. His statement, "an hour is coming and has now come" (John 4:23), is an indication that Jesus' purpose was to bring about a major change in worship. His plan is to restore worship to spiritual communion with Him so that He can be glorified through it.

The Gospel in the Synoptic Gospels

Mark 1:1 is considered by some to be the title of the book itself: "The beginning of the gospel of Jesus Christ." The story of His whole life is "the gospel."

Jesus' life emphasized the centrality of worship. It is highly significant that both at the beginning and the end of His ministry, Jesus purified the temple, showing His zeal for God's designated place of worship for the Jewish people. The Gospel of John describes Jesus' first Passover after His baptism (John 2:13-21). He was virtually unknown when He expelled the vendors and moneychangers for exploiting those who desired to worship God.

Just before His crucifixion, Jesus again cleansed the temple (Matt. 21:12-13; Mark 11:15-18; Luke 19:45-48). The very last public act was His observation of the sincere worship[5] of the widow as contrasted with the external, self-serving worship of the Jews (Luke 21:1-4). Then Jesus judiciously departed from the temple (Matt. 24:1), much as the glory of God left the temple in Ezekiel's day (Ezek. 10:18-19).

Jesus' teaching stressed worship. Matthew 4:23 and 9:35 are almost identical. They stand like bookends summarizing that phase of Jesus' public ministry. An example of each of the activities listed in these

[5] The word used for offering implied a sacrificial gift (*dōron*) offered to God. This offering was an act of worship, which included an offering of the widow's life (*bíos*).

verses is given, including "proclaiming the gospel of the kingdom." What was the gospel Jesus proclaimed? In the Sermon on the Mount, Jesus shares the attitudes and actions that characterize the participants in His kingdom. He describes the heart of a true worshiper, condemning the hypocritical worship of the religious people of His day.

When Mary poured the alabaster bottle of perfume on Jesus, the disciples were indignant (Matt. 26:7). Jesus pointed out that Mary had done something very special and added, "Truly I say to you, wherever this gospel is preached in the whole world, what this woman has done will also be spoken of in memory of her" (Matt. 26:13). Her expression of worship is a part of the gospel.

The Gospel in Acts

The message Philip preached to the Ethiopian eunuch is mentioned in Acts 8:35, "Beginning from this Scripture he preached Jesus to him." It would have been nice if Luke had included Philip's sermon outline with references. We see, however, the same content of the gospel that we have seen previously: Jesus and His fulfillment of Old Testament prophecies. We know Philip included His death because of the reference to Isaiah 53.

The eunuch was transformed into a worshiper and "went on his way rejoicing" (Acts 8:39). He had come to Jerusalem to worship (v. 27), and he discovered that the key that opened the door to God's presence was in Jesus Christ.

The Gospel in Romans

In the beginning of the book of Romans, Paul describes himself as a "bond-servant" or slave of Christ who has been set apart or appointed for the gospel (Romans 1:1). Since the gospel is the principal subject of the book of Romans, Paul defines it in the next several verses.

The first point Paul makes about the gospel is that it was "pre-promised" (v. 2). To prove this, he quoted about 60 passages from the Old Testament in the course of writing the book of Romans. He strongly linked the gospel to the writings of the prophets.

The Old Testament passages point to the heart of the gospel: It is concerning the Son, Jesus Christ (v. 3). Who is this Son? First, Paul points again to the Old Testament by calling Him the descendant of David. This is a reference to promises concerning David's descendant (2 Sam. 7:12, 16; Psalm 132:11) and speaks of His royalty and His humanity. Paul then turns his attention to the Son's deity (v. 4). His resurrection from the dead was proof He was, indeed, the Son of God, indicating He is of the same nature as the Father. This one verse speaks of His power, His holiness, and spiritual nature. Jesus Christ deserves our worship.

In 1 Corinthians 15:1-4 Paul reminds his readers of the gospel they had embraced. He says the death, burial, and resurrection of Christ were of "first importance," the heart of the gospel. It should be noted that the phrase "according to the Scriptures" is repeated twice in this passage. The fulfillment of the Old Testament prophecies is also part of the gospel. What happened almost 2,000 years ago is the object of our faith. We become personally identified with those events as we become worshipers.

The Gospel in John

"Even as You gave Him authority over all flesh, that to all whom You have given Him, He may give eternal life. This is eternal life, that they may know You, the only true God, and Jesus Christ whom You have sent" (John 17:3).

Jesus, in His prayer, makes no apologies for the sovereignty of God in salvation. He said, "Even as You gave Him authority over all flesh," indicating His absolute power or control over all humanity. For what purpose did the Father gave Him this authority? It was "That to all whom You have given Him, He may give eternal life."

Jesus then defines eternal life: "That they may know You, the only true God, and Jesus Christ whom You have sent" The essence of eternal life is an intimate knowledge of the Father and the Son. It is about worship. It is about walking by the Holy Spirit. Intimacy with God is the essence of eternal life and it is based upon a correct understanding of the Father and the Son.

Philip asked Jesus to show the disciples the Father. Jesus said that whoever has seen Him has seen the Father also (John 14:9). The only way to have a true knowledge of the Father is through a true knowledge of the Son. The character of the Father is manifest through the Son. For so many years, I thought the gospel was the plan of salvation. Some with whom I shared the gospel embraced the plan without embracing the Person. When Jesus Christ is presented as God who became flesh and lived among us, who died for our sins and rose again to give us new life, and who is sitting at the right hand of God, some are drawn by their desire to worship Him.

THE REJECTION OF THE GOSPEL

As a result of the fall, people not only cannot worship God, they utterly refuse to do so. In Romans 1, Paul says, "The wrath of God is revealed from heaven against all ungodliness and unrighteousness of men who suppress the truth in unrighteousness" (v. 18).

The wrath of God is against "ungodliness." This word means a lack of reverence or worship.[6] This sets the tone for Romans 1, which describes the essence of the fall as the rejection of worship. This doesn't contradict the idea in the last chapter that there are "potential worshipers" in whom God has planted a desire to worship Him. In my own life, I was very irreverent, even though I wanted to know what it meant to worship Him. I shudder to think of some of the things I said and did in those days.

The rejection of worship starts with a rejection of the truth. The word for "suppresses" (v. 18) means to press downward as though you are trying to deny the inevitable.

When I play with the kids in the pool, I hold the ball underwater between my knees. I have pushed it down so they can't see it. As soon as I release it, it pops up to the surface. This passage teaches us that man is suppressing some truth about God that has caused God to pour out His wrath. However, when man releases the suppression, he is forced to face the truth.

The suppressed truth is His invisible attributes, specifically "His eternal power and divine nature" (v. 20). These are "clearly seen" by

---

[6] In chapter 2, we defined worship using the word "godliness" or *eusébeia* in the Greek. This word means to live in awe, reverence, or fear of God. Ungodliness is *asébeia*, the absence of such worship. A form of this word is used three times in Jude 15.

every human being through nature. "His eternal power" is infinite both in space and in time. His sheer power alone should lead men to worship Him. Not only that, but His "divine nature" or position should lead us to submit humbly to Him in worship.

"For even though they knew God, they did not honor Him as God or give thanks, but they became futile in their speculations, and their foolish heart was darkened. Professing to be wise, they became fools" (vv. 21-22).

They knew God's character, but refused to honor and give thanks. They refused to worship Him, because, if they did, people would have to give up their personal godhood and declare Him God.

Since people did not want to honor the true God and let go of their personal deity, they had to make a substitute god that would serve them. The rest of the passage tells how "They exchanged the glory of the incorruptible God for an image in the form of corruptible man and of birds and four-footed animals and crawling creatures" (v. 23). They "worshiped and served the creature rather than the Creator" (v. 25). Idolatry was born because people refused to worship the one true God.

Of course, the result was a darkening of their hearts (soul or mind) and the defilement of their bodies.

Verse 25 says, "They exchanged the truth of God for a lie, and worshiped…." In the original, an article is in front of "lie"—more accurately, "the lie"—indicating a specific lie that Paul had in mind. Jesus describes Satan as the "father of lies" (John 8:44), again indicating that the devil is the source of this lie.

What is the lie? The big lie is we can be like God, knowing good and evil. We can make our own moral decisions independent of God because we ourselves are sovereign. We know what is best. And most importantly, a god will not bow down before another God.

This passage reminds me of my graduate training in biology. Most biologists I know, even though they accept evolutionary theory, are not adamant about it. Two people in my department were more militant about it toward me than any other students. I asked them both why they were so against God.

The first said he had been wounded in Vietnam. As he lay bleeding on the battlefield, he could hear the mortars being launched, wondering if the next would land on top of him. Pondering the horror of his situation, he decided there was no God.

The other person who rejected God said he suffered a car accident his senior year in high school. As he lay recovering in the hospital bed for an extended period of time, he had time to think. He decided if God existed, He either didn't care or He was impotent.

Emotional decisions made at difficult times of life led them to dedicate themselves to proving their foolish conclusions correct. They basically refused to worship God and were trying to justify their decisions with an intellectual smokescreen, including evolution.

This passage indicates that people are lost, not because they are ignorant of God's existence, but because they refuse to worship Him. They prefer self-worship.

If John 17:3 teaches that eternal life is knowing God, and Romans 1 says man doesn't want to even acknowledge Him, we must conclude, then, there is no spiritual life in man.

THE APPLICATION OF THE GOSPEL
(WHAT HAPPENED AT THE CROSS)

Based on what we have said until now, we might conclude that if everyone would renounce false worship and start worshiping the one true God, everyone would be saved.

There is one problem: Nobody has the ability to worship. People are dead spiritually and have no means by which to connect with God (Eph. 2:1). Their minds are darkened; they can't understand God (Eph. 4:18). There is no desire to worship God, and there is no means by which a sinner can approach Him. Total depravity is the inability to worship God.

Something had to change in us to make us worshipers. Only God could bring about that change. He has chosen some to become worshipers and to be conformed to His image. Not only that, but He had to provide access into His presence.

I had dated a young woman for three-and-a-half years before I met my wife. Near the end of that relationship, I had become a follower of Jesus. The girl soon broke up with me, complaining the old Bruce had died. I said that was ridiculous; I was still Bruce. It was years later that I realized she was right. Something very real changed in me.

A little over a year after arriving in Brazil, I prepared an Easter message based on Romans 6. I was intrigued by Paul's emphasis on the death of the old man and the corresponding birth of the new. It was then I realized the old Bruce, who was incapable of worshiping anyone but himself, had been crucified. The old Bruce, who was a slave to his flesh and sin, had died. The old Bruce, who had been under Satan's control, was no more.

The Death of the Old Man

In Romans 6, the term "baptism" is not speaking of the ordinance, but of a total identification with Christ at conversion. Verse six tells us that we should know, "That our old self was crucified with Him [Christ] that our body of sin might be done away with, so that we should no longer be slaves to sin" (Rom. 6:6).

I used to think I was a dirty, rotten sinner going to hell. After I "accepted Jesus," I figured I was a dirty, rotten sinner going to heaven. That is far from the truth. Something real happened in my life. I had been born again and now I was truly a new person. The old Bruce who was incapable of worshiping God was dead and a new worshiper was born.

How does the gospel turn us into worshipers? What happens? As David Needham writes,

> Contrary to much popular teaching, regeneration (being born again) is more than having something taken away (sins forgiven) or having something added to you (a new nature with the assistance of the Holy Spirit); it is becoming someone you had never been before. This new identity is not on the flesh level, but the spirit level—one's deepest self. This miracle is more than a "judicial" act of God. It is an act so REAL that it is right to say that a Christian's essential nature is righteous rather than sinful.[7]

The Birth of the New Man

At the moment of conversion, the old man who is incapable of worshiping is crucified. Not only was the old self crucified with Him, it

---

[7] Needham, p. 61.

was also buried with Him (Rom 6:6). A burial happens only when there is a death.

Our old self was put to death with Christ. Faith in His death on the cross implies that it is not just a historical fact or a judicial action, but it is, in fact, the spiritual experience of every true Christian.

Our sins are washed away and a new self is generated within us "so we too might walk in newness of life" (Rom. 6:4). We are essentially different people. There are many implications of this new life, including freedom from the dominion of sin (Rom. 6:7, 18, 22), death (Rom. 6:9), the law (Rom. 6:15; 7:3), and the flesh (Rom. 8:12). This new reality is foundational to Christian growth and should be included when we present the gospel.

The new man or the "new spirit" can be called a person's heart (Eph. 1:18; 2 Tim. 2:22), the inner man (Eph. 3:16; 2 Cor. 4:16; Rom. 7:22), and the human spirit (Rom. 8:16). They basically refer to the same aspect of our being.

OUR SPIRITS WERE MADE TO HAVE COMMUNION WITH GOD.

WE WORSHIP IN SPIRIT (JOHN 4:23).

OUR SPIRITS BEAR WITNESS THAT WE ARE HIS CHILDREN (ROM. 8:16).

WE COMPREHEND SPIRITUAL TRUTH IN OUR SPIRITS (1 COR. 2:15).

OUR SPIRITS MAKE US GOD-CONSCIOUS.

The spiritual man[8] is able to discern spiritual truths that others cannot understand.

For our purposes in this book, the most important aspect of this new reality and the birth of the new man is the restoration of worship. We not only have access to God now, but we are actually joined to Him spiritually with unprecedented intimacy. Paul said, "But the one who joins himself to the Lord is one spirit with Him" (1 Cor.

---

[8] *Pneumatikós* (Greek) refers to what is spiritual. In this context, it refers, not to a more committed Christian than the so-called "carnal" Christian, but one who has been enlightened spiritually by the Lord, one who has become a worshiper.

6:17). This is possible only because the old has been destroyed and we have new spirits that were raised with Christ.

This incredible truth is the basis of our worship. No other creature in the universe, including angels, can experience being one spirit with Him.

Our spirits had to be completely regenerated (transformed) and not just reformed. Our whole being was stained with sin and was incapable of worshiping God. Our inner beings had to be destroyed and re-created to become spotless before Him so that we could join our spirits with His in worship. That is why our bodies are now sanctuaries of the Holy Spirit (1 Cor. 6:19). Our growth depends on our learning to live this reality in worship.

To summarize, when a person identifies with the death of Christ, the "old man" who is incapable of worshiping God dies. Through identification with the resurrection of Christ, a new inner person is born. The desire of this new inner person is to worship God. Because of the "flesh," the new person is easily distracted from the presence of God and, as a result, may sin.

Christian growth is not the result of self-effort in overcoming sins, but comes through strengthening the inner person through worship and the indwelling of the Holy Spirit. In the next chapter, we will discuss the role of worship in discipleship.

THE PROCESS

Although there is a moment in which a person repents of his old life, puts his trust in Christ, and becomes a new person, a process leads up to that event. The process is known as the calling.

The gospel itself involves a complete change of a person's worldview. The basic questions about our existence are reevaluated, based on the truth of God's Word. That doesn't happen overnight. We cannot expect such a change to happen in the course of a short conversation. There is a process by which the Holy Spirit opens a person's eyes to his or her need along with the offering of a solution through Jesus Christ.

At times this can be a long process and, at other times, relatively short. The Bible gives a number of examples of this process.

AN EXAMPLE IN HEALING

*After spitting on his eyes and laying His hands on him, He asked
him, "Do you see anything?" And he looked up and said, "I see
men, for I see them like trees, walking around." Then again He
laid His hands upon his eyes; and he looked intently and was
restored, and began to see everything clearly* (Mark 8:23-24).

The cure of the blind man at Bethsaida is the only recorded miracle
in which Jesus did not heal someone instantly. This miracle is
mentioned only in Mark and comes at a time when the disciples
were having trouble grasping Jesus' mission. It serves as an effective
illustration of how God opens the eyes of a person progressively.

This miracle did not reflect Jesus' inability to cure or that somehow He did not exercise enough power. He asked the man what he
was seeing, not because He did not know, but for the benefit of those
present.

The context gives a clue as to why Jesus cured this man in steps.
Before this incident, Jesus had just fed the 4,000 in Gentile territory
and had a confrontation with some Pharisees demanding a sign. As
they were going across the Sea of Galilee, Jesus warned the disciples,
"Watch out! Beware of the leaven of the Pharisees and the leaven of
Herod" (Mark 8:15).

Having no idea what Jesus was saying, they figured He was
concerned that they had not brought bread with them. That should
have been the least of their concerns since Jesus had just fed thousands
of people on two different occasions.

Aware of their lack of spiritual perception, Jesus asked, "Why do
you discuss the fact that you have no bread? Do you not yet see or
understand? Do you have a hardened heart? Having eyes, do you not
see? And having ears, do you not hear?" (Mark 8:17-18).

Although it is very dangerous to use Jesus' miracles as allegories,
He Himself used the cure of one man's blindness to illustrate His
ability to open people's spiritual eyes (John 9:39).

AN EXAMPLE IN TEACHING

In Mark's account, after curing the blind man, Jesus asked His
disciples the most important question of all time: "Who do you say

that I am?" (Mark 8:29). After Peter, as the spokesman for the group, answered correctly that He is the Christ, Jesus curiously warns them "to tell no one about Him" (v. 30).

It becomes clear why Jesus did not permit them to announce the news about the arrival of the Messiah. When Jesus taught them about His ensuing suffering and death, Peter "began to rebuke Him" (v. 32). A suffering Messiah was not what the disciples had in mind. Their eyes were in the process of being opened.

God had revealed to the disciples that Jesus was the Messiah. This was the first step in the process. The second step was the comprehension of the death and resurrection of Christ. When God revealed that piece of the puzzle, they became worshipers (Matt. 28:17).

THE ENGLE SCALE

To make people aware of the process of calling people to the gospel, Dr. James Engle developed what is known as "The Engle Scale."[9]

-10	Awareness of the supernatural
- 9	No effective knowledge of Christianity
- 8	Initial awareness of Christianity
- 7	Interest in Christianity
- 6	Awareness of basic facts of the gospel
- 5	Grasp of implications of the gospel
- 4	Positive attitudes to the gospel
- 3	Awareness of personal need
- 2	Challenge and decision to act
- 1	Repentance and faith in Christ
0	The New Birth

This scale is useful, but it focuses too much on a cognitive awareness, rather than the progressive conviction of biblical truth as the Holy Spirit opens the potential worshiper's spiritual eyes.

THE WORSHIP SCALE

I am proposing a modification of this scale that leads potential worshipers to become fruitful worshipers. I like to think of it as a

[9] James Engle, *What's Wrong with the Harvest?*

thermometer that measures a person who is heating up until he hits zero, which is the freezing point in the Centigrade temperature scale. The person "thaws out" at that point and becomes a worshiper.

0. Birth of a new worshiper

1. Personal identification with the resurrection of Christ
2. Personal identification with the death of Christ

3. Conviction of judgment

4. Conviction of righteousness

5. Conviction of sin

6. Conviction that God has outlined how He wants to be worshiped in the Bible
7. Conviction of the existence of a supreme being who deserves to be worshiped

Some of these "steps" have been elaborated already, but others have not been presented. We will briefly look at the steps and define them as seeds leading to a person's becoming a worshiper.

7. **CONVICTION OF THE EXISTENCE OF A SUPREME BEING WHO DESERVES TO BE WORSHIPED**
According to Romans 1:18-20, there is really no such thing as an atheist. Every human being is conscious of the supernatural and the presence of a supreme being. Those who profess to be atheists are living in denial of what they know to be true.

This first step is not just an acknowledgement that God exists, but that He deserves to be worshiped. One report indicated that

99 percent of Brazilians believe in a supreme being. However, many feel this god exists to serve them somehow. Worship is an appeasement of their god or a way of obtaining his favor to get something in return.

6. **CONVICTION THAT GOD HAS OUTLINED HOW HE WANTS TO BE WORSHIPED IN THE BIBLE**
If God truly exists, then He has certainly communicated to us how we are to approach Him.

Cain tried to "worship" God without faith (Gen. 4:3; Heb. 11:4) and made an unacceptable offering.

Aaron's sons, Nadab and Abihu, burned "strange fire before the LORD" (Lev 10:1). Their offense was they did not approach God in worship in the way He had determined.

The Jews in Isaiah's day performed the right rituals that God had ordered, but their attitudes were wrong (Isaiah 1:10-15).

That is why Moses said to Pharaoh that they would "sacrifice to the LORD our God as He commands us" (Ex. 8:27). When God told Moses to do something, he did it. This conviction goes beyond a desire to know more about the Bible or about God. The motivation is to worship God in the way He has ordered in His Word.

5. **CONVICTION OF SIN**
The Spirit came to "convict the world concerning sin and righteousness and judgment" (John 16:8). Notice how the Spirit convicts of sin, "Because they do not believe in Me" (v. 9). A real conviction of sin comes from understanding and believing Jesus. Unbelief, of course, is the heart of sin. Where there is unbelief, there is *ungodliness* or a lack of worship.

Potential worshipers know they are not worshiping God. They become conscious of the sin that keeps them from God.

4. **CONVICTION OF RIGHTEOUSNESS**
Also, the Spirit uses the life of Jesus to convict them of righteousness, "Because I go to the Father and you no longer behold Me" (v. 10). Jesus is the perfect standard of righteousness. It is impossible

for potential worshipers to observe the life of Jesus and think they can somehow become righteous on their own.

3. **CONVICTION OF JUDGMENT**
The Spirit also convicts of judgment. John 5:22-23 tells us the Father "has given all judgment to the Son, so that all will honor the Son even as they honor the Father…who sent Him." The Son is to be worshiped as the Father is worshiped, because God has given Him the role of judging men and angels.

Did you ever stop to think that one of the horrors of hell is that people there will never be able to worship God? They will finally understand the joy from which they will be excluded for eternity. They "will pay the penalty of eternal destruction, away from the presence of the Lord and from the glory of His power" (2 Thess. 1:9). They will never be able to experience true worship. That is hell.

2. **PERSONAL IDENTIFICATION WITH THE DEATH OF CHRIST (REPENTANCE)**
The human mind produces remorse as a result of embarrassment or negative consequences of a person's actions. True repentance leads to faith and a definite change. "Repentance" is a strong word. It means turning one's back on evil and false worship and turning toward God.

The parable of the prodigal son illustrates repentance very well. After losing everything, the son found himself in a helpless condition. In Portuguese, we say that he found himself "at the bottom of the well." The following is not a formula to be followed to repentance, but it illustrates the attitude of a repentant person.

The Bible says, "He came to his senses" (Luke 15:17). The first step in repentance is that God must open our eyes to the reality of our situation. I read that 86 percent of Brazilians think they are going to heaven, indicating that most are not conscious of their sinful state. I wouldn't be surprised if the percentage is pretty high in the U.S., too. Do we realize that pig food is starting to look good to us?

The second step in repentance was his confession, "Father, I have sinned" (Luke 15:18). Notice that he does not say "against you," but that he had "sinned against heaven, and in your sight." He recognized that his sin wasn't just humiliating, it was an offense against the holiness of God. He was willing to confess that.

Finally, he returned to his father and the relationship was restored.

1. PERSONAL IDENTIFICATION WITH THE RESURRECTION OF CHRIST (FAITH)

As I related in chapter 4, students told me, "Everybody has a lot of faith here in Brazil." But I wondered what they meant by "faith." Would they understand salvation by faith?

For many, faith has become either an intellectual affirmation of a doctrinal statement or a strong religious sentiment. Some think of faith as a strong desire that enables a person to create a new reality. I heard on the radio the other day that faith is "the tool God has given us to receive everything we desire." That, by the way, was not an off-handed remark, but part of a well-thought-out advertisement for a popular church.

The leading Greek lexicon defines "faith" as "Trust in His power and nearness to help. To be convinced that He exists and that His revelations and disclosures are true."[10] The second part of that last statement is important. We need not only to believe that God does exist, but act upon what He has said. As noted earlier, Neil Anderson writes, "Faith is the biblical response to the truth, and believing the truth is a choice…Faith is something you *decide to do,* not something you *feel like doing*…Faith does not *create* reality; faith *responds to* reality"[11] (emphasis original).

The act of faith that brings one to salvation is intimately tied to worship. At that point, there is a surrender of one's personal godhood and submission to God. There can no longer be a trust in one's merit, ability, or goodness. Faith is the ultimate act of worship.

0. CONVERSION (THE BIRTH OF A NEW WORSHIPER)

Many people think conversion means switching religions or

---

[10] Bauer et al.
[11] Anderson, *The Bondage Breaker*, p.191.

turning over a new leaf. Conversion, however, is the transformation of a rebel into a worshiper. Although the person may have been attracted by worship, now the door has been opened into God's presence, into the Holy of Holies to finally enter into true worship.

THE HARVEST

Bob Dylan sang, "You're gonna have to serve somebody." If he means serving as a form of worship, he *was* absolutely right. People, by nature, have an inborn need to worship something. Some worship idols, while others worship themselves. Some worship their religion; others worship materialism.

Conversion is a change of the object of our worship. Let's look at a few biblical descriptions of conversion from the standpoint of worship.

A BLIND MAN'S CONVERSION

Jesus said, to him, "You have both seen Him, and He is the one who is talking with you." And he said, "Lord, I believe." And he worshiped Him (John 9:37-38).

The seven signs of the book of John often provoked a strong reaction from the religious leaders of Jesus' day. The healing of the blind man was no exception.

Initially, the blind man didn't know Jesus from Adam. When Jesus asked him to go wash, he did so in faith. When people questioned him as to how his healing had happened, he gave credit to, "the man who is called Jesus" (John 9:11).

When questioned by the Pharisees, he said, "He is a prophet" (v. 17). He also indicated that he was "God-fearing" or a worshiper[12] (v. 31) and "from God" (v. 33).

Jesus then revealed Himself to him as "the Son of Man" (v. 35), indicating His humanity. The man then addressed Him as "Lord"[13] (v.36).

---

[12] Although Jesus is God, He modeled a worship life-attitude in His humanity.
[13] This is more than just a respectful address; it is a confession of His authority and possibly deity (*kúrios*).

Upon his believing, the process came to fruition: "He worshiped Him" (v. 38). This is what the process of evangelism is all about, coming to realize progressively who Jesus is. The newly sighted man made his first profession of faith and became a worshiper.[14]

CALLING ON THE NAME OF THE LORD

Whoever will call on the name of the LORD will be saved" (Rom. 10:13; cf. Joel 2:32; Acts 2:21).

"Calling upon the name of the Lord" is typically thought of as a crying out to Christ for salvation in the "sinner's prayer." This expression occurs nine times in the Bible and is usually related directly or indirectly to worship and prayer.

The Bible says that after repenting, salvation comes from believing and confessing the Lord (Rom 10:9). Salvation is often accompanied by a visible act of worship.

Averbeck affirms, "The expression 'call on the name of the Lord' is seeded throughout the Old Testament and on into the New Testament, often as the *words* of worship in the context of worship *actions*."[15]

The first use of the expression implies that with the birth of Enosh, Seth and his righteous line started to worship the LORD (Gen. 4:26).

Abraham is said to have twice called upon the name of the Lord. Both times it was related to an altar he built for worship (Gen 12:8; 26:25).

In Psalm 116 the writer mentions calling upon the name of the Lord four times. The first two references are related to his supplication (vv. 2 & 4). His last reference, however, is clearly related to worship as he says, "to You I shall offer a sacrifice of thanksgiving, and call upon the name of the LORD" (v. 17).

Supplication in the Old Testament was linked to worship. Many of the great prayers were oozing with praise with the actual request

---

[14] *proskuneō* - Although this word can mean simply to prostrate oneself before someone, the context clearly indicates that he became a worshiper. It can be construed as an aorist ingressive indicating that this was just the beginning of his worship of Jesus. Bauer et al. indicate that this refers to Jesus, "who is revered and worshiped as Messianic King and Divine Helper."

[15] Averbeck, "Worshiping God in Truth," in Bateman, p. 130.

based on some aspect of God's character. It is probable that the psalmist is not just saying he offered up prayers to the Lord, but that he worshiped the Lord "because He has inclined His ear to me" (v. 2). The supplication of verse 4 was probably in the context of worship.

In Zephaniah's prophecy, God said that after He has poured out His wrath, He will save people from every nation. He said, "I will give to the peoples purified lips, that all of them may call on the name of the LORD, to serve Him shoulder to shoulder" (Zeph. 3:9).

Ananias admonished Paul to come to faith in Christ, saying, "Now why do you delay? Get up and be baptized, and wash away your sins, calling on His name" (Acts 22:16).[16] Paul's cleansing was associated with his becoming a worshiper.

The Corinthian church, which was having trouble seeing beyond their own local body, was told they were saints together "with all who in every place call upon the name of our Lord Jesus Christ, their Lord and ours" (1 Cor. 1:2). The use of the present tense verb indicates that it was not just a one-time event, but a constant worship of God. Because of a common worship, they were bonded to other local bodies.

According to these passages, worship is not only the golden thread that is woven into the lives of believers, it is also the first act of a believer, occurring at the same time as saving faith is exercised.

THE IMPACT OF A WORSHIPING CHURCH

> *But if all prophesy, and an unbeliever or an ungifted man enters, he is convicted by all, he is called to account by all; the secrets of his heart are disclosed; and so he will fall on his face and worship God, declaring that God is certainly among you* (1 Cor. 14:24-25).

Salvation is the result of a person's coming to grips with his own sinfulness and the reality of the one true God. At that point, the person realizes his need for the Savior.

---

[16] The commands to be baptized and to wash away his sins are two distinct acts. According to this passage, calling upon the name of the Lord is what washed away his sins, expressing the means by which the cleansing takes place.

In Paul's explanation of spirituality and the use of gifts, he uses the example of a local body that has come together with all the members using their gifts to edify one another. There is no indication that the prophecies are directed specifically at the unbeliever. What convicts and calls the sinner to account is the manifestation of God's presence among the body through the exercise of their gifts. It wasn't necessary for the unbeliever to raise his hand, or walk down the aisle to "accept Jesus." When God is very real to each member, unity is a genuine reflection of His presence in the local body. God is glorified and made manifest in His church, and that is a persuasive witness to an unbeliever.

For they themselves report about us what kind of reception we had with you, and how you turned to God from idols to serve a living and true God (1 Thess. 1:9).

If being lost is false worship, then conversion must be a change in worship, as attested to in the Scriptures.

The conversion of the Thessalonians had a big impact because of their transformed lives. Paul tells how they "turned to God, from idols to serve a living and true God." The fact that they "turned"[17] indicates there was a rejection of the false gods and a turning to the true God. They rejected false worship.

"Serving"[18] indicates a recognition of God's lordship and submission as a slave to Him.

The "lordship" debate a few years ago might have been less controversial if we had understood conversion as a change of worship. People are rebellious self-worshipers. Conversion is a giving up of that rebellion and submitting to God in worship. That is what repentance is all about.

A Personal Testimony

I look at my calling as a long process. I do not know exactly when I was adopted into God's family. There were many seeds planted here and there. A man came by our house selling Bibles and mentioned that God was the Creator. I listened in on a conversation when a friend

---

[17] *Epistréphō - epi* – upon (intensifier), *stréphō* (to turn) – It is a radical conversion through turning away from the false and turning toward what is true.
[18] *Douleúō* - To serve as a slave.

of my father's commented to him, "You know, Jesus Christ was the only man that never sinned." In a Sunday School classroom, I read, "For I say to you that unless your righteousness surpasses that of the scribes and Pharisees, you shall not enter the kingdom of heaven" (Matt. 5:20). I listened to *Jesus Christ Superstar*[19] and thought about Jesus. All those seeds, both good and bad, had an impact on my life, eventually bringing me to the point of becoming a worshiper.

While I was a sophomore in high school, someone shared a gospel tract with me after a Bible study for athletes. Just to be safe, I prayed the suggested prayer several times. Everyone assured me that I was *in* and had eternal life, which I could not lose, because I had prayed the prayer. I was sincerely interested in the Bible and went to studies regularly. I had my quiet times and went to church. However, I knew I was still a prisoner of sin.

During a low point four years later, I woke up one Sunday morning and was getting ready to go to church. I had been out at the bars the night before, and I realized there was something wrong with that picture. I was convicted of sin in my life, as I had never been before. I played a tape recording of a song a friend of mine had written, adapting the words to an old bluegrass song called, "Fox on the Run." The words to the song started,

> Sunday morning early, I woke at the break of dawn,
> I asked my Lord and Savior if somehow I'd gone wrong.
> He said, "Oh, you of little faith, I'm right here by your side.
> If somehow you'll but come to Me this day I'll be your Guide.

The Lord broke me. I had come to the end of myself and my fleshly religiosity and truly was regenerated. I became a worshiper of the Lord Jesus Christ that day.

The process took four years. I am convinced that what slowed down the process was a false belief that the prayer I had prayed years earlier had saved me. I didn't seek salvation any further because I believed I was saved, and everyone around me confirmed it. I was not a worshiper, however, and my life showed it.

---

[19] *Jesus Christ Superstar* often had some pretty accurate insights into the lives of the main characters in the gospel narrative. Everyone, that is, except Jesus. The authors missed the boat in not understanding that Jesus is God and, consequently, they portrayed Him in a blasphemous manner.

The change was dramatic. I no longer loved the world. Instead, I loved Jesus Christ. Before, I did things I knew I shouldn't be doing, but deep down, I wanted to. Now, after becoming a worshiper, I still sinned but it was different. I realized that sinning was somehow inconsistent with who I was.

WHAT WE DO IN BRAZIL

The fruit from our evangelism is drawing attention among our churches in Brazil as well as other groups. People sometimes ask us to train them in our "methods." Although we do have easy to use, in-depth material, the key is not in the methods but in the spiritual life that is passed on.

Second, since we are reproducing spiritual life in potential worshipers, we focus on one-on-one studies so people are able to see what a real worshiper looks like close up. We have developed individual Bible studies that any believer can use to study with friends, relatives, or casual contacts.

Third, we recognize that evangelism is a process, involving sowing and harvesting with quite a bit of work in between. Our evangelists know it is a long and sometimes discouraging investment of time. They persevere because their ministries are a result of worship and not focused on results.

After the initial contact using the Seven Signs from the book of John, we continue with the story of Nicodemus because he saw signs and wanted to know more. We contrast his story with the story of the Samaritan woman. By this time, if they stick with the studies, most people realize they need to take a stand in relation to this Jesus. We finish this first stage by contrasting the rich young ruler with Zaccheus. These stories emphasize that people are not saved by works. By this time, it is easy to identify the people who are truly interested in knowing God. They are reading their Bibles during the week, and they raise good questions. In many cases, some of their friends will have started to criticize them for going overboard with their search to know God.

A number of years ago, we wrote an interactive study called "The Purpose of Life." It has been very successful because it is easy to use and helps people to come to grips with the issues related to salvation. It has eight studies, each one emphasizing intimacy with God. We don't use terms such as "accept Christ" or "make a decision." At the end of this series of studies, we challenge the people to enter into an intimate relationship with Christ.

If someone sticks with the studies and participates, it takes about five months to complete. Some people come to faith relatively quickly. Others take almost a year. We allow the Holy Spirit to work in people's lives, and we don't force a decision.

Doing these studies is almost like a live illustration of the parable of the sower. Some people reject us immediately (the seed sown alongside the path). Others show interest and then start making excuses for not continuing (the seed sown in shallow soil). Others drag on and on, and it never seems that they go anywhere (the seed sown among the thorns). Those who come to Christ get involved in the church and are soon doing studies with others (the good soil). Those who know the Bible have a much easier time understanding the church as a worshiping community rather than simply an organization or a denomination.

As a result of writing this book, I went back over our material and made sure we were indeed sowing the seeds of worship. We emphasize "an intimate relationship with God" so that salvation is not seen as an end in itself, but as a means to becoming a worshiper. This leads naturally into our discipleship material.

CONCLUSION

People are not transformed from selfish rebels into worshipers overnight. Coming to see God and His purpose for one's life is a process. The worshiping evangelist understands the process involved in sowing and harvesting and is patient, allowing the Holy Spirit to work. As potential worshipers are exposed to Jesus through the Word of God and to His presence in the life of the worshiping evangelist, they are drawn into fellowship with Him. Conversion is the life transformation that occurs when the old, irreverent inner person is crucified with Christ, and becomes a new worshiper in Christ.

THE PARADIGM SHIFT

Most people recognize that evangelism cannot be a cold presentation of the gospel, but needs to be filled with life. Few people, however, see evangelism as an expression of worship. Seeing evangelism as on a par with praise, flowing from worship, will make sharing our faith anything but mechanical.

EVANGELISM AS AN EVENT	EVANGELISM AS WORSHIP
1. EMPHASIS ON THE METHOD • The right verses • The right examples	1. EMPHASIS ON THE RELATIONSHIP • With God • With the potential worshiper
2. EVANGELISM IS ONLY HARVESTING	2. EVANGELISM INVOLVES • The process of planting • The process of watering • The moment of harvesting
3. PROGRAM BASED The plan of salvation presented in impersonal programs	3. RELATIONSHIP BASED Jesus Christ is presented in direct contact between believers and potential worshipers
4. BIBLE PREACHING Selected isolated verses with illustrations	4. BIBLE DISCOVERY The potential believer actively discovers the truth through studying passages of Scripture
5. RECRUIT CHURCH MEMBERS	5. DISCOVER POTENTIAL WORSHIPERS
6. THE PLAN OF SALVATION	6. THE PERSON OF SALVATION: Jesus

WHERE TO START

1. **REFLECT ON YOUR OWN LIFE.**
   a. How did God prepare your life to bring you to the point of becoming a worshiper?
   b. Which people were instrumental in impacting your life? How?
   c. What struck you about Jesus Christ?
   d. Spend some time thanking God for your salvation.

2. **STUDY THE PEOPLE AROUND YOU.** The best way to learn evangelism is not by attending a seminar, but by listening to what the unbelievers around you are saying.
   a. Where are most of the people you know on the "worship scale"?
   b. What do they believe?
   c. What don't they believe?
   d. What is the biggest barrier for them in understanding the gospel?
   e. How do they view professing Christians?
   f. How do they view you?

3. **READ THE GOSPEL OF LUKE.** The more we know Jesus, the better able we are to share Him with others.
   a. Notice how Jesus treated sinners.
   b. Notice how Jesus dealt with the religious people.
   c. Write down every quality you find of Jesus. Stop to worship Him for those qualities.
   d. Tell God after every chapter that you want to be more like Jesus.

4. **INVITE SOMEONE TO DISCOVER JESUS.** Instead of sharing the plan of salvation, invite him or her to discover Jesus with you through the Bible.

DISCUSSION QUESTIONS

1. What can we learn from creation about the reason God made us?

2. How did the fall affect our worship?

3. How does Jesus Christ restore worship?

4. Why do we say evangelism is a process?

5. Why is it important to understand that the old self was crucified?

6. What about your salvation?
   a. Is it possible that when you first made a decision, you weren't really saved?
   b. When did you really become a worshiper?
   c. How do you know you are a worshiper of the Lord today?
   d. How can you grow in your worship?

7. In light of this chapter, how should we evangelize?

8. How is conversion a change of worship?

9. What struck you about the worship scale?

10. Where do you think most people with whom you have contact fall on the "worship scale"?

11. What is the most important thing you learned from this chapter?

Chapter 13

WORSHIP
AND
DISCIPLESHIP

HELPING PEOPLE BECOME LIKE CHRIST
THROUGH WORSHIP

But we all, with unveiled face, beholding as a in a mirror the glory of the Lord, ARE BEING TRANSFORMED INTO THE SAME IMAGE *from glory to glory, just as from the Lord, the Spirit* (2 Corinthians 3:18).

SEED TRUTH: DISCIPLESHIP IS THE PROCESS BY WHICH WE HELP OTHERS LIVE A HOLY LIFE THROUGH HELPING THEM TO GROW IN WORSHIP AND TO LEARN HOW TO WALK BY THE SPIRIT. *The key to helping people live a victorious Christian life does not come from religious rules lived out in one's own strength, but from growing in spiritual understanding through worship. Disciples are transformed into the image of Christ to the degree of their spiritual understanding of their position in Him and His work in their lives. Discipleship involves developing the spiritual disciplines in one's life. These spiritual disciplines weave worship into the fabric of a person's being.*

I had been a missionary for about 11 years when I woke up to the fact that my ministry was not rooted in worship. Theoretically, I knew that and had it as my goal, but in reality something was missing.

One day, I was meditating on the book of Galatians in *The MacArthur Study Bible*. He claims, "The central theme of Galatians (like that of Romans) is justification by faith."[1] In other words, these two books explain that a person's salvation is not based on any moral or religious merit, but on God's grace that is applied to one's life through trusting in Jesus. Certainly, these books make it clear that salvation through self-effort is impossible.

I had always heard and accepted that justification by grace through faith is the theme of Galatians and I still believe that. However, I wondered if there were another reason Paul was defending salvation by grace alone.

As I continued reading, I began to think that maybe Paul was building his case for salvation by faith to demonstrate that sanctification also was not a result of human effort. Maybe the Judaizers were not questioning the importance of grace at the moment of conversion, but that progress or maintaining one's relationship with God depends on adherence to the law. In other words, they may have conceded that salvation is by grace through faith initially, but sanctification is by works through the law. If salvation must be maintained by our efforts or if progress depends on following the law, then salvation is no longer by grace. If human effort plays any role in any part of the process, "Grace is no longer grace" (Rom. 11:6).[2]

Then the words jumped off the page at me, "This is the only thing I want to find out from you: did you receive the Spirit by the works of the Law, or by hearing with faith? Are you so foolish? Having begun by the Spirit, are you now being perfected by the flesh?" (Gal. 3:2-3).

---

[1] MacArthur, *Study Bible*, p. 1787.

[2] Galatians deals with the issue of justification by grace through faith as well as sanctification principally because, when there is legalism, there is a tendency to confuse the two. Justification by grace inevitably leads to sanctification, but the two are distinct. Justification is a legal declaration of our right standing with God at the moment of salvation because of the work of Christ, while sanctification is the life-long process by which we are conformed to His image. Both are the work of God's grace and not self-effort. The Judaizers, like so many religious people today, claim it is necessary to sanctify oneself before one can claim to be justified. (See MacArthur, *Faith Works*, pp. 87-104, for a complete discussion of the relationship between justification and sanctification.)

What about me? How much of my own life is the result of fleshly effort? How much of my own ministry is from me? Do I really think I can please God through my own efforts?

In retrospect, very little of my ministry was glorifying God. My good works and my obedience were not flowing from worship, but were coming mostly from me. That means God's character was not shining forth from me. Worship was not being expressed.

Once again I started my search of what it meant to be a worshiper. I wanted to learn how to walk by the Spirit as Paul told us in Galatians 5:16. I asked God to show me how much of my life was lived by the flesh, rather than the Spirit. This is a dangerous prayer. He showed me and it was not a pretty sight. However, I grew through those times, and my marriage and my relationship with my children changed.

When you are raising teenagers, you don't always know what they are thinking. Our oldest son, Josiah, went away to college and, at the suggestion of his teacher, sent me a paper he had written about what he had observed in my life.

He said, "In recent years he has made it his focus to investigate and apply the meaning of being a true worshiper of God. His desire to walk in the Spirit (as opposed to living by the flesh) has led him to pursue a growing life of prayer and devotion. This desire he has to always be growing demonstrates his humble attitude that he doesn't have everything figured out."[3]

Those of you who are reading this book can easily be fooled by my words. I can hide behind the pulpit or lectern when I am speaking. I think I can even fool myself into thinking I have really changed. But my son's words gave me hope that God was working, such that even those who lived closest to me perceived it. Now I have a passion to help others become worshipers. That is the essence of discipleship.

Reproducing worship in the lives of others cannot be reduced to some sort of methodology. There are no "three steps to spiritual

---

[3] Josiah D. Triplehorn, *Admiration*, an unpublished classroom assignment. Used by permission.

maturity" or "five booklets" to walking with God or "How to worship God in four easy lessons." However, there are some principles that can guide us in passing our worship lives on to others. If this were not possible, worship might be lost from one generation to the next.

When I began to disciple people, I was groping in the dark, partly because so much was lacking in my own walk with God. I had no idea where I was going with them or what I was doing. I am sure I grew and learned more than the people with whom I was working.

Early in my teaching career at a Christian college, I made a few critical remarks to my office mate about the spiritual development of the students. He said, "If you don't like it, why don't you leave?" I later apologized for grumbling and he apologized for reacting so strongly. However, I knew what the students really needed was discipleship and not more preaching.

At that point, I decided that I would light a candle rather than curse the darkness. I started discipling students. Although the students had three required chapels and three required church services per week in addition to Bible classes, they hungered for someone who could meet with them one-on-one and model worship to them. By the time I left, I was discipling more people than at any other time in my life. Because of that, I came to love the school. It was a time of great growth in my walk with Christ because I was in the beginning stages of my own discovery of worship.

> DISCIPLESHIP IS ONE BEGGAR TELLING
> ANOTHER BEGGAR WHERE TO GET FOOD.
> BETTER: DISCIPLESHIP IS ONE THIRSTY PERSON TELLING
> ANOTHER THIRSTY PERSON WHAT NEW WINE IS,
> WHERE TO FIND IT, AND HOW TO DRINK DEEPLY.

My first pastor said that discipleship is one beggar telling another beggar where to get food. I will modify that analogy slightly: Discipleship is one thirsty person telling another thirsty person what new wine is, where to find it, and how to drink deeply. This chapter explores how to help others grow in their worship.

THE MARRIAGE METAPHOR

When a couple leaves on their honeymoon, everything is new. There is an excitement of finally being together. For many couples, the newness of the relationship wears off and within a few months they fall into a routine. The marriage grows stagnant.

On the other hand, some couples, starting with their honeymoon, are constantly learning new ways to express their love to each other. They never become satisfied with the depth of their relationship, but are always communicating and learning more about how to please each another and become better friends.

Like marriage, discipleship is all about deepening our intimacy with God. Many Christians, although genuinely saved, fall into a routine of religious activities after the initial excitement of their new life in Christ wears off. They become stuck in a rut and cease striving to deepen their walk with Him.

A growing disciple of the Lord learns how to worship God in a variety of ways and situations. He or she gleans new truths from the Word and gains new insights from other believers, leading to new heights in the worship of God. His prayer life is not a list of requests, but a dynamic interaction with the Lord. Of course, as he grows in his worship, his life overflows in the fruit of obedience, love, and influence on those around him. He glorifies God in his life showing forth God's character.

A worshiper is never satisfied, but always desires a closer walk with God.

THE VINE METAPHOR

My grandparents' yard was probably one of the most productive plots of ground I have ever seen. Although it was smaller than an acre, they grew more than 20 different kinds of produce. Meals always included fresh, frozen, or preserved vegetables and fruits they had grown and harvested themselves. One of my favorites was the grape pies.

My father did not have quite as much success with his grapes as my grandfather. He asked my grandfather how he pruned them every year. Pruning, of course, is necessary so that all the plant's energy in the spring goes into fruit production rather than producing more leaves. My father, the scientist, wanted a systematic way of pruning. My grandfather seemed just to cut off whatever buds looked as though they weren't going to be productive.

As a first-time homeowner, I also wanted to fill my yard with fruit-bearing trees. I remembered the grape pies my grandmother and mother made, so I bought two grapevines at a nursery. Leaves budded from both vines in the spring, but as summer wore on, it appeared that one of them had died, undoubtedly as a result of my neglect.

The next spring I was pleased that new grape leaves started budding on the lower end of the dead grape vine. What I didn't realize until later was that the fruit-bearing vine itself had died, and the hearty, pest resistant rootstock was sending up runners that would never bear edible fruit. Although the branch had been grafted into the rootstock and it appeared to have taken hold, there was never a vital contact between the two and it died.

Of course, my experiences with grapes come to mind every time I read Jesus' words: "I am the true vine, and My Father is the vinedresser. Every branch in Me that does not bear fruit, He takes away; and every branch that bears fruit, He prunes it, that it may bear more fruit" (John 15:1-2).

Jesus is the strong rootstock that provides all the spiritual life for the branches. The branches (Christians) that have a vital link to the vine will bear fruit. If we *abide* in Him as worshipers, we will bear *fruit* because His life will be flowing through us.

Of course, none of us bears the fruit that we should. That is why the Father prunes us, taking away not just sinful activities that impair our ability to bear fruit, but any relationship or activity that stands in the way of our relationship with Him. God doesn't want to produce a bunch of leaves, but real fruit. He works with us so we will progressively bear more.

Although it appears that Jesus is teaching that someone can lose his salvation when he speaks of taking away an unfruitful branch,

He is, in fact, describing a person who has never established a vital relationship with Him. As a result, there was no fruit—like with my grapevine.[4]

What does it mean to abide? The word means to live, take up residence, remain or continue.[5] It is a permanent, dependent relationship, which, in this context speaks of the intimacy with God that comes through a worship relationship.

We draw our life from the vine through worship as we fear, honor, and love Him. We express our worship by glorifying Him through our words and lifestyles. Obedience and good works are the fruit of abiding in the vine.

Discipleship is about helping the branch establish and develop a vital link with the vine (a worship life-attitude). Discipleship is also helping cultivate that life so that Christians bear *much fruit*, demonstrating that they are, indeed, disciples (having a lifestyle that glorifies God).

---

[4] Various efforts have been offered to explain this passage. Some have suggested that these were believers who did not bear fruit and so were "cut off." This interpretation suggests that salvation is by works that are necessary to maintain one's salvation. However, verse six says they were cut off because they were not abiding, not because they didn't bear fruit. They were not bearing fruit because they were not abiding.

Others have suggested that the phrase "takes away" should be translated "lifted up" which is one of the possible translations of *aírō*. The idea is that a branch that has not been supported by the arbor would be unfruitful and must be raised up off the ground so it can become productive.

Bauer et al., however, take this in the sense of removing and translate it as "cut off." Also, the throwing away of the non-abiding vines and the fact that He "casts them into the fire, and they are burned" (John 15:5) speaks of judgment.

The key to understanding this passage is to understand what Jesus is saying when he says "in Me." There is a tendency to project Pauline terminology, particularly from Ephesians, onto Jesus' words, taking "in Me" to be locative or positional, implying that the vine indeed has a worship relationship with God.

However, the Greek word order could make the prepositional phrase refer, not to the branch, but to the means of bearing fruit. The *en* would be interpreted instrumentally. Thus, the phrase should be translated, "Any branch not bearing fruit through Me is cut off." Thus, it becomes obvious that this is neither an unfruitful Christian (an impossibility) nor a person who was saved and lost his or her salvation (also an impossibility).

[5] *Ménō.* This word means to live or dwell somewhere either in a literal or figurative sense. It carries the idea of a relative permanence. Bauer et al. say that it is a favorite term of John's, used "to denote an inward, enduring personal communion."

WHAT IS A DISCIPLE?

I was asked to be part of a disciplinary board to confront a student who had been caught smoking pot. Apparently, he was one of several guys who were partying together. When one of the key individuals had some dope to sell, he would put a box of cereal in his dorm window. The kids dubbed it the "Captain Crunch Connection."

The kid was scared, but very honest with us. The board asked all kinds of questions, including many irrelevant ones. Finally, I asked if he knew the Lord before this happened. It seemed like getting caught had sincerely broken him. He said, "Oh, yeah. I went forward in church two years ago. But even as I was kneeling at the altar, I knew that I was going to continue to do my own thing."

After the student left the room, I commented that maybe he didn't know the Lord. One of the other members of the board said, "Oh yes, he was saved before. Salvation is free. It's discipleship that costs."

I do believe that salvation is a free gift. It is by grace through faith, but somehow the board member's statement didn't sit well with me.

Tozer, in *I Call it Heresy*, writes, "Apart from obedience, there can be no salvation, for salvation without obedience is a self-contradictory impossibility. The essence of sin is rebellion against divine authority."[6]

Essentially, the gentleman on the disciplinary committee had said that salvation was free and a person could go to heaven with an unrepentant and rebellious heart. However, if the person would so choose, he could follow Jesus and pay the price, but that was independent of his salvation.

As I look back on it today, it wasn't that the student needed to get his life straightened out or give up something. It wasn't a question of his sincerity or whether he prayed the right prayer. It wasn't even a question of his accepting the lordship of Christ. If he had become a worshiper of the Lord, his whole inward bent toward life would have changed. One very key element of worship is submitting to God and subordinating our dreams and life to His glory.

Since some consider discipleship to be a "second step" or a deeper commitment to God that's unrelated to salvation, I set out to discover what a disciple really is. Here is what the Scripture teaches.

---

[6] Tozer, *I Call It Heresy*, p. 11.

LIKE HIS TEACHER

A disciple is not one who is interested only in learning, but he is determined to become like his teacher. Jesus said, "It is enough for the disciple that he or she become as his teacher..." (Matt. 10:25). A disciple's goal is that the character of the Lord Jesus Christ is formed within him or her.

LIVING IN GOD'S WORD

Jesus said, "If you continue in My word, then you are truly disciples of Mine" (John 8:31).[7] A disciple will not casually listen to the words of his teacher, but he will hang on everything he says. Our goal is that the very words of Jesus become implanted into our lives, becoming part of our DNA. From our innermost being, the Word of God is lived out.

LOVING OTHERS

The greatest outward evidence that we are disciples of Jesus is the way we love one another. Jesus gave His disciples "A new commandment" (John 3:34-35). The Old Testament has commands to love (Lev. 19:18, 34; Deut. 10:19). What was new is the standard, "even as I have loved you." The love that Christ desires from His disciples is the same sacrificial love with which He loved us when He laid down His life for us.

BEARING FRUIT

Jesus told us, "My Father is glorified by this, that you bear much fruit, and so prove to be My disciples" (John 15:8). I am often asked whether Jesus is talking about leading people to Christ or about reflecting Christ in one's life.

Can the two be separated? If we are reflecting Christ through worship and spontaneously sharing the Word with others, people around us will be impacted. It is not about the number of people who come into a relationship with Christ. That is for the Lord to decide. However, there is really no such thing as a fruitless Christian. The influence on people around us is the fruit of being His disciple.

---

[7] Jesus used the word *ménō* ("live, dwell") in this passage as well. It is also interesting to note that Jesus used the word *logos* for His word, indicating that it is the whole of His message as recorded in the Scriptures.

Notice that Christ is glorified when we bear fruit because His character is shown forth.

COMMITMENT TO FOLLOW JESUS

This point is undoubtedly what troubled the person who defended the salvation of the student being expelled. Jesus said, "If anyone...does not hate his own father and mother and wife and children and brothers and sisters, yes, and even his own life, he cannot be My disciple" (Luke 14:26). Some think that such a demand sounds like a works salvation. Others think it is a call to a deeper commitment some time after salvation. Jesus reiterated this standard when He said, "None of you can be My disciple who does not give up all his own possessions" (Luke 14:33).

Renouncing everything is not a work that earns one's salvation, but it is one of the key attitudes necessary to become a worshiper. It is honoring Christ or making Him our treasure. Jesus said, "No one can serve two masters; for either he will hate the one and love the other, or he will be devoted to one and despise the other" (Matt. 6:24). In the context, He is speaking of material wealth, but the principle applies to every area of our lives. A person cannot be a worshiper of God if God is not the most important thing in his or her life.

When God prohibited worship of other gods, He said, "I, the LORD your God, am a jealous God" (Ex. 20:5). God wants us all for Himself. True worship cannot be divided. We must honor and value God exclusively. I never understood that until I learned Portuguese. We have the words, *inveja* and *ciumes,* which can both be translated "jealous." The distinction is that *inveja* means to be envious of the attention someone is receiving or of someone's possession. *Ciumes,* on the other hand, is wanting something all for yourself. God is a "ciumento" in that He wants us to be exclusively His in our love and worship. True worship cannot be divided with anything. We honor or value Him alone.

SUMMARY

A Disciple Is a Christian.

Acts 11:20 mentions some "men of Cyprus and Cyrene, who came to Antioch and began speaking to the Greeks also, preaching the

Lord Jesus." These amazing men, who are not identified by name, started the first church among Gentiles. This church they started sent out the first missionary team that eventually led to the evangelization of Europe and the rest of the world.

The changed lives of the people were so noticeable that the Bible tells us, "The disciples were first called Christians in Antioch" (Acts 11:26). It is clear that being a disciple is not a calling to a higher commitment, but it is simply being a Christian. There is no distinction between a disciple and a Christian. Both are called to the same commitment.

Those who called them Christians meant it as an insult. They probably said, "Oh, these are the people who are always talking about Christos, the Christ-people, the Christians."[8] It soon became an honor to bear Christ's name because it implied that they bore His image. He was glorified in their lives.

A Disciple Is a Worshiper!

Contact discovery is finding potential worshipers. The process of evangelism is opening the door of worship to those who are being drawn into an intimate relationship with Jesus. Discipleship is cultivating that relationship.

Christian growth is not picking ourselves up by our bootstraps and trying to live up to the high standard that Christ set. Nor is it looking at the qualities of a disciple and making them our goal. Every one of the qualities of a disciple flows from worship. God is glorified in them as we fear, honor, and love Him.

WHAT IS DISCIPLESHIP?

Discipleship is the heart of the Great Commission and should be at the very center of the ministry of the church. It is critical to the life of the church.

Neil Cole comments,

> The command that God gave us was to make and multiply disciples, not cell groups or churches. Jesus does want to build His kingdom through church planting and multipli-

---

[8] F. F. Bruce, *Commentary on the Book of Acts*, p. 241.

cation, but His plan is to do so by multiplying disciples. It begins here—with the basic unit of the church—then it spreads through every pore in the body of Christ. But if we do not start here, if we skip this God-ordained step, we can work and work and work until we turn blue and drop dead and we will not see multiplication happen.[9]

The Great Commission is to "make disciples" or to "disciple[10] the nations" (Matt. 28:19-20). He doesn't tell us to multiply church members, but followers of Jesus. He mentions two phases[11] in the process.

First, He says, "…baptizing them in the name of the Father and the Son and the Holy Spirit" (v. 19). Although Jesus is describing the mode of water baptism in this passage, He also has in mind the spiritual reality behind the act as part of discipleship.

When a person is baptized, he or she comes under a new authority and has a new position. As Bauer, Gingrich, and Danker say, "Through baptism, the one who is baptized becomes the possession of and comes under the protection of the one whose name he bears; he is under the control of the effective power of the name and the One who bears the name, i.e., he is dedicated to them."[12]

This submission to Christ's authority transforms the rebel into a worshiper.

The second aspect of discipleship reveals its goal: "…teaching them to observe all that I commanded you" (Matt. 28:20). The goal of discipleship is an obedient Christian life that glorifies the Lord. Obedience is the fruit of a worship life-attitude that glorifies God.

Paul is definitely not speaking of legalistic obedience. When I first became interested in the Bible, I tried to live up to the standard

---

[9] Cole, p. 52.

[10] *Mathēteúō* (Greek) means to make someone a disciple or follower. This is the verbal form of "disciple," and it occurs in only three other passages (Matt. 27:57, Matt. 13:52, Acts 14:21). It is an aorist ingressive imperative indicating that they are to begin this process that had been done in their lives. There are two present continuous active participles that describe the means of making disciples: baptizing and teaching.

[11] These two present tense participles should be taken as modal, showing how the discipleship is to be carried out.

[12] Bauer et al.

of what a Christian is supposed to be. I couldn't do it and became a hypocrite. I was a sincere hypocrite, wanting to please God. Nonetheless, I did not know the Lord.

I became a Christian when God finally opened my eyes to recognize I could do nothing to earn His favor. Even after becoming a Christian, however, many times I still tried to please God in my own strength, because my obedience was not flowing from a worship life-attitude. It was then I realized the command, "walk by the Spirit" (Gal 5:18), could be fulfilled only through worship. When this became my focus, everything began to change.

I discovered that discipleship is not so much teaching people *what* to obey, but *how* to obey. Although there will be times when we speak of specific areas of obedience, our goal should always be to strengthen the spiritual foundation of the practice and not just change the practice. We need to focus on the areas of fearing, honoring, and loving God as foundational for obedience.

ESSENTIAL ELEMENTS

Discipleship cannot be neatly divided into categories, because everything is interrelated. To give direction to our discussion, however, we will consider discipleship in three areas.

The first involves understanding our position in Christ. As we understand what happened when we entered into a relationship with Jesus, we can begin to live according to who we are in Him. These are not promises to claim, but facts to believe. Many Christians spend much of their time seeking what they already have. People believe lies from the enemy and do not understand their position in Christ. Look again at the end of chapter 8 ("Worship Transforms Our Lives") to review the series of truths that the Bible affirms about our position.

In *Who I am in Christ*, Neil Anderson says,

> The most important belief we possess is a true knowledge of
> who God is. The second most important belief is who we are
> as children of God, because we cannot consistently behave
> in a way that is inconsistent with how we perceive ourselves.
> And if we do not see ourselves as God sees us, then to that
> degree we suffer from a wrong identity and a poor image of
> who we really are.[13]

How do we learn to see God for who He is and to see our lives
as God sees us? Through worship. The truths we read in Scripture
become inner convictions through coming into His presence. We see
things as He sees them. Our minds are transformed and our behavior
is changed and our obedience flows from who we truly are.

The second area of discipleship is development of those practices
that deepen a person's worship. I call these the "root disciplines"
because they are foundational to bearing fruit. They will be discussed
a little later.

Our goal is to develop the Christian walk through worship.
Averbeck notes: "Worship is, in fact, one of the most important
principles, if not the most important all-organizing principle of the
faithful Christian life."[14]

Finally, discipleship is not complete until it has borne fruit. This
fruit, as stated above, is both our outward behavior and our impact
on those around us. It means to glorify God through shining forth
His character. Although these "fruit disciplines" flow from a life of
worship, we do not automatically practice them when we worship.
They still require discipline. Cultivating an effective life for God and
being disciplined in these practices is not the same as doing things in
our own strength. Such discipline allows us to glorify God more fully
as an expression of our worship.

Averbeck also observes that "authentic worship in spirit leads to
action in life, and this life action in turn becomes worship."[15]

---

[13] Anderson, *Who I Am in Christ*, p. 11.
[14] Averback, "Worshiping God in Spirit" in Bateman, p. 116.
[15] Ibid., p.129.

BEING AN EXAMPLE

Sometimes parents say, "Do as I say and not as I do." In other words, "My life is not a model of what you should be." Jesus condemned the hypocritical Pharisees and scribes for not practicing what they preached. He said, "Therefore, all that they tell you, do and observe, but do not do according to their deeds; for they say things and do not do them" (Matt. 23:3). Their discipleship resulted in people becoming "twice as much a son of hell" as the Pharisees and scribes (Matt. 23:15). You reproduce what you are.

Paul, on the other hand, said, "The things you have learned and received and heard and seen in me, practice these things, and the God of peace will be with you" (Phil. 4:9). Paul did not flinch from calling people to follow his example, because he was following Christ. Paul was a worshiper and he knew his life would reproduce worshipers.

As much as I pray that you, the readers of this book, become better worshipers, I know that won't happen unless you can see what a Spirit-filled life looks like. Walking with Him cannot be transferred through the written page. Worship must be modeled.

A holy life does not come from following a list of rules, no matter how biblical the standard might be. Our flesh is hostile toward God. It will not and cannot be subjected to Him (Rom 8:7). If we try to live a holy life through our will power, we end up weakening ourselves and strengthening the flesh.

On the other hand, when we drink deeply of the new wine of intimacy with God through worship, we rest in our position in Him. We come to truly believe what He has done for us and that we are right now seated with Him in the heavenly places. Our minds become filled with the Spirit's presence, and at that moment, it becomes impossible for us even to think of fulfilling the desires of the flesh.

Alas, we are so easily distracted. We put our minds on autopilot and we sin. As we learn to recognize the flesh in our lives, however, we can refocus our minds on worship and our position in Christ more quickly when we stray. We don't dwell on our specific sins, chastising ourselves, but on His forgiveness. As David learned, restoration of fellowship is sweet and leads us to a deeper sense of worship (see Psalm 32).

As we grow, we spend more time fixing our minds on whatever is true, honorable, right, pure, lovely, of good repute, excellent and worthy of praise (Phil. 4:8) and less time on the things of this world. It is not that we are unconscious of this world, but we are now seeing it through God's eyes. Our perceptions and affections have changed. When we are distracted and stumble, our fellowship is quickly restored, as we give ourselves to worship again.

Obviously, we are all in the process, or should be, of learning how to walk by the Spirit and live out a worship life-attitude. The most important part of our ministry is an authentic life. We reproduce what we are, not what we say.

That is why transparency through one-on-one discipleship is so important. Paul writes, "Show yourself an example [to] those who believe" (1 Tim. 4:12). A few verses later (v.15) he makes it clear that Timothy should be growing so that his "progress will be evident to all."

I am certainly not a model of perfection to those I am discipling. And I shouldn't pretend to be. However, I believe that those around me can attest to the fact that I am seeking and growing. If a discipler is not growing, then neither will those he or she is discipling.

Remember, discipleship is not indoctrinating others into our religion, teaching them behaviors, but it is modeling and passing to others the joy of the Spirit-filled life that reflects the character of Christ.

THE GOAL

THE SUPREME GOAL OF THE CHRISTIAN LIFE IS WORSHIP.

Therefore, the Great Commission is to make worshipers. Knowing this, we will evangelize differently, we will train our leaders differently, and most importantly, we will disciple differently.

Someone asked one of our missionaries whether our model was cell- or celebration-centered. He replied, "Neither, we are discipleship-centered." Discipleship is the key to making worship a part of a person's life. If discipleship is weak or not focused on building worshipers, the celebrations and small groups will usually become centered on the leader, with little participation from the others present.

There are four basic models for discipleship, each with a different goal. Each of them has its strengths and weaknesses.

MODELS OF DISCIPLESHIP

Based on Follow-up

Since traditional evangelism is based on making quick decisions, people who respond usually have little or no idea what their decision means. Follow-up based discipleship is geared to give a few essentials about Christ's life, death, and resurrection so the person has a rudimentary understanding of the plan of salvation. The goal is to integrate the person into the church, assuming that is where he will learn how to walk with God through involvement.

It is important for a person to evaluate the decision he made to follow Christ. Was it an emotional response to a stirring message? Are other people's opinions or desires entering into the decision? Has God already been making His presence felt? What gives the person confidence that he or she has indeed come into a relationship with Christ?

It is important, also, for the new believer to understand his position before God and to understand what happened when he became a new person. The new worshiper needs to understand that, although salvation is an individual commitment made between him and God, he now has become a part of the body of Christ. God does not intend for us to live the Christian life isolated from other believers.

These truths are an important beginning for discipleship, but there is much more ahead as the person grows in worship and church involvement. Most people will progress only if they have someone to model the Christian life and accompany them in their development.

Based on Transferability

Some discipleship programs have focused on developing material that produces reproducers. They are geared toward getting people involved in evangelizing and discipling others as quickly as possible.

In biology, we know that various factors affect the growth of a population such as number of offspring, gestation period, period of fertility, life expectancy, and time between generations. Surprisingly, the most important factor in population growth is the time between generations. In other words, growth in a population is not influenced by how many babies an organism has or how quickly it can reproduce, but principally by the period of time between birth and when the organism starts to reproduce.

That is true for evangelism and discipleship, also. That is the reason we stress that evangelism and discipleship have to be transferable so we can involve everyone as quickly as possible.

> IT IS NOT HOW MANY PEOPLE SOMEONE WINS TO THE
> LORD OR HOW QUICKLY HE CAN WIN THEM,
> BUT HOW QUICKLY HE CAN EQUIP THE NEW BELIEVERS
> TO REPRODUCE.

Discipleship that is not transferable is not discipleship. However, *what* we are transferring to others is even more important. Our goal is not to reproduce evangelists, but worshipers. If we are not giving people spiritual depth, our discipleship will be just another program.

Based on Accountability

More and more people are realizing how important accountability to one another is, as they face many distractions and temptations. We all need somebody to ask us the hard questions because we all have our areas of weakness and irresponsibility. This can happen in various contexts, but it all comes down to people meeting one-on-one or in groups of three in the context of commitment, transparency, and confidentiality.

These need to be times of confessing sins to one another. Steps need to be taken to bring about real change and growth. Our goal is not to reform our behavior externally, because we know that someone is going to ask us about that area, but to focus on building intimacy with Christ. In other words, the question is not, "Did you have your quiet time this week?" but "Did you meet with God for fellowship with Him this week?" It is not, "Did you read your Bible?" but "Did you hear God's voice through His Word this week?" It is not, "Are you spending time with your wife?" but "Does your relationship with your wife glorify God?" And so on.

Based on Content

Having a solid biblical base is crucial to our relationship with God. The disciple's growth comes through Bible reading and study. Without it, our knowledge and love for God will be, at best, only superficial.

There is a tendency away from teaching today and a move toward personal discovery. However, if a solid biblical foundation is not laid, the student will fall prey to every wave of doctrine.

In Brazil we have noted that as soon as we start studying with someone, so-called evangelical neighbors who have never before talked to them about the Lord will be there with some sort of strange doctrine or experience trying to pull them into their group. If people don't know the Word, they are easy prey to those who teach error.

COMPLETE DISCIPLESHIP IN CONTEXT

Discipleship should be a combination of all these elements with an emphasis on worship. There is follow-up, content, transparency, accountability, and reproducibility. It is not a program, but a relationship between two friends with the same life goals.

Discipleship is about making sure a person knows who he is in Christ, convinced that he truly has entered into a relationship with Him and not just embraced a religion.

Discipleship is about a relationship in which there is transparency and accountability so that intimacy with God can be passed to the other. It is much more than a weekly meeting with someone described as "dentist office discipleship," in which you "drill it into him or her" once a week.

Discipleship is about reproducing reproducers. The ideal result of discipleship is that one who was discipled begins to disciple others. There is a great need for more people to be involved in this ministry.

Discipleship is about learning the Bible. In a one-on-one setting, things become so much clearer. Real understanding can take place.

Most of all, discipleship is about helping others develop a life of worship, resulting in transformed lives. We need to see, as Ryan says, that "Worship is the tip of the spear point of personal and cultural transformation. Without it, no genuine and lasting Christian growth can occur for any of us, nor can any meaningful change in our world take place."[16]

Since our goal is to pass our worship relationship to others in such a way that it is transferable, it cannot be carried out effectively in a classroom or small group. Jesus preached to huge multitudes and housefuls of people. However, that was not where He had the most influence. The real impact of Jesus' life was in the lives of the twelve.

Although Jesus taught them regularly as a group, He would often withdraw with them in groups of three or four and even one-on-one.

Jesus did everything with His disciples. They saw Him preach to the crowds and reach out to needy people. Jesus had them at His side when He was being rejected and criticized. The disciples would ask Him questions and He would, in turn, ask them questions to make them think and evaluate their lives.

THE PROCESS OF DISCIPLESHIP

Discipleship is a relationship, but that does not mean there is no plan or direction. There is a process by which a person grows, and as we disciple people, we should know how to cultivate a life of worship in them.

THE ENGLE SCALE

Engle didn't stop his scale with salvation, but continued with the discipleship process.[17]

- 1 Evaluation of the decision
- 2 Initiation into the church

---

[16] Ryan, p. 9.
[17] Engle.

- 3   Beginning to disciple others
- 4   Growth in understanding of the faith
- 5   Growth in Christian character
- 6   Discovery and use of gifts
- 7   Christian lifestyle
- 8   Stewardship of resources
- 9   Prayer
-10   Openness to others/Effective sharing of faith & life

THE WORSHIP SCALE

As with evangelism, I have made some modifications to emphasize the role of worship in Christian growth.

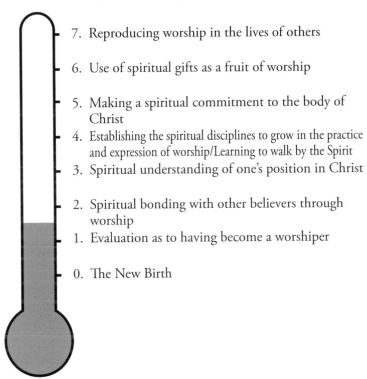

7. Reproducing worship in the lives of others

6. Use of spiritual gifts as a fruit of worship

5. Making a spiritual commitment to the body of Christ

4. Establishing the spiritual disciplines to grow in the practice and expression of worship/Learning to walk by the Spirit

3. Spiritual understanding of one's position in Christ

2. Spiritual bonding with other believers through worship

1. Evaluation as to having become a worshiper

0. The New Birth

The evangelism scale shows the "thawing" process, reaching the melting point at conversion. This scale shows the new believer "heating up" as he grows in his relationship with God.

The New Birth

At this point, the person becomes a worshiper. The door has been opened and now it is possible to begin growing in intimacy with God.

Evaluation of Becoming a Worshiper

Every new worshiper, to walk confidently with God, needs to have a conviction that he indeed has eternal life. The Gospel of John was written that "believing you may have life in His name" (John 20:31). The first epistle of John was written "so that you may know you have eternal life" (1 John 5:13). The latter text was not written merely to give assurance to those who have "asked Jesus into their lives," but rather, it refers to the entire preceding content of the epistle.

In 1 John the author describes the inner and outer qualities of a real worshiper. He says a believer is someone who has fellowship with God (1:3), is cleansed from all sin (1:7), walks in the light (1:7), abides in Him (2:6), loves the Father (2:15), is anointed (2:20), is a child of God (3:2), is of the truth (3:19), is from God (4:4), and overcomes the world (5:4). All these describe the believer's position and true identity.

He also says a worshiper will readily confess his sins (1:9), keep God's Word (2:5), conduct his life as Jesus did (2:6), love his brother (2:10), persevere in the body (2:19), confess the deity of the Son (2:23), practice righteousness (2:29) and purify himself through hope (3:3). Those are some of the things a worshiper does as an overflow of a relationship with Christ. Those acts glorify God.

When a person becomes a worshiper, his attitudes and actions will change greatly. MacArthur writes, "Genuine assurance comes from seeing the Holy Spirit's transforming work in one's life, not from clinging to the memory of some experience"[18] Of course there is a growth process that takes one's whole life. However, right from the beginning there is a new direction and a desire to eliminate those things that stand in the way of worship.

Bonding with Other Believers

Worshipers will be drawn to other worshipers. That does not mean a person will immediately become a member of a church, but there will be a closeness with other worshipers with whom he has contact.

---

[18] MacArthur, *Gospel According to Jesus,* p. 23.

David said, "As for the saints who are in the earth, They are the majestic ones in whom is all my delight" (Ps. 16:3). There is a natural affinity between worshipers.

We will discuss this bond in the last chapter.

Understanding One's Position in Christ

You may have studied Ephesians and even preached or taught the book. You feel like you understand what Paul wrote and can follow his description of the believer and the church in the first three chapters. However, biblically speaking, comprehension is different from understanding something cognitively.

Paul knew that giving the Ephesians the facts would not be enough. He knew these truths needed to be assimilated into the Ephesians' lives spiritually. That can take place only through prayer and worship.

Notice that he prayed for a "spirit [state or condition] of wisdom and of revelation" through intimacy with Him (Eph. 1:17). As important as study is to provide the basis for this kind of knowledge, only intimacy[19] with Him can lead to comprehension. Commentaries, as useful as they are, can never enlighten the eyes of one's heart (Eph. 1:18).

In Ephesians 3, Paul prayed that they would be "strengthened with power through His Spirit in the inner man"(Eph 3:16). That spiritual strengthening would help them to comprehend the greatness of the church (v. 18) and the love of Christ. How can you ever understand something that "surpasses knowledge"? (v. 19).

Spiritual truth can be implanted into our lives only through worship. When our study leads us to worship God for the truths we learn, they become part of our lives. God's Spirit illumines our spirits, leading to an understanding that is beyond our natural capabilities. We begin to see as never before.

Spiritual Disciplines

The spiritual disciplines are more than religious practices, although every one of them can turn into such a task.

---

[19] *epígnósis* in the Greek.

We call them spiritual disciplines principally because they are *spiritual*. They are not some fleshly attempt to gain God's favor. The goal of each one is spiritual and it is motivated by a desire for intimacy with God.

Discipline requires effort and initiative. I have trained for football, lacrosse, baseball, track, and distance running. Many times I would have preferred to stay in bed or relax somewhere. However, I had a goal to improve and to help my team.

Although a holy, fruitful life flows from our worship, it is not entirely passive. After giving very specific instructions, Paul told Titus (2:11-12), "For the grace of God has appeared, ...instructing[20] us to deny ungodliness and worldly desires...." That means as we focus on the grace of God, it should lead us to turn our backs on those things that still are attractive to our flesh, but interfere with our worship.

Commitment to the Body of Christ

A new worshiper immediately has an affinity to other believers and is immediately part of the body of Christ spiritually. Although noted as the fifth step, making a commitment to the church should happen relatively soon after one enters into a relationship with Christ. At this point, the believer identifies publicly with Jesus Christ and His body through baptism.

Using Spiritual Gifts

Because of his commitment to the church, the believer desires to serve the body through the gifts God has given him.

In the first section of this book, we drew extensively from Romans 12:1-2 to describe true worship. Paul urges the Romans to have sound judgment as to their role in the body of Christ, not giving undue importance to their own individual role, but to see themselves as part of the whole. Paul admonishes them to exercise freely the gifts God has given them in serving others (Rom. 12:6-8).

---

[20] *Paideúō* (Greek) from which we get the word "pedagogy." It is used of the training a father gives his son. As a present participle, it means that this instruction that comes from the grace of God is continuous.

The Corinthians, on the other hand, saw their spiritual gifts as a measure of their spirituality[21] rather than a means to serve the body. The admonition to love in 1 Corinthians 13 touches the very core and motivation for the use of the spiritual gifts. Although the passage is often read at weddings, Paul uses love in a broad sense, not even mentioning love's object. I believe he is speaking principally of love for God (worship) that invariably translates into love for the body of Christ. Our love is expressed through serving the church with our spiritual gifts.

Reproducing Worshipers

As we discover contacts and evangelize, we are looking for lives into which we can plant the seeds of worship. As we disciple others, we are developing worship in their lives.

There is an ongoing need in everyone's life for discipleship and accountability. So how do we know when discipleship has reached its goal? Discipleship is complete when the Christian has developed life attitudes (worship), is expressing worship outwardly (glorifying God), and is reproducing his intimacy with God in others. God takes pleasure in reproducing His spiritual life in other people.

OUR POSITION IN CHRIST

To grow as a disciple of Christ, we must understand our position in Him. I had a student who spent weeks pondering the expression "in Christ" in Ephesians 1. He had trouble because there are several ways the expression can be interpreted in the Greek.

"In Christ" is an expression of our position that comes through our relationship with Him. If you take a dollar bill and put it in your Bible, whatever happens to your Bible will also happen to the dollar bill. If you lose your Bible, you lose the dollar bill. If the Bible gets wet or burns, the dollar bill will likewise become moist or charred.

It is the same way with Christ. When we are "in Christ," our lives have become so identified with Him that His destiny becomes our destiny.

---

[21] The subject of 1 Cor. 12-14 is not just about spiritual gifts (*chárismata*), but touches on the whole subject of spirituality (*pneumatikos,* 1 Cor. 12:1). The Corinthians thought the *chárismata* they had were a measure of their *pneumatikós* or spirituality.

Three Greek prepositions are associated with believing. One means literally to believe "upon Christ."[22] He is the foundation and basis of our belief. Another expression is directly translated believing "in Christ,"[23] indicating He is the object of our belief. The most common expression, however, is literally believing "into Christ."[24] It implies movement and direction as we place our lives into Him.

Our position in Christ is based upon faith. Believing, however, is much more than an intellectual assent to the facts about Jesus. It is believing "into" Christ. It implies that our trust in Him is so deep we have tied our destiny to Him. We are in Him. That is why the expression occurs some 15 times in Ephesians.

Let us look at a few key statements about our position in Christ as elaborated in the book of Ephesians.

BLESSED BY GOD (EPH.1:3)

In the evangelical world in Brazil, it seems that people are always chasing after the latest experience. There is always something new, such as the time God was supposedly transforming people's dental restorations into gold. (I think if it were from God, He would have given them real teeth, which are better than any restoration). Some people are always seeking something amazingly supernatural from God, as if their spiritual experience were lacking in some way without it.

The good news is that anyone who is in Christ is already complete in Him. There is no need to seek something more from outside to become complete in Christ (Col. 2:10). We have already received *every* spiritual blessing. Everything has already been granted to us for "life [salvation] and godliness [a holy life of worship]" in Christ (2 Pet. 1:3).

Having received every spiritual blessing at salvation, however, does not mean we are currently walking according to who we are in Christ. That is why there are admonitions to walk in a worthy manner, that is, walk in a way that corresponds with who you are (Gal. 5:25; Eph. 4:1; Phil 3:16; Col. 1:10).

---

[22] *Epi Christo* (Dative or Locative).
[23] *En Christo* (Dative or Locative). This is a locative sphere.
[24] *Eis Christon* (Accusative).

My father has a computer with some powerful programs. He has no idea how to use most of what he has, and is content to play games and check his e-mail. That is how most Christians live. They have no idea of how much they already have received. Because of their ignorance, they are not living the life God has for them. They are not walking according to who they are.

The expression, "in the heavenly places," is used several times in Ephesians. In 2:5-6, it says we were "co-made alive" through Christ, "co-raised" with Christ, and "co-seated"[25] "in the heavenly places" with Christ. He says this is a present reality, not something in the future. That is why we have been blessed with every spiritual blessing in the heavenly places. That is a reason to "bless the blessed God" (praise Him).

CHOSEN BY THE FATHER (EPH. 1:4-5)

No one who studies the Bible would dispute that God has *chosen* people before the foundation of the world. The debate is usually as to *why* or *how* He chose them.[26] Rather than debating *how* or *why*, I want to focus on the question of the ultimate purpose of God's election. However the selection was made, for what were they were chosen? Remember, when God chooses someone for a purpose, it will come about. God has two basic goals for His elect.

First, they were chosen to be "holy and blameless" (v. 4). Paul could be thinking of our position as being holy in Christ now, but the same words are used in Ephesians 5:27 referring to the final destiny of His bride, the church. That means God has chosen them to be perfected or sanctified. He has the end in mind. We will be holy and blameless when He transforms us into His image after the rapture.

The second goal of His choice is "adoption as sons" (v. 5). That too could be positional since the Bible says we are now sons of God

---

[25] All of the verbs, *suzōopoiéō, sunegeírō,* and *sugkathízō* are aorist, meaning that they are completed actions, and they all have the suffix – *sun* indicating they were done because of our association with Him. That is why I translated them "Co-made alive," etc.

[26] Calvinists affirm that God made this choice as an act of His sovereign will and caused the chosen to believe. Others say He chose them because, in His omniscience, He knew who would believe. The question is *how* did God choose them and *why* did He choose them.

(1 John 3:1 KJV), but more likely, it refers to our future state. Romans 8:23 indicates our adoption will be complete when our bodies are redeemed. Again, this points to our destiny, which is to be perfect, just like Jesus. We will become conformed to the image of Him whom we worship.

What would it do to a football team if they knew they were destined to win the national championship? Would it affect their play? You bet it would! Some might relax, but real champions want to play like champions and such destiny should make them work even harder to win.

Now what does that do to you, knowing you are destined to be holy and blameless? It should affect how you live. It should make you pray and strive to be what God wants you to be and what you ultimately will become.

By the way, Paul did tell why the Father chooses people: "to the praise of the glory of His grace" (Eph. 1:6). He has chosen so that what He has done will manifest His wonderful grace.

Redeemed by the Son (Eph. 1:7-12)

Since slavery no longer exists in our country, the only common usage of the word "redemption" is in relation to supermarkets' redeeming coupons. But the term was rich for the Jews who had been redeemed from slavery in Egypt. A price had been paid to free them from bondage.

Actually, slavery does still exist in our world, but people don't want to admit it. People are slaves to their desires (food, sex, entertainment, etc.), slaves to sin, slaves to death, and slaves to the law. They go to therapists, attend conferences, and read books to try to deny it, but the fact is people are slaves. They may kick a habit for some time, but eventually they will have another master that controls them. As Mark Twain said, "Giving up smoking is the easiest thing in the world. I know because I have done it thousands of times."

Jesus Christ came to save us and to set us free from every kind of slavery. In Romans 6-8, Paul gives us more insight into our redemption to help us live holy lives. Look at what the Bible declares:

"No longer slaves to sin" (Rom. 6:6).

"He who has died is freed from sin" (Rom. 6:7).

"Death no longer is master over Him" (referring to Christ, but implying that it is true of us as well; Rom. 6:9).

"Consider yourselves to be dead to sin" (Rom. 6:11).

"Though you were slaves to sin, you became obedient from the heart" (Rom. 6:17).

"Having been freed from sin" (Rom. 6:18).

"But now having been freed from sin" (Rom. 6:22).

"You also were made to die to the Law" (Rom. 7:4).

"But now we have been released from the Law" (Rom. 7:6).

"For the law of the Spirit of life in Christ Jesus has set you free from the law of sin and of death" (Rom. 8:2).

"We are under obligation, not to the flesh, to live according to the flesh" (Rom. 8:12).

I call this section of Romans, "The Christian Emancipation Proclamation." Although we still succumb to the influence of sin, we have been set free from its dominion. We are no longer slaves of sin, obliged to obey as we once were.

After the Civil War, a plantation owner called his slaves together and told them he had received a copy of the Emancipation Proclamation, and now that the war was over, he was obliged to read it. After reading it, he said, "You are welcome to stay on the plantation, but I can't pay you anything for your work. The war took all my money. But you can work the land and keep a portion."

Upon hearing those words, some of the slaves went off to make a new life for themselves. There were struggles, but those who stuck with it, believing in their freedom, did well. Others had no idea what to do because they had known nothing but slavery. They became sharecroppers. They did not live too differently than they did as slaves. Although they were legally free, they continued to be used by their former master.

How would those slaves have lived if they knew they were truly free and began boldly to live the reality of their liberty? Would they have allowed their former masters or racist groups to rob them of that freedom? I don't think so.

What if we really believed we were free from sin? What if we drank deeply of the new wine? Would we ever want to go back? I don't think so. We worship our Redeemer who set us free and that is liberating.

By the way, Paul also tells us why Christ redeemed us. It wasn't for our personal comfort or so we could do our own thing that we were set free, but that we "would be to the praise of His glory" (Eph. 1:12). We were set free to be able to worship and glorify Him through our lives.

Sealed by the Spirit (Eph. 1:13-14).

The most radically different part of Ephesians 1 concerning our position in Christ is in reference to the Holy Sprit. There is nothing in the Old Testament that is comparable. The passage says, "…having also believed, you were sealed in Him with the Holy Spirit of promise."

What defines the church and makes it distinct from Israel is the baptism of the Holy Spirit. What makes someone a Christian is the regeneration of the Spirit. His sealing gives us a guarantee of our future glorification. His indwelling is what makes us holy worshipers. These are the most misunderstood or ignored doctrines in the Bible.

For years, I was confused about 1 Cor. 12:2, "You know that when you were pagans, you were led astray to the mute idols, however you were led." Then I discovered two truths, one from personal study and the other from living in Brazil.

As I mentioned in chapter 2, I believe the topic of 1 Cor. 12-14 is not spiritual gifts, but the action of the Holy Spirit in our lives. Obviously, the spiritual gifts are the biggest part of the discussion, but Paul wanted his readers to see that the action of the Holy Spirit goes well beyond the manifestation of the sign gifts. In fact, Paul showed that real spirituality is not in what gifts you have, but in edifying others in love. The Corinthians were confused about the operation of the Holy Spirit in their lives.

Second, I discovered that the pagan religions of Corinth more closely resembled Brazil's Afro-spiritism than I had ever imagined. Clinton Arnold did a detailed study of the Greco-Roman and Oriental religions in the regions where Paul ministered. He describes the rites, amulets, prophecies, sacrifices, and necromancy associated with the various deities in the ancient world. He even mentions the offering of sacrificial meals at crossroads that we often see around Brazil. As Arnold described Paul's world, it was as if he were describing Belém.[27]

In Brazilian spiritist sessions (Macumba), the spirit comes down upon those who are open, leading them to some bizarre behaviors caused by real demonic powers. When the sessions are over, the possessed person usually remembers nothing.

For that reason, I have stopped using the expression "controlled by the *Spirit*" and started seeking what it means to walk by the Spirit.

Needham points out that the term "controlled by the Spirit" is not biblical and is a recent invention. He said,

> The biblical phrases are "led by the Spirit," "walk by the Spirit," and "filled by the Spirit." None of these imply what "Spirit control" would appear to suggest. I can only assume that the reason some have chosen this new terminology is because their concept of the work of the Holy Spirit is that He desires to restrain, to hold back, to work against the tendencies that a child of God normally would have. Hence He must "control" rather than "lead" or "strengthen" or "fill." This I believe fails to correspond to the emphasis of new covenant personhood.[28]

One more thing: Paul tells us God sealed us with the Spirit "to the praise of His glory" (Eph. 1:14). The Spirit leads us into worship and allows our lives to reflect His glory.

In summary, the Father has chosen us to make us holy worshipers, the Son has set us free to worship and glorify God, and the Holy Spirit has sealed us as eternal worshipers, empowering us to have constant fellowship with Him and reflect that intimacy in everything we do. The work of the Father, the Son, and the Holy Spirit on our behalf is said to be "to the praise of His glory," like a chorus after each section (Eph. 1:6, 12, 14).

---

[27] See Clinton E. Arnold, *Powers of Darkness.*
[28] Needham, p.16.

UNDERSTANDING OUR POSITION (EPH 1:15-23)

Some people think they can skip Bible study and allow the Holy Spirit to reveal truth to them. But, as we emphasized in chapter 4, we need to pour ourselves into our study of the Scriptures, giving our hearts to understanding (Ezra 7:10). However, we also need to realize that even at the end of our studies, if the Holy Spirit has not worked in our lives, we have not grasped the passage. If we want to truly comprehend the Scriptures, our study needs to be combined with worship and prayer as a single experience, humbly allowing the Holy Spirit to lead us into the truth.

SPIRITUAL DISCIPLINES

The goal of our discipleship is to live an obedient Christian life. This obedience is not a legalistic burden that is to be carried out in our own strength, but a joyful overflow of walking by His Spirit. Spiritual disciplines help us learn how to be led by the Spirit and are foundational to growth and living in His strength.

We cannot even start to think of spiritual disciplines as a seven-step process to becoming a worshiper. We can do everything *right* and yet see no results. There is no formula or methodology.

Richard Foster says, "By themselves, the Spiritual Disciplines can do nothing; they can only get us to the place where something can be done. They are God's means of grace. The inner righteousness we seek is not something poured on our heads. God has ordained the disciplines of the spiritual life as means by which we are placed where He can bless us."[29]

At times, there is a fine line between religious duties and spiritual disciplines. The difference is in the goals and motivations. If we read our Bibles as a religious duty, we may feel good about ourselves, because we did what was expected of us, but we may not have really met with God. On the other hand, spiritual disciplines are practiced, not as an end in themselves, but as a means of becoming more intimate with God. Just doing the disciplines is not a guarantee we will grow spiritually, but it puts us in a position to meet with God.

[29] Foster, p. 6.

If we are not practicing the spiritual disciplines, it is certain we are not growing.

WHY SPIRITUAL DISCIPLINES?

As we said earlier in this chapter, we call them spiritual disciplines because they are spiritual and not fleshly and because they are disciplines and not duties. We do not rely on our own abilities to seek God, but allow Him to draw us into the practice. They are never to be done mechanically, but we rely on the power of His Spirit working in us. Our goals are spiritual, and not self-interest.

The mark of a discipline is that you practice something you might not feel like doing, but you sincerely do it because you have a higher goal. It is not will power, but a longing for the results.

When I ran my first marathon, I had to start training well in advance. Many times I did not feel like getting out of bed to run 20 miles in the cold after a hard week's work. But I did it. I had a higher goal, which was to complete the marathon in less than four hours. I knew I would not be able to finish the 26.2 miles if I did not prepare. Once I rolled out of bed and got up the hill out of our subdivision, there was satisfaction. Getting out the door was the hardest part.

I don't always feel like reading my Bible and praying. I am sometimes tired or thinking of all the other things I have to do. But I do it. There are no shortcuts. If I am going to be a worshiper, I need to be in the Word. At times I do it more out of duty than as a discipline. I feel like I need to read through a few chapters and I do it. Ten minutes later, I forget what I read. Other times, I confess to God that I am anxious and I place it into His hand, telling Him of my desire to worship Him through His Word. As I open up the Scriptures, they come alive.

The seven disciplines come from John 17. In this prayer just before He death, Jesus reviewed His life before the Father. His goal had been to give eternal life to His followers (v. 2).

Then He defined eternal life, "This is eternal life, that they may knowYou, the only true God, and Jesus Christ whom You have sent" (v. 3) Jesus defined eternal life as intimacy with God.

Jesus not only taught His disciples about a worship lifestyle, but He modeled it. He said, "I glorified You on the earth, having accomplished the work which You have given Me to do" (v. 4). To glorify God is to show forth His character. Glorifying God through our words, attitudes, and actions is what worship is all about. Jesus lived a life of worship in all He did.

In my discipleship training, I ask people to draw a tree. Inevitably, many people draw a tree without roots and without fruit. I tell them their trees are not biblical. Healthy plants require a good root system, and they will produce fruit.

The metaphor of the plant is scattered throughout Scripture. One of the clearest is Jeremiah 17:5-8.

People who trust in their natural abilities or other people may do fine during the rainy season, but wither and die during the dry season. On the other hand, those plants that have been transplanted near streams will have a constant source of water so they are not dependent on climatic conditions, but will always be green.

When we first came to Brazil, we lived in the central highlands where there truly are dry and wet seasons. In the wet season, everything is green, but then months would pass without rain. Flying over the area in the dry season shows how true this metaphor is. Everything is brown except for thin strips of green in the valleys where the streams flow. Plants there remain green year-round.

Intimacy with God is our life. If we are transplanted to be near Him, there is a constant source of life. We will not only bear fruit in the good times, but will continue to do so in the bad times. We are not tossed to and fro by our circumstances, because we are seated in the heavenlies in fellowship with Him.

Discipleship is not telling people what fruit they should be bearing and letting them struggle to do so. That would be like the farmer going out in the orchard and admonishing his trees to bear better apples.

What does the farmer do? He feeds the roots with water and fertilizer. He knocks down the weeds that compete for resources. He focuses on the roots, because he knows a plant with a good root system will bear good fruit. He makes sure his plants have a constant source of the water they need to bear fruit.

When we disciple people, we need to develop an effective root system so they can learn to extend their roots into their relationship with God and drink deeply of the new wine. The root disciplines develop our fear, honor, and love for God. This requires spiritual discipline, putting ourselves into a position of hearing from the Lord and allowing Him to draw us.

Bearing fruit is also a spiritual discipline. If we lack discipline, we can inhibit the Lord's producing fruit through us.

THE FRUIT DISCIPLINES
- Stewardship
- Sanctification
- Sending
- Fellowship

THE ROOT DISCIPLINES
- Name
- Word
- Prayer
- Fellowship

THE ROOT DISCIPLINES

The First Discipline: the Name

Jesus said, "I manifested Your name to the men whom You gave Me" (v. 6). Jesus did not just say, "His name is God" or "His name is Yahweh." God's name implies His revealed character. That is why a study of the Hebrew names of God is enlightening (see chapter 4). But it is more than just knowing His name or character. It is our worship response. Our lives respond in worship as we learn who He is.

Jesus prayed, "Holy Father, keep them in Your name, the name which You have given Me, that they may be one, even as we are" (v. 11). His character is a protection for us (v. 12) and is able to unite us in the same way the Father and the Son are united.

The Second Discipline: the Word

The Word of God is central to discipleship. The key to any discipleship system is "the unleashing of God's word into the lives of people.

The Lord made it clear that the word of God is the seed of new life."[30]

Jesus said, "They have kept Your word" (v. 6). He didn't just give them content, but He implanted the Word into their lives. They received the words and believed (v. 8). That is why He said, "I have given them your word; and the world has hated them, because they are not of the world, even as I am not of the world" (v. 14). This implies that when the disciples received the Word from Jesus, their lives were transformed so they no longer fit into the world system. They were transformed spiritually into the image of Jesus and were thus seated with Him in the heavenly places.

The Word not only saved them, it was sanctifying them, as well. Jesus prayed, "Sanctify them in the truth; Your word is truth" (v. 17).

The Third Discipline: Prayer

In this passage, Jesus doesn't say He taught them to pray, but He had certainly modeled it (Mark 1:35; 6:46; Luke 6:12). He prayed, "I ask on their behalf; I do not ask on behalf of the world, but of those whom You have given Me; for they are Yours" (v. 9).

Jesus added, "I do not ask on behalf of these alone, but for those also who believe in Me through their word" (v. 20). This does not divide the prayer into two sections, one for the disciples and the other for the rest of us, but it all applies to us. He extended His prayer to all who would believe in the future, much as I pray for my unmarried children's future spouses and their children.

Jesus' prayer life was so strikingly different from the disciple's mechanical prayers that they asked the Lord to teach them to pray. They realized what they were doing was nothing like His prayers.

The Fourth Discipline: Fellowship

Many Christians consider fellowship to be a group of Christians having a good time together. There is nothing wrong with that, of course, but real fellowship is a sharing together of what we have in common: our worship of God.

---

[30] Cole, p. 66.

In this prayer, Jesus emphasized the importance of unity. He prayed, "that they may be one, even as We are" (v. 11). And He prayed, "that they may all be one; even as you, Father, are in Me and I in You, that they also may be in Us"(v. 21). He declared that His glory was to be in us, "…that they may be one, just as We are one; I in them, and You in Me, that they may be perfected in unity" (vv. 22-23). He also asked, "that the love with which You loved Me may be in them, and I in them" (v. 26).

It is God's will for us to be one. This is not a social unity or a legal unity. It is a unity that is reflected in the Trinity. It is very plain that Jesus is praying that the same fellowship that exists in the Godhead should be reflected in His church.

THE FRUIT DISCIPLINES

The Fifth Discipline: Stewardship

When we think of stewardship campaigns, we usually are talking about giving money. It is important to contribute to God's work, but stewardship goes far beyond giving just money. Jesus said, "Now they have come to know that everything You have given Me is from You (v. 7) and "All things that are Mine are Yours, and Yours are Mine; and I have been glorified in them" (v. 10).

Stewardship means recognizing God as the source and owner of all things. He has placed everything we have into our hands for one purpose: to glorify God Himself. We are to worship God with all our resources. How we use them should demonstrate that He is our treasure and not anything on this earth.

All the money you have is from Him. Honor Him with your money.

All the time you have, every year, every month, every day, and every minute is from Him. Worship him with your time.

Your body is a gift from God. Glorify Him with your body.

The abilities, gifts, and talents you have are from Him. Worship Him with all that you do.

God has placed your family into your hands. Honor God as a family.

The pleasures and fun times, the trips and vacations are from Him. Let them be an overflow of worship.

414 WORSHIP, THE GOLDEN THREAD

Your life is from Him. Let your life be an overflow of worship and glorify Him.

The Sixth Discipline: Sanctification

Jesus said to the Father, "I do not ask You to take them [the disciples] out of the world, but to keep them from the evil one" (v. 15). Sanctification is not isolation, but living in the world in such a way that we impact the world and not vice versa. Rules will usually isolate us from any impact on the world, because our flesh always finds a way around the rules to satisfy its worldly desires. Jesus defined sanctification when He said, "Sanctify them in truth; Your word is truth" (v. 17). Real sanctification comes from worship through His Word; it is the fruit of worship.

The Seventh Discipline: Sending

Jesus said, "As You sent Me into the world, I also have sent them into the world" (v. 18). Jesus reiterated that He was leaving them in the world, knowing others would believe in Him through their testimony.

Sharing our faith is an overflow of our transformed life as we glorify Him with our testimony, but it is still a discipline. We need to make time to share our faith and we must be alert for opportunities God opens up for us. It is both spontaneous and planned.

Missions is the fruit of worship. Warren Wiersbe writes, "When missions is divorced from worship, the human need can become more important than the divine glory;" [31] Jesus was careful not to spend all His time healing, because He came to preach the good news (Mark 1:34-39).

The Eighth Discipline: Fellowship (the same as the fourth)

Fellowship is both a root and a fruit discipline. When we interact with other believers, we grow in our worship and intimacy with God. The closer we are to other believers, the closer we are to God.

This unity has an impact in the world. Jesus prayed for unity "so that the world may believe that You sent Me" (v. 21). Further, this

---

[31] Wiersbe, p. 15.

unity will show the world that the Father "loved them, even as [He] loved [Jesus] (v. 23).

What We Do in Brazil

Currently, our discipleship is a combination of accountability groups and the study of the spiritual disciplines in two workbooks. The first book is geared to establishing a basic walk with God (*First Steps*) and the second is focused on understanding our part in the body of Christ (*The Church: The Body of Christ*). We also have auxiliary material aimed at answering questions that new believers ask (*Important Questions 1* and *2*). For spiritual problems that stem from demonic oppression, we have developed a booklet based on Neil Anderson's "Bondage Breaker" material.

Finally, we have *Becoming One,* a book that deals with the marriage relationship.

We stress that the material is not as important as the interaction. The notebooks provide direction for the time together and make sure that certain key concepts are being transferred. The discipler must be transparent and willing to ask and be asked the hard questions about his or her walk with the Lord. Above all, we strive to make sure everything is transferable.

The churches that have developed the most have been those that have maintained their vision for discipleship. We can promote worship in the church services, special meetings and spiritual families, but there is no substitute for the one-on-one encounter to pass on a worship life-attitude. When we get away from the discipleship relationship, worship can quickly become an empty practice.

Conclusion

Discipleship is not just a program to introduce someone to the church. It is a relationship between two people that brings both into a deeper walk with God. The more mature believer models a life of worship, being transparent with every aspect of his life. There is accountability, and biblical content is passed on, helping the younger believer to walk by the Spirit and in fellowship with God. The end result is that the person being discipled not only develops as a worshiper of the Lord Jesus Christ, but also he or she, in turn, is able to pass on spiritual life to others.

Discipleship is fundamental in forming strong churches. The body of Christ is made up of worshipers. Although teaching and preaching are essential, worship is best passed on through the transparency of an intimate relationship between two believers. Worship is developed through the practice of spiritual disciplines. These are more than religious obligations; rather they are practices that develop one's worship and its expression.

Discipleship is helping others learn how to drink deeply of the new wine and weave the golden thread of worship into every aspect of their lives. Discipleship is about the multiplication of worshipers.

PARADIGM SHIFT

Discussions of discipleship are usually focused on the method rather than the goal. How discipleship is done is not as important as what it achieves. The goal in discipleship is worship and not merely to introduce the person to the church's culture. Discipleship is a lifelong process of developing intimacy with God through the practice of the spiritual disciplines.

INDOCTRINATING MEMBERS	PREPARING WORSHIPERS
1. OBJECTIVES • To get new members • To acquire the correct practices in order to attend church • To perform religious duties (Bible reading, prayer, church attendance, tithes, etc.) • To conform one's behavior to the acceptable standard of the church	1. OBJECTIVES • To have intimacy with God • To develop spiritual maturity so as to be able to participate actively at the church • To practice the spiritual disciplines in order to develop intimacy with God (Bible meditation, communion with God, worship, fellowship with others that have a relationship with God) • To develop the "roots" of the Christian life so as to bear fruit
2. CONTENT • Doctrine of the church • Religious practices	2. CONTENT • Basic doctrine to be able to understand our position in Christ • The spiritual disciplines

INDOCTRINATING MEMBERS	PREPARING WORSHIPERS
3. **METHOD** • A teaching time • A few lessons 4. **RESULT** • Dependence of the discipler • Passivity	3. **METHOD** • A relationship • A lifelong process 4. **RESULT** • Dependence on God • Involvement • Worship

Where to Start

1. **Start with your own life.** Continue praying that people will see God's character in your life and glorify Him. Ask God to allow His light to shine before others so that they might be led to thirst for a deeper walk with Him.

    a. *Ask God to show you where you have fleshly attitudes.* God will allow circumstances and people to come into your life to bring to the surface those hidden fleshly areas in your life.

    b. *Ask God to give you understanding of your position in Him.* Study and read Romans 6 and Ephesians 1 and 2 for the next several weeks with an attitude of prayer and praise, asking God to help you see the truth of who you are. Review the truths and lies at the end of chapter 8 in this book.

    c. *Fix your mind upon Christ in worship so you can walk by the Spirit.* Our minds are so fleshly and so easily distracted from His presence. Ask God to help you discipline your mind so you can see things from His perspective and have His mind-set. Have a one-track mind to worship.

2. **Pray for someone to disciple.** Allow God to bring people into your life in whom you can invest your life. You will grow more than the other person.

3. **Start discipling.** You are assuming a responsibility to pray specifically for that person to become a worshiper. Find or develop a list of accountability questions to ask one another. Read material together that will enable you to pass on to the other person what the Lord has taught you about walking with Him.

DISCUSSION QUESTIONS

1. What is discipleship?

2. What is the goal of discipleship?

3. How can you pass on your worship experience with the Lord to others?

4. What has been your experience in discipleship, both discipling and being discipled?

5. What are the spiritual disciplines? Why are they important?

6. What is the difference between a spiritual discipline and a religious obligation?

7. Which disciplines are lacking in your life?

8. Explain what you learned from the metaphor of the plant.

9. How would accountability help you become a better worshiper?

10. How might it help you to be more fruitful?

11. Why is it easy to let discipleship slide by the wayside?

12. What will you do differently as a result of reading this chapter?

Chapter 14

WORSHIP
AND
LEADERSHIP

DISCOVERING AND TRAINING LEADERS
THROUGH WORSHIP

WHILE THEY WERE WORSHIPING *the Lord and fasting, the Holy Spirit said, "*SET APART FOR ME *Barnabas and Saul for the work to which I have called them"* (Acts 13:2 NIV).

For GOD, WHOM I SERVE IN MY SPIRIT IN THE PREACHING OF THE GOSPEL *of His Son, is my witness as to how unceasingly I make mention of you"* (Romans 1:9).

SEED TRUTH: PEOPLE ARE CALLED TO SERVE GOD IN THE CONTEXT OF WORSHIP, RESULTING IN A MINISTRY THAT FLOWS FROM THEIR GROWING INTIMACY WITH GOD. *Religious people, if they are active, respond to a subjective, emotional need to serve and try to do the Lord's work in their own strength. A true calling to service starts with worship. When we bow down before God, His desires become our desires and we respond, offering ourselves to Him. Any other motivation for ministry will result in frustration, ineffectiveness, and burnout. A leader is one who has the golden thread of worship woven into the fabric of his life and is able, in the Lord's strength, to help others weave worship into their lives.*

I was drawn to missions in the Americas during graduate school. In the course of running after insects in Mexico, Guatemala, Peru, and Colombia, I found Latin Americans were very open to talk about spiritual matters.

After graduating, Lisa and I spent three months in Brazil and were moved by the spiritual needs in Belém. We decided we wanted to be missionaries in Brazil, confirming a commitment we had made before we were married. The recognition of a need, however, does not constitute a call.

After I started teaching at Liberty University and going to seminary, I began to lose my passion for missions. Our home was nestled in the woods up in the Blue Ridge foothills, and I enjoyed being 45 minutes from the Blue Ridge Parkway. I had great colleagues on the faculty, and the students were fun. I enjoyed my job, and life was going great for me.

One day, my department chairman walked into my office and announced he could get a master's degree in biblical studies in one year. By this time, I was in the "someday-we-are-going-to-the-mission-field" stage of preparation. I was plodding along on my Masters of Divinity degree and was still a few years away from graduating. Now, this friend told me how I could get a master's degree in a year. I thought, "Wait a minute, that means I could be on the mission field in a year!"

I didn't say anything to Lisa that night. All I could think was, "In one year, we could be on the mission field." All my fears and doubts about being a missionary came into play. I thought of every reason that wasn't realistic.

The next morning in prayer, I kept thinking, "One Year." I told God I was willing, but I wanted it to be clearly from Him. Although it was a struggle, there was a real brokenness and yielding to Him in worship.

Still thinking about "one year," I went to my Greek class. We were studying participles. One of the types of participles that we studied is called an "attendant circumstance participle." Dr. Sauer said this type of participle takes on the characteristic of the main verb and is on par with it. If the main verb is a command, the participle should be translated as a command.

The example he used is Matthew 28:19, "Go therefore and make disciples of all the nations." "Go" is a participle. "Disciple" is an imperative. He mentioned an article that had translated it, "As you go, disciple the nations." Dr. Sauer explained that it was an incorrect translation. "Go" should, in fact, be translated as a command.

Someone in the back of the room spoke up and said, "Dr. Sauer, are you saying we are all called to the mission field?" That certainly got my attention!

Dr. Sauer said, "Fellows, you're in seminary because you feel called to ministry. The command to "go" is here. You need to knock on the door of missions to see if God is calling you. If He closes the door as He has for me, then stay."

I left Greek class in tears. Many people go out of Greek class in tears, but for other reasons. But I knew God had spoken to me. At the same time, I was still a doubter like Gideon, needing further confirmations (Judges 6:36-40). God graciously led me through my indecision.

Years later, I was reading Lisa's Bible and I found this note written in the front, "2-7-87. Bruce just called me from Liberty to say that God had spoken to him strongly about missions today, in his prayer time *and* in Greek class! I think this is a turning point for us!"

Every time I went to Greek class, I felt as if I were standing on holy ground in God's presence as we studied His Word. The way the class was conducted made it a worship experience for me, and that day was no exception. I am convinced that worship is the basis for a calling into any kind of leadership, even when it is in a Greek class. Every time I have widened my horizons in ministry, it has been through worship.

I have invested a lot of time in training leaders and working with those who are already in leadership. One factor that is central to the leader's effectiveness and perseverance is worship. Is he a worshiper? That is the bottom line.

The absence of worship, intimacy with God, will certainly lead to spiritual failure. I grieve when I remember a prominent leader in our fellowship who had started a church, a school, a missions organization and led our national organization for some years. I had often tried to become better acquainted with him, to share with him about spiritual things, but he seemed uninterested. I naively thought, "Well, he is not very deep spiritually, but he is very dedicated and hard working."

We were shocked to discover from several women that this leader had sought improper relationships with them. We should not have been surprised, however, having recognized his lack of intimacy with God.

We have developed a worship-based leadership training system called RETREL (a Portuguese acronym for Leadership Training Network). The biblical knowledge our trainees gain is implanted in their lives through worship. Their character is formed through worship, and their ministry training is presented as an overflow of worship.

The first group through the training was made up of ordinary guys, men who worked in "the fruitful fruit stand." I think only one of them had a high school education. These men started their Christian lives with a focus on worship. Their discipleship developed their worship. When they participated in RETREL, the "seeds" that were planted in their lives began to bear fruit, and they have started three new churches in the last two years.

As John Wesley said, "Give me one hundred preachers who fear nothing but sin and desire nothing but God, and I care not a straw whether they be clergymen or laymen; such alone will shake the gates of hell and set up the kingdom of heaven on earth."[1]

In other words, "Give me a hundred worshipers and regardless of how talented or educated they are, God will change the world through them."

Who is God looking for to lead His church? Worshipers.

In this chapter, we consider the importance of worship in calling, training, developing, and maintaining leaders.

MARRIAGE METAPHOR

This is more of an analogy than a metaphor. It is more of a testimony than a teaching.

I believe a quality marriage will impact other people. People are hungry, not to hear theories and philosophies, but to see and learn from two people who are genuinely in love and functioning as a team.

After teaching our leadership training material in one of our churches, a leader told me he had never heard anyone talk about being

---

[1] Wesley, From a letter to Alexander Matwher, 6 August, 1777. Quoted in E. M. Bounds. *Power Through Prayer*, p.101.

one with his wife as I had. I asked him if there was anyone in his church he considered as having a model marriage.

He said, "No," and asked if he could come to my house to spend the day with me to learn more about the subject. He invited two other men from the church to join him.

When they came, I told them how God had brought Lisa and me together, about my failures along the way and our growth as a couple. We spent a good deal of time looking at Ephesians. I made it clear that it was worship that transformed me and not any marriage enrichment methodology.

The greatest impact on their lives that day, however, was my wife. Toward the end of the day, I invited the men to ask Lisa any questions they wanted. Our marriage was laid open before them, and they could see firsthand how worship had transformed our marriage.

All of them commented later that the study, our transparency, and personal interaction as a couple had helped their own marriages.

Leadership is about influence. Mature worshipers build worship into the lives of others by their teaching and living examples of both successes and failure.

LEADERSHIP METAPHORS

There are many metaphors in the Bible for leaders. In 2 Timothy 2 alone, Paul compares the leader to a soldier, an athlete, and a farmer. In our leadership training system, we use three principal metaphors: ambassador, servant, and shepherd.

THE AMBASSADOR

Paul uses this metaphor in 2 Corinthians 5:20 and Ephesians 6:20 to describe a king's envoy or representative. An effective ambassador needs to know and trust the "king" whom he represents.

A leader, of course, is a representative of the Lord Jesus Christ. The only way to effectively know Him is through worship. Instead of simply memorizing attributes, our training is designed to enable the student-disciple through his worship to experience them as life-giving truths. The person will not only begin to see God's character embedded in his life, but his trust in Him will grow.

Psalm 9:10 says, "And those who know your name will put their trust in You." Those who have intimate knowledge of God will trust Him.

I decided to put this principle to the test in my own life during the development of RETREL. I can wax eloquent on the sovereignty of God, but what would happen if I truly saw God as sovereign? I decided to focus my mind in worship on His sovereignty for a few weeks.

I noticed that the usual little irritations of life no longer affected me as much as before.

We were traveling to visit a church, and the kids were sleeping in the back of the car. I stopped for gas and went into the convenience store to pay. As I was about to get back into the car, Lisa told me the kids were starting to awake and asked if I could get them something to snack on.

When I came back to the car a second time, Lisa commented, "Boy, you really have changed, haven't you?"

"What do you mean?" I asked.

She explained that a couple years earlier I would have gotten all bent out of shape and grumbled if she had asked such a favor.

A good ambassador knows his king and that leads him to trust the one who sent him. Worshiping God for His sovereignty enabled me to know His sovereignty in a new way. This led me to trust in His control over all things. Further, I was beginning to see His hand around me in ways I had never seen before and to know Him in new ways. The result was His peace and patience lived out practically. I was beginning to act like a good ambassador who truly trusted His King.

Only a worshiping leader can be an excellent ambassador, because only then can he reflect the glory of his King.

THE SERVANT

There are four Greek words for "servant" and Paul uses them all to describe himself.

One of the most common words, *doúlos,* describes a common slave and is translated as "bond-servant." The word speaks of Paul's humble commitment to serve the Lord (Phil. 1:1).

A second type of servant is a table waiter or *diákonos* from which we get the word "deacon" (sometimes translated "minister"). This kind of servant is very trustworthy, because if anyone wanted to poison the king, he had to have access to the food over which this servant is responsible. (See Col. 1:23.)

A third kind of servant is a household steward or *oikonómos*.[2] Potiphar had trusted his entire household into Joseph's hands because Joseph was faithful. This reminds the leader of the great responsibility the Lord has entrusted into his hands. It is also a reminder that God is Lord of His church and His ministry. They are not ours, but have been entrusted to us. (See 1 Cor. 4:1.)

Probably the most astounding word Paul uses is *hupērétēs,* which describes a galley slave. Do you remember those old movies with the slaves chained to the oars? You cannot get much lower than that. (See 1 Cor. 4:1.)

Before Paul was saved, he was a prideful, self-righteous Pharisee. God humbled him on the way to Damascus and transformed him into a worshiper. Paul described himself as the chief of sinners (1 Tim. 1:15-17). In gratitude for his salvation, Paul offered himself to the Lord in service.

Paul generally describes himself as a servant, but as a servant of the Lord Jesus Christ. He served God by serving others. His humble, servant attitude was an overflow of his worship. Humility is foundational for intimacy with God.

Teaching the disciples to be servants

The disciples had been jockeying for the best of the twelve thrones Jesus had promised them (Matt 19:28). To them, leadership meant comfort and privilege. John and Mark had even gone so far as to have their mother, Jesus' aunt, ask for the most important places in the kingdom, at His side (Matt. 20:20-21; see, also, chapter 10).

Jesus answers, "You know that the rulers of the Gentiles lord it over them, and their great men exercise authority over them. It is not this way among you, but whoever wishes to become great among you shall be your servant" (Matt. 20:25-26). Jesus completely reverses their thinking. He gives a new standard for leadership.

Jesus modeled servant leadership. When different people asked Him to come, He came (Mark 5:22-24; Luke 7:2-6). When He was

---

[2] This word literally means "law of the house."

asked to leave, He left (Mark 5:16-18). When He was tired, He still served (Mark 1:32-34; 3:20; 6:30-34). He even added, "Just as the Son of Man did not come to be served, but to serve, and to give His life a ransom for many" (Matt. 20:28).

To drive this home to His disciples, Jesus stopped and asked two blind beggars, "What do you want Me to do for you?" (Matt. 20:32). He put Himself in the position of a servant to two men the crowd considered insignificant.

I think of how I can be so disconnected from people when I get busy. How many times have I passed by people in need just like the priest and the Levite in the story of the Good Samaritan? (Luke 10:31-32). Jesus was so different from us. Worship, however, is able to make us more like Him.

Developing servanthood

Although God's purpose was for Israel to be a theocracy, with Himself as their king, He knew they would want a government like all the nations around them. He put a provision for the king in the law.

The king was instructed to have his own personal copy of the law and to read from it, "That He may learn to fear the LORD his God" (Deut. 17:19). In other words, his daily Bible reading was to produce real worship as a life-attitude. This worship was to make sure "that his heart may not be lifted up above his countrymen" (v. 20).

The only way the king would have a right perspective on his own life would be through worship.

When a leader lets worship slide, he becomes open to all kinds of problems. They say that gold, glitter, and girls are the downfall of leaders. They become attractive when there is a lack of humility, which stems from neglect of worship.

David had come to the point that he thought he was too important to go out to war with his army, as was the custom. His adultery occurred when he stopped being a humble servant. He had been focused and dependent on God while he was running from Saul, but later David had taken his eyes off the Lord.

Only a worshiping leader can be a servant, because in worship we can see ourselves and others as God does.

THE SHEPHERD

The Portuguese word for "shepherd" is the same as "pastor." Unfortunately, the evangelical world in Brazil uses this word as a title, rather than as a metaphor for leadership.

The best way to understand this metaphor is to look at God's condemnation of the mercenary shepherds of Israel in Ezekiel 34. God's words show us what they should have been doing. They should have been.

1. Feeding the flock (vv. 2-3).
2. Helping the wounded (v. 4).
3. Seeking the wayward (v. 4).
4. Guiding them (v. 5).
5. Protecting them (v. 5).

Jesus, of course, is the model shepherd. He set the standard when He said, "I am the good shepherd; the good shepherd lays down His life for the sheep" (John 10:11). By the same token, leaders of the church need to lay down their lives for the sheep rather than seeking any personal benefit.

Jesus asked Peter three times if he loved Him (John 21:15-19). After every affirmation of his love, Jesus admonished him to give himself for the sheep as a fruit of this love. Loving and worshiping Jesus means we love His flock and want to give our lives for the church.[3]

As a matter of fact, Jesus prophesied that Peter would indeed give his life for the flock (v. 19).

Only a worshiping leader will be able to lead His flock, because he is willing to lay down his life for the church as a fruit of his worship.

WORSHIP AND THE CALL

The "Call" is very subjective in most people's thinking. It is often an emotional response to a need. A perusal of my books on

---

[3] As a side note, most people are aware that Jesus' question was whether Peter loved Him sacrificially (*agapáō*), while Peter's responses were affirmations of strong friendship with Jesus (*philéō*). I don't believe these are synonyms as many have affirmed. It seems that Peter was afraid to say he loved Jesus sacrificially after having denied Him three times. Such a sacrificial love for Jesus (worship) will lead us to lay down our lives for the sheep.

evangelism, discipleship, church-growth, and missions revealed that people generally focus on the needs in those areas rather than on worship. The real call to ministry takes place when people respond to the call to be worshipers.

Logan observes, "Worship must describe the state of being in [the leaders'] lives as well as a regular activity in which they participate. Scripture shows that worship both precedes and produces ministry."[4]

There was never one specific calling in my life, but a series of God-given opportunities. As I learned about worship, I was faithful to respond in ministry. God allowed me to continue to grow and He opened new doors along the way.

When I taught at Liberty University, I started discipling a new student who seemed to be floundering. God must have been pleased, because He sent another. Then another. As I was getting ready to leave Liberty to come to Brazil, one of my students observed that I was going to Brazil to do full-time what I had already been doing at Liberty part-time, evidencing God's call upon my life.

THE CALLING OF THE DISCIPLES

The disciples were also called progressively to a deeper involvement. Their first calling was a result of John the Baptist's testimony. When the disciples asked Jesus where He was staying so that they could have more time with Him, He said, "Come, and you will see" (John 1:38, 46). They had not seen a miracle, yet they followed Him.

During that first year, His disciples were present when He changed water into wine (John 2:1-11), cleansed the temple for the first time (John 2:13-22), pronounced the healing of the official's son (John 4:46-54), and performed various other miracles not specifically recorded. Some of them may have been present when he talked to Nicodemus (John 3:1-21) and they came in on the tail end of His conversation with the Samaritan woman (John 4:1-42). They even witnessed how He handled being rejected at Nazareth (Luke 4:16-31).

It was after more than a year that Peter fully came to grips with who Jesus was. After the miraculous fishing expedition, Peter "fell

---

[4] Robert Logan, *Beyond Church Growth*, p. 78.

down at Jesus' feet, saying, 'Go away from me, Lord, for I am a sinful man, O Lord!'" (Luke 5:8). Peter was ready to be trained as a leader then. His worship caused him to realize how sinful he was and led him to fall before Jesus and call Him, "Lord."

Jesus' response was, "Follow Me, and I will make you become fishers of men" (Mark 1:17). This was a process[5] that would transform these ordinary men into worshiping leaders.

The final step of their calling came when Jesus "summoned those whom he Himself wanted" (Mark 3:13). In this phase of their calling, they were appointed so that "they would be with Him [worship] and that He could send them out to preach [glorifying God]" (v. 14).

When the Great Commission was given, it was in the context of worship (Matt 28:17). It seems that all the great men of the Bible were called in the context of worship.

THE CALLING OF MOSES

In chapter 2, we talked about Moses' being called when he was 40 (Acts 7:23-29). He knew God had called him to free the Jews from slavery. He tried to do it in his own strength and ended up fleeing for 40 years. It was in the context of worship when he was before the burning bush that God called him and he went out in God's power (Exodus 3, 4). Moses would have surely quit in the years ahead if worship hadn't been the basis of his commissioning.

The key to Moses' boldness was that he was a worshiping leader, called in the context of worship.

THE CALLING OF DAVID

Why was King David a man after God's own heart (1 Sam 13:14)? It is because he was a worshiper. He began his "ministry" by calming the evil spirit in Saul with his musical praise (1 Sam 16:23). A quick reading through the Psalms shows David's priority of worship and how it flowed from his life in all circumstances. Despite his shortcomings and sins, David delighted in the presence of God (Ps. 16:11).

David became famous when he defeated Goliath. His motivation for going against the giant was because Goliath had "taunted

---

[5] The Greek verb *gínomai* usually indicates some sort of change. It could be translated, "I will make you to become fishers of men."

the armies of the living God" (1 Sam. 17:26, 36, 45). He went out to battle "in the name of the LORD of hosts" (1 Sam. 17:45).

Even when David sinned with Bathsheba, the grace and forgiveness he received from God deepened his worship, as expressed in Psalm 32. When he sinned by taking the census, he averted the plague by worshiping God, which led to his ultimately buying the temple mount (2 Sam. 24:18-25).

The key to David being a successful leader was not his skill or determination, but it was his deep longing for God.

THE CALLING OF EZEKIEL

Ezekiel was called into a difficult ministry. As a priest (Ezek 1:3), he witnessed firsthand the corruption of the Jewish system of worship that ultimately led to Jerusalem's destruction. God allowed him to look right into the heart of "the wicked abominations that they are committing here" (Ezek. 8:9). He saw the way the religious leaders of his day were worshiping idols in the temple itself.

In spite of all that corruption, one of the key themes of Ezekiel is the "glory of the LORD" (Ezek 1:28, 3:12, 23, 10:4,18-19; 11:23; 43:4-5; 44:4.) This stands in stark contrast to the false worship that characterized his day. In fact, Ezekiel personally witnessed one of the saddest scenes in the Bible when God removed His glory from the temple, essentially dooming it to destruction at the hands of the Babylonians (Ezek 10:18-19).

The most difficult aspect, however, of Ezekiel's ministry was the resistance of those to whom he ministered. His calling was not the encouraging ordination services we have today. God told him they were a rebellious,[6] stubborn, and obstinate group of transgressors who would not listen (Ezekiel 2).

God instructed Ezekiel, "Go to the exiles, to the sons of your people, and speak to them and tell them, whether they will listen or not, 'Thus says the Lord God'" (Ezek. 3:11). God told Ezekiel up front the going would be rough.

I think many of us have the romantic idea that a missionary's day is filled with Bible studies with eager students. Before moving to Brazil,

---

[6] In eight short verses, God described them as rebellious six times.

I could imagine a group of us studying the Bible under a mango tree with a light breeze blowing. Although there are moments like that, there are many frustrations. Most of us understand the reality of Ezekiel's experience very well. A vast majority of the people will turn a deaf ear. And many who do listen will not apply what they hear. Some will even turn against you.

But just to make sure Ezekiel's focus was on God's glory and not the results of a difficult and frustrating ministry, God took him to the throne room. "Then the Spirit lifted me up, and I heard a great rumbling sound behind me, 'Blessed be the glory of the LORD in His place.' And I heard the sound of the wings of the living beings touching one another and the sound of the wheels beside them, even a great rumbling sound" (Ezek. 3:12, 13). This is one of many heavenly visions that motivated him.

Ezekiel was able to persevere in a difficult ministry because he was a worshiping leader, called in the context of worship.

THE CALLING OF PAUL

Paul was saved after having a vision of the glorious light of the Lord (Acts 9:3-9). Actually, the vision made him aware of his sinfulness and of Christ's lordship. God did not give him an immediate solution to his sin problem, but allowed him to sit under the weight of his sin for three days before sending a reluctant Ananias to explain to him about Jesus (Acts 9:10-19).[7]

We know Ananias told Paul that he would be God's instrument to spread the Word among the Gentiles (Acts 9:15). We also know

---

[7] It is difficult to determine with certainty when, during these three days, Paul was really saved. He was certainly made aware of who Jesus was and his own sinfulness on the road to Damascus. He obeyed what Jesus had told him to do by going into the city and waiting. Ananias called him "Brother Saul," which could indicate he was already saved, but that address was after the imposition of hands (Acts 1:17). The fact that Paul was filled with the Spirit at that point does not necessarily mean the Spirit did not already indwell him, but Spirit's presence in his life had not been mentioned up to that point. Paul was immediately baptized, which normally happened in those days in conjunction with conversion. Paul's account in Acts 22:16 includes an admonition by Ananias to "wash away your sins [by means of] calling upon His name,"indicating that Paul was being called to be saved. When Paul asked Jesus what he should do, he was not told to repent or believe, but only directed to Damascus to wait for further instructions.

Paul did not sit around for several years waiting for that to happen. He immediately started proclaiming the Word after his conversion (Acts 9:20).

Paul was specifically called and separated for missions after a year in Antioch. Barnabas, who was a prophet[8] and Paul, a teacher, had successfully raised up a leadership team. The group was together and, "while they were ministering to the Lord and fasting, the Holy Spirit said, 'Set apart for Me Barnabas and Saul for the work to which I have called them'" (Acts 13:2).

The New International Version translates this, "while they were worshiping the Lord," which more accurately reflects the original meaning.[9] It was during this time that the leadership had set aside as a time for worship that the Holy Spirit called Paul and Barnabas.

Maybe that is why Paul said in Romans 1:9, "[The] God whom I serve [worship] in the preaching of the gospel of His Son...." Paul recognized that his evangelism was an overflow of worship[10]

Despite opposition, Paul was able to spread the gospel throughout much of the known world of his day and to raise up leaders in the fledgling Christian communities because he was a worshiping leader, called in the context of worship.

THE CALLING OF ISAIAH

Of all the examples of people being called, the account of Isaiah's experience had the greatest impact on my life.

In the late 1980s, I heard John MacArthur speak on this passage in such a way that I entered into the pages of the Bible. This message was important in my own calling to become a missionary by bringing

---

[8] The name, Barnabas, is translated, "Son of Encouragement" (Greek: *Paráklēsis* – to exhort). We tend to think of a prophet only as one who tells the future. The purpose of such prophetic utterances is to exhort people to live a holy life. That is consistent with the encouragement (*parakaléō*) that he gave the young body when he came to Antioch. The grammar of Acts 13:1 divides the group into prophets (Barnabas, Simeon, and Lucius) and teachers (Manaen and Saul).

[9] *Leitourgéō* from where we get the work "liturgy" is a word used of those who were performing priestly service. The present temporal participle indicates that the calling took place while they were worshiping.

[10] *Latreúō* – This is also a worship term used of priestly service, but carries a deeper, spiritual connotation in the New Testament, referring to those who worship "in spirit" (Phil 3:2-3).

me into a deeper worship of the Lord. I will be borrowing liberally from what I heard that night.

The Fruitless Nation

Let me sing now for my well-beloved a song of my beloved concerning His vineyard. My well-beloved had a vineyard on a fertile hill. He dug it all around, removed its stones, and planted it with the choicest vine. And He built a tower in the middle of it and hewed out a wine vat in it; then He expected it to produce good grapes, but it produced only worthless ones (Isaiah 5:1-2).

The calling of Isaiah really starts in chapter five, providing a backdrop of the spiritual climate of Israel. The first two verses are a parable, picturing Israel as a fruitless vineyard. The owner had invested money, time, and effort in providing the best conditions for a profitable venture. He planted the best vines in a fertile land that he himself had cleared. He dug a moat and built a tower to protect it. In anticipation of a bumper crop of succulent grapes, he even put in a wine vat.

God had planted Israel "on a fertile hill" (Isa. 5:1). They were at a kind of crossroads between three continents, a place where they could be a light. He dug it all around, making a moat to protect them. He gave them the law to preserve the holiness of His people. He removed the stones, expelling the Canaanites before them. The Jewish race is the choicest vine, having some of the most brilliant minds in business, law, medicine, science, and entertainment. They are a beautiful people. He built a tower (Jerusalem) and built in a wine vat (the sacrificial system).

God had invested so much in the Jews. Imagine His disappointment at the state of His people. It was a far cry from what He had planned for them: "In you all the families of the earth will be blessed" (Gen. 12:3). He described the fruit of His investment as worthless or wild grapes.

I once saw wild grapes that were larger than any I had ever seen and I tried some, specifically thinking of this passage of Scripture. They were horrible! I could not spit them out quickly enough. God said,

"[I] looked for justice, but behold, bloodshed; For righteousness, but behold, a cry of distress" (Isaiah 5:7).

I know the disappointment of working hard and not seeing fruit. Most Brazilians do not like sweet corn, preferring what we call field corn. My missionary colleague, Dan Green, and I decided to plant some corn at a friend's farm. I did as my grandmother had done and planted a row every week, putting in fertilizer, thinning the row, and doing everything I knew to have some sweet corn. Dan harvested it one day and brought my share over to the house. There were a dozen ears that were only a couple of inches long. You can imagine my disappointment. I didn't know kernels could form on such small ears.

I also know the disappointment of investing in the lives of people, training them, only to have them reject the truth.

I cannot read this passage without examining my own life. God has blessed me so much, placing me at the most significant time in human history and given me so many resources to serve Him. Have I borne the fruit He desires? I asked myself the same thing the night MacArthur spoke.

The Cause of Fruitlessness

Why had Israel wandered so far from God's purposes for them? Why did they not bear fruit? Why were they so corrupt?

The latter part of Isaiah 5:24 gives us the answer: "For they have rejected the law of the LORD of hosts, and despised the word of the Holy One of Israel." Verse 13 says, "Therefore, My people go into exile for their lack of knowledge." The Jews had rejected God's Word. By calling God "the Holy One of Israel" and "the LORD of hosts," it is obvious that, by abandoning His Word, they had lost sight of who He is and thus strayed from worshiping the true and living God. Without God's Word, there can be no worship.

That Israel had stopped worshiping God was manifest in a series of six "woes." They are expressions of pain and displeasure, leading to condemnation. The first three woes were barriers to worship and the last three were results of a lack of worship. These woes are true of any nation, church, or individual who has walked away from intimacy with God.

Woe to those who add house to house and join field to field (Isaiah 5:8). "Land speculators had begun putting together huge estates."[11] Israel had become consumed with materialism as we have today.

When I was in college, I worked summers at a farm near the Ohio State University airport. When we baled hay, I enjoyed riding on the hay wagon, sitting six bales high, as a tractor pulled us through farmland along a little two-lane road. Today, the same road is six lanes wide and lined for miles with stores and fast-food places, an evidence of increasing materialism.

Nothing is wrong with having nice houses or stores, but material wealth catches our eyes and takes our attention off God. Materialism is a common barrier to worship and I feel it every time I return to the U.S.

It seems like more "things" mean more problems. Something always needs to be fixed and we turn from the holy presence of God to the "things" of this world.

Woe to those who rise early in the morning that they may pursue strong drink; who stay up late in the evening that wine may inflame them! (Isaiah 5:11). The focus of this passage is pleasure and entertainment. Although there is certainly nothing wrong with having a good time, it also can become our focus and take our eyes off worship. God continued, "They do not pay attention to the deeds of the LORD, nor do they consider the work of His hands" (v. 12). Clearly, their pleasure seeking had led Israel away from worship.

The real problem is where we find pleasure. Worshipers find pleasure and fulfillment in their relationship with God.

Our youngest son Jonathan thinks a certain amusement park is the greatest place on the planet. It is one of those "must visit" places for our family when we go to the U.S. As I enter the gates, I am always struck by the word "amusement." "To muse" is to be in a state of deep thought or contemplation. "To a-muse" means to be without any deep thinking.

Maybe that is why they spend millions each year to build an even higher and faster thrill ride, to keep us from thinking, at least for one day.

Such amusements can take away from our deep contemplation and worship of God. Just as Israel became consumed with pleasure,

---

[11] MacArthur, *Study Bible*, p. 961.

people today are more drawn to entertainment than they are to worship.

Woe to those who drag iniquity with the cords of falsehood, and sin as if with cart ropes (Isaiah 5:18). This is open sinfulness. In fact, verse 19 is an arrogant challenge to God: "Let Him make speed, let Him hasten His work, that we may see it." God is so much more patient than we are.

I regularly pass in front of a huge church that promises prosperity, all the while milking millions out of the poor of Brazil. All around me I see the huge idols that keep people in bondage, blinding their eyes to the truth. Why does not God strike down these buildings and statues? Because He has not done so, people think He approves.

What was once done in secret, because it was generally considered shameful, is now on afternoon talk shows. It is as if people are pushing the limits further and further in the false belief that God does not even notice.

This is the result of a blatant rejection of worship. There is no fear of God.

These first three "woes" (materialism, pleasure seeking, and open sinfulness) are the biggest barriers to worship in our society, in our churches, and even in our personal lives.

Woe to those who call evil good, and good evil; who substitute darkness for light and light for darkness (Isaiah 5:20). Today, there is an inversion of values, indicating that people are distancing themselves from God.

Those who stand up for the truth are called "extremists" or "intolerant," while evil is applauded all around us. This happens when worship is rejected. A faulty view of God leads to faulty values.

Woe to those who are wise in their own eyes and clever in their own sight! (Isaiah 5:21). We all are probably arrogant in one way or another. Even in the church, there seems to be a "you can't tell me anything I don't already know" attitude. Our opinions and evaluations sometime take precedence over what God says. God's Word and simple truths no longer amaze us.

God answered Job's questioning by saying, "Will you really annul My judgment? Will you condemn Me that you may be justified?" (Job 40:8).

Arrogance comes from a lack of worship. When we are not worshiping God, we tend to worship ourselves.

Woe to those who are heroes in drinking wine and valiant men in mixing strong drink, who justify the wicked for a bribe, and take away the rights of the ones who are in the right! (Isaiah 5:22). Israel was suffering from corrupt leadership. Drunken judges were bribed to distort justice.

A few years ago, I was asked to lead the national ministerium here in Brazil. The only agenda I had was worship and accountability. We devoted time in our meetings to nothing but worship, prayer, and confession of our sins. Most of our leaders are godly men and participated eagerly.

One day, one of my friends told me there were three pastors who did not like the agenda, but preferred arguments, debates, and business sessions. This puzzled me. It soon became evident that the presence of God made these men uncomfortable. We later discovered there were serious problems in their lives that had negatively affected some of our churches for years. All three are no longer leaders in our churches.

Inversion of values, arrogance, and corrupt leaders are all a reflection of the lack of worship in Israel. They had all the right "forms" of worship. They did all the right things that God had commanded, but He said,

> "What are your multiplied sacrifices to Me?" says the Lord. "I have had enough of burnt offerings of rams, and the fat of fed cattle, and I take no pleasure in the blood of bulls, lambs or goats. When you come to appear before Me, who requires of you this trampling of My courts. Bring your worthless offerings no longer, their incense is an abomination to Me. New moon and Sabbath, and the calling of assemblies—I cannot endure the iniquity and the solemn assembly. I hate your new moon festivals and your appointed feasts, they have become a burden to Me; I am weary of bearing them" (Isaiah 1:11-14).

God could not stand their "worship" any longer.

The Judgment

The rest of Isaiah chapter 5 speaks mostly of judgment against the worshipless nation. He describes the removal of His divine protection, resulting in their being consumed and trampled (v. 5). He described Israel as being like an abandoned vineyard (v. 6). Fire was to consume them like stubble (v. 24). In the latter part of the chapter, he describes the fierce army He had prepared to judge Israel, predicting the invasion by Assyria and ultimately Babylon about 150 years later.

MacArthur added a chilling thought to this chapter, saying, "If God did not spare a covenant people, neither would He spare a non-covenant people." Whether we think it is fair or not, there will be a judgment day for those who refuse to worship God.

The Vision

In the middle of this quagmire of religious and political hypocrisy, God called Isaiah into the throne room (Isa. 6). To top it off, it was "the year of King Uzziah's death" (739 B.C.) (v. 1). He had been a good king and God had preserved the Jews, despite the underlying religious corruption.

Uzziah was a worshiper, at least initially, as attested by the fact that "he did right in the sight of the LORD" (2 Chron 26:4). The Bible tells us that "he continued to seek God in the days of Zechariah, who had understanding through the vision of God; and as long as he sought the LORD, God prospered him" (2 Chron 26:5). We are told he did fantastic engineering, agricultural, and military feats.

One has to wonder what sort of man Zechariah was. How did he encourage the king to seek God? Some 30 different Zechariahs are mentioned in the Scriptures and nothing is known about this man other than what is written here.

Apparently, when the prophet's influence ended, Uzziah stagnated in his worship. The Bible says, "But when he became strong, his heart was so proud that he acted corruptly, and he was unfaithful to the LORD his God, for he entered the temple of the LORD to burn incense on the altar of incense" (2 Chron 26:16). Uzziah became angry when the priests opposed him (2 Chron. 26:19). To humble this arrogant king, God struck him with leprosy until the day he died.

Now the king was dead and the nation was in a huge crisis. Isaiah was taken into the presence of God and he saw Yahweh on a throne, lofty and exalted (Isa. 6:1). According to John, it was Jesus Christ whom Isaiah saw (John 12:41). The train of the glorious robe filled the temple. As Keil and Delitzsch say, "As far as the eye of the seer could look at first, the ground was covered by this splendid robe. There was consequently no room for any one [sic] to stand."[12]

Isaiah saw seraphim surrounding the throne, mentioned only here in Scripture, apparently different from cherubim mentioned by Ezekiel. They are important angels that apparently have a high function of constant worship and praise.

Keil and Delitzsch describe the scene, "Whilst these seraphim hovered above on both sides of Him that sat upon the throne, and therefore formed two opposite choirs, each ranged in a semicircle, they presented antiphonal worship to Him that sat upon the throne."[13]

The fact that the seraphim covered their faces suggests that, even though they are exalted beings, they could not look directly on the glory of God. The covering of the feet is also an act of reverence to show "the depth at which the creature stands below the Holiest of all."[14]

As MacArthur pointed out, "Two wings covered the faces of the seraphim because they dared not gaze directly at God's glory. Two covered their feet, acknowledging their lowliness even though engaged in divine service. With two they flew in serving the One on the throne." Thus, four wings related to worship, emphasizing the priority of praise. "The fact that four of the six wings were used in worship, speaks of the priority of praise."[15]

As they surround the throne, the seraphim cry out to one another, "Holy, Holy, Holy, is the LORD of hosts" (v. 3).[16] They were discussing among themselves how utterly holy God is. It is "His veiled or hidden glory"[17] that has become manifest to Isaiah.

When the Apostle John was led into the throne room, cherubim are singing the same song (Rev 4:8). Apparently, the angels did not

---

[12] Keil and Delitzsch, Volume 7. Isaiah, p. 190.
[13] Ibid. p. 192.
[14] Ibid. p. 191.
[15] MacArthur, Study Bible, p.963.
[16] Yahweh Sabaoth
[17] Keil and Delitzsch, Isaiah, p.192.

exhaust the subject of the depth of His holiness, because eight hundred years later, they were still just as amazed.

One problem in our modern culture is that we do not take time to reflect and meditate. We think, "Yeah, I know God is holy" and quickly move on to the next subject. But the seraphim constantly stand in awe of His holiness.

Why is "holy" repeated three times? Obviously it is a reference to the Trinity: Holy is the Father, Holy is the Spirit, Holy is the Son. However, the Bible never repeats any other attribute of God three times. Its threefold repetition is also emphatic, because every aspect of His character is Holy, separate, and beyond anything human. He is holy in His love, in His wisdom, in His righteousness, in His mercy, etc.

The sound of the voices of the seraphim was so deep and loud, that the very foundations of the temple vibrated (v. 4). I am sure that Isaiah's insides rattled, also, at the thunderous sounds.

The very first requirement for being a godly leader is a deep, personal knowledge of God's holiness. Worship begins with seeing God for who He is. Leadership also begins with fixing our eyes on God's glory.

The Brokenness

Just how would you feel if you were in Isaiah's shoes at that moment? What Isaiah saw is beyond anything we could ever imagine. Worship depends upon our ability to contemplate God, and Isaiah was seeing Him as never before. His sovereign control of all circumstances stands out. Uzziah's death did not rattle God, nor did Israel's religious corruption. He, as the sovereign Lord of the entire heavenly host, was still sitting on the throne.

The most obvious reaction would be a keen awareness of our own sin. The light of His presence penetrates into our inner motivations and thoughts, exposing them for what they are. Nothing is hidden from His presence.

Samson's father, Manoah, after seeing the angel of the Lord, said to his wife, "We will surely die, for we have seen God" (Judges 13:22). He knew that he, a sinful man, had been in the presence of a Holy God.

Peter came to the same conclusion after seeing Jesus' sovereignty over nature when the disciples' catch of fish burst their nets. He said, "Go away from me Lord, for I am a sinful man, O Lord!" (Luke 5:8). It was in the context of this brokenness that Jesus called him to the next stage of his training and said, "Do not fear, from now on you will be catching men" (v. 10).

WORSHIP ALWAYS LEADS TO A DEEP CONSCIOUSNESS OF
NEED AND DEPENDENCE UPON GOD'S GRACE.

Brokenness is probably best described as becoming "poor in spirit" (Matt. 5:3). When we are broken, we come to the end of ourselves and realize we are beggars before God, deserving nothing and receiving only what He gives us by His grace. It leads us to mourn because of our sinfulness (Matt. 5:4) and to hunger and thirst for righteousness (Matt. 5:6).

Brokenness as part of a leader's worship is essential. No longer is there any room for self-sufficiency, self-confidence, or self-promotion. There is no leaning upon one's abilities or worthiness. We must cast ourselves upon Jesus in utter dependence.

Although God has broken me many times, one time changed me most dramatically. I was just learning what it meant to walk by the Spirit and was hungry for more. It seemed God was leading me to new heights of worship, but something happened that took me to one of the lowest points in my life. I was made to reevaluate everything and throw myself upon God as never before.

A couple of weeks later, I was talking with my wife as I rinsed the dishes, and suddenly she began to cry for no apparent reason. When I asked why she was tearful, she said it was because I was being the friend she had always dreamed I would be. My growing intimacy with God had brought about a change in my relationship with my wife.

Since that time, so much has changed. Brokenness is part of my worship. The more aware I am of God's presence, the more I lose any sense of my own importance, ability, or worthiness. He said, "To this one I will look, to him who is humble and contrite of spirit, and who trembles at My word" (Isa. 66:2). Isaiah had realized that back in chapter 6.

Leaders who do not have a deep concept of the holiness of God are not broken before Him, and those who are not broken are in risk of becoming arrogant, self-sufficient, and ineffective.

The Cleansing

Isaiah needed cleansing, so one of the seraphim took a burning coal from the altar and touched his mouth with it. The seraphim said, "Behold, this has touched your lips; and your iniquity is taken away, and your sin is forgiven" (Isa. 6:7).

Just to think about this should make us recoil. Our lips have one of the highest concentrations of nerve receptors in our bodies. Imagine the pain involved in a hot coal touching your lips!

Cleansing is necessary, but painful. Isaiah recognized his lips were unclean, and so God cleansed them.

Worship not only shows the glory of God and breaks us because of our sinfulness, but His presence cleanses and transforms. (See chapter 8, "Worship Transforms Our Lives.") A leader who has been cleansed is "useful to the Master, prepared for every good work" (2 Tim. 2:21).

Obviously, this is a process. If we wait until we have been fully cleansed, we will never do anything for God. I have seen in my own life how God has gradually, patiently taken away attitudes and motivations that were not pleasing to Him. I have never claimed to be a pattern of perfection, but I do strive to be a model of growth. I try to let the leaders I work with see my weaknesses and failures. They know I am not perfect, but they do know I am growing.

Paul told Timothy, "Take pains with these things; be absorbed in them, so that your progress may be evident to all" (1 Tim. 4:15). He asked Timothy to doggedly pursue a godly life with the result that his progress, not his perfection, might be obvious to all around him. Timothy was to be a model of a growing Christian. That way, he would not be so far ahead that no one could follow him any more.

Leaders must be in the process of being transformed in God's presence.

The Call

Now Isaiah was ready. God had prepared him. The Lord said, "Whom shall I send, and who will go for Us?" (Isa. 6:8). The "Us," of course refers to the Trinity and not a council with the seraphim, nor is it a literary device.

Paul said he "was not sent from men nor through the agency of man, but through Jesus Christ and God the Father, who raised Him from the dead" (Gal. 1:1). It was the Spirit who said, "Set apart for Me Saul and Barnabas for the work to which I have called them" (Acts 13:2). Isaiah was no different.

It is likely that Isaiah volunteered, not because he thought he was the most qualified, but because there was no one else. He did not brazenly say, "Here am I, send me" (Isa. 6:8), but he knew there was no other.

When I was considering going to Brazil, I asked my Greek teacher, Dr. Sauer, for advice. He said, "If you go to Brazil, there will be another person to take your place on the faculty at Liberty. However, if you don't go to Brazil, there probably won't be anyone who will go to do what you will be doing."

I asked him how I could be sure it was God's will for us to go to Brazil. He said, "Bruce, we give ourselves much more credit for making these decisions than we deserve. 'The mind of man plans his way, but the Lord directs his steps.' (Prov. 16:9). You focus on walking with God, and you will make the right decision."

I found his words to be true. Our goal is to focus on worship instead of trying to figure out what our ministry should be. When we raised our support to be missionaries, I did not talk about our needs and what great things we were going to do. I spoke on worship, using this very passage from Isaiah, as a matter of fact. I said we were going to Brazil, not to make converts, but to discover worshipers.

When I was the missionary-in-residence at Grace College in Winona Lake, Indiana, a few years back, I decided I wouldn't try to talk people into become missionaries. If I could talk them into it, Satan could certainly talk them out of it. I talked about worship and tried to help people walk with God. If they are worshiping God, they will be broken and cleansed. Then God will call them into whatever ministry He has for them.

The Reality

To paraphrase Isaiah's commissioning sermon, God told him, "No one is going to listen. No one is going to understand. No one is going to repent. No one is going to be transformed" (Isa. 6:9-10).

That didn't matter to Isaiah. Since he was called in the context of worship, he would not get caught up in the ups and downs that come with the ministry.

I have always admired people who can handle a number of problems at the same time, but stay at peace. A friend of mine calls it "plate spinning," thinking of the circus juggler who keeps a number of plates spinning at the end of a stick.

When I faced problems, my concentration would be broken. I found it hard to concentrate when one of my "plates" would start to wobble. My reaction usually was to go stare at the TV for an hour just to get my mind off things.

As I have learned to focus on worship rather than ministry, however, I have been able to "set [my] mind, on the things above, not on the things that are on earth" (Col. 3:2). From that perspective, knowing my "life is hidden with Christ" (v. 3), I can see everything from His perspective. The problems of the ministry, rather than detracting from worship, actually draw me into His presence.

Nevertheless, Isaiah asked God the obvious question. "Lord, how long?" (Isa. 6:11). "How long do you want me to keep banging my head against a wall?" (author's paraphrase).

God's response was that Isaiah should be faithful until all was destroyed. Perseverance is so important in the ministry, especially missions. Real fruit takes time and there are always roadblocks, resistance, and opposition. Faithfulness and perseverance are possible only when worship is the foundation of the calling.

People who are called by romantic notions of living in another culture or because their hearts have been tugged by the needs overseas will not last on most fields.

At times I see many powerful things happening, people becoming involved in evangelism and discipleship, people being transformed by the gospel. Other times, it feels like everything is falling apart and I wonder if the years we have invested in Brazil have had any impact at all.

Why are we still here? Because we were saved to worship, we were transformed by worship, we were called through worship, our ministry is to make worshipers, and our ultimate goal is to see heaven filled with worshipers.

THE GOAL OF MINISTRY

Although Isaiah 6 is bleak and God's description of Isaiah's ministry is dismal from a human standpoint, the chapter ends on a hopeful note. God says "the tenth," "the stump," and the "holy seed" will respond (v. 13).

These are the chosen ones, the potential worshipers who will one day bow themselves before God. That is what makes the ministry worthwhile, when we know there are those who will one day join "the great multitude which no one could count, from every nation and all tribes and peoples and tongues, standing before the throne and before the Lamb…" (Rev. 7:9). This group will join in the seven-fold perfect praise to God (Rev. 7:12). Then we will experience the depth of what worship is all about.

Paul said, "…I endure all things for the sake of those who are chosen, so that they also may obtain the salvation which is in Christ Jesus and with it eternal glory" (2 Tim. 2:10). Paul was willing to stick with it through the tough times, because his ultimate goal was to help those who would come to experience eternity in God's presence.

WHAT WE DO IN BRAZIL

If what we have discussed in this book is true, the only effective way to train leaders is to develop them as worshipers. We have shown that every kind of ministry is an outflow of intimacy with God. I am not suggesting we add another course to the seminary curriculum called "Worship 101." What we need, instead, is to integrate worship into every aspect of the training.

Everything we are looking for in a leader is the fruit of worship.

1. An excellent character is the fruit of worship (1 Tim. 3).
2. A strong marriage and healthy family life are the fruit of walking by the Spirit (Eph. 5).
3. Dedication to the ministry is an overflow of our intimacy with God (1 Tim 4).

4. A love for people comes from loving God first (1 John).
5. A vision for ministry comes from being in God's presence (Isa. 6).
6. Skills and competence are made effective through worship.

The question is, "How does one person help others grow in their intimacy with God?" And then, "How can we spot leaders who are worshipers and who will, in turn, be faithful to stimulate worship in others?"

AT THE BEGINNING

When I first arrived in Belém, I was asked to take over the Bible Institute, a once vibrant training tool that had since closed. I had a three-fold plan. First, I made the program Bible-based, teaching biblical theology rather than systematic theology. Rather than discuss topics as arranged by a theological system, we studied books of the Bible and treated the theological issues as they came up in the text. The most important aspect of that procedure was that I made sure to emphasize the underlying theme of worship as we went through the books of the Bible.

Second, because more is "caught" than "taught," I sought to be an example as a worshiper. I sought to make worship a priority in my life and model it. That probably changed my life more than the students.

Paul said, "The things you have learned and received and heard and seen in me, practice these things, and the God of peace will be with you" (Phil. 4:9). In the three previous verses, he had admonished them to place their anxieties before the Lord and focus on those things that pertain to His character. In other words, worship instead of worry.

While he was in Philippi, Paul modeled what he said here (see Acts 16:12-40). When they were unjustly thrown in prison, instead of worrying and complaining, Paul and Silas worshiped (v. 25). (See chapter 5).

Finally, I spent time meeting one-on-one with students who are humble, sensitive to the Spirit, and fear God. We cannot expect to pass worship on to others unless we are willing to have a close relationship with trust and transparency. I have mentored a number of people; some went nowhere in their spiritual journey, while others are doing great things for the Lord and being an example in their dedication and sacrifice for the Lord.

Although classes, lectures, and sermons help, there is no substitute for one-on-one contact with people when training leaders to be worshipers. Information and techniques can be taught in the classroom, but worship is transferred through a relationship.

A NEW START

After about eight years of training leaders in a seminary/Bible institute context, I spent some time reflecting on where we needed to go. I felt there was something missing in this approach. Several principles began to take shape.

First, the training had to be *transferable*, that is, those trained should be able to train others. Most teacher-centered leadership training programs are not transferable. Many of those who try to start Bible Institutes in their local churches, try to imitate their seminary curriculum. Without full-time staff to invest in this endeavor, the quality of the training may suffer.

My desire was that the leader in the local church would be able to transfer the content, the spiritual life, the attitudes, and practices of an excellent servant of Jesus Christ to those within his church. If the training were highly academic, that could never happen. By being worship-based and emphasizing principles, it is something that leaders have been able to implement.

Second, it was important for the training to be *accessible*. I teach at Word of Life Bible Institute here in Belém. It is set up about as well as any training course I have seen. Since it is a smaller institution, there are good relationships built between the students and faculty. The students are given both good academic training and practical experience.

As good as it is, however, it is not accessible to everyone. It is best suited for high school graduates who have above average intelligence, are single, and have a source of funding. Right away, that eliminates the vast majority of our believers.

In planning RETREL, it was important that those being trained did not have to relocate away from their local churches and didn't need to have a strong academic background or even a certain level of intelligence. It had to be inexpensive, because most of our believers struggle to make ends meet.

Third, and probably most obvious to those reading the book, it had to be *spiritual.* Our goal was to make godly, worshiping leaders who served as models, not just in their behavior, but also in their intimacy with God. Our goal is that they worship God in their hearts and glorify God through their lifestyle.

Finally, all the ideas presented had to be interrelated or *integrated.* A good friend of mine, who trains leaders in another country, becomes irritated when people say, "He teaches theology. I teach the practical material." Theology is practical! It is our failure to see the truth of Scripture as a whole that creates such an artificial divide.

One of the biggest problems of training programs is that the techniques that are taught often blatantly contradict the theology that is espoused. It seems that people are so bound by traditions in their practices that they don't see the discrepancy between the biblical facts, principles, and practices.

That is especially true in evangelism as we noted in the introduction to this section. The noble goal of making evangelism as transferable as possible has often led to a streamlining of the message to the point that it does not reflect the gospel that Jesus proclaimed. Those methods have become so sacred to some, that to question them is like questioning the Scriptures.

That is one of the reasons I wrote our own evangelism material, so the methods would be consistent with the facts and principles the Bible teaches. I also developed the material so that it would be culturally relevant to Brazilians.

With these goals in mind, I attended a leadership training conference with our mission. We were challenged to think in terms of *the soil, the seed, the sower, and the fruit.*[18] To summarize what we learned, the soil are those being trained. We need to consider how the students learn, and prepare them to receive the "seed" (concept). The seed is the biblical truth being conveyed whether it be a fact, a principle, or a practice. The sower is the teacher. The seed needs to

---

[18] See Tom Julien, "Four Laws for Effective Communicators."

impact the sower for the message to be conveyed. Finally, the fruit is the result of the seed truth being successfully conveyed in the life of the student.

James 1:21 summarizes many aspects of what was conveyed at that conference: "Therefore, putting aside all filthiness and all that remains of wickedness, in humility receive the word implanted, which is able to save your souls." The word that is so striking in this passage is "implanted," unique to this verse in the New Testament. It means, "to be inborn" or "to become part of one's very nature."

The Word of God, when implanted, does not just become head-knowledge or theory, but penetrates into the very core of a person's being. As was said at the conference, "Our goal is not to transplant biblical knowledge, but implant biblical culture." In other words, the attitudes and values of a person are conformed to the scriptural way of thinking. It is not forced; it is integrated into one's very being. God's thoughts have become our thoughts.

The "soil, " the student, needs to prepare himself by laying aside those external and internal barriers that impede the implantation process (filthiness and wickedness) and he must be ready to be changed in "humility."

The fruit is mentioned in verse 22, when the students become "doers of the word, and not merely hearers."

The question is how best to implant into our lives the seeds from the Scriptures. How can the truth of Scripture be transformed from biblical knowledge to biblical culture? How can truth be transferred from the head to the heart so that we live what we preach?

Soon after the conference, a pastor friend of mine who knew of my interest in worship gave me *How to Worship Jesus Christ* by Joseph S. Carroll. What Carroll says struck me just right and at just the right moment. In discussing Martha and Mary, he writes:

> Now the *attitude* of faith must become an *act* of faith. Next comes the test: "Take ye away the stone." Is the attitude of faith to be followed by the act of faith? Is the profession to be followed by the performance? They are all gathered at the graveside. Only one person speaks. It is Martha. And what does she say in verse 39? "Lord, by this time he stinketh: for

he hath been dead four days." Where is her faith now? It is one thing to make a profession; it is quite a different thing to perform.[19]

He makes it clear that Martha's theology did not match her practice, because she was not a worshiper. Mary, on the other hand, as David, had chosen the one thing that was really important, to sit at the Lord's feet and contemplate His glory (Psalm 27:4; Luke 10:42). As Carroll says, "David chose to be occupied with the One he loved and to seek for Him with all his heart. Mary, too, chose the better part, and it was not taken from her."[20] Carroll indicates that Mary acted according to her profession (theology) because she was a worshiper.

THE BIRTH OF RETREL

After seeing the need for some changes, participating in the conference, and reading Joseph Carroll's book all at about the same time, I was ready to develop a new system for training leaders.

What would happen if, instead of only studying the sovereignty of God, we would study, hear a lecture, talk about it with others who are also studying, interact with unbelievers, and then go before God, worshiping through several passages related to sovereignty? What would be the impact of following up all that with some exercises to train our minds to see God's sovereign hand around us and respond throughout the day in worship to His presence?

I chose 60 seed truths from Scripture that I felt would be necessary for an effective leader to have "implanted" into his life. Each lesson has a summary, a metaphor, a detailed outline of a passage related to the seed, group discussion questions, exercises, but most importantly worship-exercises. The last one has made the difference, according to those who have done the training.

RETREL is a decentralized system for raising up leaders in local churches. There is no need for anyone to relocate or quit his job to participate. It has been challenging both to highly educated pastors as well as to inexperienced people who have only been a short time in the Lord (accessible). Although I am still the principal teacher,

---

[19] Carroll, p. 29.
[20] Ibid.

three leaders have taken the course and are teaching it in their local churches (transferable). The seeds are all based on the three leadership metaphors explained earlier in this chapter. Each lesson builds on the previous lessons (integrated). Most important of all, the course has built worship into the lives of the leaders (spiritual).

So far, 60 people have gone completely through the material, taking a little more than two years on average. About a third of them are involved in some sort of church-planting ministry. I estimate that two-thirds of them have integrated worship as a life-attitude. Those who have not been changed have basically chosen to attend only the classes, ignoring the worship exercises.

The most gratifying result I have heard from RETREL is that several people have said they have a "new Bible." What they mean is that they used to read it and enjoy it. Now it has become a worship manual for them. The result has been that the Bible has truly become implanted in their lives and they are no longer just hearers, but doers.

CONCLUSION

Since worship is the golden thread of the Christian life and ministry, it follows that worship should be central to the calling, the training, and the practice of ministry. A leader, above all else, must be a person who models worship. By integrating worship as foundational in the training process, we assure that scriptural truths become implanted into the leader's life at the center of his thinking and attitudes. He will honor, fear, and love God from the depth of his being. When that happens, his conduct and ministry overflow from his intimacy with God to influence those around them. His life will glorify God. A worshiping leader is an excellent ambassador because he reflects the glory of the King.

The Paradigm Shift

It is often assumed that biblical knowledge will translate into spiritual life. Although those who hunger for worship flourish when taught solid doctrine and on hearing careful exposition, those who do not have that hunger can often become arrogant with increased knowledge. They often do more harm than good to the body of Christ. I have seen examples of both.

Worship will never become central in the lives of believers and our churches if leaders are not modeling it.

EDUCATING AUTHORITIES	LIBERATING SERVANTS
1. Selection process <ul><li>A youth</li><li>The calling</li><li>Enrollment in a theological program</li><li>Approval by vote of the church</li></ul>	1. Selection process <ul><li>A person with experience</li><li>Demonstration of a spiritual life and worship</li><li>Demonstration of a fruitful life</li><li>Recognition of the community and those outside</li></ul>
2. Training <ul><li>Classes</li><li>Internship within the church organization</li><li>A three-year degree program</li><li>Theology memorized</li></ul>	2. Training <ul><li>Experience in evangelism and discipleship</li><li>A mentor</li><li>Classes</li><li>Internship with a variety of experiences</li><li>A lifetime</li><li>Biblical truths implanted through worship exercises</li></ul>

EDUCATING AUTHORITIES	LIBERATING SERVANTS
3. LEADERSHIP STYLE • Authoritarian • Based on position • The congregation is expected to support the leader's ministry. • Only one leader. **4. QUALITIES SOUGHT** • Education • Talent • Ability to administer • Eloquence	**3. LEADERSHIP STYLE** • Servant • Life as an example • Supports the ministry of the members • A group of leaders **4. QUALITIES SOUGHT** • Spirituality • Gifts • Humility • Love for others

WHERE TO START?

FOR TRAINERS

1. **EVALUATE HOW YOU SELECT POTENTIAL LEADERS.**
   a. Have you selected them through prayer?
   b. Have they shown themselves to be faithful?
   c. Have they been called through worship?

2. **EVALUATE THE "SEEDS" YOU ARE PLANTING.**
   a. Is the knowledge you are passing along building a worship life or intellectual pride?
   b. Does the character you desire to form in your students flow from walking by the Spirit or from legalistic effort?
   c. Are the skills you are building in your students flowing from worship?

3. **EVALUATE YOUR METHODS.**
   a. Are you modeling a worship life to your students?
   b. Are you being transparent with those you are training?
   c. Are you spending time one-on-one with those in whom you are investing?
   d. Are you learning from your students?

4. **PRAY.**
   a. Pray God would show you in whom you should invest.
   b. Pray for your own life, that it would demonstrate forth a worship life-attitude.
   c. Pray for those you are training, that God would open their spiritual eyes so that they would have spiritual understanding of the Scriptures and be worshipers.

FOR TRAINEES

1. TAKE TIME TO WORSHIP. If you are learning in a classroom situation, it is easy to become bogged down in assignments, tests, and grades and lose sight of the glory of God. Never let business squeeze out your worship life.

2. FIND A MENTOR WHO IS A WORSHIPER. Find a spiritually mature person who is dedicated to the Word of God and is a worshiper. Meet regularly with that person. Make sure you are transparent so that he or she can help you grow.

3. CHECK YOUR CALLING AND MOTIVATION. Are you interested in serving the Lord because you want to be obedient and use your gifts, or do you have a burning desire to see God glorified? Study Isaiah 6 and make it personal.

DISCUSSION QUESTIONS

1. How are leaders typically chosen?

2. How have you been called to serve the Lord? What evidences do you see?

3. Why is worship important in the call?

4. What do you feel are the essential elements of leadership training?

5. What should we look for in a leader?

6. What most struck you from the Isaiah passage?

7. How is a leader like an ambassador?

8. What do we learn about leadership from the servant metaphor?

9. In what ways are leaders like shepherds?

10. How would you design a leadership training system for those with whom you are working?

11. Who should we be training?

12. Why is a mentor so important in raising up leaders?

13. What did you learn from the way the author prepared leaders in Brazil?

Chapter 15

WORSHIP
AND
THE CHURCH

COMING TOGETHER TO WORSHIP TOGETHER

But if all prophesy, and an unbeliever or an ungifted man enters, he is convicted by all, he is called to account by all; the secrets of his heart are disclosed and so HE WILL FALL ON HIS FACE AND WORSHIP GOD, declaring that God is certainly among you (1 Corinthians 14:24-25).

In order that the manifold wisdom of God might now be made known through the church to the rulers and the authorities in the heavenly places (Ephesians 3:10).

SEED TRUTH: WHEN WORSHIPERS ARE UNITED SPIRITUALLY IN GOD'S PRESENCE, BELIEVERS ARE EDIFIED AND HIS PRESENCE IS MANIFEST TO THE UNBELIEVERS. *Unity among the body of Christ is a result of worship and, in turn, results in worship. Small groups enable people to stimulate one another to worship. Larger gatherings enable the body to manifest Christ's presence through corporate worship. The structure of the local church gives direction to the body, enabling growth in intimacy with God and in outreach to find new worshipers. The gathering together of believers to worship God is also a powerful witness to unbelievers. Although God's Spirit dwells in each believer individually, there is a special corporate indwelling of the*

Spirit when they gather to express in community what they have been doing in their individual lives. The body of Christ and its ministry are tied together by the golden thread of worship.

After two years of working with the churches in Belém, Brazil, several of us realized it was time to start a new church with a different vision. Although the people with whom I was studying had learned to worship God, they were finding difficulty expressing their worship in the context of their local church. It was not just a question of music styles, but their concern involved evangelism, discipleship, and fellowship. They needed new wineskins for the new wine of the intimacy with God they were seeking.

Brazilians, by nature, are much more expressive, relational, and uninhibited than Americans. A dozen Brazilians at any sporting event can out-cheer a thousand North Americans. Their parties are livelier and every activity seems to be a joyful celebration. Watching a movie is even an event in which people participate. This is why it seems so unnatural for Brazilians to sit quietly in pews through praise time and preaching.

On the other hand, too many religious groups have catered to the fleshly side of this natural enthusiasm. They focus on a hyped-up experience rather than real worship of God. People hire unsaved professional musicians to create an emotionally charged atmosphere with no thought of coming into the presence of God. Many people live from one religious high to the next.

As a missionary, I want to know how Brazilians worship together, experiencing and expressing their love for God as a group. In order to answer that question, we must first ask, "What is corporate worship?"

WORSHIP MUST BE A PERSONAL PRACTICE
BEFORE IT CAN BE EXPERIENCED AS A GROUP.

Up to this point, we have focused principally on individual worship (Part 1) and its impact on our lives and ministries (Part 2). In this final chapter, we go a step further to look at worship as a community. Worship must be a personal practice before it can be experienced as a group. I am not referring to merely getting together to sing and pray, but joining our hearts into one to exalt the Lord.

This is going to stretch all of us because we live in an individualistic society. We not only have to be completely grounded in our understanding of worship individually, but we also need to understand that the church is much more than a group of individuals. Then we can join together our hearts to worship Him.

In some of the better-led praise times in which I've participated, I have seen that a number of those participating were having intense personal experiences with the Lord. There was, however, no bonding together in the presence of God. They were all in the same room, focused on God, but were not joined in their seeking. Even in our worship we can be individualistic. I think there are very few of us who have entered into God's presence as a group. It is my prayer that we would all move on to new heights in our understanding and practice of worship through joining our hearts together in His presence as we reflect on what the Scriptures teach.

We are going to combine three steps of the ACT strategy mentioned in the introduction to this section in this last chapter. Small groups, corporate worship, and leadership structure are all interrelated when it comes to worship, and we will treat each in this closing chapter.

THE BODY METAPHOR

There are many metaphors for the church, notably, the bride (Eph 5:25-27), the temple (Eph 2:20-22), the vineyard (John 15) and the flock (Acts 20:28). All these have their equivalents in the Old Testament referring to Israel—all except the body.

Having taught human anatomy for a number of years, I can appreciate the organic unity this metaphor describes. The very life of the body depends on the unity of the structure. Virtually every action involves the whole body. Although the basic unit of life is the cell, the body is much more than a collection of individual cells. Each cell makes up part of a tissue with cells of similar structure. Each organ is made for a specific function that unifies a number of different kinds of tissues. The organs work together in the various systems (nervous, circulatory, digestive, etc.) to carry out a specific function in the body. All the systems, organs, tissues, and cells are coordinated to make one single organism.

There is no room for individuality, arrogance, or an inferiority complex in the body. What matters is the one living organism. Everything works together for the whole.

This kind of unity was never experienced by Israel. It was impossible without the presence of the Holy Spirit in regenerated men and women.

The church can be described as a body (community), rather than merely a group of individuals that congregate, because of the presence of the Holy Spirit in each member. The baptism of the Holy Spirit is what defines the church.

John the Baptist predicted it: "He [Jesus] will baptize you with the Holy Spirit…" (Matt. 3:11).

Jesus promised it: "You will be baptized with the Holy Spirit not many days from now" (Acts 1:5).

The disciples remembered it happening to them on the day of Pentecost, surprised that the Gentiles were also receiving the Spirit. "And I remembered the word of the Lord, how He used to say, 'John baptized with water, but you will be baptized with the Holy Spirit'" (Acts 11:16).

Paul declared that it was a universal experience that united the church: "For by one Spirit we were all baptized into one body, whether Jews or Greeks, whether slaves or free, and we were all made to drink of one Spirit" (1 Cor 12:13).

John MacArthur says,

> Spirit baptism brings the believer into a vital union with Christ. To be baptized with the Holy Spirit means that Christ immerses us by the Spirit, thereby giving us a common life principle. This spiritual baptism is what connects us with all other believers in Christ and makes us part of Christ's own body. Baptism with the Spirit makes all believers one. It is a fact, not a feeling.[1]

---

[1] MacArthur, *Charismatic Chaos*, p. 189.

This spiritual union comes about because our spirits are transformed, making us alive in Christ. The Bible teaches that "the one who joins himself to the Lord is one spirit with Him" (1 Cor. 6:17). By becoming one spirit with Him, we become one spirit with everyone who has joined himself to the Lord. That is why Paul talks about the "fellowship of the Spirit" (Phil. 2:1) and the "unity of the Spirit" (Eph. 4:3).

THE BAPTISM OF THE SPIRIT, THEN,
IS WHAT MAKES THE CHURCH THE "BODY."

Since Christ has chosen to fill it with "the fullness of Him who fills all in all" (Eph. 1:23), we can think of the church as the second incarnation of Christ.

Although we are all baptized (1 Cor. 12:13), indwelt (Rom. 8:9), and sealed with the Holy Spirit (Eph. 1:13), we are not constantly filled with the Spirit automatically (Eph. 5:18). Nor are we walking by the Spirit on a regular basis (Gal. 5:16) or being strengthened by the Spirit (Eph. 3:16). We often grieve (Eph. 4:30) or quench the Spirit (1 Thess. 5:19).

Walking by the Spirit is key to the unity of the church. Whether or not we are doing it will be seen in the way we relate to one another. It is significant that the one of the results of being filled with the Spirit is to "be subject to one another in the fear of Christ" (Eph. 5:22). This mutual submission, which is to be done in the context of worship (fear), is manifest in the way wives treat their husbands (Eph. 5:22-24), husbands treat their wives (25-33), children treat their parents (Eph. 6:1-3), parents treat their children (Eph 6:4), employees treat their employers (Eph. 6:5-8), and the way employers treat their employees.

The opposite of walking by the Spirit is walking in the flesh. As we pointed out earlier, seven of the fifteen manifestations of the flesh have to do with interpersonal relationships (Gal. 5:19-20).

The bottom line is this: The full expression of the fullness of the body of Christ depends on its members being filled with the Spirit and "being diligent to preserve the unity of the Spirit in the bond of peace" (Eph. 4:3). Notice, we are to preserve what God has already created—the unity of the Spirit—not try to create it ourselves. By the same token, walking by the Spirit is integrally tied with walking in worship. When that happens, the church is no longer a collection of individuals, but a single body, tied together by the golden thread of worship.

WHAT IS THE BODY?

If you ask people to describe their church, they will typically focus on the forms. Perhaps they will mention their programs or the building. Normally they mention the pastor. Often they will describe the style of the service as being liturgical, traditional, contemporary, seeker-sensitive, etc.

THE SPIRITUAL BEFORE THE ORGANIZATION

Many people start churches by putting the structure in place first and then going out to reach the people to fill it. They rent buildings, buy instruments, chairs, and a pulpit and organize the program. Someone described this approach to church planting as "The Kevin Costner Method." In his film, *Field of Dreams,* the mantra is "If you build it, they will come."

As I was writing this chapter, I received a letter from a friend in another city. He expressed concern about the lack of effective organization among our national fellowship here in Brazil, a concern I share. He told me it was necessary to separate the organizational aspects of the church from the spiritual. That is something I cannot do. The forms and structure must begin with worship. We cannot organize a church and somehow inject spiritual life into it after structures are in place.

Obviously, organization is important. Without it, the church becomes ineffective and may be vulnerable to division because of the lack of clearly defined goals. Organization and spirituality are not mutually exclusive, but should go hand in hand. However, if we divide our thinking, looking at them as two separate categories, we become blind to the beauty of the bride of Christ and will stifle the expression of worship as a body.

As people have looked at the church through managerial eyes, organizational metaphors have begun to replace biblical metaphors to describe the church. Pastors are seen as CEOs and evangelism as sales. Worst of all, the church's business and social aspects become the focus of attention and energy. Even the "worship" becomes more technical, taking on the form of a performance. Not only is individual worship stifled, but also corporate worship becomes almost non-existent.

FORM, FUNCTION, AND ESSENCE

One of my students became a missionary and was sent to an Indian tribe here in Brazil. He excitedly told me there were a number of converts, and they were beginning to train some of the Indians as pastors. I was saddened when he said these potential leaders were being sent to their denomination's seminary in the state capital.

Perhaps they went to the city with a number of questions in their minds as new believers: "After our training, as we go back to the tribe…

> …in what kind of place should we meet?"
> …when should we gather?"
> …how often should we get together?"
> …what should we do when we meet?"
> …how can we best help those who gather understand
>   God's Word?"
> …how should we express our love for God together?"

When they go to the capital, these leaders will learn how to "do church" and later will try to imitate what they have seen in the city, which is so different from their tribe's culture. These questions will be answered for them and they will begin to define church by its forms instead of its essence.

What would have happened if the missionaries had limited their teaching about the church to only what is written in the Bible? They would probably have come up with some answers to those questions that we might never have considered. Of course, helping them understand what the Bible says about the church without mentioning forms would be extremely difficult because we all read the Bible, especially the book of Acts, through the lens of our own cultural expression of the church. It is easy to imagine the Ephesians church with pews and a pulpit as we have today. We may be tempted to think of the leadership of the Antioch church sitting around a table in a boardroom.

I once met an African pastor who lamented that it is probably no longer possible to discover what a truly African church looks like. I have to wonder what a truly Brazilian church should look like. This goes much deeper than just adapting the music and preaching styles to the culture. Perhaps we should ask, "What *is* the Brazilian church?"

Before we started our first church, I spent two months meditating on the church to see what seeds we needed to plant. In other words, we had to answer the questions, "Why does the church exist?" and "What is the church?" Once we answered these questions, we could begin to answer a third question, "What will it look like when it sprouts in Brazilian soil?" The answer would help us to understand what forms were most appropriate.

The question "Why does the church exist?" is a little easier to answer. The Grace Brethren Statement of Faith, which is fairly representative of what most evangelical groups believe, says that believers are organized into local churches "for worship, for edification of believers, and for worldwide gospel witness...." This is a good definition of the church's purpose and can be represented by this triangle:

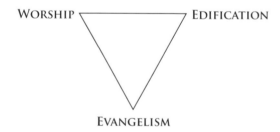

WORSHIP   EDIFICATION

EVANGELISM

We have seen how *evangelism* is more than just "Jesus in your mouth," but also "Jesus in the community." It is not just an individual activity; the Great Commission was given to the church. Our corporate witness is part of evangelism (John 17:20-23).

Edification is a second important ministry of the church (Eph. 4:11-13). When we become part of a local church, we don't just make a commitment to attend services and give our offerings to the organization, but we take on a mutual responsibility for edifying one another. Edification is not just the pastor's job.

Worship is the third purpose for our existence as a body (Rom. 15:5-6). As we learn how to worship God individually, we are drawn together with other worshipers to exalt His name together. Being in God's presence together encourages us to worship Him individually in the times we are not with each other. Corporate worship should not be limited to worship services, but should be woven into all our interactions, whether sports, business meetings, or social times.

As important as it is to know why the church exists, God did not bring His bride into being just to fulfill those functions. Although all of them should be part of the DNA of a local church, the church is more than what she does. Jesus formed His body as a manifestation of His glory, and that is demonstrated in relationships. We used this triangle to express the essence of the church in chapter 10.

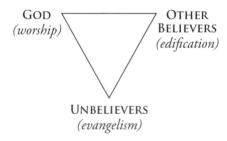

So worship, edification, and evangelism are more than functions of the church, but should be visible manifestations of His glory through our relationships with God, other believers, and unbelievers. That is why if individual *and* corporate worship are not the golden thread of the church, woven into its fabric, then our praise, edification, and evangelism will be weak and ineffective.

THE FULLNESS OF THE BODY

To describe the church as *a* body is not quite accurate. It is more precisely *the body of Christ*. So what is the difference between His body and any other human body?

First, we need to understand who Jesus is. During His incarnation, Jesus was completely God. The Bible says, "For in Him all the fullness[2] of Deity dwells in bodily form" (Col. 2:9; cf. Col.1:19). This means that the sum total, full measure or even super abundance of the attributes of God were in Christ's earthly body.

Second, Paul describes the church as, "His body, the fullness of Him who fills all in all" (Eph. 1:23). The church is more than a body, it is *His* body, and it also is filled with the fullness, just as His earthly body was. Paul is not referring to any one individual having the totality of Christ's character. It would be blasphemous even to suggest that. However, he does say that God has chosen to express the totality of His character in the church.

Third, Paul describes the mature church as having "the unity of the faith [doctrine] and of the knowledge [intimacy] of the Son of God." He says that this state "belongs to the fullness of Christ" (Eph. 4:13).

How can a church ever express this reality? Apparently, it begins with understanding who we are in Christ. In Ephesians chapter 1, Paul explains who we are in Christ as individuals (Eph. 1:3-14). He then prays for a spiritual understanding of that position (Eph. 1:15-2:10).

It also seems essential that we understand the church. Paul explains how the barriers that existed between human beings were broken down in Christ (Eph. 2:11-18), explaining that what unites us is our common access to His presence because we are all individually indwelt by the same Holy Spirit (Eph. 2:18). Not only that, but the Holy Spirit also indwells us as a "holy temple" referring to the church (Eph. 2:21).

While there are different interpretations of this passage, as we mentioned in chapter 10, I understand the context to indicate that the church, the body of Christ, is the focus of Paul's teaching here. To paraphrase and simplify the essence of the prayer:

> *I pray that the Father would strengthen you spiritually in your inner man so that Christ may be at home in your hearts. Then*

---

[2] *Plērōma* in the Greek. It is used seven times in the NT to refer to Christ or His church. See John 1:16.

you will be able to comprehend what is the breadth and length and height and depth of the church and to know the love of Christ that you, as a church, may fully express the fullness of the character of God (Eph. 3:14-19, author's paraphrase).

The strengthening of the inner man with the power of the Holy Spirit is foundational to all of this prayer. Worship is the exercise that strengthens our spirits. The result is divine comprehension of the body of Christ and His love as expressed in the church. This spiritual understanding results in the church as a whole, not just the individual, manifesting the plenitude of Christ's character.

If we don't have a biblical vision of the church, we will never see the church as a body, but only as a collection of individuals.

WE CAN NEVER SEE THE TOTALITY OF CHRIST'S CHARACTER EXPRESSED IN THE CHURCH APART FROM WORSHIP.

Is it really possible for a diverse group of people to come to a spiritual understanding of their position in Christ and the essence of the church and live these truths? Can this "glory in the church" shine forth through a local church?

God is "able to do far more abundantly beyond all that we ask or think…." Why? Because of His "power that works within us" (Eph. 3:20).

To summarize, when believers understand their position in Christ, they will be drawn to other worshipers. When this group comes to a spiritual understanding of the church, they will express the fullness of His character as a group in their worship. If an unbeliever is present, he will be convicted by God's presence and moved to worship, also (1 Cor. 14:24-25).

BEING THE BODY

Paul expresses his desire for the Roman church to live the reality of the body of Christ, saying, "Now may the God who gives perseverance and encouragement grant you to be of the same mind with one another according to Christ Jesus, that with one accord you may with one voice glorify the God and Father of our Lord Jesus Christ" (Rom. 15:5-6).

God is patient and encouraging,[3] but He also grants such qualities to those who worship Him as His character is formed the worshipers. Paul focused on these qualities because those attitudes are essential to Christian unity.

Paul asks that God would give them unity in having "the same mind" and being of "one accord," meaning that they are to have the same mind-set, thinking, and goals.

The result of God's character being formed in individuals is unity. The result of unity is a worshiping body. Paul describes the church as having one voice[4] to "glorify the God and Father of our Lord Jesus Christ."

This is more than just singing the same songs while sitting in the same building. It means that they have joined their hearts together so they might express the glory of God corporately.

Commenting on this passage, MacArthur observes,

> The consummate purpose of Christian unity, however, is not to please other believers, as essential as that is, but to please the Lord, both inwardly and outwardly and both individually and corporately. It is only when His people are in *one accord* and worship Him *with one voice* that they truly and fully *glorify the God and Father of our Lord Jesus Christ.*[5]

THE WORSHIP OF THE BODY

If worship is a life-attitude for the individual, the same must be true for the body of Christ. In other words, worship as a body is not restricted to those times when we are engaged in praise.

Protestant churches refer to the gathering of believers as "worship services" and they should be. Actually, it is a redundant expression,

---

[3] Literally, he says that He is the "God of patience (*hupomēnō*) and encouragement (*parakaleō*)." This could be a descriptive genitive, describing God as having these qualities, but it is more than likely an ablative source, meaning that God is the one who grants these qualities to believers.

[4] Literally, with one mouth.

[5] MacArthur, *NT Commentary; Romans 9-16*, p. 314.

because "service," in this context refers to acts of worship. But what happens in these services?

No one would dispute that singing is very important when the body comes together. I have heard of churches banning music for a period of time so the church might learn that music is not the only way to express worship. The Psalms are full of calls to sing to God. Even in the New Testament, singing is considered part of our edification (Eph. 5:19; Col. 3:16; 1 Cor. 14:26).

Some view music as a form of entertainment with the focus on the style or talent of the musicians rather than on God's presence. This could be true of both traditional and contemporary music. Others view music as merely a warm-up for the message, allowing time for everyone to arrive to hear the pastor. The worship leader must be very intentional to bring the body together to see God during that time.

The message is not just a session in which information is passed, although I have heard many sermons that were only that. Sound doctrine (1 Tim. 1:10, 6:3; 2 Tim. 1:13, 4:3; Titus 1:9, 2:1), however, is more than just correct teaching. It also means that life-giving truth is being taught.[6] A gifted teacher can exposit the Word in such a way that the hearers are brought into the presence of God. Bible teaching is foundational to corporate worship because everyone hears from God and is brought into the same experience through the Word.

Prayer is also important. The whole body should be joining with one another so that the praises, thanksgiving, and petitions are corporately brought before God. In many churches in Brazil, when one person starts to pray, everyone starts shouting his own prayers at the same time, making an awful commotion. I cannot think of a more individualistic practice. Instead of quietly agreeing with the one praying, each person feels the need to say his own prayer.

Are your experiences in your worship services individualistic or corporate? It all has to do with the mind-set and not so much the style. That is why understanding the body is essential to corporate worship.

Form, however, can have an influence. In many worship services, people slip into their pews and slip out without any interaction with those around them. That is why something as absurd as "drive-in churches" developed. That way people don't even have to sit next to

---

[6] *Hugiaínō* in the Greek can also refer to physical health.

each other in the pew. It may be a good way to reach some people who have a reticence to going into a church building, but there is certainly no expression of the beauty of the bride.

Corporate worship is not just what happens on Sunday morning. Worship can happen in small groups, business meetings, accountability groups, discipleship, Adult Bible Fellowships, Sunday School, Vacation Bible School, sports outreaches—everything. Of course, it all depends on our mind-set.

When I am in a business meeting or any other activity and I sense that those around me have lost sight of the presence of God or do not see what we are doing as an expression of worship, I often ask God how I can bring them into His presence with me, that they would somehow enter into my experience with Him.

EDIFYING THE BODY: SMALL GROUPS

Discipleship teaches us how to worship individually. Small groups teach us how to worship with others with a united spirit.

Many good books have been written on small group dynamics, including the importance of building community, evangelism, edification, use of spiritual gifts, and sanctification. Other than as an occasional synonym for praise, however, worship is not extensively mentioned in the literature.

The early church met in the homes (Acts 2:46; 5:42; 20:20; Rom. 16:5; 1 Cor. 16:19), which is one of the practical reasons there was unity. The Bible describes them as "devoting themselves…to fellowship…" (Acts 2:42), having "one mind" (Acts 2:46), and having "one heart and soul" (Acts 4:32).

Obviously, the presence of the Holy Spirit united the believers in the early church. They were committed to edifying one another and so were always together.

Hebrews 10:25 is often used to berate Christians for missing church on Sunday morning, "…not forsaking our own assembling together, as is the habit of some…." The whole context of the verse, however, is often overlooked.

We believe the book of Hebrews was written to small groups of Jews living in Rome. They were facing persecution and were wavering in their commitment to Christ.

The verses preceding this passage tell us we now have access "to enter the holy place by the blood of Jesus by a new and living way which He inaugurated for us through the veil, that is, His flesh" (Heb 10:19-20).

Imagine the Jewish believer reading this. Every time he went to Jerusalem and entered the temple, he was made aware that he did *not* have access to God's presence. He could never enter the Holy of Holies. Intimacy with God was unthinkable.

However, in this passage, the Jewish believer is told he is able to come into God's presence. That is why there was an invitation to come. The author of Hebrews admonished, "Let us draw near." This is an invitation to salvation, to become a worshiper.

A second admonition was given that says, "Let us hold fast…" (v. 22). That is, let us remain firm in our convictions.

Certainly, sharing in small groups strengthens our convictions, especially in the face of persecutions. Seeing God at work in other believers is very important to me, reaffirming my beliefs as being very real.

The third exhortation is "And let us consider how to stimulate one another to love and good deeds" (v. 24).

We are not told whom we are to love and so it is unclear whether the author is speaking of fellowship love, which most commentators assume, or loving God. Either is possible in this context. Jesus combined the two in what is called "The Great Commandment" (Matt. 22:34-40). The two are inseparable. If we love and worship God, we will love one another. The "good deeds" are the practical expression of our love for God and for each other. This means we are to help one another glorify God through our love and good deeds.

The passage can be translated one of two ways.[7] 1) "Stimulate one another to practice love and good deeds." In this case, the gathering together has the function of encouraging us to worship, to love one another, and to do good. 2) "Stimulate one another by means of

---

[7] The author of Hebrews used a genitive. If he meant it as an objective genitive, it would be translated "stimulate love and good deeds." However, if his intention was a subjective genitive it could be translated "love and good deeds stimulate." This vagueness could have been averted with a simple preposition. I believe the author purposely left it vague because both are true.

love and good deeds." In other words, the community itself, by its worship, love, and good deeds actually encourages the living out of our Christianity. Although the former is probably the intent, both are true. Getting together to worship and do good to one another stimulates worship and doing good to one another. We can actually help each other enter more fully into God's presence.

The first step in our time together is to see *God* as a group. That means looking at the same passage of Scripture with each person sharing what he or she learned about God. Worship starts with the Scriptures (in spirit and truth—John 4:23). It is not a teaching, but each person helping each other see God's character in a passage. I like to use the passages in Isaiah 40-50, which are rich in their description of the one true God.

Each person looks at the Scripture individually and praises God for the qualities he or she has found. It becomes collective worship when people share with one another what they have discovered.

The second step is turning the group *inward*, allowing God's Spirit to shine the light on areas that are not pleasing to Him, areas that are barriers to worship. There are a number of passages to use, or it may be helpful to use some sort of spiritual inventory list. David asked, "Who can discern his errors?" (Psalm 19:12). The answer is no one. But God's Word and His Spirit can show us those hidden faults.

When people have allowed God to deal with them individually, it can become *collective brokenness* where there is confession of sin. We are told, "Confess your sins to one another, and pray for one another..." (James 5:16).

The praying for one another describes the *collective cleansing and restoration.*

Although it was a group of leaders, it was in a small group setting that Paul and Barnabas were called to missions (Acts 13). Part of worship is *offering of ourselves* to God, offering ourselves in service however He chooses to use us. If the group does that, the calling is a group venture. That is why the other leaders in Acts 13 "fasted and prayed and laid their hands on them [Paul and Barnabas]" (v. 3). The group felt a part of the call and thus a part of the ministry.

Perhaps the deepest part of corporate worship is when the group is silent before God, in awe, loving and enjoying His holy presence *together.*

Because we are so individualistic in our thinking about our walking with the Lord, it is hard for us to conceive of real corporate worship. Although nothing is wrong with closing our eyes during a group praise time, we can be doing it to shut out the presence of everyone around us to focus on God. Our goal is for each person to know Him individually, but our worship should never be individualistic.

Although we like our NIVs and NASBs, there is one great advantage of the King James Version of the Bible. Modern English does not distinguish between the second person singular "you" and the plural. The old Elizabethan English has the singular "thee" and "thou" and the plural "ye." As a result we usually assume the "you" in our Bibles is speaking to the individual rather than the group. We typically think of many passages as talking about the Christian, when, in reality, they are referring to the church. Consider the following passages in the King James Version:

> But ye shall receive power, after that the Holy Ghost is come upon you: and ye shall be witnesses unto me both in Jerusalem, and in all Judea, and in Samaria, and unto the uttermost part of the earth (Acts 1:8).

> Know ye not that ye are the temple of God, and that the Spirit of God dwelleth in you? (1 Cor. 3:16).

> In whom ye also are builded together for an habitation of God through the Spirit (Eph. 2:22).

> I therefore, the prisoner of the Lord, beseech you that ye walk worthy of the vocation wherewith ye are called (Eph. 4:1).

All these passages are in the context of the church, but are often applied to the individual. Obviously, we cannot read the church into every passage that says "ye" in the KJV, but maybe we should start thinking more collectively when we read the Bible. For example, "Ye are the salt of the earth...Ye are the light of the world" (Matt 5:13-14) might be speaking of us not only as individual Christians, but also as a church.

Corporate worship is best learned in small groups. There is more freedom and involvement in a small group setting. A stronger bond exists in a more intimate community so it is easier to worship collectively.

I don't in any way want to give the impression that the worshiping community meets together only to worship and praise corporately. If they learn how to be one in God's presence, then times of recreation, service, and socializing are also lived out in His presence and are a different expression of worship. Every joint activity will glorify God.

CELEBRATING THE BODY: THE WORSHIP SERVICE

When small groups are experiencing worship, a larger celebration becomes more of a corporate worship time as well. Basically, corporate worship should be what we just described, only on a larger scale, with a few differences. Obviously, it will not be as intimate nor will there be the freedom that exists with a smaller group, but there can and should be a powerful corporate sense of God's presence.

UNITED IN GOD'S PRESENCE

It is easier to do almost everything with a small group than with a larger group. This is especially true in trying to unite a diverse group in the presence of the Lord. When a larger group of people gathers, each person brings with him or her a variety of life circumstances and almost everyone is in a different spiritual state.

Think of Sunday morning and attending church. Some worshipers may have just had a major fight with their spouse on the way to church while running late. Others may have just spent the night in prayer and Bible study. Others are weighed down by guilt and shame; still others are experiencing victory in their walk with the Lord as never before. Some have just begun to walk with the Lord while others have known Jesus for half a century. Some have shared their faith with several people during the week; others have never talked to anyone about Jesus. It is no small task to help this group experience God's presence together.

The key is the preaching and teaching of the Word of God in the celebration. It must be sound doctrine.

The only way the group can be united is for everyone to see God and hear from Him together. Traditionally, we think of music in the beginning of the service as a warm-up for the main event, the preaching. However, music may get people's mind off their problems and onto the Lord, but it doesn't necessarily bring them together nor bring them into God's presence as the Word of God does. A testimony that is focused on God's work in someone's life can bring the whole group to be in awe of God together.

For that reason, it might be interesting to place the teaching of the Word of God at the beginning of the corporate celebration. In that way, the preaching can enable the whole group to see God together and then afterward respond in praise.

The teaching could be followed by sharing among the people so that bonds can be created among those sitting close to one another. Perhaps a couple of people with cordless microphones could create more interaction by interviewing worshipers. Involvement also has the effect of reinforcing the message. Many times someone else's insights concerning the message have more impact on our lives than the message itself.

Music and prayer are powerful tools to reinforce the truth of Scripture. The teaching should be followed with songs that relate to the message along with praise/prayer times, allowing small groups within the larger group to respond to the teaching.

There is a scriptural precedent for dividing the larger group into small groups to talk about the message. Ezra did it when he read the law after returning to the land. As Ezra read, a number of men were scattered among the people who "explained the law to the people while the people remained in their place…translating to give the sense so that they understood the reading" (Neh. 8:7-8).

It would be very appropriate to follow the teaching with an exhortation to obey the passage.

Although it may seem strange to us, the early church apparently would have more than one message in a meeting. Paul instructed, "Let two or three prophets speak, and let the others pass judgment" (1 Cor. 14:29). He also indicated there was more than one type of message given in the public services, "Until I come, give attention to the public reading of Scripture, to exhortation and teaching" (1 Tim. 4:13).

Barnabas, whose name means, "Son of Encouragement or Exhortation," was a prophet and Paul was a teacher (Acts 13:1)[8] When Barnabas arrived in Antioch, he *encouraged* them (Acts 11:23). The actual teaching ministry started when Saul arrived (Acts 11:26). This combination seems to be important in their teamwork. Later, Paul picked Silas to take Barnabas's place on the team since he also was a prophet who encouraged others (Acts 15:32).

Although the prophetic gift that involved new revelation ceased during the apostolic era, the prophetic gift of exhortation did not. A healthy church today will have both teachers and prophets (preachers or exhorters) speaking to the church.

Ezra led the returning Jewish exiles in an incredible corporate celebration. They came together with a common purpose to hear from God and "gathered as one man" (Neh. 8:1). They had already put aside their individualism before the meeting started.

It is obvious they did not come together as a religious obligation because when Ezra read the Word, "the people were attentive" to the Bible despite standing and listening for about six hours (Neh. 8:3). When people attend a meeting only as a religious duty, there is no hunger to understand God's Word.

The people were joined to one another through small group interaction, discussing the Word until they understood (Neh. 8:7).

The people responded together. The Word of God always elicits a response, especially when there is teaching and exhortation. As in Nehemiah's day, when "all the people were weeping when they heard the words of the law" (Neh. 8:9), so after a message today, there should be a time of reflection and sometimes confession and brokenness.

Good leadership will know whether to lead the people in a joyful time to conclude the meeting together—"to celebrate a great festival" (Neh. 8:12), to "be still" (Neh. 8:11), or to have a "solemn assembly" (Neh. 8:18). Whatever the response, it should be because "they understood the words which had been made known to them" (Neh. 8:12).

Corporate worship is not directed by a talented musician, a clever showman, or a charismatic speaker, but by the Spirit of God leading

---

[8] The conjunction *té* divides the list in two groups, corresponding to prophets (Barnabas, Simeon, and Lucius) and teachers (Manaen and Saul).

the people to respond to the Word of God. The person who has the ability to lead a group into God's presence must first be a worshiper himself, and he must have a vision for what it means to be in God's presence corporately. He is excited about coming together before the Lord, and he is able to share that excitement. Only a certain few have this gift and even fewer have the vision.

TRANSPLANTING FORMS

As we look at the styles of worship services in various parts of the world and in different denominations, we are struck with the great variety, even within a single local body. Is there a right way to worship God? Is there a way to worship God that is inherently wrong?

The essential truth or the "seed" of authentic worship is constant: God is seeking worshipers, and they are to join together to love, encourage, and exhort one another. The major factor that determines *how* they will choose to do that is their culture, or what we call the "soil," in which the seed truth is planted.

Missionaries often make the mistake of bringing cultural "soil" into their new setting, instead of observing and working with the soil of the people to whom they have been sent. They imagine that every soil is basically the same, so they simply do what they did in their home country. The result is a "colonial" church, a church merely transplanted from a foreign country. The nationals simply consecrate the traditions taught by the founding missionaries, and, as a result, it becomes almost impossible for them to think of doing church any other way.

A "syncretistic church," on the other hand, develops when the church's styles and even doctrines have become so well adapted to the soil that it has lost all connection with the original seed. The essence of the belief system is completely lost while some outward forms are retained. When this happens, people feel so at home in the church, they become a part of it without converting. The practices and beliefs of the church are so in line with the popular religion of the culture that there is no need to change.

On a trip to Guatemala, I visited the oldest church building in the Americas. Down the center row were platforms with different colored rose petals. When I asked the guide what it meant, he told me it was an ancient Indian practice of offering the petals to the gods. One color was for fertility, another for health, and a third for prosperity. It didn't really matter that what they were doing conflicted with Roman Catholic doctrine. They "converted" to Catholicism in name only.

In every culture there are "high religions" (what people profess to believe) and "folk religion" (what they actually believe and practice). It is not uncommon for a people group to shift their high religion while maintaining their folk religion.

In Brazil, the high religion has always been Catholicism, while the folk religion is African or European spiritism. The high religion in Brazil has shifted, as people have switched from being Catholic to Pentecostal. However, the majority of the people have remained spiritist in their convictions and in their approach to life while professing evangelical doctrines and singing Christian music. In other words, they still believe in curses, in the power of certain objects and rituals to protect them spiritually, and in the prophecies of their future uttered by seemingly "illuminated" individuals. Their salvation is based on works, and blessings are earned through vows, rituals, and sacrifices. One such church's blending of spiritist rituals and symbols together with prosperity theology has attracted people in droves.

The "indigenous" church is one that has truly sprung up from the natural soil. It is solid biblically, maintaining the scriptural seed while not repressing spontaneous cultural expression. These churches grow spontaneously, but not nearly as quickly as the syncretistic church.

THE "INDIGENOUS" CHURCH IS ONE THAT HAS TRULY SPRUNG UP FROM THE NATURAL SOIL. IT IS SOLID BIBLICALLY, MAINTAINING THE SCRIPTURAL SEED WHILE NOT REPRESSING SPONTANEOUS CULTURAL EXPRESSION.

So then, worship is our seed. Intimate knowledge of the true God builds in us inner attitudes of honor, fear, and love. This naturally leads to a spontaneous expression of praise. One of these expressions will be in musical form. And each of the church types described above will have very noticeable distinctions in its praise.

Colonial praise is an imposition of forms and styles of expression that are not natural to the culture. There is a repression of spontaneity. Leaders become fearful that people will be attracted to just the music, or that worldly styles will influence their choices. They forget that music is a valuable tool for teaching doctrine as well as expressing love for God. The authors of all the old hymns understood that principle. The music style of the old hymns was generally in line with the popular music of the day, though it expressed deep biblical truths.

A syncretistic praise focuses more on the form and appeals to the fleshly elements within the culture rather than flowing from intimacy with God. The appeal is in the rhythm or style. Often the words are superficial, even reflecting wrong doctrine.

An indigenous praise style is one that is natural for the people to sing, and a biblical message comes through clearly. When this is true, people throughout the week are singing the song to themselves, while in conscious communion with God. The time of corporate worship on Sunday will help focus our minds on worship individually throughout the week.

One day, my son popped a CD in the car sound system. It was what I call "Cookie Monster music" (guttural shouting like the Sesame Street character). He told me the lifestyle and message of the band were very solid. I told him that at times I have heard pretty wild Christian music that seemed to be a genuine expression of praise while others are inclined to say, "See, we can rock just like the world." Personally, I didn't care for the music; it is a different culture from mine, but that does not make it wrong.

Of course, the polemic about music styles has been around for a long time, as the church has passed through so many different "soils," soils of times and places. As Nelson comments, "Unfortunately, we tend to be ignorant of the history of music in the life of the church. The church has often struggled with which kinds of music are appropriate for worship and which musical instruments, if any, are appropriate for worship."[9] He went on to trace some of the controversies over styles since the time of the Church Fathers.

[9] Nelson, "Voicing God's Praise: The Use of Music in Worship" in Bateman, p. 147.

Richard Foster says that "we can be indifferent to the question of a correct form for worship. The issue of high liturgy or low liturgy, this form or that form, is peripheral rather than central. We are encouraged in our difference when we realize that nowhere does the New Testament prescribe a particular form of worship." [10]

It is not the form of praise that is important; it is the source, the seed. If the seed is fleshly, the praise will be too. If the seed is real worship and the fear of God, it may sprout up in many different forms, all glorifying God.

Stallter, speaking of cultural differences in expressions of worship, describes the difficulties people have in adjusting to different styles as "worship shock."[11] There is a tendency to criticize rather than recognize the presence of God and "be expanded as we learn what our culture has withheld from us."[12] Worship styles need to be dynamic. We should always be looking at other cultures and examining our own methods to come up with new ways to express worship that are culturally relevant.

Instead of looking at differences in worship with suspicion or criticism, we should allow ourselves to be enriched by the diversity. Whether they are ethnic, geographical, or generational differences, by stripping off our own cultural blinders, we can see God more clearly in His fullness. That is why Paul commented to the isolationist Corinthians that they were "saints by calling, with all who in every place call upon the name of our Lord Jesus Christ, their Lord and ours" (1 Cor. 1:2). Paul saw worship as transcending any one culture or geographical location.

Stallter raises a rhetorical question, "One wonders how much of this is God's intention in order that we might have a fuller, richer understanding of Himself. Is it possible He expects us to learn from each other?"[13] Of course He does! When friends from the U.S. visit us and become involved with Brazilian believers, both groups are enriched in their understanding of God and worship. And we also need to learn from the generational differences. Maybe we would see God more clearly that way, as Stallter has suggested.

---

[10] Foster, p. 139.
[11] Tom Stallter, "The Challenges of Multicultural Worship" in Bateman, p. 277.
[12] Ibid. p.277.
[13] Ibid. p. 282.

HOW DID WE GET WHERE WE ARE?

How did the church lose sight of worship and reduce it to a form? Why have we become so institutionalized? Why are we not more united? What happened in these almost 2,000 years? Why is the church losing its relevance? Can we recover the beauty of the bride?

In Acts 20, Paul warned the Ephesians elders about what would happen after he left them. Keep in mind that Paul had not yet written the book of Ephesians, describing the beauty of the church. He alerted them that "savage wolves will come in among you, not sparing the flock." (v. 29), referring to persecution. He advised them that some within the church would be "speaking perverse things" (v.30), describing the heretical divisions, including Gnosticism, that would affect the church. Those who advocated heresies would also try to "draw away the disciples after them" (v. 30), creating political division among the brethren.

Instead of setting up a well-defined doctrinal system or a strong leadership structure, Paul committed the church "to God and to the word of His grace" (v. 32). He felt that a worshiping community, guided by spiritual leaders, committed to God and to His Word, would be safe against those attacks.

However, when the events Paul had warned about started happening, the church leadership panicked. They did what is done so often today: They circled the wagons and strengthened the hierarchy in order to achieve unity.

As Jim Petersen comments, "They achieved their goals, but at an awful price. They created a clergy-laity caste system, which put the average believer out of business in terms of his or her ministry in the gospel. The freedom experienced in the New Testament period vanished as the authority of the bishops grew."[14] I would add that the hierarchy not only stifled ministry and the community, but made worship into an event instead of a life-attitude.

David Bosch comments on the early church's response: "Its white-hot convictions, poured into the hearts of the first adherents, cooled down and became crystallized codes, solidified institutions

---

[14] Petersen, p. 89.

and petrified dogmas. The prophet became a priest of the establishment, charisma became office and love became routine." [15]

> THE HOPE FOR THE CHURCH TODAY IS TO RECAPTURE
> WORSHIP AND TO WEAVE IT BACK INTO THE FABRIC
> OF THE CHRISTIAN LIFE AND THE CHURCH.

We need to seek the new wine and be willing to change the wineskins that hold it; otherwise, they will burst.

I sense the current generation of youth wants to see genuine Christianity more than anything else. They are broader in their tastes than I, and they seem to have a genuine zeal for the holiness of God. My son told me recently he did not like the way I joked around at a baptism service because he thought I was irreverent, not promoting a worshipful atmosphere. I was pleasantly surprised, but at the same time embarrassed.

If the church does not recapture the genuine worship of the first church, we won't cease to exist, because God always preserves a remnant. It will continue, however, to weaken with very few continuing in the faith. And "when the Son of Man comes, will He find faith on the earth?" (Luke 18:8).

GUIDING THE BODY: LEADERSHIP STRUCTURE

Again, there are many great books written about different leadership structures, advocating elder-based, board-based, congregational, or pastoral leadership. Although I believe in a plurality of leaders and the autonomy of the local church, there seems to be some flexibility in Scripture (see Acts 15).

Whatever leadership structure is chosen, worship should predominate the decision-making process. Business meetings and worship are not incompatible. If they are separated, decisions will be made in the flesh and not be glorifying to God.

---

[15] David Bosch, quoted in Petersen, p. 90.

In *choosing leaders*, we often elect those who are willing, active, or give large gifts to the church. When the early church was faced with a leadership crisis because they had outgrown their ability to serve some of the widows, they allowed the church to choose leaders to take some of the burden off the apostles.

They were to choose "men of a good reputation, full of the Spirit and of wisdom" (Acts 6:3). Did you ever wonder why it was so important for someone to have these qualities just to deliver meals?

It indicates that every kind of work in the church is spiritual and should be done as an overflow of worship so that it glorifies God. There should be no division between the administrative and spiritual areas of ministry. Everything is spiritual when dealing with the body of Christ.

Because of his martyrdom in Acts 7, Stephen was one of the most notable of the seven selected that day. He was:

1. Full of the Spirit (Acts 6:3,5,10; 7:55).
2. Full of wisdom (Acts 6:3,10).
3. Full of faith (Acts 6:5).
4. Full of grace (Acts 6:8).
5. Full of power (Acts 6:8).

He was a worshiper and for that reason, as he was passing from this world, he was given a glimpse of the glory of God (Acts 7:55).

Paul warned us not to "lay hands upon any one too hastily and thereby share responsibility for the sins of others" (1 Tim. 5:22). If we just look at a potential leader's curriculum vitae and his outward behavior, we can't immediately tell whether he is a worshiper.

As Paul says, "The sins of some men are quite evident, going before them to judgment..." (1 Tim. 5:24). It is easier to discern when they are *not* worshipers, than to quickly tell if they are. On the other hand, the deeds of a worshiper, in time, "are quite evident" (v. 25). Those deeds will glorify God.

Whether the *structure* is a pastor with a deacon board, an official board, an elder board, or whatever, two things are necessary. 1) There must be a priority of worship over administration. 2) There must be accountability within the leadership so that each person is growing in his worship.

In Acts 6, the seven Hellenistic Jews were appointed to relieve the apostles of one of their responsibilities so they could dedicate themselves to "prayer and to the ministry of the word" (v. 4). As we have said, serving meals was considered an outflow of worship and was carried out by godly men. However, it was essential that the apostles be undistracted by the church's social outreach. Although everything is to flow from worship, there is still a need for undistracted time to focus on the presence of the Lord, especially for those leading the church.

The leadership of the church at Antioch separated themselves for "ministering to the Lord and fasting" (Acts 13:2). It seems their worship as a group was so intense they chose not to be distracted even by food. Worship was the priority on their agenda.

Having multiple leaders of a church provides the advantage of accountability, especially in persevering and growing in worship. The ministry can easily become one's focus, and intimacy with God can be put on the back burner. The excuse is usually that, "After all, we are working for the Lord."

Finally, godly leadership needs to have a *vision* for worship as the golden thread to be woven into every aspect of church ministry. They should be asking the following questions:

1. Are we leaders modeling a worship life-attitude?

2. Are the people in every level of ministry in our church making worship the priority?

3. Are we attracting potential worshipers or merely religious inquirers?

4. Are people who are converting becoming transformed worshipers?

5. Is our discipleship focused on building a worship life-attitude?

6. Are our small groups helping people learn how to join their hearts in corporate worship?

7. Do our larger gatherings focus on the Word of God to bring the group into God's presence?

8. Is our leadership training system focused on developing worshipers?

9. What is the biggest barrier to worship in our midst? Is there sin? Indifference?

10. What can we change to become a better worshiping church?

It should be the goal of every church to find and develop worshipers and send them out to impact the world. The leadership of the church is responsible to make sure these goals are achieved.

REPRODUCING THE BODY: CHURCH MULTIPLICATION AND MISSIONS

It is only appropriate to finish this book looking at the glory of God in missions.

The book of Revelation is about worship. One of the most important events occurs when the Lamb (Jesus Christ) steps forward to take the book from the hand of Him who sits on the throne (the Father) (Rev. 5:9).

It seems best to regard the "scroll" as a Roman "testament" that tells the promise of the inheritance of the Kingdom.

Only Jesus is worthy to take the scroll and inherit the earth. When He does so, all heaven erupts in praise. The worship motive behind this is stated in Revelation 5:9.

> And they sang a new song, saying, "Worthy art Thou to take the book and to break its seals; for Thou wast slain, and didst purchase for God with Thy blood men from every tribe and tongue and people and nation."

It is quite clear that the new song is a fresh vision of God and a new motivation for worship. It is because Christ has redeemed people, not just from every country, but also from every people group.

Why did He do that? In Revelation 7:9, John saw the fruit of the 144,000 Jewish evangelists from the Tribulation.

> After these things I looked, and behold, a great multitude, which no one could count, from every nation and all tribes

and peoples and tongues, standing before the throne and before the Lamb....

Here we have a truly international, ethnically diverse group before God. What are they doing? They are joining together in intense worship before God. It started with the four living creatures (Rev. 4:8), continued with the addition of the 24 elders (Rev. 5:8-10), grew stronger with the angels (vv. 11-12), expanded to include "every created thing" (v. 13), and finally reached a crescendo when the international enclave of saints joined in the chorus. Listen to what they are singing.

> "Amen, blessing and glory and wisdom and thanksgiving and honor and power and might, be to our God forever an ever. Amen" (Rev. 7:12).

It starts with an "Amen" and finishes with an "Amen." Seven eternal qualities are attributed to God by this huge, diverse group.

We can conclude from this that Jesus Christ died to redeem an ethnically diverse group of people to reflect His glory with *perfect* worship. That is why there is a seven-fold praise expressed.

This is eternal. Revelation 21:26 says, "They shall bring the glory of the nations into it." That means a culturally diverse group will offer the glorious and eternal worship. The ethnic distinctions will be, as Gordon Chandler refers to them, a "divine mosaic."[16]

THE GOAL OF MISSIONS

Heaven is about enjoying perfect fellowship with the Triune God. The New Jerusalem is full of the glory and honor of God.

The goal of missions is to fill heaven with a diverse group of worshipers, each contributing to the eternal glorification of God.

One of the best missions statements comes from a statement of faith drawn up by the elders of John Piper's church. It says,

> The ultimate aim of world missions is that God would create, by His Word, worshippers who glorify His name through glad-hearted faith and obedience. Missions exists because

---

[16] Gordon Chandler, *God's Global Mosaic: What We Can Learn from Christians Around the World* quoted by Stallter in Bateman, p. 277.

worship doesn't. When this age is over, and the countless millions of the redeemed fall on their faces before the throne of God, missions will be no more. It is a temporary necessity. But worship abides forever. Worship, therefore, is the fuel and the goal of missions.[17]

THE CALLING TO MISSIONS

If worship is our goal, then it should be our call.

I heard of a missionary who resigned because that particular field was "no longer meeting my needs." Since when do we go to the mission field to meet *our* needs? Certainly that is not the reason for going.

Brazil is fast becoming a missionary *sending* country, rather than a missionary *receiving* field. Our churches are starting to have missionary conferences to reach out into the unreached people groups.

In one such conference, the *needs* in other parts of the world were stressed. If the need is our motive for going, we will probably return from the field. Those who are most in need of the gospel are often those who are most resistant. They don't think they need you and won't want you there, at least initially. That can be discouraging.

Although obedience to the Great Commission is important, that, too, should not be the principal motive for missions.

The real call to commit our lives to missions, whether it be praying, giving, or going is *worship*. As worshipers, our goal should be to see Jesus Christ honored and glorified. If worship is our greatest joy, it should be our passion to see more and more people from a culturally diverse group bowing down to Him. He can never be fully glorified by a culturally homogenous group. The fullness of His character will be reflected in the nations before the throne.

To Him be the glory, forever and ever, Amen.

WHAT WE DO IN BRAZIL

Brazil is more of what is called a "collective culture" and tends to be more event-oriented. People are drawn to large and loud groups. Small groups tend not to be so attractive. The first missionaries to Brazil

[17] Piper, *Don't Waste Your Life*, p. 162.

came more than a century-and-a-half ago and introduced traditional religious forms. These styles have become sacred and difficult to change. Brazilians tend to look to a centralized, authoritarian leadership to solve their problems, and that is reflected in the church.

One of my goals as a missionary has been to weave the golden thread of worship into the Brazilian church, not change its style. It has been my prayer that when the Brazilian church begins to live a worship life-attitude, it will begin to discover culturally relevant ways to express it in their small groups, leadership styles, and corporate praise times.

I wish I could close this book with a stellar example of how the Brazilian church has truly become a worshiping body. Although there are bright spots, we still have much to learn. More and more of our churches are experimenting with different styles in their corporate celebrations, using more than one speaker and encouraging interaction between members.

One of our churches recognized that when they were meeting in their homes, they were more unified and more spontaneous in their praise. They decided to turn their building into a home, furnishing it with sofas, tables, a kitchenette, and plastic tables spread around the room. During the service, they sit around tables and interact with each other about the message.

There is one more point that might be the key to this whole section of the book: Those who have been drawn by worship, evangelized in the context of worship, and discipled to develop their worship, have a much easier time entering into and starting spiritual communities than those who have a merely religious background.

Leadership training must begin when people are being evangelized. Otherwise, we will have to go back later to rebuild the whole foundation of their Christian life to help them to become worshipers.

In chapter 11, I briefly mentioned Nonato's story. I first met him when I started teaching in our seminary. He had been studying there for quite some time and was being trained to be a pastor. He participated in a somewhat legalistic church. During the time he was my student, we started the "Community of Life" church, and he became pastor at his own church.

Those who were graduating with Nonato wanted to have a special service at our new church, Community of Life, to celebrate finishing the seminary course. Three different men preached that night, interspersed with music, testimonies, and exhortations for the new graduates. We were not a very large group, but we were alive, active, united, and involved.

Nonato was amazed. Although his church was much larger and older, it was not nearly as alive or involved. He invited us to join him in an evangelistic outreach in a neighborhood a couple of kilometers from his house. Several of us joined Nonato, but no one from his church came. After a few weeks, he informed the group of new contacts, "I am handing you over to Community of Life. I want you all to be active Christians."

A few months later, Nonato called to tell me he was resigning as pastor and wanted to be a part of our church. I urged him instead to pray about starting a new church.

Having found a mission field, he wanted to introduce me to some of his contacts. He asked me if I would help train him in our church-planting methods.

I told him, "Nonato, it is not about methods. It is about intimacy with God. You are a faithful pastor, but you don't have intimacy with God." When I returned a week later, he confessed he was taken back by the statement, but came to the conclusion that I was right. He needed to find intimacy with God.

As I started working with him, I discovered that he had never been discipled. He had a number of personal problems he had tried to conquer on his own.

Little by little, he began to understand what it means to worship God. He became less and less mechanical in his ministry and began to replace his harsh exterior with a very tender, loving manner. He went to several church-planting clinics and learned how worship should be incorporated into his life and ministry.

He began to meet with a small group of believers right away. However, as he evangelized out of an overflow of worship and led people into a worshiping relationship with Christ, the meetings started giving way to a worshiping community. The new believers were active in sharing their faith and were walking with God.

The first class of RETREL was made up of six people from his church, mostly relatively new believers who had been saved through worship evangelism. These were the people from the "fruitful fruit stand." Of those six, three have moved to the interior and are involved in a new church plant. Two more are taking turns manning their fruit stand and going out to their hometown about three hours outside of Belém. The sixth is Nonato himself. He is mentoring those who are planting the churches.

Although this church is only eight years old, it is involved in five different locations where they are trying to start new churches. Nonato himself still laughs and shakes his head at what God has done. He says, "Before, my goal was to get people into my church. I didn't care about discipleship. Now, my goal is to make worshipers. I don't even ask people to come to my church, but they are coming."

Those who see worship as an event rather than a life-attitude to be woven into the fabric of life have trouble entering into a worshiping community. Although many people have caught the vision for worship, there is not a "method" or "trick" to this important transformation from the religious to the spiritual.

The old saying, "You can lead a horse to water, but you can't make him drink," can be applied to evangelism. Jesus said, "The wind blows where it wishes and you hear the sound of it, but do not know where it comes from and where it is going; so is everyone who is born of the Spirit" (John 3:8). No one can create a movement of God's Spirit in the life of another for salvation or for developing as a worshiper, but we see the results of the Spirit's work.

That is why prayer is important. Start praying for your own life. Pray that God will open your eyes and teach you what it means to be a worshiper. I pray that for myself almost every day, first thing. Pray also for those around you. I can think of no greater reward than knowing my life would somehow be a catalyst for others to worship God. I want to have the golden thread of worship woven into my life, so that I can be a part of that process in others.

CONCLUSION

The church is made up of individual Christians who have been transformed from rebels to worshipers. Not only has the door been opened into God's presence, but also believers have now drunk deeply of intimacy and are continually growing in their *practice* of worship. Their life is not divided into a thousand interests, but they have one purpose: to grow in their worship of God. Their divided lives have been tied together by this divine purpose.

It is only natural that these worshipers will be drawn to others who share the same intimacy with God and the same love for God's Word. They will not be bound up by traditional wineskins, but will desire to find the best ways to express their worship corporately, first in small groups, then spilling over into larger gatherings.

A commitment among these worshipers will develop, as they organize themselves into spiritual communities, committing themselves to the edification and expansion of Christ's church, not as an organization, but as a living body. The golden thread of worship will tie them together as they subordinate their individuality to the body and for the glory of Jesus Christ their Lord. Amen!

PARADIGM SHIFT

This paradigm and the previous shift summarize those at the end of the other chapters. Here, we compare the "Solid Church" to a "Worshiping Community." The former may have stability, but its strength is in the structure and not in its dependence on God's presence. Some of the churches in Revelation 2-3 were praised for resisting false doctrine and remaining firm in the face of opposition. It is obvious, however, that their strength did not come because they were worshiping God. They were relying on the strength and tradition of the institution rather than on the presence of the Living God.

A SOLID CHURCH	A WORSHIPING COMMUNITY
1. SMALL GROUPS • Evangelism • Edification • Fellowship	1. SMALL GROUPS • Encourage individual worship through the Word • Learn corporate worship
2. LEADERSHIP SELECTION • By education • By talent	2. LEADERSHIP SELECTION • By worship • By the fruit of worship
3. LEADERSHIP STRUCTURE • Organizational • United by the task • Mobilize the church for ministry	3. LEADERSHIP STRUCTURE • Worship based • United by worship • Incorporate worship into all levels of ministry
4. WORSHIP SERVICE • Passive listening • Congregational singing • Same order of service: Prayer, praise, preaching, and prayer	4. CELEBRATION • Praise in response to the Word • Active participation • Culturally dynamic

WHERE TO START?

1. ASK GOD TO GIVE YOU A SPIRITUAL UNDERSTANDING OF THE CHURCH. Pray the prayer in Ephesians 3:14-21 several times this week. Ask Him to strip away all the human perceptions of the body so you can clearly see His bride through His eyes.

2. IF YOU ARE MARRIED, START THERE. Paul said the oneness experienced in a marriage is comparable to the relationship between Christ and His church. If we do not learn what it means to experience spiritual oneness with our spouses, we will never understand nor experience it on the level of the church.

3. PASS A SPIRITUAL VISION OF THE CHURCH TO YOUR LOCAL BODY. If we focus on changing forms and styles, we will meet with resistance. If our emphasis is on helping people experience the new wine of worship, however, the new wineskins will come with time. Work on weaving the golden thread of worship into your own life and into the life and ministry of your church. God will create a bond of spiritual unity, as you practice the reality of being one spirit with Him (1 Cor. 6:17).

DISCUSSION QUESTIONS

1. How have this chapter and this book changed your view of the church?

2. What role do small groups play in promoting worship in the church?

3. How have you experienced unity in worship in a small group setting?

4. Imagine a worship service or celebration in which the whole group comes together in God's presence. How do you see that happening?

5. How can we free ourselves of the individuality that exists in our thinking about the church?

6. How much structure is needed for a church to give continuity to its worship and ministries?

7. How should we choose our leaders?

8. What should a 21st-century American church look like?

9. What are your thoughts about music styles?

10. What is the difference between appealing to the flesh and being culturally relevant in music styles?

11. How can we recapture the essence of worship and begin to experience the reality of the church?

Afterword

Just as I was working on some finishing touches to this book, my wife asked me the haunting question of what I wanted to see happen through this book.

I want to add my voice to the many who are crying out for real worship. It is my dream that the ideas expressed here will help fuel a genuine spiritual change in these end times.

This book is intended to present a whole new perspective on our lives. As has happened to many people in Brazil, it should give us a new perspective on the Bible, seeing it now as our manual of worship. It is my hope that it will provide a new purpose and focus in our lives. This will produce a newfound holiness, as we live out worship as a life-attitude, glorifying God.

This book should change the way we do evangelism. Instead of looking for converts to fill our pews, we will pray and seek for worshipers to be integrated into Christ's body. No longer will evangelism be a task to be performed, but a genuine overflow of our love and worship of God. There will be a respect for the process of the calling out of individuals to be incorporated into the bride of Christ. The gospel will become relevant to a whole new generation of believers who want to see real Christianity.

This book should lead us to a different outlook on discipleship, as we seek to change people's values, instead of their behavior. We will implant biblical culture into their lives instead of transplanting knowledge and behavior codes.

This book should help raise up leaders. People should be called to ministry, not out of a sense of duty or because of the needs, but because of their love for God. Those who are willing to bow before Him in worship will have no regard for their personal benefit in their desire to serve God. All of us should be willing to obey the command to go, sacrificing our personal comfort so that others might become worshipers. As Piper says, "God seldom calls us to an easier life, but always calls us to know more of Him and drink more deeply of His sustaining grace." [1]

This book should change the way we train leaders. Instead of picking the talented, we will choose the spiritual. On every level, leaders will be trained to worship through worship for worship. Those whom God is calling to be leaders should desire above all else to be worshipers, and our training should start with developing worship in their lives. Worship is not only the goal, but also the means by which training takes place as the Word is planted in them in God's presence. Finally our leaders should be instruments to promote worship in others.

This book should help change the way we do church. No longer will we be the dry, irrelevant institutions that are trying to draw people from the world into our buildings. We will no longer be grain bins for storing the harvest, but seed distribution centers, sending out worshipers into the world to sow the gospel.

I am probably overly optimistic. Writing this book has changed me. I finished my first draft exactly two years to the day after that car ride in the Volkswagen in Uberlândia when I was challenged to think about what makes our movement here in Brazil different. I am a different person today, having studied and deepened my convictions about worship.

Can these changes really take place? My hope, my prayer, and my worship is "to Him who is able to do far more abundantly beyond all that we ask or think, according to the power that works within us, to Him be the glory in the church and in Christ Jesus to all generations forever and ever. Amen" (Eph. 3:20-21).

---

[1] Piper, *Don't Waste Your Life,* p. 178.

Works Cited

Allen, Ronald and Gordon Borror. *Worship: Rediscovering the Missing Jewel.* Portland: Multnomah Press, 1982.

Anderson, Neil T. *The Bondage Breaker.* Eugene, Ore.: Harvest House Publishers, 1990.

_____ *Who I Am in Christ.* Ventura, Calif.: Regal Books, 2001.

Arnold, Clinton E. *Powers of Darkness, Principalities and Powers in Paul's Letters.* Downers Grove, Ill.: InterVarsity Press, 1992.

Bateman, Herbert W. IV. *Authentic Worship: Hearing Scripture's Voice, Applying Its Truths.* Grand Rapids: Kregel, 2002.

Bauer, Walter; F. Wilbur Gingrich; and Frederick W. Danker. *A Greek-English Lexicon of the New Testament and Other Early Christian Literature.* Chicago: University of Chicago Press, 1979.

Bayly, Joseph. *The Gospel Blimp.* Grand Rapids: Zondervan, 1960.

Best, Harold. *Music Through the Eyes of Faith.* San Francisco: Harper and Row, 1993.

Bounds, E. M. *Power Through Prayer.* Grand Rapids: Baker Book House, 1980.

Briscoe, Stuart and Jill. *The Family Book of Christian Values.* Colorado Springs: Christian Parenting Books, 1995.

Bruce, F. F. *Commentary on the Book of Acts.* Grand Rapids: William B. Eerdmans, 1954.

Carroll, Joseph. *How to Worship Jesus Christ.* Chicago: Moody Press, 1984.

Cole, Neil. *Cultivating a Life for God.* Carol Stream, Ill.: Church Smart Resources, 1999.

Douglas, J. D., Philip W. Comfort, and Donald Mitchell, Editors. *Who's Who in Christian History.* Wheaton: Tyndale House Publishers, 1992.

Eadie, John. *Commentary on the Epistle of Paul to the Ephesians.* London: Griffin, Bohn, and Co., 1981.

Engle, James F. *What's Wrong with the Harvest?: A Communication Strategy for the Church and World Evangelization.* Grand Rapids: Zondervan, 1975.

Foster, Richard J. *Celebration of Discipline.* New York: Harper and Row, 1978.

Gibbs, Eddie. *ChurchNext: Quantum Changes in How We Do Ministry.* Downers Grove: InterVarsity Press, 2000.

Gribble, Florence Newberry. *Undaunted Hope, the Life of James Gribble.* Winona Lake, Ind.: BMH Books, 1984.

Guyon, Madame. *Experiencing the Depths of Jesus Christ.* Augusta: Christian Books, 1975.

Julien, Tom. *Inherited Wealth: Studies in Ephesians.* Winona Lake, Ind.: BMH Books: 1976.

Keil, C. F. and F. Delitzsch. *Commentary on the Old Testament. Volumes 1 & 7. The Pentateuch.* Grand Rapids: William B. Eerdmans, 1986.

Kittel, Gerhard, and Gerhard Friedrich, editors, *The Theological Dictionary of the New Testament, Abridged in One Volume.* Grand Rapids, Michigan: William B. Eerdmans, 1985.

Lawson, James Gilchrist. *Deeper Experiences of Famous Christians.* Uhrichsville, Ohio: Barbour Publishing, 2000.

Lewis, C. S. *The Lion, the Witch and the Wardrobe.* New York: Collier books, 1950.

Logan, Robert E. *Beyond Church Growth.* Grand Rapids: Baker Book House, 1989.

MacArthur, John F. Jr. *Charismatic Chaos.* Grand Rapids: Zondervan, 1992.

_____ *Faith Works: the Gospel According to the Apostles.* Dallas: Word, 1993.

_____ *The Gospel According to Jesus.* Grand Rapids: Zondervan, 1988.

_____ *The MacArthur Study Bible.* Nashville: Word Publishing, 1997.

_____ *The MacArthur New Testament Commentary: Matthew 1-7.* Chicago: Moody Press, 1985.

_____ *The MacArthur New Testament Commentary: Matthew 8-15.* Chicago: Moody Press, 1987.

_____ *The MacArthur New Testament Commentary: Romans 1-8* Chicago: Moody Press, 1991.

_____ *The MacArthur New Testament Commentary: Romans 9-16* Chicago: Moody Press, 1994.

_____ *The MacArthur New Testament Commentary: 1 Corinthians.* Chicago: Moody Press, 1984.

_____ *The MacArthur New Testament Commentary: Galatians.* Chicago: Moody Press, 1994.

_____ *The MacArthur New Testament Commentary" Ephesians.* Chicago: Moody Press, 1986.

_____ *The MacArthur New Testament Commentary: Hebrews.* Chicago: The Moody Bible Institute, 1983.

_____ *The Ultimate Priority.* Chicago: Moody Press, 1983.

Morgenthaler, Sally. *Worship Evangelism: Inviting Unbelievers into the Presence of God.* Grand Rapids: Zondervan, 1995.

Needham, David C. *Birthright: Christian, Do You Know Who You Are?* Portland: Multnomah Press, 1979.

Packer, J. I. *Knowing God.* Madison: InterVarsity Press, 1973.

Petersen, Jim. *Church Without Walls.* Colorado Springs: Navpress, 1992.

Pinckney, Coty. "Suffering and Joy," a sermon on Mark 10:32-52 at Community Bible Church, Williamstown, MA 4/2/00. <http: tcpii.tripod.com/mark10c.htm.>

Piper, John, *The Dangerous Duty of Delight.* Sisters, Ore.: Multnomah Publishers. 2001.

_____ *Desiring God.* Sisters, Ore.: Multnomah Publishers, 2003.

_____ *Don't Waste Your Life.* Wheaton: Crossway Books, 2003.

_____ *Let the Nations Be Glad! The Supremacy of God in Missions.* Grand Rapids: Baker Books, 1993.

Ridenour, Fritz. *How to Be a Christian without Being Religious.* Ventura, Calif.: Gospel Light Publications, 1967.

Robinson, Jeff. "Romanian Josef Tson Recounts God's Grace Amid Suffering." *Baptist Press, News with a Christian Perspective,* July 19, 2004. www.bpnews.net.

Ryan, Joseph, "Skip." *Worship: Beholding the Beauty of the Lord.* Wheaton: Crossway Books, 2005.

Smethurst, Dave. "I Got Off at George Street." www.baptistboard.com.

Spurgeon, C. H. *"The Axe at the Root – A Testimony Against Puseyite Idolatry."* http://www. spurgeon.org/sermons/0695.htm.

_____ *The Treasury of David.* Nashville: Thomas Nelson Publishers, 1985.

Stone, Nathan J. *Names of God.* Chicago: Moody Press, 1944.

Tozer, A. W. *I Call It Heresy.* Harrisburg, Pa.: Christian Publications, 1974.

_____ *The Knowledge of The Holy.* India: Alliance Publications, 1961.

_____ *Whatever Happened to Worship?* Camp Hill, Pa.: Christian Publications, 1985.

Van Dyk, Leanne. *A More Profound Alleluia: Theology and Worship in Harmony.* Grand Rapids: William B. Eerdmans, 2005.

Vine, W. E. *An Expository Dictionary of New Testament Words.* Old Tappan, N.J.: Fleming H. Revell, 1940.

Warren, Rick. *The Purpose Driven Church.* Grand Rapids: Zondervan, 1995.

_____ *The Purpose Driven Life.* Grand Rapids: Zondervan, 2002.

Webster's New Collegiate Dictionary, 8th edition. Springfield, Mass.: Merriam-Webster.

Wiersbe, Warren. *Real Worship: Playground, Battleground, or Holy Ground?* Grand Rapids: Baker Book House, 2000.